PEGGY DAVIES CERAMICS

INCORPORATING

Kevin **KF** Francis

Tea with Clarice Cliff
Released February
1997. **SOLD OUT**

Young Clarice
SOLD OUT
Issue Price £130.00

Susie Cooper
Issue Price £145.00
SOLD OUT

Lo La Palooza
Released June '97
SOLD OUT
Issue Price £149.00

Persian Dancer
Issue Price £115.00
SOLD OUT

Pyjama Girl
Released November 1998
Issue Price £175.00

D-Day Landings
Limited Edition 750
£147.00

Charlotte Rhead figurine
Limited Edition of 950 worldwide
SOLD OUT
Issue Price £195.00

Approximate average height is 9 inches.

PEGGY DAVIES CERAMICS

Peggy Davies Ceramics, the sole producers of Kevin Francis ware, established by the world renowned ceramic artist Peggy Davies, is at the forefront when it comes to design and quality in the world of Limited Edition, hand crafted, hand painted ceramic art.

Celebrating ten years of producing the world's most intricate pieces in 1997, the Kevin Francis range has become much sought after, so much so that there is now an investment label on these quality items. Our range is being added to approximately four times a year. To join our free register of Collectors for regular brochures, or to find out more about the thriving Kevin Francis Collectors Guild,
write, phone or fax Rod Davies or Rhys Davies
Peggy Davies Ceramics
Freepost Mid 16669, Stoke-on-Trent, ST4 1BJ
Tel: 01782 848002   Fax: 01782 747651   Email: rhys@kevinfrancis.co.uk
Website: www.kevinfrancis.co.uk

MILLER'S

collectibles

collectibles

MADELEINE MARSH *GENERAL EDITOR*

2002/3
VOLUME XIV

MILLER'S COLLECTIBLES PRICE GUIDE 2002/3

Created and designed by
Miller's
The Cellars, High Street
Tenterden, Kent, TN30 6BN
Tel: 01580 766411
Fax: 01580 766100

General Editor: Madeleine Marsh
Managing Editor: Valerie Lewis
Production Co-ordinator: Kari Reeves
Editorial Co-ordinator: Deborah Wanstall
Editorial Assistants: Kim Cook, Maureen Horner
Production Assistants: Gillian Charles, Clare Gillingham, Ethne Tragett
Advertising Executive: Jill Jackson
Advertising Co-ordinator & Administrator: Melinda Williams
Advertising Assistant: Jo Hill
Designer: Philip Hannath
Advertisement Designer: Simon Cook
Indexer: Hilary Bird
Jacket Design: Victoria Bevan
Production: Angela Couchman
Additional Photographers: Dennis O'Reilly, Robin Saker
North American Consultants: Marilynn and Sheila Brass

First published in Great Britain in 2002
by Miller's, a division of Mitchell Beazley,
imprint of Octopus Publishing Group Ltd,
2–4 Heron Quays, London E14 4JP

© 2002 Octopus Publishing Group Ltd

A CIP catalogue record for this book is
available from the British Library

ISBN 1-84000-620-X

Whilst every care has been exercised in the
compilation of this guide, neither the authors
nor publishers accept any liability for any financial or other
loss incurred by reliance placed on the information contained in
Miller's Collectibles Price Guide

Illustrations by CK Digital, Whitstable, Kent, England
Printed and bound by Rotolito Lombarda, Italy

Front cover illustrations:
Lucie Attwell's Story Book, published by Dean, c1930, 10 x 9in (25.5 x 23cm). **£50–55/$70–80** ▦ MEM
A Cornish Ware flour shaker, early mark, 5½in (14cm) high. **£45–50/$65–75** ▦ TAC
An orange straw cloche hat, 1920s, 8in (20.5cm) diam. **£50–55/$70–80** ⚹ CCO

How To Use This Book

I t is our aim to make this guide easy to use. In order to find a particular item, turn to the contents list on page 7 to find the main heading, for example, Ceramics. Having located your area of interest, you will see that larger sections have been sub-divided by subject or maker. If you are looking for a particular factory, maker, or object, consult the index, which starts on page 454.

114 CERAMICS • T. G. Green

T. G. Green

A T. G. Green Cube teapot, cream jug and sugar bowl, decorated in Dickens Days pattern, 1930.
£150–200
$220–300 ⊞ CAL

Ten T. G. Green plates, decorated in blue with white spots, 1930–50, four 9in (23cm) diam, six 7in (18cm) diam.
£35–45
$50–70 ➹ BBR

A T. G. Green salt shaker, decorated with blue and white bands, 1930–50, 5in (12.5cm) high.
£12–15
$15–20 ➹ BBR

Backstamps
Over the years T. G. Green used a number of different marks. On Cornish Ware a shield-shaped mark, appearing in both black and green, was used from the late 1920s until the second half of the 1960s. From 1968 until the late 1970s this was replaced by a Target mark designed by Judith Onions. In the 1980s, a modern church mark was used. In 1987, T. G. Green was taken over by Cloverleaf, who introduced a cloverleaf backstamp.

Cross Reference
See Colour Review (page 147)

A T. G. Green Cornish Ware flour shaker, decorated with blue and white bands, with handle, 1930–50, 5½in (14cm) high.
£120–160
$175–225 ⊞ CAL
The handled flour shaker is a rare item in Cornish Ware.

▶ A T. G. Green biscuit barrel, decorated in blue with white spots, blue domino mark, 1930–50, 5in (12.5cm) high.
£350–450
$500–650 ⊞ CAL

Further reading
Miller's Collecting Kitchenware, Miller's Publications, 2000

A T. G. Green sugar bowl, decorated with blue and white bands, 1940s, 5in (12.5cm) diam.
£15–20
$20–30 ⊞ TAC

◀ A T. G. Green Cornish Ware trio, decorated with Morning Glory pattern, 1950s, plate 7in (18cm) diam.
£50–60
$75–90 ⊞ CAL

A T. G. Green mug, decorated with yellow and white bands, 1940s, 4in (10cm) high.
£25–30
$35–45 ⊞ TAC

Caption
provides a brief description of the item including the maker's name, medium, date, measurements and in some instances condition.

Cross Reference
directs the reader to where other related items may be found.

Information Box
covers relevant collecting information on factories, makers, care, restoration, fakes and alterations.

Price Guide
these are based on actual prices realized shown in £sterling with a US$ conversion. Remember that Miller's is a PRICE GUIDE not a PRICE LIST and prices are affected by many variables such as location, condition, desirability and so on. Don't forget that if you are selling, it is quite likely you will be offered less than the price range. Price ranges for items sold at auction tend to include the buyer's premium and VAT if applicable.

Source Code
refers to the 'Key to Illustrations' on page 444 that lists the details of where the item was sourced. The ➹ icon indicates the item was sold at auction. The ⊞ icon indicates the item originated from a dealer.

Further Reading
directs the reader towards additional sources of information.

Acknowledgments

We would like to acknowledge the great assistance given by our consultants who are listed below. We would also like to extend our thanks to all the auction houses, their press offices, dealers and collectors who have assisted us in the production of this book.

ANTIQUE AMUSEMENT CO
Mill Lane, Swaffham
Bulbeck, Cambridge CB5 0NF
(Amusement & Slot Machines)

BEVERLEY/BETH
30 Church Street
Alfie's Antique Market
Marylebone
London NW8 8EP
(Ceramics)

ALAN BLAKEMAN
BBR Elsecar Heritage Centre
Wath Road, Elsecar, Barnsley
Yorks S74 8AF
(Advertising, Packaging, Bottles, Breweriana)

MARILYNN & SHEILA BRASS
PO Box 380503, Cambridge
USA MA 02238-0503
(Cookery)

JIM BULLOCK
Romsey Medal Centre
5 Bell Street, Romsey
Hants SO51 8GY
(Military Medals)

DR D. DOWSON
Old Tackle Box
PO Box 55, Cranbrook
Kent TN17 3ZU
(Fishing Tackle)

ANDREW HILTON
Special Auction Services
The Coach House, Midgham Park
Reading, Berks RG7 5UG
(Commemorative Ware)

DAVID HUXTABLE
S03/05 Alfies Antique Market
13–25 Church Street
London NW8 8DT
(Advertising Tins)

KEN LAWSON
Specialized Postcard Auctions
25 Gloucester Street
Cirencester GL7 2DJ
(Postcards)

PAUL MULVEY
Cloud Cuckooland
12 Fore Street
Mevagissey
Cornwall PL26 6UQ
(Photographs)

MARK OLIVER
Bonhams
101 New Bond Street
London W1Y 9LG
(Decorative Arts)

GAVIN PAYNE
The Old Granary
Battlebridge Antique Centre
Nr Wickford, Essex SS11 7RF
(Telephones)

MALCOLM PHILLIPS
Comic Book Postal Auctions
40–42 Osnaburgh Street
London NW1 3ND
(Comics)

ALVIN ROSS
Oxfordshire
(Puppets)

MAUREEN SILVERMAN
Planet Bazaar
149 Drummond Street
London NW1 2PB
(Sixties & Seventies)

DOMINIC WINTER
The Old School
Maxwell Street, Swindon
Wiltshire SN1 5DR
(Books)

Contents

Introduction

As we at Miller's know only too well, anything and everything can be collectable. New sections in this year's guide range from hot water bottles, to Tupperware, to wallpaper. As these examples show, an object doesn't have to be expensive in the first place to become collectable in the future. Many of the items in this book were designed to be discarded and some, for example pot lids and bottles, have literally been rescued from rubbish tips. But as the saying goes – where there's muck, there's brass – occasionally lots of it, as the lucky bottle digger who excavated a Victorian poison flask in the shape of a coffin discovered (see Record Breakers pp429). What makes such items desirable is their rarity. Disposable or ephemeral objects tend by their very nature to get thrown away, hence the value of those that escape the trashcan. Objects in this year's guide include a *Daily Mail* No. 1 from 1896, a pair of torn tickets for a Beatle's concert, football programmes, and the first ever Christmas card which made a record price of £22,350 ($32,400) when at auction.

As ever, this guide is full of surprises and where else would you find a pair of collectable wellies (see pp390). Interest in antique fashion has expanded considerably over the past couple of years, to the extent that some major stores now have vintage departments. Clothing illustrated here ranges from Victorian dresses to a pair of 1970s Nylon Y-fronts (see pp399). In addition to Costume and Textiles, there are also individual sections on Handbags, Cosmetic Accessories and Jewellery.

For those with more traditionally masculine tastes, we feature Automobilia, Aeronautica and Railwayana. For the first time, we devote a special section to crime and the macabre hobby of collecting memorabilia connected with famous criminals. Countering this, we also have collectables associated with the police, and in the wake of the events of 11 September 2001, we look at the history of firefighters, with a selection of objects commemorating their courage over the decades. Other new subjects this year include Black History and Memorabilia, and Politics, which includes a wide range of items both serious and satirical.

There are all sorts of reasons why objects become collectable. Nostalgia is a powerful spur. Many people will no doubt remember playing with the Barbies in our doll section, or the Dinky, Corgi and Matchbox cars illustrated in toys. Condition is all important when it comes to such objects, and price ranges reflect the difficulty of finding examples that have escaped the cheerfully destructive hands of children. If you grew up hiding behind the sofa to watch the Daleks on television, you will enjoy our section on *Doctor Who*, and how much people are prepared to spend to recapture their childhood TV memories is demonstrated by the thousands of pounds paid at auction for original props and puppets from series such as *Doctor Who* and *Thunderbirds*.

Our rock and pop section will take you back to your teenage years, whether you were a punk or a Beatles fan. Whilst in Radios and Gramophones you might even find the original machines on which you listened to your favourite music.

The objects in *Miller's Collectables Price Guide* reflect every aspect of human life. In our bathroom section we lift the lid on Victorian lavatories and the history of sanitation. In ceramics we look at Cornish Ware and how humble kitchen storage jars can be worth hundreds of pounds. We go out into the garden to find some valuable garden gnomes and we also look at the collectable owl. We celebrate the sweet childhood images of Mabel Lucie Attwell, and take a peek at the naughty world of Erotica. The earliest items shown in this book date from before Christ, whilst our Collectables of the Future page suggests which of today's purchases might well become the antiques of tomorrow.

The great joy of compiling, and hopefully reading this book is the infinite variety of objects there are to collect, and the fascinating stories behind them. If you have an interesting collection yourself or there are further subjects you would like to see covered by this guide, please let us know. Also if you would like to become a member of the Miller's Club do contact us. Club members are invited to nominate candidates for the BACAS – the British Antiques and Collectables Awards – which were started by Miller's to recognize excellence in the industry. We value your input and we look forward to receiving your suggestions. Thank you for your support and as ever happy hunting!

Advertising & Packaging

A Conrad W. Schmidt boxwood paper knife,
late 19thC, 12in (30.5cm) long.
£55–65
$80–95 ⊞ MLu

A Lancashire Insurance Company pottery capital matchstriker,
1910, 3in (7.5cm) high.
£25–30
$35–45 ⊞ HUX

◄ **A Hudson's Soap dish,** enamelled, chipped, 1900–20, 14¼in (36cm) wide.
£400–450
$600–650 ⚒ BBR

A Lever's Toilet Soaps revolving display case, glass to four sides, the interior fitted with three graduated glass shelves, 1890–1900, 23¾in (60.5cm) high.
£1,300–1,500
$2,000–2,200 ⚒ BBR

An Iceberg Cigarettes packet, in red and brown, 1910, 3½in (9cm) high.
£90–100
$130–150 ⊞ HUX

A Royle's Mantle, Costume and Family Mourning Warehouse wooden coat hanger, 1910–20, 16in (40.5cm) long.
£18–20
$20–30 ⊞ MRW

A Cherry Blossom shoe-shine stand, with red and black lettering and cherries, 1920–30, 12in (30.5cm) high.
£550–600
$800–900 ⚒ BBR

> Items in the Advertising & Packaging section have been arranged in date order within each sub-section.

An Ingram's Omega Whirling Spray, in brown and black, 1920, 11in (28cm) long, in original box.
£18–20
$20–30 ⊞ HUX

▶ **A Kiwi Boot Polish metal turntable display stand,** with red kiwi on top, and nine tins of Kiwi Boot Polish, 1920–30, 14½in (37cm) high.
£110–130
$160–190 ⚒ BBR

An Ovaltine pottery jug and mug, transfer-printed in brown, red and yellow, 1920, jug 8in (20.5cm) high.
£80–100
$115–145 ⊞ SMI

A Fyffes bananas yellow cardboard display, 1920s, 10in (25.5cm) high.
£50–55
$75–80 ⊞ HUX

A Cooperative Wholesale Society pistol-shaped glass sweet container, with original contents, c1920, 6in (15cm) long.
£35–60
$50–100 ⊞ MURR

A Five Cents copper display soda glass, c1920, 5½in (14cm) high.
£150–170
$200–250 ⊞ MSB

▶ A Bovril pine box, 1920–30, 10in (25.5cm) wide.
£15–20
$20–30 ⊞ AL

A Perrier Water paper fold-up fan, 1920–30, 8¾in (22cm) long.
£12–14
$15–18 ⊞ HUX

An Aero chocolate bar shop dummy, c1930, 4½in (11.5cm) long.
£12–15
$15–20 ⊞ HUX

A cardboard egg box for 24 eggs, c1930, 12in (30.5cm) long.
£22–26
$30–35 ⊞ AL

A Chocolat Lanvin stand-up litho-graphed tin display, in red and gold, c1930, 6½in (16.5cm) long.
£45–55
$60–80 ⊞ MSB

A papier-mâché sweet container, modelled as a roasted turkey, German, c1930, 7in (18cm) long.
£75–85
$110–125 ⚒ MSB

A Mr Therm brass cap badge, designed by Eric Fraser for Gas Light & Coke Co, 1930s, 2in (5cm) long.
£25–30
$35–45 ⊞ REN

A Strawberry tak-home Sundae paper cone, 1935, 4½in (11.5cm) high.
£15–20
$20–30 ⊞ MSB

◀ A pair of shop display joints of ham, 1930s, 18in (45.5cm) long.
£50–60
$75–100 each ⊞ SMI

Cross Reference
See Colour Review
(page 65–66)

A Puritan Soles coloured rubberoid bust of a Puritan, with red and white raised lettering, 1930s–40s, 11in (28cm) high.
£170–200
$250–300 ⚲ BBR

A Crawford's Biscuits metal ice-cream wafer maker, 1940s, 5in (12.5cm) high.
£35–40
$50–60 ⊞ HUX

An EKCO glass advertising tile, for use as a shop window decoration, 1955, 8in (20.5cm) square.
£25–30
$35–45 ⊞ GM

A Zippo lighter tape measure, 1960s, 3in (7.5cm) long.
£15–20
$20–30 ⊞ COB

A Wrigley's Spearmint Chewing Gum dummy pack, 1960s, 3in (7.5cm) square.
£8–10
$10–15 ⊞ HUX

◀ A Pillsbury Dough boy rubber doll, American, 1971, 7in (18cm) high.
£12–15
$15–20 ⊞ MRW

◀ A Rapitan cardboard sun reflector, with silver surface, Canadian, 1960s, 26in (66cm) wide.
£10–12
$15–18 ⊞ RTT

▶ A Coca-Cola seat, in the shape of a Coke bottle top, 1950s, 14in (35.5cm) diam.
£30–35
$45–50 ⚲ SAF

A Durex illuminated plastic sign, c1955, 12in (30.5cm) long.
£30–35
$45–50 ⊞ HUX

The word condom has been in use since the early 18th century and is said to be named after Colonel Condom, a British Guards Officer who wanted to protect his troops from venereal disease. Condoms were made of everything from cloth to animal intestines until the introduction of vulcanized rubber in the mid-19th century. In 1932, the London Rubber Company launched Durex, the name derived from the sheath's most important features: Durability, Reliability and Excellence.

Advertisement & Showcards

A Marston, Thompson & Evershed advertisement, depicting a multi-coloured picture of the brewery buildings, 1890–1900, 35 x 45in (89 x 114.5cm), framed.
£600–700
$870–1,000 ⚒ BBR

A Dicker's Dorset Sausages pressed cardboard advertising sign, early 20thC, 10½in (26.5cm) wide.
£20–24
$30–35 ⊞ RUSS

A Gallaher Limited tobacco and cigarette advertisement, depicting multi-coloured portraits of famous people, 1910–20, 28 x 22½in (71 x 57cm), framed.
£200–220
$300–320 ⚒ BBR

An Edison Bell Needles showcard, holding various gramophone needle tins, 1920s, 12in (30.5cm) high.
£100–125
$140–180 ⊞ MURR

A Harris Bacon stand-up cardboard cut-out figure of a seated pig, in pink and brown, some surface marks, 1930s–40s, 29in (73.5cm) high.
£80–90
$115–130 ⚒ BBR

A Whiteway's Cydrax cardboard display stand, 1930s, 12in (30.5cm) high.
£35–50
$50–75 ⊞ MURR

An Ovaltine cardboard cut-out advertising display, 1940s, 19in (48.5cm) high.
£45–55
$65–80 ⚒ DW

An ICI shop cardboard display advertisement, yellow and white lettering on a red ground, c1956, 12in (30.5cm) high.
£12–15
$18–20 ⊞ MRW

A Carnation Milk showcard, c1960, 12in (30.5cm) high.
£15–20
$20–30 ⊞ HOP

Enamel Signs

Enamel signs were a common form of street decoration from the 1880s (when manufacturing techniques were developed) until the 1950s, when they were generally replaced by paper posters and tin signs. Popular locations included not just shops, but trams, omnibuses and above all train stations.

The expansion of the railways not only allowed signs to be distributed around the country but also provided advertisers with a captive audience. W H Lever negotiated a special contract with the train companies and personally chose the sites for Lever products such as Sunlight Soap, particularly favouring the walls around the station booking office. Soap manufacturers were among the first to use

enamel signs and other makers soon followed suit. By their very nature enamel signs were durable and, unlike today, advertising campaigns were long-running. Famous images such as Fry's Five Boys – 'Desperation – Pacification – Expectation – Acclamation – Realization, It's Fry's' – permeated the national consciousness, making this a desirable sign today.

Values of enamel signs depend on subject, age, and size. Smaller, domestically convenient sizes are popular, as are unusually shaped examples that depart from the traditional rectangle. Condition is an important factor although, since signs were hung outside for decades and often carelessly removed, in most instances some wear and tear is unavoidable.

A J. A. Nadeau cast-iron and tin watchmaker's trade sign, with traces of gilt, the tin dial painted front and reverse with Roman numerals in black on a cream ground, some wear, American, 19thC, 49¾in (126.5cm) high.
£950–1,150
$1,400–1,600 ↗ SK(B)

A Brasso Metal Polish enamel advertising sign, black and white lettering on a green ground, chipped, 1900–20, 24in (61cm) high.
£230–250
$330–360 ↗ BBR

► A Hudson's Soap enamel advertising sign, black and white lettering on a green ground with red borders, outer border retouched, 1900–20, 18in (45.5cm) wide.
£100–110
$145–160 ↗ BBR

An R. White's Mineral Waters enamel advertising sign, blue and white, c1910, 24in (61cm) high.
£90–100
$130–150 ⊞ HUX

A We Deliver to All Parts Daily tin-on-board advertising sign, 1920s, 13in (33cm) wide.
£75–85
$110–125 ⊞ HOP

A Fry's enamel advertising sign, depicting a schoolboy looking into a sweetshop window, minor chips and rust spots, 1910–20, 14in (35.5cm) high.
£850–900
$1,200–1,300 ⚒ BBR

A Rowntree's Chocolates enamel advertising sign, white lettering on a dark blue ground, with a black and white picture of Rowntrees No. 3 Factory York, coloured coat-of-arms to either side, minor chips and rust, 1910–20, 30in (76cm) wide.
£800–850
$1,200–1,300 ⚒ BBR

A Fry's Chocolate enamel advertising sign, depicting five boys, white lettering on a blue ground, surface damage, chips and rust spots to outer edge, 1920–30, 18in (45.5cm) wide.
£60–70
$90–100 ⚒ BBR

An Arthur Davy's Yorkshire Polony enamel advertising sign, white and yellow lettering on a blue ground, with red polony links, some surface damage and chips to edge, 1920–30, 24in (61cm) wide.
£180–200
$250–300 ⚒ BBR

A Milkmaid Sweetened Condensed Milk enamel advertising sign, black lettering on a red ground, 1930s, 12in (30.5cm) square.
£75–100
$100–150 ⊞ MURR

Miller's is a price GUIDE not a price LIST

◀ **An Orange Maid enamel advertising sign,** double-sided to stand outside a shop, yellow and white lettering on a blue and red ground, 1940–50, in a wooden frame.
£25–30
$35–45 ⚒ BBR

An Oxo Cube enamel double-sided advertising sign, the reverse inscribed 'Oxo Makes All Meat Dishes', red and cream on a blue ground, slight rusting, 1930–40, 13½in (34.5cm) square.
£60–70
$90–100 ⚒ BBR

▶ **A Ruston Power tin advertising sign,** red lettering on a white border with yellow, green and black centre, 1950s, 30in (76cm) diam.
£50–70
$75–100 ⊞ JUN

A Swan Vestas enamel advertising sign, white lettering on a black ground, c1950, 15in (38cm) high.
£40–50
$60–80 ⊞ CRN

Tins

A Huntley & Palmer's biscuit tin, decorated with golfing and polo scenes in green, blue and yellow, c1890, 7in (18cm) diam.
£270–300
$400–450 ⊞ HUX

A Colman's Mustard tin, decorated with a scene from Queen Victoria's Diamond Jubilee, 1897, 8in (20.5cm) wide.
£150–170
$220–250 ⊞ TMa

▶ **A Huntley & Palmer's biscuit tin,** modelled as a set of books, brown, cream, red and green, c1901, 3½in (9cm) wide.
£100–120
$145–175 ⚒ DN

A Fry's 'Tourist' Chocolate tin, decorated with a mountain scene, c1910, 4¾in (12cm) wide.
£200–225
$300–330 ⊞ HUX

A Smith's Schooner Navy Cut tobacco tin, black lettering on a gold ground, 1880–90, 6in (15cm) wide.
£150–200
$200–300 ⊞ MURR

A B. Muratti, Sons & Co Kaiser Wilhelm Gold Tipped Cigarettes tin, decorated with Kaiser Wilhelm in black, gold, red and yellow, 1905, 4¼in (11cm) wide.
£225–250
$320–360 ⊞ HUX

A McVitie & Price biscuit tin, decorated with the Pied Piper of Hamelin in green, blue, yellow and red, 1890s, 10in (25.5cm) wide.
£150–200
$220–300 ⊞ MURR

A Rowntree's sweet tin, modelled as a rugby ball, c1900, 2in (5cm) long.
£90–100
$130–150 ⊞ MRW

A Clarnico tin, modelled as a golf club, 1910–20, 5¾in (14.5cm) long.
£170–190
$250–275 ⚲ BBR

A Pascall tin, modelled as a rifle, 1910–20, 6in (15cm) long.
£180–200
$250–300 ⚲ BBR

A Fullers Earth Cream tin, decorated in pink, green, red and cream, 1920s, 2in (5cm) diam.
£7–10
$10–15 ⊞ YR

A Sharp's Super Kreem Toffee tin, decorated with Sir Kreemy Nut feeding a macaw in blue, black, yellow and green on an orange ground, 1930, 9in (23cm) high.
£85–95
$125–145 ⊞ TMa
Sharp's introduced their Macaw trademark c1915, along with the slogan 'Sharp's Toffee Speaks For Itself'. Five years later they added the figure of Sir Kreemy Nut.

An Abonne cigar tin, decorated with six raised cigars, c1925, 4½in (11.5cm) square.
£30–35
$45–50 ⊞ HUX

A World Cup Willie's Football tin, modelled as a football, inscribed 'Lovell's Newport Mon' with black lettering on orange, on a green circular base, 1966, 5½in (14cm) high.
£60–70
$90–100 ⚲ BBR

▶ **A Cadbury's Smash tin,** 1984, 5in (12.5cm) high.
£10–12
$15–20 ⊞ YR
1980s tins featuring Martians are more valuable than 1970s examples.

A Maison Lyons eight-sided sweet tin, decorated with a party scene in blue, yellow, red and green, c1920, 6in (15cm) wide.
£35–50
$50–75 ⊞ MURR

A Bulwark Cut Plug Tobacco tin, decorated with a nautical scene in blue and white, 1920s, 7in (18cm) wide.
£15–20
$20–30 ⊞ COB

A Cadbury's Milk Tray Chocolates tin, decorated in brown, green and yellow, 1950s, 7in (18cm) wide.
£10–12
$15–20 ⊞ RTT

Aeronautica

A Britannic Aeroplane wooden advertising plaque, 1910, 13in (33cm) wide.
£60–65
$90–100 ⊞ COB

An RFC brass badge, 1915, 1½in (4cm) diam.
£30–35
$45–50 ⊞ COB

A bust of Louis Bleriot, by Leo Roussel, commemorating the first flight across the English Channel in July 1909, 8in (20.5cm) high.
£400–450
$580–650 ⊞ AU

A tapestry, depicting the Spirit of St Louis and Lindbergh, with other pilots, American, 1928, 59in (150cm) wide.
£350–375
$500–575 ⊞ AU

A vesta case, commemorating Eastbourne Jubilee Aviation Rally and Garden Party, June 1933, 2½in (6.5cm) wide.
£250–300
$350–450 ⊞ AU

A Swiss Lever Superior Aeroplane Timekeeper watch, base metal, 1920, 2in (5cm) diam.
£40–50
$60–80 ⊞ COB

An airman's emergency kite, 1930s, 21in (53.5cm) long.
£75–85
$100–125 ⊞ COB

A United Airlines passenger brochure, with map and pictures, 1949, 9 x 12in (23 x 30.5cm).
£20–25
$30–40 ⊞ J&S

A wooden model aircraft, 1938, 29in (73.5cm) wide.
£130–150
$190–220 ⊞ COB

A model of a DC3 aeroplane, mounted on a metal sphere, on a black base, 1940s, 14in (35.5cm) high.
£250–300
$350–450 ⊞ COB

▶ **A London Airport badge,** 1960s, 1in (2.5cm) diam.
£5–8
$8–12 ⊞ COB

A BOAC pottery tankard, c1960, 5in (12.5cm) high.
£15–20
$20–30 ⊞ HUX

Balloons & Airships

It was a bag filled with hot-air that enabled man to fly. This was discovered by French inventors Joseph and Etienne Montgolfier who, on 5 June 1873, launched the first unmanned balloon flight. Three months later they sent up a larger balloon at Versailles containing the world's first air passengers: a rooster, a duck, and a sheep. The earliest manned balloon flights took place later that year. One pioneer landed in a French village only to be attacked with pitchforks by inhabitants, terrified at the appearance of this unnatural flying monster.

Airships (also known as dirigibles) evolved from the balloon. The first successful airship was created by Henry Giffard of France in 1852. Numerous refinements took place in France and Germany in the second half of the 19th century, with the introduction of an internal combustion engine (1872), the electric motor (1883) and the rigid airship (1897). Ferdinand Graf von Zeppelin of Germany produced rigid airships from c1900 which were used to bomb Paris and London during WWI. Developments continued in the interwar years, but after a succession of disasters culminating with the destruction of the Hindenburg in 1937, the airship was virtually abandoned as a viable means of air travel. Its precursor, however, the hot-air balloon, still remains in flight, with famous balloonists including Richard Branson. Memorabilia relating to both these early forms of air transport is very collectable, and rarities attract strong prices.

A pearlware plate, depicting Graham's balloon flight from White Conduit House, printed in red, c1828, 9½in (24cm) diam.
£400–450
$580–650 ⊞ AU

A hand-painted balloon plate, inscribed 'adieu' (farewell), in red, green and blue, French, c1840, 9in (23cm) diam.
£450–500
$650–720 ⊞ AU

▶ A black and white photographic postcard, depicting a hot-air balloon, French, 1906, 5½in (14cm) long.
£23–25
$30–35 ⊞ WI

◀ A Balloon Post postcard, 'Life-Boat Saturday', slight corner creasing, 1903.
£1,000–1,200
$1,500–1,750 ✦ VS
Although dated 29 August 1903, this balloon was not flown until 5 September as it had an accident just as it was taking off from Manchester. It was therefore flown from Alexandra Palace on 5 September with much of the mail being dropped at various areas in London. This card has a clear Enfield cachet, '1.15pm 8th September 1903', being sent to Manchester with receiving cachet '9.45pm' on the same day.

A swivelling watch fob, with a hot-air balloon scene engraved on stone, c1900, 2in (5cm) long.
£60–70
$90–100 ⊞ MRW

A Royal Doulton Hudson Fulton celebration plate, depicting different modes of air travel, 1909, 10in (25.5cm) diam.
£300–350
$450–500 ⊞ AU

A colour illustration postcard, depicting a hot-air balloon scene, German, 1909, 5½in (14cm) high.
£23–25
$30–35 ⊞ WI

A Carlton ware model of an airship, crested, 1914–18, 4¾in (12cm) long.
£50–60
$75–90 ⊞ RUSS

A brass airship searchlight, by Pittsburgh Electrical Specialities Co, American, late 1920s, 7½in (19cm) long.
£175–200
$250–300 ⊞ AU

▶ A blue and white ceramic plate, commemorating the first Atlantic crossing by a hot-air balloon and gondola, 1958, 10in (25.5cm) diam.
£65–75
$95–110 ⚒ RCo

A brass airship ashtray, c1910, 8in (20.5cm) long.
£120–130
$175–200 ⊞ COB

Five Ogden's cigarette cards, depicting different hot-air balloons, from a set of 50, 1912.
£250–275
$350–400 ⊞ WI

A bronze commemorative plaque, for a balloon event, German, 1928, 3½in (9cm) long.
£350–400
$500–600 ⊞ AU

A Royal Doulton jug, depicting a pre-WWI aviation scene including an airship, 1910–12, 6½in (16.5cm) high.
£750–850
$1,100–1,250 ⊞ AU

A model airship, 1916, 38in (96.5cm) long.
£400–450
$580–650 ⊞ COB

Six photographs of an R101 airship leaving its mooring, 1931, 3¼in (8.5cm) long.
£25–30
$35–45 ⊞ J&S

A Poole plate, decorated with an airship design, 1980s, 6in (15cm) diam.
£18–20
$20–30 ⊞ DCA

Amusement & Slot Machines

An Automatic Amusement Co spinning dial fortune teller, The Gypsy, first patented c1889, 24in (61cm) high.
£750–850
$1,100–1,250 ⊞ HAK

A Mechanical Trading Co grip test machine, London, c1895, 18in (45.5cm) high.
£3,000–4,000
$4,500–5,800 ⊞ HAK

A Société Générale D'automatique electric pig, Paris, c1898, 32in (81.5cm) high.
£7,000–8,000
$10,200–11,500 ⊞ HAK

▶ **An Automatic Sports Co machine,** with football game, London, c1896, 32in (81.5cm) high excluding stand.
£4,000–4,500
$5,800–6,500 ⊞ HAK

Insurance values

Always insure your valuable collectables for the cost of replacing them with similar items, regardless of the original price paid. Both dealers and auctioneers can provide a valuation service for a fee.

Antiquities

◄ **A Mycenaean one-piece violin-bow style bronze brooch,** complete with pin, spring and catchplate, green patina, 13thC BC, 3¾in (9.5cm) long.
£85–95
$125–140 ⊞ ANG

An Egyptian limestone fragment, with blue-filled hieroglyphs, part of an inscription suggesting the words 'palace' and 'governor of', Middle Kingdom, 21st–18thC BC, 9¼in (23.5cm) high.
£700–800
$1,000–1,150 ➶ Bon

A Mycenaean pottery jug, with simple painted decoration, 13th–11thC BC, 5½in (14cm) high.
£200–220
$300–330 ⊞ HEL

A Mediterranean alabaster vase, with decorated rim, 8th–6thC BC, 3in (7.5cm) diam.
£230–270
$330–390 ⊞ HEL

◄ **A group of Egyptian glazed faïence amulets,** late Dynastic Period, 8th–4thC BC, ½in (1cm) long.
£20–30
$30–45 each
⊞ HEL

An Etruscan terracotta votive head of a female, hair dressed beneath a diadem, traces of pink slip on the lips, 4thC BC, 9in (23cm) high.
£500–600
$720–870 ➶ Bon

An Egyptian carved steatite amulet, modelled as a cat, late Dynastic Period, 8th–4thC BC, ½in (1cm) high.
£70–80
$100–115 ⊞ HEL

A Campanian terracotta askos, modelled as a dove with folded wings, the body with white slip, the beak-shaped spout with traces of red slip, with perforated filler hole and black strap handle, 7¾in (19.5cm) long.
£800–1,200
$1,150–1,750 ✗ P
Ex-Bomford Collection.

A fragment from a Samian ware red glass bowl, with moulded decoration, 1stC, 4in (10cm) square.
£45–50
$65–75 ⊞ HEL
This fragment was found in London in the 1940s.

▶ **A Roman pottery jug,** with trefoil lip and single handle, 2nd–4thC, 3½in (9cm) high.
£50–60
$75–90 ⊞ Sama
This ancient Roman vessel was found in the Holy Land.

A Roman aubergine glass jug, with outfolded rim, tall cylindrical neck, rounded shoulder tapering to narrow base and rectangular handle, 1stC, 4¼in (11cm) high.
£1,000–1,100
$1,500–1,600 ✗ Bon

A Roman marble cinerary urn, the top of architectural outline, the base deeply carved in relief with ram's head, birds and festoons with anthemion motif to the sides, and carved inscription to Mepidus, 1st–2ndC, 11in (28cm) high.
£4,300–4,500
$6,250–6,500 ✗ CMS

A medieval silver ring brooch, with wide outwardly curving rim complete with pin engraved with owner's initials BN, 14th–15thC, 1¼in (3cm) diam.
£35–40
$50–60 ⊞ ANG
This rare item was found in Lincolnshire.

A medieval silver-gilt annular brooch, with hand-tooled flower devices with twisted loop, complete with pin and most gilding, 1¾in (4.5cm) diam.
£340–380
$490–570 ✗ Gle

A Tudor knife, found in London, c1600, 7in (18cm) long.
£30–35
$45–50 ⊞ BSA

A Roman bone lidded pyxis, the exterior carved with two figures, one of a plump old woman, naked, holding a staff and carrying a round container, the second figure of Eros, naked, carrying two containers, dark brown patina and repaired crack across middle, 3rdC, 2¼in (5.5cm) high.
£850–950
$1,250–1,380 ✗ Bon

▶ **A silver fork,** with ivory handle, the silver ferrule with two prongs, recovered from the River Thames, c1680, 5½in (14cm) long.
£90–100
$130–145 ⊞ ANG

Architectural Salvage

A carved oak corbel, c1660,
11in (28cm) high.
£1,800–2,000
$2,600–3,000 ⊞ SEA

A granite pillar,
17thC, 83in
(211cm) high.
£850–950
$1,250–1,350
⊞ RECL

**A Portland stone
balustrade,** from a
set of 32, 18thC,
32in (81.5cm) high.
£150–180
$220–260 ⊞ OLA

An oak door, with
original frame, c1799,
75in (190.5cm) high.
£750–1,000
$1,100–1,500 ⊞ OLA

**A selection of Victorian
terracotta crown chimney pots,**
some with brown saltglaze finish,
c1890, largest 54in (137cm) high.
£70–120
$100–170 each ⊞ HOP

**A mid-Victorian ham stone
Dorset/Devon window surround,**
39in (99cm) high.
£225–250
$320–360 ⊞ OLA

A copper-domed chimney vent,
with revolving blade centre section,
plaque inscribed 'Ewart
& Son Ltd Ventilation Engineers
346–350 Euston Road London
NW', c1900.
£130–150
$190–220 ⚒ RTo

**A selection of galvanized dolly
tubs,** c1930, largest 26in (66cm) high.
£15–20
$20–30 ⊞ HOP

▶ **A pair of brass wall
plaques depicting the
lion and the unicorn,**
one inscribed 'George V
ᴀᴅ1910–1936', the other
'King George's Field',
1936, 11in (28cm) high.
£360–400
$500–600 ⊞ OLA

Door Stops & Boot Scrapers

A Regency cast-iron boot scraper, 16in (40.5cm) wide.
£120–180
$160–260 ⊞ OLA

A Victorian cast-iron boot scraper, 14in (35.5cm) wide.
£75–85
$110–125 ⊞ HCJ

◀ **A cast-iron boot scraper,** with pierced, arched ends and a rectangular tray base, ex-Pitchford Hall, 19thC, 14in (35.5cm) long.
£70–80
$100–120
⚒ WBH

A brass cupid door stop, 1850, 17in (43cm) high.
£260–290
$380–440 ⊞ GBr

▶ **A painted cast-iron door stop,** modelled as a stork with its beak in a jar, from Aesop's Fables, 19thC, 11½in (29cm) high.
£950–1,050
$1,400–1,500 ⚒ S
This door stop was always used by the actor Sir Ralph Richardson to keep his dressing room door ajar, hence its high value.

A rampant lion cast-iron door stop, 1860, 15in (38cm) high.
£165–185
$240–270 ⊞ GBr

Heating

A wrought-iron adjustable pot stand, French, c1750, 23in (58.5cm) long.
£225–250
$320–360 ⊞ SEA

A wrought-iron warming stand, 18thC, 13in (33cm) long.
£35–40
$50–60 ⊞ HCJ

A pair of wrought-iron fire dogs, French, 18thC, 22in (56cm) high.
£440–480
$650–700 ⊞ SEA

A Regency cast-iron hobbed register grate, 37in (94cm) high.
£500–600
$720–870 ⊞ WRe

A brass coal scuttle, in the shape of a helmet, with embossed flower and foliate panels, foliate loop handle with turned ebony grip, on a spreading foot, 19thC, 22in (56cm) high, with matching shovel.
£450–500
$650–720 ⚒ AH

A painted wooden fire surround, the pilasters with pendant harebells, early 19thC, 76in (193cm) wide.
£190–220
$275–325 ⚒ WBH

A Victorian cast-iron and tiled forward grate, 38in (96.5cm) high.
£450–500
$650–720 ⊞ WRe

A cast-iron tiled combination grate, c1900, 48in (122cm) high.
£500–550
$720–800 ⊞ WRe

◄ **A Petrolux paraffin stove,** early 20thC, 27in (68.5cm) high.
£70–80
$100–120 ⚒ SWO

► **An Ideal Standard cast-iron radiator,** on four column feet, restored, 1920–50, 21in (53.5cm) long.
£220–250
$320–360 ⊞ OLA

A Coalbrookdale cast-iron fire basket, c1840, 36in (91.5cm) wide.
£2,000–2,400
$3,000–3,500 ⊞ ASH

A pair of cast-iron figural andirons, modelled as brownies with green glass eyes, illegible foundry mark, losses to log rests, American, late 19thC, 15½in (39.5cm) high.
£650–750
$950–1,100 ⚒ SK(B)

A pine and brass coal box, c1920, 18in (45.5cm) long.
£70–80
$100–120 ⊞ OLA

Art Deco

An Art Deco walnut sideboard,
with Bakelite and chrome handles,
60in (152.5cm) wide.
£425–475
$620–690 ⊞ HSt

**An Art Deco set of three chrome wall
lights,** 14in (35.5cm) high.
£300–500
$440–720 ⊞ ASA

◀ **An Art Deco Vitascope
electric mantel clock,** with
automated ship movement,
in a light green Bakelite
case, 12¾in (32.5cm) high.
£340–380
$500–600 🔨 AG

▶ **An Art Deco
enamelled glass scent
bottle,** 5in (12.5cm) high.
£65–75
$95–115 ⊞ TWAC

A Katzhütte bust, Austrian,
1930s, 8in (20.5cm) high.
£350–400
$500–600 ⊞ MD

**A ceramic stylized
model of a kangaroo,**
by Mougin Frères,
Nancy, French, 1920s–30s,
15in (38cm) high.
£150–175
$220–250 ⊞ ZOOM

◀ **An Art Deco-style
lady's platinum-cased
cocktail watch,** set with
82 diamonds, 1930s.
£550–600
$800–900 🔨 WilP

An Art Deco silver and enamel pin, with a central
cartouche depicting St Christopher, ½in (1cm) wide.
£75–85
$110–120 ⊞ DRJ

Art Nouveau

A brass aide-memoire, c1900, 2½in (5cm) high.
£20–30
$30–50 ⊞ VB

A copper jardinière, in the shape of a cauldron, on three swept supports terminating in spade-shaped motifs, with two handles, unmarked, 1885, 12¾in (32.5cm) diam.
£160–180
$230–260 ➤ P(B)

▶ A table lamp, with shell shade, on a Tiffany-style anodized base, American, c1900, 17¾in (45cm) high.
£400–440
$580–650 ➤ WilP

A gold and mother-of-pearl pendant brooch, c1900, 1½in (4cm) wide.
£350–450
$500–650 ⊞ ASA

A copper vase, attributed to WMF, the hammered body with stylized plant forms, with applied geometric brass handles, on a spreading foot, base marked with running ostrich within a lozenge, 1905, 11¾in (30cm) high.
£230–250
$330–360 ➤ P(B)

A sterling silver and plique-a-jour enamel pendant, the shaped plaque decorated with blue-grey plique-a-jour enamel in a trellis and floral vine design, with cabochon green and pink stones and a rose-cut diamond, 1910, 2¾in (7cm) long.
£600–700
$850–1,000 ➤ SK

A Montjoye enamelled glass vase, by Legras, French, c1900, 11in (28cm) high.
£380–450
$575–650 ⊞ OND

▶ An Art Nouveau carved mahogany photograph frame, 13in (33cm) high.
£85–95
$125–145 ⊞ AMR

◀ A Hancock & Sons Morrisware vase, designed by George Cartlidge, decorated with red flowers and blue and purple foliage on a mottled green ground, green printed factory mark, green painted signature, after 1918, 6¼in (16cm) high.
£1,000–1,200
$1,500–1,750 ➤ S(S)

A silver and enamel brooch, with yellow metal inlay, maker's mark 'A.J.S', Birmingham 1912, 2in (5cm) wide.
£100–120
$145–175 ➤ DD

Arts & Crafts

A silver beaker, by James Dixon & Sons, with punchwork decoration, on three ball feet, Sheffield 1888, 3¼in (8.5cm) high, 5.25oz.
£260–300
$360–440 ➤ **F&C**

A brass coal scuttle, with repoussé decoration, 1895, 16in (40.5cm) long.
£100–120
$145–175 ➤ **SWO**

A silver necklace, set with two black cabochon moonstones and four blister pearls within a pierced and foliate border, late 19thC/early 20thC, 19in (48cm) long.
£425–495
$620–720 ➤ **S(S)**

An oak cabinet, by Goodall Lamb & Heighway, with overhanging cornice above a panel door and metalware hinges, the lower section fitted with three short drawers and three open shelves, on a block base, c1890, 78in (198cm) high.
£550–650
$800–950 ➤ **P(B)**

> **Miller's is a price GUIDE not a price LIST**

A copper charger, c1890, 17in (43cm) diam.
£350–450
$500–650 ⊞ **ASA**

A copper blind convex mirror, embossed with butterflies and birds, with butterfly wing and mother-of-pearl detail, late 19thC, 16in (40.5cm) diam.
£530–580
$750–850 ➤ **GAK**

▶ **An oak and copper plant stand,** with stylized floral embossed panels, on four square legs, c1900, 27½in (70cm) high.
£180–220
$220–320 ➤ **P(B)**

An Art Nouveau brass wall clock, the square brass dial with embossed Roman numerals and Celtic banding, with brass weights and pendulum, Scottish, 10¾in (27.5cm) square.
£200–250
$300–350 ➤ **TRM**

◀ **An Art Nouveau oak wall cabinet,** the cupboard door with pottery plaque inset depicting dancing figures, recess and side shelves with carved motifs, Dutch, 27in (68.5cm) wide.
£375–425
$550–620 ➤ **TRM**

Mabel Lucie Attwell

At the turn of the century, children's illustration was one of the few artistic areas where women could compete on an equal footing with men, and none were more successful than Mabel Lucie Attwell (1879–1964). The ninth child of a London butcher, Attwell put herself through art school by selling drawings for one guinea a piece. She began illustrating children's books and postcards in the 1900s and, together with her husband, artist Harry Earnshaw, she also worked in advertising. Attwell's greatest fame, however, came after WWI, partly inspired by necessity when in 1916 Harold, who had joined the Artists' Rifles, had his right arm blown off, which left her financially responsible for their family of three children. She fulfilled the task admirably.

In the inter-war years Mabel Lucie Attwell became a household name. Her famous bun-cheeked infants, the antithesis of her own long, strong-boned face and said to be inspired by her daughter Peggy (b1909), appeared on everything from biscuit tins to bathroom plaques and advertised every conceivable product from toothpaste to the London Underground. Attwell characters were turned into dolls and games. Shelley china was decorated with the 'Boo-Boos' (a series of roly-poly fairies), and the young princesses Elizabeth and Margaret both ate from Attwell nursery ware. There were endless books and annuals; countless postcards and greetings cards (in 1941 alone postcard sales topped two million).

Although her professional career never faltered, Attwell's personal life was marked by tragedy. One son died from pneumonia aged 20, the other never fully recovered from a serious car crash. Her husband became increasingly ill from his war wounds and died in 1937. Her drawings, however, never lost their cheerful charm. Attwell merchandise is still being produced today, there is an active collectors' club and demand for vintage material (the earlier the better) continues to rise.

Mabel Lucie Attwell, three *Boo-Boos* books, with green, brown and red jackets, 1920–22, 5 x 6in (12.5 x 15cm).
£90–110
$130–160 ⊞ MEM

◀ **Mabel Lucie Attwell,** *Little So Shy* cut-out book, by Valentines & Sons, 1910, 11in (28cm) high.
£150–160
$220–240 ⊞ MEM

J. M. Barrie, *Peter Pan & Wendy*, illustrated by Mabel Lucie Attwell, published by Hodder & Stoughton, 12 mounted colour plates, in original yellow cloth binding, 1924, 9 x 7in (23 x 18cm).
£110–130
$160–190 ⊞ BIB

A Mabel Lucie Attwell nursery plate, decorated in yellow, green and red on a pale blue ground, 1930s–40s, 9in (23cm) diam.
£80–100
$115–145 ⊞ I&M

A Mabel Lucie Attwell cut-out calendar, by Valentines & Sons, with the figure of a golfer in shades of brown, on a wooden base, 1930s, 9in (23cm) wide.
£175–185
$250–270 ⊞ MEM

A Shelley Mabel Lucie Attwell nursery plate, decorated in yellow, green, black and red on a white ground, c1930, 7in (18cm) diam.
£130–150
$190–220 ⊞ BD

A Mabel Lucie Attwell warming dish with lid, decorated in yellow and green, c1930, 8in (20.5cm) diam.
£200–225
$300–330 ⊞ MEM

A Shelley Mabel Lucie Attwell nursery mug, decorated in blue, pink and green, 1930s, 4in (10cm) high.
£175–195
$255–285 ⊞ BD

Two porcelain Mabel Lucie Attwell toothbrush holders, decorated in yellow, brown, red and blue, German, c1934, 4in (10cm) high.
£90–120
$130–150 each ⊞ MEM

A Mabel Lucie Attwell Nestol advertising puzzle, 1934, 9 x 7in (23 x 18cm), in original box.
£180–200
$250–300 ⊞ MEM

A pack of Mabel Lucie Attwell Dorma white bed sheets, unopened, 1930s, 20in (51cm) long.
£80–90
$115–130 ⊞ MEM

Two Mabel Lucie Attwell Bijou Mottoes, by Valentines & Sons, decorated in pink, blue yellow and green, 1930–40, 3 x 5in (7.5 x 12.5cm), framed.
£15–20
$20–30 each ⊞ MEM

► **A Mabel Lucie Attwell kitchen jotter,** decorated in yellow, blue and red, c1950, 12 x 6in (30.5 x 15cm).
£15–17
$20–25 ⊞ CRN

Two Mabel Lucie Attwell postcards, 1950s.
£5–10
$10–15 ⊞ MEM

A Mabel Lucie Attwell
cut-out calendar, by
Valentines & Sons, Dundee,
1953, 10in (25.5cm) high.
£35–45
$50–70 ⊞ MEM

► A Mabel Lucie
Attwell Peek
Frean's biscuit
tin, c1960, 8in
(20.5cm) diam.
£20–30
$30–50 ⊞ MEM

An Old Hall stainless
steel children's plate,
in original blue box with
Mabel Lucie Attwell design,
c1960, 8in (20.5cm) diam.
£25–35
$30–50 ⊞ MEM

► A Mabel
Lucie Attwell
Kinnerton's
Easter chocolate
box, 1992,
9in (23cm) wide.
£20–25
$30–35 ⊞ MEM

*Lucie Attwell's Story for
a Poppet,* published by
Dean, 1961, 8 x 5in
(20.5 x 12.5cm).
£16–18
$20–25 ⊞ J&J

A set of eight Mabel
Lucie Attwell Huntley
& Palmer's biscuit tins,
1960s, 5in (12.5cm) diam.
£120–140
$170–200 ⊞ MEM

A Mabel Lucie Attwell
Memories of Yesterday
porcelain jam pot, in
green and brown, c1992,
3½in (9cm) high.
£35–45
$50–70 ⊞ MEM

Three Mabel Lucie
Attwell Memories of
Yesterday lapel badges,
one inscribed 'Memories UK
Mabel Lucie Attwell Club',
c1990, 3in (7.5cm) high.
£5–8
$10–15 each ⊞ MEM

Autographs

Buzz Aldrin, a signed colour photograph, half-length, wearing a white spacesuit, an image of the moon in the background, c1969, 10 x 8in (25.5 x 20.5cm).
£200–220
$290–320 ✒ VS

Fred Astaire, a signed photograph, 1940s, 10 x 8in (25.5 x 20.5cm).
£300–340
$450–500 ⊞ SDP

Cross Reference
See Rock & Pop
(page 329)

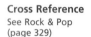

Lauren Bacall, an autograph and photograph, mounted, 1970s, 10 x 8in (25.5 x 20.5cm).
£50–60
$75–90 ⊞ SDP

The Beatles, signatures of all four Beatles on a piece of brown paper, adhesive marks not affecting signatures, 1964.
£1,000–1,100
$1,500–1,600 ✒ DW
A note of provenance states that the signatures were obtained by W. F. Charlton, Director of British Airways Helicopters, during the filming of *A Hard Day's Night*. '...they had use of Mr Charlton's office, he met them on a daily basis and came to the conclusion that they were a really nice group of young men.'

Enid Blyton, an autograph letter expressing satisfaction that her books were on the reading list in school, 1959, 3½ x 5½in (9 x 14cm).
£300–330
$450–480 ⊞ IQ

Napoleon, a letter written by Mounier and a photograph, both signed by Napoleon, mounted, 1813, 9 x 7in (23 x 18cm).
£900–1,000
$1,300–1,500 ⊞ IQ

Sir Adrian Boult, a postcard showing Boult, half-length, in old age studying a score, 1939, 6 x 4in (15 x 10cm).
£55–65
$80–95 ✒ DW

Leslie Caron, a signed photograph, mounted, 1950s, 10 x 8in (25.5 x 20.5cm).
£35–38
$50–60 ⊞ SDP

Charlie Chaplin, a signed photograph, 1930s, 7 x 5in (18 x 12.5cm).
£450–500
$650–720 ⊞ SDP

José Collins, a signed silver print by Dorothy Wilding, Royal Photographer, also signed by Wilding, 1932, 20 x 13in (51 x 33cm).
£180–200
$250–300 ⊞ BoC

Arthur Conan Doyle,
a signed sepia
postcard, c1910.
£650–750
$950–1,100 ✒ VS

**Edward, Duke of Windsor
and Wallis, Duchess of
Windsor,** a signed printed
leaflet with details of the
landing arrangements
issued by the Cunard Line
for the voyage of RMS
Queen Elizabeth from New
York, 18th April 1956, also
signed by Ginger Rogers,
minor staining.
£240–280
$350–400 ✒ VS

Harry H. Corbett, a signed and
inscribed photograph, three-quarter
length, late 1950s–early 1960s,
10 x 8in (25.5 x 20.3cm).
£100–120
$145–175 ✒ VS

◀ **Charles Darwin,** a signed
attendance register for the
Philosophical Club of the Royal Society,
with the signatures of John Tyndall,
Lyell, Richard Patridge, Muller and
15 others, with pencil minutes of the
meeting and observations of procedure
and scientific matters discussed,
dated 22nd November 1855, 2°.
£850–950
$1,250–1,350 ✒ DW

Isadora Duncan, a signed photograph, and unsigned photograph,
mounted, 1919, largest 9 x 5in
(23 x 12.5cm).
£675–750
$975–1,100 ⊞ SDP

Aleister Crowley, a signed note, 'in haste –
O.K. will expect you at Mr Chase', with
photograph, mounted, 14 x 17in (35.5 x 43cm).
£315–350
$450–500 ⊞ IQ
English writer and black magician, Aleister
Crowley (1875–1967), first became
interested in the occult at Cambridge. He
went on to form his own order, the Silver
Star, and settled for several years in Sicily
with a group of disciples. Rumours of drugs,
orgies and sacrifice abounded leading to
his expulsion from Italy. Many of those
associated with him died tragically. Crowley
gained the reputation of 'the wickedest
man alive' and, even after his death,
memorabilia connected with the 'great
beast', as he liked to be called, is still
sought after.

Walt Disney, a small signed card, London, 1935.
£700–800
$1,000–1,150 ✒ VS

**Cross
Reference**
See Politics
(page 301)

▶ **Carrie Fisher,**
a signed colour
photograph,
full-length,
wearing a *Star
Wars* costume,
1970s, 10 x 8in
(25.5 x 20.5cm).
£35–40
$50–60 ✒ VS

◀ **Margot Fonteyn,** a photograph and signed
letter, 1955, 6 x 8in (15 x 20.5cm).
£65–75
$95–115 ⊞ SDP

George Formby a signed photograph, 1936, 11 x 8½in (28 x 21.5cm).
£100–110
$145–160 ✒ VS

Jimi Hendrix and the Walker Brothers, a signed official tour programme, also signed by Scott Walker and Englebert Humperdinck, 7th April 1967, 10½ x 8in (26.5 x 20.5cm).
£1,400–1,600
$2,000–2,300 ✒ Bon

Adolf Hitler, a publicity postcard by Hoffman, signed in ink, c1937, 6 x 4in (15 x 10cm).
£1,800–2,000
$2,600–2,900 ⊞ IQ

Clark Gable, a signed copy of *The Stars and Stripes,* 'Daily newspaper of US Armed Forces in the European Theater of Operations', 28th July 1943.
£130–150
$190–220 ✒ DW
Obtained in person by a lady who worked for the American Red Cross during WWII and who 'bumped into' Gable whilst on duty. Autographs of Gable as a member of the US armed forces in WWII are rare. Unlike many of his peers, Gable had a distinguished military career.

▶ **Matt Groening,** a signed and inscribed colour still from *The Simpsons*, depicting the family, with additional ink sketch of Bart Simpson drawn to image, 19th June 1999, 8 x 10in (20.5 x 25.5cm).
£190–210
$275–300 ✒ VS

Sid James, a signed photograph, 1960s, 5 x 3in (12.5 x 7.5cm).
£135–150
$200–220 ⊞ SDP

▶ **Vivien Leigh,** a signed photograph, dressed in costume, slight surface creasing, 1940s–50s, 6½ x 5in (16.5 x 12.5cm).
£220–250
$320–360 ✒ VS

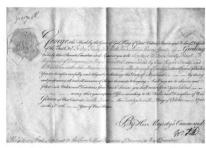

King George III, a signed military commission appointing Philip Perry an adjutant in the 21st Regiment of Dragoon (or Royal Forresters) commanded by John Manners, Marquess of Granby, countersigned by William Pitt The Elder, given at the Court at Saville House, with embossed paper seal affixed, folds, 27th October 1760.
£330–350
$480–500 ✒ VS

◀ **Jacqueline Kennedy,** a signed envelope and card expressing gratitude for expressions of sympathy following the assassination, stamped, 1964, 6 x 3in (15 x 7.5cm).
£90–100
$130–150 ⊞ IQ

Arthur Lowe, a signed postcard, wearing *Dad's Army* costume, 1970s.
£120–140
$175–200 ✒ VS

Manchester United, 11 team autographs on a single autograph album leaf, including W. Robertson, T. Jones, E. Hine, J. Griffith, S. Bamford, and Billy McKay, 1st December 1934.
£80–100
$115–145 ⚲ **DW**

Alan Alexander Milne, a signed copy of *If I May*, inscribed on the front free endpaper 'For Irene Rooke – the adorable Marion – in admiration and gratitude from A. A. Milne.', original quarter cloth binding, rubbed, worn and faded, inner front hinge cracked, New York, 1921.
£50–60
$75–90 ⚲ **WW**

Ayrton Senna, a signed colour photograph, 1990s, 9½ x 7in (24 x 18cm).
£850–950
$1,250–1,400 ⚲ **DW**

Items in the Autographs section have been arranged in alphabetical order.

▶ **George Bernard Shaw,** signed card to Mrs Lyth, Postmistress at Ayot St Lawrence, asking for three pounds' worth of three-halfpenny stamps, 23rd July 1938.
£160–180
$230–260 ⚲ **VS**

James Stewart, an original pen and ink cartoon of Harvey on white artist's card, signed, 1980s.
£240–260
$350–380 ⚲ **DW**
Harvey was one of Stewart's most successful, if somewhat curious, films. It centred on an eccentric (played by Stewart) who could see and converse with a giant rabbit named Harvey, much to the consternation of the rest of the cast who could see nothing. Stewart took pride in producing these cartoon sketches and they are much sought after today.

Field Marshal Lord Roberts, a sepia portrait, signed as Commander in Chief in India, 1880s.
£85–95
$125–140 ⚲ **DW**

Leon Trotsky, a document from the Russian civil war, signed in blue pencil, 1918, 6in (15cm) square.
£720–800
$1,000–1,250 ⊞ **IQ**

Cross Reference
See Crime (page 174)

Automobilia

A Rolls-Royce chauffeur's silver and enamel cap badge, in original box, c1913, 2½in (6.5cm) high.
£275–350
$400–500 ⊞ MURR

▶ **A cast-iron hand-operated Surrey petrol pump,** maker's plate reads 'Model CH 1 Consumer Pump. Serial No CH1/ 8431 Pat No 306358/28/ Manufactured By Avery Hardoll Ltd Oakcroft Road Chessington Surrey', 1920s, 70in (178cm) high.
£120–140
$175–200 ⚲ BBR

▶ **A Packard Luxurious Motoring advertising pamphlet,** c1920, 6 x 11in (15 x 28cm).
£12–15
$15–20 ⊞ HO

A glass posy vase, with brass fitting, from a luxury car, 1920s, 7in (18cm) high.
£35–40
$50–60 ⊞ HO

A Brooklands badge, gold lettering on light and dark blue, dated 1935, 1½in (4cm) square.
£30–35
$45–50 ⊞ COB

A motorcycle helmet shop display card, black lettering on white and orange, 1940s–50s, 10in (25.5cm) high.
£10–12
$15–18 ⊞ MRW

▶ **A collection of vehicle excise licences,** 1950s, 3½in (9cm) diam.
£5–8
$10–15 each
⊞ COB

A Seddon Diesel lorry badge, c1950.
£45–55
$60–80 ⊞ HOP
The Seddon sign was designed by B. H. Seddon, daughter of the founder.

Four key rings, 1960s,
largest 2½in (6.5cm) long.
£5–15
$8–20 each ⊞ HUX

An aluminium Hackney Carriage sign,
1950s–60s, 11in (28cm) wide.
£14–15
$18–20 ⊞ BiR

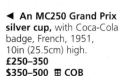

A quart oil bottle, 1950,
14in (35.5cm) high.
£3–5
$5–10 ⊞ BLM

A painted, pressed aluminium motorcycle trade plate,
GR stamp, issued in Gloucester, July 1923, 7in (18cm) wide.
£45–50
$65–75 ⊞ MW

◄ **An MC250 Grand Prix silver cup,** with Coca-Cola badge, French, 1951,
10in (25.5cm) high.
£250–350
$350–500 ⊞ COB

Number plates

Motor vehicle registration plates were first introduced in Paris in 1893, spreading to the rest of France by 1901. According to the UK press, British drivers were generally opposed to this measure considering that the number plate made the private motor car look like 'a common cab prowling for hire'. But with 5,000 vehicles now in use, Parliament was determined to exert control. The Motor Car Act, passed on 1st January 1904, stipulated both the licensing of drivers and the registration of vehicles. The first registration number 'A1' was granted to Earl Russell, the Under Secretary for Air, who had queued all night to secure it. In 1959, this plate was sold for charity for £2,500 – an early example of the collectable appeal of an interesting number plate.

An aluminium motorcycle front number plate,
issued in London, March 1960–62, 10in (25.5cm) wide.
£1–2
$3–5 ⊞ MW

Bathrooms

The Victorian period saw the building of new sewer systems, the passing of numerous acts to improve water supplies and sanitation, and a revolution in personal hygiene. The first public lavatory was opened in London in 1851, instigated by Sir Henry Cole, organizer of the Great Exhibition. Bathrooms became increasingly common in middle and upper class homes, and were filled with the latest fixtures and fittings.

In the 1880s, Thomas Crapper perfected the standard flushing toilet cistern and developed the U-bend, which prevented sewer fumes and rats from entering the house. In 1884 Jennings exhibited what was said to be the first pedestal lavatory and the same company was also responsible for introducing the oval 'picture frame' lavatory seat. Since lavatory bowls were no longer encased in wooden surrounds they became increasingly decorative, often painted with flowers both inside and out.

Other well-known manufacturers included Twyford, Brahmah, Shanks and Royal Doulton. Crapper was not the only lavatory pioneer whose name was to become immortalized in the English language. Edward Johns won an award for his WC at the 1876 Philadelphia Exhibition, hence the American colloquialism 'john'.

A walnut-framed bidet, with inset French faïence blue and white liner, floral-painted, on turned supports and stretchers, early 19thC, 23½in (59.5cm) wide.
£1,300–1,500
$2,000–2,200 ⚲ RBB

A Victorian mahogany and lead-lined toilet cistern, 22in (56cm) wide.
£550–600
$800–870 ⊞ WRe

A porcelain water fountain, with floral decoration, French, c1889, 36in (91.5cm) high.
£1,000–1,200
$1,500–1,750 ⊞ OLA

A pair of Victorian globe bath taps, refurbished, 5in (12.5cm) high.
£160–180
$230–260 ⊞ OLA

A Victorian ceramic lavatory bowl, by Stock Sons & Taylor, Birmingham, Rd No. 19753, 16½in (42cm) high.
£80–100
$115–145 ⚲ SWO

▶ **A pair of Victorian nickel-plated roll-top bath collars,** 4in (10cm) long.
£70–90
$100–130 ⊞ WRe

A pair of Shanks & Co polished brass long throw-plunger bath taps, 1¼in thread, fully reconditioned, 1895.
£300–350
$450–500 ⊞ WRe

A Staffordshire Royal washdown pedestal lavatory bowl, blue and white transfer-printed, decorated with flowers and foliage, late 19thC, 15½in (39.5cm) high.
£330–360
$480–520 🏹 **E**

A white Excelsior washdown pedestal lavatory bowl, with S-trap, 1898, 16in (40.5cm) high.
£450–500
$650–700 ⊞ **OLA**

A blue and white Excelsior washdown pedestal lavatory bowl, with S-trap, 1898, 16in (40.5cm) high.
£900–1,000
$1,300–1,500 ⊞ **OLA**

▶ **A waterfall lavatory,** with church seat and flushing cistern, bowl c1890, seat 1920, 96in (244cm) high.
£1,800–2,000
$2,600–3,000 ⊞ **C&R**

A pair of Victorian polished brass roll-top bath taps with collars, fully reconditioned, 1890s, 6in (15cm) high.
£290–330
$425–475 ⊞ **WRe**

A Morrison Ingham & Co Triton patent embossed lavatory bowl, with enclosed trap, c1895, 16in (40.5cm) high.
£900–1,100
$1,300–1,600 ⊞ **WRe**

A Doulton & Co mahogany lavatory seat, c1897.
£225–250
$325–375 ⊞ **WRe**

A pair of nickel-plated basin taps, with ½in thread, fully reconditioned, c1890, 5in (12.5cm) high.
£180–200
$250–300 ⊞ **WRe**

An Edwardian cloakroom basin, with nickel-plated taps, fully reconditioned, 22in (56cm) wide.
£500–550
$720–800 ⊞ **WRe**

▶ **A collection of enamelled iron soap dishes,** in pastel colours, French, c1900, largest 5½in (14cm) long.
£12–15
$15–20 each ⊞ **HOP**

An enamel soap, sponge and toothbrush holder, blue with a white liner, early 20thC, 7in (18cm) high.
£25–30
$35–45 ⊞ B&R

An Edwardian Bathena cloakroom basin and nickel-plated taps, reconditioned, 25in (63.5cm) wide.
£450–500
$650–720 ⊞ WRe

A pair of Art Deco bath taps, refurbished and re-nickeled, 6in (15cm) high.
£200–220
$280–320 ⊞ OLA

◄ A Royal Doulton p-trap lavatory, with nickel-plated flush pipe clip, 1930, 16in (40.5cm) high.
£400–450
$580–650 ⊞ WRe

THOMAS CRAPPER & CO.'S
Sanitary Specialities.
IMPROVED
LAVATORY BASIN.
ELASTIC VALVE CLOSET.
IMPROVED SYPHON
Water Waste Preventer.
50, 52, & 54, MARLBOROUGH ROAD, CHELSEA, LONDON, S.W.

A Thomas Crapper & Co Sanitary Specialities mounted advertisement, c1905, 16 x 12in (40.5 x 30.5cm).
£18–20
$25–30 ⊞ J&S

An Edwardian pair of Shanks & Co nickel-plated lever taps, fully reconditioned, 6in (15cm) high.
£270–300
$400–440 ⊞ WRe

An Art Deco-style nickel-plated bath spray mixer, ¾in thread, fully reconditioned, 1930s.
£450–500
$650–720 ⊞ WRe

A Twyfords high level lidded china cistern, c1910, 20in (51cm) wide.
£400–450
$580–650 ⊞ WRe

An Art Deco nickel-plated bath mixer set, ¾in thread, fully reconditioned, 1930s, 7in (18cm) wide.
£380–420
$550–650 ⊞ WRe

A brass and cast-iron heated towel rail, with fluted radiator, fully reconditioned, c1935, 37in (94cm) high.
£500–550
$700–800 ⊞ WRe

A set of wall-mounted taps and soap tray, French, 1940s, 9in (23cm) wide.
£250–300
$350–450 ⊞ OLA

Bicycles

A **Stevengraph,** entitled 'The Last Lap', woven in silk, printed label to verso, woven in Ventnor, manufactured in Coventry and London, dampstained, c1870, 2 x 6in (5 x 15cm), with original mount.
£200–220
$300–330 ✗ DW

An **Alldays & Onions bicycle anvil,** for repairing chains, c1880.
£55–65
$80–100 ⊞ BAJ

A **'La Percutante' shaft-drive gentleman's bicycle,** with black-painted frame, re-nickeled driving mechanism, 36-spoke wooden rims with aluminium linings, Christy saddle, wooden handlebars with cork grips, French, late 1890s, 28in (71cm) tyres fitted, 22½in (57cm) frame.
£900–1,000
$1,300–1,500 ✗ Bon

▶ A **Humber enamel sign,** in the shape of the Humber transfer with the running man trademark, white lettering on a black ground, marked 'Willing & Co Ltd London', late 1890s, 23½in (59.5cm) high.
£150–200
$220–300 ✗ P(Ba)

A **Penny Farthing,** with oval backbone, fluted front and rear forks, hollow rims, radial spokes, cranked down bars, U-section replaced, saddle cover, handles and pedals cut down from original, some rusting and repairs, early 1880s, rear wheel 16in (40.5cm) diam.
£800–900
$1,150–1,300 ✗ P(Ba)

A **Victorian brass and silver-plated four-turn cyclist's buglet,** by J. Higham, Manchester, stamped, 7½in (19cm) wide.
£500–550
$700–800 ✗ Bon

A **silver-plated cycling prize,** modelled as a rider wearing fashionable period cycling attire preparing to mount a penny farthing, on a wooden plinth, c1880, 7in (18cm) long.
£600–650
$870–950 ⊞ TML

A **stein,** decorated with a cycling scene, German, 1895–1900, 6in (15cm) high.
£200–230
$300–330 ⊞ AU

A **League of American Wheelmen stein,** the base with lithophane, inscribed 'Indianapolis 1898', 6in (15cm) high.
£550–650
$800–1,000 ⊞ AU

A Quadrant open-framed tricycle, with central chainwheel, 1in-pitch chain-driving fixed differential with contracting band brake, the whole on hangers from the frame, non-extended raised bars with plunger-type brake lever operating rear brake, double plate fork crown, c1899, 22in (56cm) frame .
£500–600
$720–870 ✗ P(Ba)

An Ever Ready battery wooden bicycle lamp, deep version with fluted reflector and magnifying lens, trade label to case interior, original varnished wood finish, weathered, early 20thC, 4½in (12cm) high.
£60–70
$90–100 ✗ P(Ba)

A silver-plated pewter WMF inkwell, probably presented as a trophy, c1905, 10in (25.5cm) wide.
£800–850
$1,150–1,250 ⊞ AU

► **An Excelsior bicycle,** American, c1910.
£550–600
$800–900 ⊞ YEST

A Bradbury Cycles advertising postcard.
£40–45
$60–70 ✗ VS

► **A Thanet light touring bicycle,** frame design built using silver solder, c1949.
£700–800
$1,000–1,150 ⊞ AVT

An Eagle drop-front tandem, American, 1900–05.
£1,000–1,250
$1,500–1,800 ⊞ AU

An Alldays & Onions child's bicycle, with photographs of original owner (not shown), 1914, 40in (101.5cm) long.
£400–450
$580–650 ⊞ BAJ

A Cyclops human-powered vehicle, by Burrows Engineering, Norwich, with alloy rimmed front driver/steerer, 84-tooth chain ring, 12-tooth sprocket, 26in chrome-titanium rear rim, 1986, 52in (132cm) wheelbase.
£750–800
$1,100–1,200 ✗ P(Ba)
The Cyclops is shrouded in an aerodynamic fibreglass housing and gained its name from the fact that this casing had no window. The rider viewed the road using fibre optic technology connected to a pair of goggles requiring only a minute single aperture in the housing's nose.

A Mobo Tot Cycle, 1950s.
£70–80
$100–120 ⊞ JUN

Black History & Memorabilia

This section is devoted to Black history and memorabilia. It begins with material commemorating the history of slavery and moves on to reflect on the vast amount of black memorabilia mass-produced from the late 19th century and into the 20th.

Manufactured for a predominantly white audience, the images on the objects portrayed are often stereotypical, derogatory and racist. Blacks are generally represented as servants, piccaninnies, savages or entertainers. The golly, which first appeared in *The Adventures of Two Dutch Dolls* (1895) by Florence K. and Bertha Upton, and was adopted by Robertson's jam and marmalade company in 1914, became a favourite nursery and advertising character. It is not just the images that can seem shocking, but the language, 'Darkie' toothbrushes, the 'Nigga' motorcycle repair

outfit, even the word Golliwogg itself. It was only in the 1950s/60s with the development of the Civil Rights movement and growing social and political awareness that attitudes, and as such the portrayals of Blacks on everyday domestic objects (and vocabulary), began to change.

However offensive some of these objects might seem today, they are a part of our culture and a physical representation of how Blacks were considered and portrayed by whites at a certain period in history. It is a measure of how times have changed that not only has much of this imagery become unacceptable (Robertson's have now abandoned their famous golly), but that these artefacts, made by and for a white audience, are now sought-after by black collectors (particularly in the USA).

A white metal anti-slavery ticket,
'Wilberforce For Ever', the reverse with 'Humanity Is The Cause Of The People', pierced for suspension, 1807, 1½in (4cm) diam.
£220–250
$320–360 ⊞ TML
British politician William Wilberforce (1759–1833) was a prominent figure in the abolition of the slave trade. Converted to evangelical Christianity, he promoted anti-slavery legislation in the House of Commons achieving his first success on 25 March 1807 with the passing of the bill to abolish the slave trade in the British West Indies. This did not, however, free those enslaved before the bill became law. Wilberforce continued to campaign for the Black cause. Thanks in part to his efforts, the Slavery Abolition Act he had promoted throughout his political life was eventually passed in 1833, one month after his death.

A manuscript proposal of the Royal African Company,
responding to the House of Commons' request 'for ye better settling of trade to Africa and securing of same to this Kingdom and ye Plantations', c1709, 2°.
£900–1,100
$1,300–1,600 ⋏ DW
An important document in the history of the slave trade which accelerated considerably at this time and through the reigns of the first three Georges, leading to the establishment of the British Empire in Africa and the British Colonies in America.

A manuscript letter book,
compiled by M. J. Simper, a high-status resident of Antigua, possibly a plantation owner, with detailed discussion of day-to-day conditions including sugar and rum production, trade with Britain and America, and negro slave conditions and clothing and provisions requirements, modern cloth boards, 1823–24, 4°.
£1,000–1,200
$1,500–1,700 ⋏ DW

LOCATE THE SOURCE

The source of each illustration in Miller's can be found by checking the code letters below each caption with the Key to Illustrations, pages 444–452.

A porcellaneous mug, printed with a slavery scene entitled 'Liberty Given to the Slaves', faded, c1835, 2¼in (5.5cm) high.
£80–90
$115–130 ↗ SAS

A London Anti-Slavery Convention white metal medal, by J. Davis, 1840, 2in (5cm) diam.
£220–250
$320–360 ⊞ TML

The Dandy Slave, from the *Illustrated London News*, 1861, 8 x 5½in (20.5 x 14cm).
£35–45
$50–70 ⊞ CWO

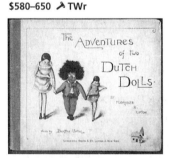

A pair of bronze figures of Moroccan boys, made in Vienna, c1890, 6in (15cm) long.
£400–450
$580–650 ↗ TWr

A pack of Golly playing cards, illustrated by and © Florence Upton for Thomas de la Rue & Co, c1900, 4 x 2¾in (10 x 7cm).
£50–55
$75–85 ⊞ HUX

Florence K. and Bertha Upton, *The Adventures of two Dutch Dolls,* first editions, original pictorial boards with cloth spines, c1895, 4°.
£170–200
$250–300 ↗ WW

A Simon & Halbig black bisque-headed doll, No. 1009, with fixed brown glass eyes, open mouth with red painted lips and nostrils and upper teeth, feathered eyebrows, dark brown wig, fully jointed composition body, wearing a pink velvet dress, underclothes, socks and leather shoes, bonnet decorated with gold coins, German, chipped, c1900, 27in (68.5cm) high.
£1,200–1,400
$1,750–2,000 ↗ Bon

> **Cross Reference**
> See Colour Review (page 71)

A group photograph of an integrated school class, c1908.
£30–34
$45–50 ⊞ VP

◄ **A photograph of a Black boy dancing Le Cake-Walk,** Paris, France, c1905.
£28–32
$40–45 ⊞ VP

A child's plate, illustrated by and
© Florence Upton, 1908–18, 10in
(25.5cm) diam.
£100–150
$145–225 ⊞ MURR

A Spin & Old Maid card game,
by Thomas de la Rue, 1910–20,
3½ x 2in (9 x 5cm).
£35–45
$50–70 ⊞ MURR

A Christmas Greeting postcard,
c1910, 5½ x 3½in (14 x 9cm).
£30–35
$40–50 ⊞ CWO

I'SE PINING FOR YOU IN DIS PAIR

**A postcard 'I'se Pining For You
in Dis Pair',** c1910, 5½ x 3½in
(14 x 9cm).
£30–35
$40–50 ⊞ CWO

◄ **Three gramophone needle tins,** with
decorated lids, c1920, largest 2in (5cm) wide.
£40–80
$65–115 ⊞ HUX

GOLDEN
SHRED

RECIPES

**A Robertson's Golly
Golden Shred Recipes
book,** c1928, 8 x 5in
(20.5 x 12.5cm).
£25–35
$40–50 ⊞ MURR

**An All-Blacks Pure
Mint sweet tin,** c1930,
5in (12.5cm) high.
£140–180
$200–250 ⊞ HUX

A Diase tin, 'Le meilleure
essence pour le moteur
humain', French, c1930,
4½in (11.5cm) high.
£30–35
$40–50 ⊞ HUX

**A Negri Vert Brillant
De Chrome tin,** c1930,
4in (10cm) high.
£22–26
$30–35 ⊞ HUX

◄ **A 'Nigga' Motor Cycle Repair
Outfit,** c1930, 4in (10cm) wide.
£40–45
$60–70 ⊞ HUX

► **Four 'Darkie' De Luxe toothbrushes,** c1930, 6¼in (16cm) long.
£10–12
$15–20 each ⊞ HUX

A collection of Norah Wellings dolls, with brown velour doll in striped trousers, various smaller dolls, two dressed as Islanders in grass skirts, with a plush cat with green glass eyes, 1930s, largest 19¼in (49cm) high.
£550–650
$800–1,000 ➶ DN

An autographed photograph of Lena Horne, by W. T. Gray, the first black woman vocalist to be featured with a white band, American, c1940.
£45–55
$65–80 ⊞ VP

A Rhum Georgetta enamel thermometer, 1940s, 11½in (29cm) high.
£32–35
$45–50 ⊞ HUX

A Combex rubberized doll, 1940–50, 6in (15cm) high.
£30–35
$45–50 ⊞ RUSS

A postcard, 'I can spare you this little lump of coal–keep it dark!', 1948, 5½ x 3½in (14 x 9cm).
£25–28
$35–45 ⊞ CWO

A pair of Murano glass novelty candlesticks, 1940–50, 24in (61cm) high.
£275–325
$400–480 ➶ Bon(C)

A WWII photograph of a black sailor, c1944.
£30–35
$45–50 ⊞ VP

A Merrythought cloth Golly, with painted button eyes and red felt mouth, c1960, 17in (43cm) high.
£100–120
$145–175 ➶ Bon

A Zulu Lulu plastic cocktails sticks card, 1950s, 9 x 11in (23 x 28cm).
£40–45
$60–70 ⊞ SpM

▶ **A Banania key ring,** c1965, 1½in (4cm) long.
£3–4
$4–8 ⊞ HUX

A Training School for Communists group photograph, including Martin Luther King and Miles Horton, Belmont Massachusetts, c1960.
£25–30
$35–40 ⊞ VP

Books

Iain Banks, *The Wasp Factory*, first edition, 1984, 8¾ x 5¾in (22 x 14.5cm).
£120–140
$170–200 ⊞ BIB

Georges Braque, *Cahier de Georges Braque 1917–1947*, edited by Maeght Editeur, Paris, with dust jacket, c1947, 4°.
£50–60
$70–90 ↗ DW

Benjamin Britten, *Tribute to Benjamin Britten on his Fiftieth Birthday*, first limited edition, signed by Benjamin Britten, published by Faber & Faber, 1966, 9 x 6in (23 x 15cm).
£85–95
$125–145 ⊞ SDP

► **Elizabeth Barrett Browning,** *Mrs. Browning*, poetical works, published by Nimmo Hay & Mitchell, Edinburgh, c1880, 8 x 5in (20.5 x 12.5cm).
£12–18
$15–20 ⊞ AnS

John Buchan, *Mr Standfast*, first edition, published by Hodder & Stoughton, 1919, 7½ x 5in (19 x 12.5cm).
£65–75
$95–115 ⊞ BAY

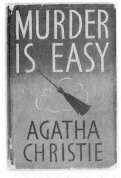

Agatha Christie, *Murder is Easy*, first edition, original dust jacket, loss to spine, 1939.
£800–1,000
$1,150–1,500 ↗ DW

◄ **Jean Cocteau,** *Le Secret Professionnel Suivi Des Monologues De l'Oiseleur*, first illustrated edition, published by Au Sans Pareil, Paris, 1925, 4°.
£900–1,100
$1,300–1,600 ↗ S

Lindsey Davis, *The Silver Pigs, A Novel*, signed presentation copy of author's first book, published by Sidgwick & Jackson, 1989, 9½ x 6½in (24 x 16.5cm).
£650–700
$900–1,000 ⊞ BIB
Copies of Lindsey Davis's first novel are scarce, hence the value of this signed presentation copy.

I. E. A. Dolby, *The Journal of the Household Brigade*, published by W. Clowes & Sons, 1879, 10 x 8in (25.5 x 20.5cm).
£40–45
$60–70 ⊞ BAY

Colin Dexter, *The Dead of Jericho*, first edition, published by Macmillan, 1981, 8 x 5¼in (20.5 x 13.5cm).
£410–460
$600–650 ⊞ BIB

Charles Dickens, *David Copperfield*, illustrated by H. K. Browne, first edition, published by Bradbury & Evans, 1850, 9 x 6in (23 x 15cm).
£450–500
$650–720 ⊞ BAY

◀ **Arthur Conan Doyle,** *The Vital Message*, author's presentation copy, inscribed 'To Lady Glenconnor with kind remembrance from a co-worker Arthur Conan Doyle', with four black and white plates, published by Hodder & Stoughton, 1919, 8°.
£320–360
$470–520 ✒ DW

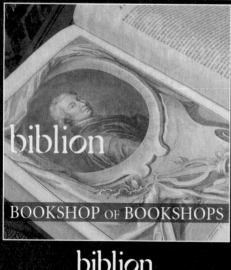

▶ **Arthur Conan Doyle,** *The Firm of Girdlestone*, first edition, published by Chatto & Windus, 1890, 8 x 6in (20.5 x 15cm).
£100–125
$145–175 ⊞ BAY

Sebastian Faulks, *A Trick of the Light*, first edition, published by The Bodley Head, 1984, 8¾ x 5¾in (22 x 14.5cm).
£450–500
$650–750 ⊞ BIB

Ian Fleming, *Dr No*, first edition, 1958, 8 x 5½in (20.5 x 14cm).
£450–500
$650–720 ⊞ BIB

◄ **Ian Fleming,** *Goldfinger*, first edition, dust jacket designed by Richard Chopping, published by Jonathan Cape, worn, stained, 1959, 8°.
£4,400–4,800
$6,500–7,000 ⚡ **DW**
Author's signed presentation copy inscribed to the front endpaper 'To Lionel, something more to read! From Ian'. This copy was given to his friend and employer Lionel Berry Viscount Kemsley, owner of Kemsley Newspapers, which included *The Sunday Times,* **for which Fleming worked as Foreign Manager. The position particularly suited him as he was allowed prolonged periods of absence in order to write his Bond novels.**

Sue Grafton, *O is for Outlaw, The New Kinsey Millhone Mystery*, first edition, published by Macmillan, 1999, 9½ x 6½in (24 x 16.5cm).
£170–190
$250–280 ⊞ **BIB**

◄ **Michihiko Hachiya,** *Hiroshima Diary, The Journal of a Japanese Physician*, published by Gollancz, 1955, 8¾ x 5¾in (22 x 14.5cm).
£20–25
$30–40 ⊞ **BIB**

Graham Greene, *The Name of Action*, first edition, published by Heinemann, dust jacket slightly worn, 1930, 8°.
£1,900–2,100
$2,700–3,000 ⚡ **DW**

Graham Greene, *Stamboul Train*, first edition, published by Heinemann, dust jacket worn, 1932, 8°.
£400–450
$580–650 ⚡ **DW**

Cross Reference
See Colour Review
(page 72–74)

Nick Hornby, *Fever Pitch, A Fan's Life*, first edition, 1992, 8¾ x 5¾in (22 x 14.5cm).
£250–275
$350–400 ⊞ **BIB**

Ernest Hemingway, *A Farewell to Arms*, first English edition, published by Jonathan Cape, rebound in leather by Bayntun, 1929, 7½ x 5in (19 x 12.5cm).
£320–360
$470–570 ⊞ **BAY**

Georges Hugnet, *Pablo Picasso*, with six etchings by Pablo Picasso, first edition, one of 200 copies, binding signed by Pierre Lucien Martin, 1961, original wrappers, 1941, 12°.
£700–800
$1,000–1,150 ⚄ S
Picasso produced six illuminations in wash which surround the four parts of the poem. The images were then reworked by him in etching and printed. He drew three female cubist heads for the work and a large female figure, the interior of which contained Hugnet's surrealist text.

Jerome K. Jerome, *My Life and Times*, first edition, author's presentation copy inscribed 'To Carl Hentschel from his affectionate friend Jerome K. Jerome, 16.9.26', with cigarette card portrait of author, 1926, 8°.
£230–260
$330–380 ⚄ DW
Carl Hentschel was the original model for Harris, one of the *Three Men in a Boat.*

Edward Lear, *Journals of a Landscape Painter in Southern Calabria*, first edition, with 20 tinted litho plates and two maps, in later cloth gilt binding, 1852, 8°.
£400–500
$580–720 ⚄ DW

Henry Mayhew, *London Labour and the London Poor; a Cyclopaedia of the Condition and Earnings of Those That Will Work, Those That Cannot Work, and Those That Will Not Work*, published by Griffin, Bohn & Co, in four volumes, with wood engravings, 1861–62, 8°.
£750–800
$1,100–1,200 ⚄ DW

▶ **Rev F. O. Morris,** *A History of British Birds*, second edition, in six volumes, with 355 hand-coloured engraved plates, 1870, 8°.
£5,000–5,500
$7,250–8,000 ⚄ DW

A. A. Milne, *The Red House Mystery*, first edition, signed by the author, dust jacket, 1922, 8°.
£2,200–2,400
$3,200–3,500 ⚄ BBA
This is Milne's first piece of detective fiction, written for his father, to whom it is dedicated.

Patrick O'Brian, *The Thirteen Gun Salute*, first edition, published by Collins, 1989, 9 x 5½in (23 x 14cm).
£140–180
$200–250 ⚄ AHa

William Morris, *The Defence of Guenevere and other poems by William Morris*, illustrated by Jessie M. King, black and white plates, Kelmscott Press, 1904, 8°.
£300–350
$450–500 ⚄ DW

▶ **Ellis Peters,** *Saint Peter's Fair, The Fourth Chronicle of Brother Cadfael*, first edition, 1981, 8 x 5in (20.5 x 12.5cm).
£250–300
$360–440 ⊞ BIB

◀ **Iain Pears,** *The Raphael Affair*, published by Gollancz, 1990, 8 x 5½in (20.5 x 14cm).
£250–300
$360–440 ⊞ BIB

Pigot & Co, *British Atlas,* part three only, 18 hand-coloured engraved maps, c1830s, oblong 2°.
£420–450
$620–650 ↗ DW

Terry Pratchett, *The Colour of Magic,* first edition, signed by Colin Smythe, boxed, 1983, 8 x 6in (20.5 x 15cm).
£6,000–6,500
$8,700–9,400 ⊞ BIB

Ian Rankin, *Knots & Crosses,* first edition, signed, 1987, 8¾ x 5¾in (22 x 14.5cm).
£1,250–1,500
$1,800–2,200 ⊞ BIB

Herbert Read, *Unit One, The Modern Movement in English Architecture, Painting and Sculpture,* first edition, dust jacket, 1934, large 8°.
£120–150
$175–225 ↗ DW

William Shakespeare, *Twelfth Night or What You Will,* illustrated by W. Heath Robinson, published by Hodder & Stoughton, 1908, 10 x 8in (25.5 x 20.5cm).
£125–150
$180–220 ⊞ BAY

> **Further reading**
> *Miller's Antiques Price Guide,* Miller's Publications, 2002

▶ **Henry M. Stanley,** *In Darkest Africa,* third edition, two volumes, published by Samson Low, 1890, 9 x 6in (23 x 15cm).
£350–400
$500–600 ⊞ BAY

P. F. Warner (ed), *British Sports and Sportsmen, Cricket and Football,* limited edition, No. 572 of 1,000, with plates and illustrations, c1933, 14½ x 10½in (37 x 26.5cm).
£100–150
$145–225 ↗ RTo

◀ **Ellen Terry,** *The Story of My Life,* first edition, signed by author, published by Hutchinson, 1912, 8 x 6in (20.5 x 15cm).
£40–50
$60–80 ⊞ SDP

Children's Books

Richard Adams,
Watership Down, first edition, author's signature inserted, with folding map, Published by Rex Collings, dust jacket, 1972, 8°.
£1,500–1,800
$2,200–2,600 🏹 BBA

Aesop's Fables,
illustrated by Arthur Rackham, first edition, published by William Heinemann, with 13 colour plates, 1912, 8 x 6in (20.5 x 15cm).
£130–160
$200–230 ⊞ BAY

Aesop's Fables,
illustrated in colour by Edward Detmold, first trade edition, published by Hodder & Stoughton, 1915, 11 x 9in (28 x 23cm), with box.
£325–375
$460–560 ⊞ BAY

◄ **Enid Blyton,** *A Prize for Mary Mouse*, published by The Brockhampton Press, 1950s, 3 x 6in (7.5 x 15cm).
£10–12
$15–20 ⊞ OCB

Hans Anderson, *Fairy Tales and Legends*, illustrated by Rex Whistler, first edition, published by Cobden Sanderson, 1935, 8 x 6in (20.5 x 15cm).
£40–50
$60–80 ⊞ BAY

Cicely Mary Barker, *The Lord of the Rushie River*, published by Blackie & Son, c1940, 6 x 4in (15 x 10cm).
£40–45
$60–70 ⊞ J&J

◄ **Enid Blyton,** *Noddy's Own Nursery Rhymes*, first edition, 1958, 10 x 9in (25.5 x 23cm).
£85–95
$125–145 ⊞ BIB

Insurance values

Always insure your valuable collectables for the cost of replacing them with similar items, regardless of the original price paid. Both dealers and auctioneers can provide a valuation service for a fee.

◄ **Harmsen van der Beek,** a full page illustration from *Noddy Meets Father Christmas*, by Enid Blyton, 1953–54, 6½ x 4¾in (16.5 x 12cm).
£3,000–3,300
$4,400–4,800 ⊞ BRG
Noddy was created in 1949 by Enid Blyton who described the character in words and Harmsen van der Beek who visualized him. Noddy was instantly successful and 24 books were published. Beek died in 1953 and Enid Blyton in 1968 but new books, records and videos are still being published worldwide every year. Other artists have illustrated Noddy since Beek, but all follow his original visualization. With sales in excess of 200 million books worldwide in 20 languages, Noddy books are still on the Top Ten list in countries as diverse as Australia and Japan. Noddy translates into Oui Oui (France), Doddi (Iceland) and Hilitos (Spain). The current value of Noddy merchandising is in excess of £35 million (US$50 million) annually and there is considerable interest in period Noddy material.

A Bookano stories pop-up book,
1930s, worn, 8 x 7in (20.5 x 18cm).
£20–30
$30–50 ⊞ A&J

*Walt Disney's Version
of Pinocchio,* published
by Collins, 1940, 11 x 9in
(28 x 23cm).
£60–70
$90–100 ⊞ SDP

**Rev Charles Lutwidge Dodgson (Lewis
Carroll),** *The Hunting of the Snark,* illustrated
by Henry Holiday, first edition, published by
Macmillan, 1876, slim 8°.
£550–600
$800–900 ⚒ DW

◄ **Kenneth Grahame,** *The Wind in
the Willows,* illustrated by Arthur
Rackham, first trade edition,
published by The Heritage Press,
1940, 10 x 7in (25.5 x 18cm).
£350–400
$500–600 ⊞ BIB

► **Joan Hickson,** original artwork for
Postman Pat, comprising a double
page spread of eleven paintings,
1970s, 15 x 11in (38 x 28cm).
£300–345
$450–500 ⊞ BRG

A. A. Milne, *When We Were Very Young*, illustrated by E. H. Shepard, first edition, published by Methuen & Co, 1924, 8°.
£4,400–4,800
$6,500–7,000 ✍ **BBA**
With this book is a dust jacket for the second edition.

Frank Richards, *Lord Billy Bunter*, first edition, published by Cassell, 1956, 7 x 5in (18 x 12.5cm).
£40–50
$60–80 ⊞ **BIB**

◄ **Jonathan Swift,** *Gulliver's Travels*, illustrated by Arthur Rackham, first edition, published by Dent, 1909, 9 x 7in (23 x 18cm).
£130–150
$200–220 ⊞ **BAY**

◄ **A. A. Milne,** *The House at Pooh Corner*, illustrated by E. H. Shepard, first edition, published by Methuen & Co, 1928, 8 x 5in (20.5 x 12.5cm).
£500–550
$720–800 ⊞ **BIB**

A. A. Milne, *Winnie-the-Pooh* and *The House at Pooh Corner*, Russian text by Boris Zakhoder, illustrated by B. Diodorov and G. Kalinovskiy, dust jacket, New York 1967, 8°.
£225–275
$320–400 ✍ **BBA**
The dust jacket reads 'Winnie-the-Pooh has become a Russian bear. His name has been changed to Vinni-Pukh, and he converses in the Russian language as if he had spent his entire life on the banks of the Volga.'

A. A. Milne, *The Pooh Calendar*, designed by A. E. Taylor, illustrated by E. H. Shepard, published by Methuen & Co, 1930, 4°, and *The Christopher Robin Calendar,* 1929.
£700–800
$1,000–1,200 ✍ **BBA**

Louis Wain, *Daddy Cat*, published by Blackie & Son, 1914, slim 8°.
£350–400
$500–600 ✍ **DW**

Cookbooks

Proven Recipes Showing the uses of the Three Great Products from Corn, published by the Corn Products Refining Co, c1925, 6½ x 5½in (16.5 x 14cm).
£12–15
$15–20 ⊞ **MSB**

Grandma's Old Fashioned Molasses Recipes, published by Boston Molasses Co, 1930, 7¼ x 5¼in (18.5 x 13.5cm).
£7–10
$10–15 ⊞ **MSB**

◄ *Mrs Beeton's Every-Day Cookery,* published by Ward Lock & Co, 1909, 8 x 6in (20.5 x 15cm).
£30–35
$40–50 ⊞ **SMI**

An R. H. Quine's ice-blue glass bottle, wedge shaped, with flat base, embossed 'poison' to both sides of shoulder, '4oz' to base, patent 1893, 5¾in (14.5cm) long.
£375–425
$550–620 ✦ BBR

▶ A cobalt-blue poison bottle, modelled as a submarine, embossed 'Poison' across the body, with registered number to base, restored, 1900–20, 3in (7.5cm) wide.
£60–70
$90–100 ✦ BBR

Five cobalt-blue glass poison bottles, c1900, largest 5in (12.5cm) high.
£6–7
$9–12 each ⊞ QW

◀ A stoneware ginger beer bottle, with wired stopper, black transfer-printed 'Ginger Beer P. Sullivan Beaconsfield', around a portrait of Cecil J. Rhodes in a foliate wreath, with entwined initials to reverse, 1900–20, 11in (28cm) high.
£120–140
$170–200 ✦ BBR

A Boots stoneware ginger beer bottle, c1900, 7in (18cm) high.
£20–25
$30–35 ⊞ QW

A Walker's Universal Mixture clear glass hexagonal bottle, for veterinary medicine, 1920s, 7in (18cm) high.
£5–6
$8–10 ⊞ BoC

A commemorative Coronation Ale bottle, with stopper and seal, embossed 'Reading', with original label dated 'June 22 A.D. 1911', 8¼in (21cm) high.
£35–40
$50–60 ⊞ HUX

Boxes

A walnut snuff box, the central medallion depicting Frederick the Great mounted on a horse, dated 1749, 3½in (9cm) diam.
£150–175
$225–255 ⊞ MB

A engine-turned yew snuff box, c1810, 3¼in (8.5cm) diam.
£100–120
$145–175 ⊞ MB

▶ **A brass-bound mahogany box,** with brass military-style handles and original Bramah lock, mid-19thC, 11in (28cm) wide.
£270–300
$400–440 ⊞ OTT

A lady's Victorian burr-walnut travelling box, the vanity compartment complete with mirror to underside of lid, cut-glass bottles and jars, with silver-plated top, lift-out tray, above a drawer with writing slope, 12¼in (31cm) wide.
£650–700
$900–1,000 ↗ TRM

A burr walnut snuff box, c1800, 3½in (9cm) wide.
£130–150
$200–220 ⊞ MB

A William IV rosewood vanity box, inlaid with mother-of-pearl, c1830, 12in (30.5cm) wide.
£500–600
$720–870 ⊞ MB

An oak-veneered tea caddy, with hinged lid, c1860, 7in (18cm) long.
£180–200
$260–290 ⊞ MRW

A table snuff box, with pentagon design in ebony, mahogany and tulipwood, ivory centre, c1820, 3½in (9cm) diam.
£100–120
$145–175 ⊞ MB

A burr-elm veneered campaign tea caddy, c1840, 4in (10cm) wide.
£200–220
$290–320 ⊞ MRW

A Tunbridge ware stamp box, c1860, 2in (5cm) square.
£60–70
$90–100 ⊞ MB

A tin gloves box, c1870, 12in (30.5cm) long.
£40–45
$60–70 ⊞ TMa

▶ A Tartan ware
box, c1880,
2in (5cm) high.
£35–40
$50–60 ⊞ VBo

A Mauchline ware
sycamore beaker box,
with a printed illustration
of North Parade,
Eastbourne, containing a
medicine beaker, 1880,
3in (7.5cm) high.
£60–70
$90–100 ⊞ MB

A tin box, with looped
carrying handle and
strap closure, c1880,
11in (28cm) high.
£15–20
$20–30 ⊞ AL

▶ A tin deed
box, with
leather strap
fastening,
c1880, 16in
(40.5cm) wide.
£15–20
$20–30 ⊞ AL

◀ A Tunbridge
ware stamp
box, with
George V stamp
on lid, c1930,
1½in (4cm) high.
£65–75
$95–115 ⊞ VB

Breweriana

A silver claret label,
London, c1820,
2in (5cm) wide.
£145–165
$200–240 ⊞ CAL

**An S-shaped silver
decanter label,** by
George Unite, 1846,
1½in (4cm) high.
£115–135
$165–195 ⊞ CAL

Five Wedgwood ceramic bin labels, Cowslip, Madeira,
Moselle and Rum stamped verso 'Wedgwood', and
No. 10 stamped verso 'Charles Farrow, London', 19thC,
5½in (14cm) wide.
£400–450
$580–650 ⚲ P(B)

A cast-iron cork press, modelled as a crocodile, late
19thC, 11½in (29cm) long.
£200–250
$300–350 ⚲ P(B)

**A Dunville's Whisky
enamelled pub tray,**
with blue lettering on a
white ground, late 19thC,
12in (30.5cm) diam.
£80–100
$115–145 ⊞ CAL

**A Brontë Yorkshire
Liqueurs miniature flagon,**
of French brandy and
honey, the paper label with
a shoulder portrait of
one of the Brontë sisters,
1900–30, 3in (7.5cm) high.
£20–30
$30–45 ⊞ ES

**A Buchanan's Black & White Whisky
advertisement figure,** modelled as
a pair of Scottish terriers, together
with a letter from James Buchanan
& Co, early 20thC, 11in (28cm) high.
£200–240
$290–350 ⚲ P(B)
The accompanying letter confirms
that these figures were distributed
throughout the world, and the
last price paid for them, in 1939,
was 3s 9d.

**Miller's is a price GUIDE
not a price LIST**

**A Royal Doulton Wm. Younger
& Co advertising ashtray,** white
with black lettering, 1920s,
6in (15cm) high.
£35–50
$50–75 ⊞ MURR

**A Johnnie Walker advertising
jug,** red and black lettering on a
white body, 1920s, 6in (15cm) high.
£40–50
$60–80 ⚲ BBR

An Old Taylor Bourbon Whiskey rubberoid advertising figure of a jockey, with yellow shirt, blue waistcoat and white jodhpurs, 1920–30, 14¾in (37.5cm) high.
£120–140
$170–200 ✗ BBR

A Sandeman ceramic advertising figure, wearing a black cloak and hat, holding a red glass, on an oblong plinth, 1930–40, 15¼in (38.5cm) high.
£55–65
$80–100 ✗ BBR

A William Lawson's Scotch Whisky rubberoid advertising figure of a bare-fisted fighter, Bob Fitzsimmon, on a plaster-filled plinth, 1920–30, 13½in (34.5cm) high.
£320–350
$450–500 ✗ BBR

A Teacher's Scotch Whisky rubberoid advertising figure of a schoolmaster, holding a diploma, 1920–40, 14½in (37cm) high.
£200–250
$300–350 ✗ BBR

▶ **An Old Grans Special Scotch Whisky advertising water jug,** c1930, 8in (20.5cm) high.
£65–95
$95–145
⊞ MURR

◀ **A Buchanan's Black & White Scotch Whisky advertising water jug,** c1930, 7in (18cm) high.
£85–130
$120–190
⊞ MURR

▶ **A Canadian Club Whisky wood and composite advertising figure,** modelled as an ice hockey player, 1940–50, 10in (25.5cm) high.
£150–200
$220–280
⊞ MURR

A Ricard Anisette ceramic water jug, light brown with blue interior, 1950s, 6½in (16.5cm) high.
£18–20
$25–30 ⊞ HUX

Three whisky advertising measurers, Dewar's White Label, Queen Anne Scotch Whisky, and Teacher's Highland Cream, c1950, 2in (5cm) wide.
£12–14
$17–20 ⊞ HUX

An articulated wooden bottle stopper, modelled as the head and neck of a clown, painted in red, white, black and green, c1950, 4in (10cm) high.
£18–22
$25–30 ⊞ CAL

A Clinch & Co shop display advertisement, 1950s–60s, 11 x 8in (28 x 20.5cm).
£18–20
$25–30 ⊞ MRW

A Pernod advertising water jug, c1960, 11in (28cm) high.
£10–12
$15–20 ⊞ HUX

A Noilly Prat Vermouth carafe, c1960, 7in (18cm) high.
£10–12
$15–18 ⊞ HUX

Cross Reference
See Colour Review (page 76)

◀ **A bottle of 'The Macallan 25 year old Anniversary Malt' whisky,** distilled 1962, bottled 1987, with wooden crate.
£120–140
$170–200 🔨 P(B)

A Gaymer's Cyder plastic back-bar figure, of a town crier, wearing a magenta, red, black and white costume, c1960, 6¼in (16cm) high.
£20–25
$30–35 ⊞ HUX

A Watney's Ale Jubilee advertising figure, modelled as a porcelain dray horse in the shafts of a wooden wagon bearing three barrels, produced for the Queen's Silver Jubilee, 1977, 15in (38cm) long.
£40–45
$60–65 ⊞ Mo

A Royal Doulton Greene King Lambeth plaque, of a king wearing pale green and ermine robes, with gold orb, sceptre and crown, on a purple carpet, 1960–70, 23in (58.5cm) high.
£130–150
$190–220 🔨 BBR

A Beswick Worthington E back-bar figure, modelled as two rugby players, 1970s, 10in (25.5cm) high.
£130–175
$200–250 ⊞ MURR

A Mabel Lucie Attwell Swan Pen shop advertisement, 1925, 15in (38cm) high.
£180–200
$260–300 ⊞ MEM

A Mabel Lucie Attwell motto soap set, by the British Legion, 1920–30, 6in (15cm) long.
£45–50
$65–75 ⊞ MEM

A Shelley Mabel Lucie Attwell three-piece tea service, comprising toadstool teapot and cover, sugar bowl and elf milk jug, decorated in polychrome enamels, printed marks to base, 1930s, elf 6in (15cm) high.
£650–750
$950–1,150 ⋔ Pott

A Mabel Lucie Attwell Diddums celluloid doll, 1930s, 13in (33cm) high.
£180–200
$260–290 ⊞ MEM

A Mabel Lucie Attwell biscuit tin, c1935, 8in (20.5cm) high.
£225–250
$325–375 ⊞ HUX

A Shelley Mabel Lucie Attwell Flying pattern sugar basin, 1930, 7½in (19cm) diam.
£350–400
$500–600 ⊞ BD

The Lucie Attwell Kiddy's Cutlery, spoon and pusher, c1940, in original box, 5in (12.5cm) long.
£35–45
$50–65 ⊞ MEM

The Lucie Attwell Hanky House, cardboard with pull-down front revealing seven handkerchiefs and picture, marked at side, late 1930s, 6in (15cm) long.
£145–165
$200–250 ⊞ MEM

◄ **A Mabel Lucie Attwell cut-out plywood string holder,** 1930s, 6¾in (17cm) high.
£85–95
$125–140 ⊞ MEM

► *Lucie Attwell's Super Book of Fun No 3,* Dean first edition, 1969, 10 x 8in (25.5 x 20.5cm).
£50–55
$75–80 ⊞ BIB

A 15ct gold suspension medal, for the Thomas Reid Five-mile Championship, St Helen's Bicycle Club, 24th May 1882.
£570–630
$800–950 ⊞ **AU**

A Calcott Bros display poster, full-colour lithograph mounted on a W. H. Smith advertising distribution department canvas stretcher, some damage, 1890s, 30 x 50in (76 x 127cm).
£250–300
$350–450 ↗ **P(Ba)**

A German glass stein, with metal mounts, painted with a cycling scene, 1895–1900, 10in (25.5cm) high.
£525–575
$750–850 ⊞ **AU**

A German china figure of a lady cyclist with billowing dress, the underside depicting a saucy image of her rear view, c1900, 7in (18cm) wide.
£400–450
$580–650 ⊞ **AU**

A French carved cheroot holder, surmounted by a figure of a lady cyclist, c1900, 6in (15cm) long.
£500–600
$720–870 ⊞ **AU**

A Coventry Eagle Bicycles framed card advertising sign, c1910, 32in (81.5cm) high.
£550–650
$800–950 ⊞ **JUN**

A Royal Doulton stein, depicting male and female cyclists, 1914–18, 6½in (16.5cm) high.
£580–650
$850–950 ⊞ **AU**

A Swift pacing bicycle, with wooden rims and leather saddle, 1910.
£750–850
$1,100–1,250 ⊞ **JUN**

A Raleigh advertising card, framed, 1920s, 22 x 30in (56 x 76cm).
£300–350
$450–500 ⊞ **JUN**

A Raleigh Chopper Mark II bicycle, 1974–75.
£400–450
$580–650 ⊞ **TBoy**

A Venetian blackamoor torchère stand, 19thC, 40in (101.5cm) high.
£1,700–2,000
$2,500–3,000 ⚡ S
Ex-Ralph Richardson.

▶ **A Negronoir Café Exquis advertising sign,** c1930, 14in (35.5cm) high.
£70–75
$100–110 ⊞ HUX

A Simon & Halbig bisque-head mulatto doll, with weighted brown glass eyes, open mouth with upper teeth, dimpled chin, on a fully-jointed composition body, incised '12, S&H 1039, DEP', Germany, c1910, 25in (63.5cm) high.
£1,200–1,400
$1,750–2,000 ⚡ Bon

A Lyons' Tea money box, Germany, 1925, 6in (15cm) high.
£270–300
$400–440 ⊞ HUX

A Banania Tapioca tin, 1925, 7in (18cm) high.
£20–25
$30–35 ⊞ HUX

A Negronoir Café Exquis advertising sign

A Mr Golly soft toy, by Deans Rag Book Co, 1950s, 13in (33cm) high.
£60–70
$90–100 ⊞ TAC

A theatre programme, for *The Black and White Minstrel Show*, 1962, 8¾in (22cm) high.
£3–4
$4–6 ⊞ HUX

An 'I's got an idea' greetings card, c1950, 5in (12.5cm) high.
£6–7
$9–10 ⊞ CWO

▶ **A Robertson's Golden Shred plaster illuminated display figure,** 1963, 28in (71cm) high.
£850–900
$1,250–1,300 ⚡ BBR

A Sphinx pin, modelled as a blackamoor, 1960s, 4in (10cm) high.
£40–45
$60–65 ⊞ CRIS

A Bakelite, wood and metal card or envelope holder, modelled as Josephine Baker, 1910–30, 8in (20.5cm) high.
£130–135
$190–200 ⊞ LBe

Louis de Bernières, *The Troublesome Offspring of Cardinal Guzman,* first edition, published by Secker & Warburg, 1992, 9½ x 6½in (24 x 16.5cm).
£175–195
$250–280 ⊞ BIB

R. D. Blackmore, *Lorna Doone,* Dulverton edition, fourth edition, original decorated cloth, published by Sampson Low Marston & Co, 1920, 9 x 7in (23 x 18cm).
£40–50
$60–75 ⊞ BAY

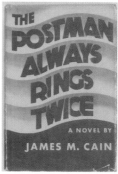

James M. Cain, *The Postman Always Rings Twice,* first edition, original orange cloth blocked and lettered in blue, original dust jacket, published by Alfred A. Knopf, New York, 1934, 8°.
£1,400–1,500
$2,000–2,200 ↗ DW

Charles Dickens, *A Christmas Carol,* illustrated by A. C. Michael, original cloth elaborately gilt-blocked, published by Hodder & Stoughton, 1911, 10 x 8in (25.5 x 20.5cm).
£190–220
$275–325 ⊞ BAY

Sir Arthur Conan Doyle, *The Memoirs of Sherlock Holmes,* first edition, illustrated by Sidney Paget, original dark blue cloth, blocked and titled in black and gilt, published by George Newnes, c1894, 8°.
£3,300–3,500
$4,800–5,000 ↗ S

Ian Fleming, *Thunderball,* author's inscription on front endpaper, published by Jonathan Cape, 1961, 7¾ x 5¼in (19.5 x 13.5cm).
£4,300–4,600
$6,250–6,650 ↗ WW

Graham Greene, *It's a Battlefield,* first edition, original cloth, dust jacket designed by Youngman Carter, published by Heinemann, 1934, 8°.
£1,100–1,300
$1,600–2,000 ↗ DW
This was the first issue to show the price of 7/6 on the front flap of the dust jacket.

Shere Hite, *The Hite Report on Love, Passion and Emotional Violence,* signed by the author, published by Optima, 1987, 9½ x 6in (24 x 15cm).
£20–25
$30–35 ⊞ BIB

Sir Walter Scott, *Lady of the Lake,* with tartan cover, 19thC, 3½ x 2¼in (9 x 5.5cm).
£40–45
$60–65 ⊞ Fai

Minette Walters, *The Sculptress,* first edition, signed by the author, published by Macmillan, 1993, 8¾ x 5¾in (22 x 14.5cm).
£50–60
$75–90 ⊞ BIB

► **Oscar Wilde,** *The Picture of Dorian Gray,* first edition, illustrated by Henry Keen, original cloth decorated and titled in gilt, published by John Lane, The Bodley Head, 1925, 10 x 7in (25.5 x 18cm).
£110–120
$160–175 ⊞ BAY

Francis Joseph
PUBLICATIONS
'Collectors Choice'

Detailed price and information books on 20th century ceramics and glass with galleries of extensive colour photographs in each. All the collector needs for identifying the wide range of valuable ceramics and glass produced over the past 100 years.

Crown Derby Paperweights First Edition £14.95

The Bunnykins Collectors Handbook £12.95

Collecting Carlton Ware – Second Edition £16.95

Pocket Dragons – First Edition £16.95

Collecting Sylvac Pottery – First Edition £16.95

Collecting Carnival Glass – Second Edition £16.95

Collecting Wade Whimsies £14.95

The Complete Clarice Cliff £12.95

Collecting Poole Pottery – First Edition £16.95

Beswick Price Guide – Fifth Edition £12.95

Collecting Moorcroft Pottery – Second Ed £16.95

Collecting Dinky Toys – First Edition £16.95.
A departure from our usual ceramic price guides into this expanding area of collecting

The Gollies Collectors Handbook £14.95

Collecting Lalique Glass – Second Edition £16.95

Collecting Pendelfin – Second Edition £16.95

Francis Joseph
Publications
5 Southbrook Mews,
London SE12 8LG
email: office@francisjoseph.com

TELEPHONE HOTLINE:
020 8318 9580

Money back guarantee of satisfaction

Cradock, *Josephine Goes Travelling*, illustrated by Honor Appleton, undated, 10 x 8in (25.5 x 20.5cm).
£15–20
$20–30 ⊞ OCB

Cicely Mary Barker, *Flower Fairies of the Wayside*, published by Blackie & Son, 1940s, 6 x 4in (15 x 10cm).
£40–45
$60–65 ⊞ J&J

Birn Bros, *Popeye the Pirate*, first edition, illustrated, c1939, 10 x 8in (25.5 x 20.5cm).
£60–70
$90–100 ⊞ BIB

Elinor M. Brent-Dyer, *Ruey Richardson – Chaletian*, first edition, published by Chambers, 1960, 7 x 5in (18 x 13cm).
£65–75
$95–110 ⊞ OCB

Jean de Brunhoff, *The Story of Babar the little elephant*, first UK edition, preface by A. A. Milne, published by Methuen, 1934, 14 x 10in (35.5 x 25.5cm).
£130–150
$190–220 ⊞ BIB

The Animals' Trip to Sea, first edition, coloured pictorial boards, published by Ernest Nister, c1895, 10 x 12in (25.5 x 30.5cm).
£130–145
$190–210 ⊞ BIB

Selma G. Lanes, *The Art of Maurice Sendak*, first edition, published by Abram, 1993, 11 x 12in (28 x 30.5cm).
£35–40
$50–60 ⊞ BIB

◄ **J. K. Rowling,** *Harry Potter and the Philosopher's Stone*, first edition, first issue, published by Bloomsbury, 1997, 8°.
£8,000–10,000
$11,500–14,500 ⚲ WW
Only 300 copies of this edition, bound in this way, were ever issued. They were destined for school libraries and clean copies are therefore hard to find. A further 200 proof copies were issued in white paper wrappers. Uncorrected proof copies, with slight cover variation, were also issued and are more common, and therefore less valuable, than this hardback first edition.

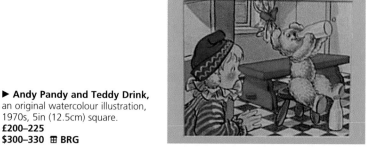

Robert Tyndall, an original watercolour illustration, entitled Noddy and the Bunkey, 1960, 6½ x 5in (16.5 x 12.5cm).
£1,250–1,450
$1,800–2,000 ⊞ BRG

► **Andy Pandy and Teddy Drink,** an original watercolour illustration, 1970s, 5in (12.5cm) square.
£200–225
$300–330 ⊞ BRG

A green Hamilton bottle, embossed 'The Scarborough Brewery Company Ltd' around 'Crystalis Waters', dolphin and fountain trademark to centre, 1880–1900, 7in (18cm) high.
£400–450
$580–650 ✗ BBR

An Old Tom flask, Chesterfield, 1840, 10in (25.5cm) high.
£275–325
$400–470 ⊞ JHo

A blue poison bottle, with remains of original paper label, 1880–1910, 4in (10cm) high.
£6–7
$8–12 ⊞ QW

A ginger beer bottle, embossed 'The Brewery, Henley-on-Thames', c1900, 7in (18cm) high.
£30–35
$45–55 ⊞ QW

A blue poison bottle, c1900, 1880–1910, 7in (18cm) high.
£10–12
$15–20 ⊞ QW

A green Codd bottle, embossed 'Crocketts Ltd Worcester', 1900–20, 8in (20.5cm) high.
£4–5
$7–10 ⊞ QW

A blue bottle, embossed 'Handysides Consumption Cure', 1890–1910, 7½in (19cm) high.
£450–500
$650–720 ✗ BBR

▶ A blue wasp-waist poison bottle, embossed 'Stephensons Patent No. 6324', 1890–1900, 7½in (19cm) high.
£1,200–1,400
$1,700–2,000 ✗ BBR

◀ A green Codd bottle, embossed 'Davies & Co, Burton Salmon' with salmon pictorial trademark to front, the rear embossed 'E. Breffit & Co Ld, Makers Castleford', 1890–1900, 7½in (19cm) high.
£170–200
$250–300 ✗ BBR

◄ A multicoloured framed advertisement for Hall's Wine, The Bloom of Perfect Health, slight surface marks, 1890–1900, 29 x 23in (73.5 x 58.5cm).
£450–550
$650–800 ➤ BBR

A Shamrock Whiskey pub mirror, produced for Kirker Greer & Co, Belfast, c1900, 36 x 28in (91.5 x 71cm).
£700–800
$1,000–1,200 ⊞ HON

A pair of Margrave Brothers whisky dispensers, advertising Pearl Irish Whisky and Excelsior Scottish Whisky, with etched, gilded and painted decoration and cut-glass conical covers, c1890, 21in (53cm) high with covers.
£1,750–2,100
$2,500–3,000 ➤ P(B)

► An articulated wooden bottle stopper, carved and painted as a man, early 20thC, 6in (15cm) high.
£35–40
$50–60 ⊞ CAL

◄ A German pottery stein, showing firefighters at work, inscribed 'Gott sur Ehr dem nächsten zur Wehr', c1908, 16in (40.5cm) high.
£1,000–1,250
$1,500–1,800 ⊞ AU
The value of this item lies in its firefighting content.

A Claymore whisky pottery advertising figure, made for Greenlees, 1900–20, 15½in (39.5cm) high.
£1,400–1,500
$2,000–2,200 ➤ BBR

◄ A Bénédictine paper advertising fan, France, c1910, 9in (23cm) wide.
£40–45
$60–65 ⊞ HUX

A Long John whisky advertising figure, made of composite material, 1930s, 10in (25.5cm) high.
£150–200
$220–280 ⊞ MURR

A Gitanes water jug, 1950s, 7½in (19cm) high.
£40–45
$60–65 ⊞ HUX

A Beswick Babycham advertising figure, c1955, 5in (12.5cm) high.
£45–55
$65–80 ⊞ HUX

A porcelain button, painted with a butterfly, late 18thC, 1½in (4cm) diam.
£180–210
$250–300 ⊞ TB

A steel button, with cut-steel and glass 'jewels', c1890, 1¼in (3cm) diam.
£25–35
$35–50 ⊞ EV

▶ **A selection of metal buttons,** hand-painted and transfer-painted, some with glass 'jewelled' centre, 1890–1930s, largest 1in (2.5cm) diam.
£2–12
$3–17 each ⊞ EV

▶ **A set of six pressed wood buttons,** hand-painted with metal shanks, c1930, 1¼in (3cm) diam.
£25–30
$35–45 ⊞ EV

Three plastic Disney character buttons, Mickey Mouse, Pluto and Donald Duck, c1940, ¾in (2cm) high.
£3–6
$5–8 each ⊞ TB

▶ **A set of five pink plastic buttons,** decorated with black poodles, 1950s, ½in (1cm) diam.
£4–5
$6–7 ⊞ LBe

A selection of Victorian glove button-hooks, the largest 2in (5cm) long.
£5–40
$8–60 each ⊞ VB

A set of six Satsuma buttons, c1870, 1½in (4cm) diam, in original case.
£430–460
$600–660 ⊞ JBB

An ivory button, painted with a finely-detailed miniature of a bird in a river landscape, under bevelled glass, set in a silver mount, mid-19thC, 1in (2.5cm) wide.
£210–275
$300–400 ⊞ TB

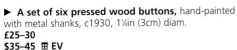

A Liberty & Co silver and enamel button, hallmarked L. & Co, Cymric, 1900–10, 1in (2.5cm) diam.
£100–120
$145–175 ⊞ TB

An Ault art pottery wryneck vase, designed by Dr Christopher Dresser, c1880, 10in (25.5cm) high.
£600–650
$850–950 ⊞ HUN

A Bargeware or Measham Ware teapot, the domed lid topped with a traditional small teapot, inscribed and dated 1914, 12in (30.5cm) high.
£300–400
$450–580 ⊞ JBL

◀ **A Bassano Scottish bagpiper,** Italy, 1950s, 11in (28cm) high.
£200–250
$300–350 ⊞ LBe

A Beswick model of Winnie the Pooh, designed by Albert Hallam, issued 1968–90, 2½in (6.5cm) high.
£45–50
$65–75 ⟋ BBR

A Don Pottery blue and white plate, 1820–34, 8in (20.5cm) diam.
£140–160
$200–250 ⊞ CAL

A Staffordshire blue and white meat platter, decorated with Wild Rose pattern, 19thC, 15in (38cm) wide.
£85–95
$125–145 ⊞ MCC

A Bonzo water jug, German, c1930, 6½in (16.5cm) high.
£175–200
$250–300 ⊞ HUX

▶ **A Burmantofts faïence jardinière-on-stand,** impressed marks, Nos. 2053/4, c1890, 40¼in (102cm) high.
£900–1,000
$1,300–1,500 ⟋ AH

A Bo'ness glazed and hand-painted bowl, with fluted rim, 1830–40, 9½in (24cm) diam.
£40–50
$60–80 ⊞ JEB

A Bovey Tracey Devon ware Toby jug, c1950, 10in (25.5cm) high.
£300–360
$450–500 ⊞ DHA

▶ **A Charles Brannam Liberty stoneware vase,** with three wrythen handles, the interior with a brown glaze, impressed marks, c1900, 11¾in (30cm) high.
£200–225
$300–330 ⟋ BLH

A Burleigh Ware coffee cup and saucer, decorated with Sunray pattern, 1930s, cup 2½in (6.5cm) high.
£40–50
$60–80 ⊞ BUR

A Burleigh Ware Budgie jug, 1930s, 8in (20.5cm) high.
£300–350
$450–500 ⊞ BD

A Carlton Ware charger, decorated with Blue Oak pattern, 1930s, 13in (33cm) diam.
£230–260
$330–380 ⊞ StC

◄ **A Carlton Ware canister,** marked 'Made in England' 1930s, 6in (15cm) high.
£85–95
$125–145 ⊞ LBe

► **A Carlton Ware Rouge Royale dish,** hand-painted in Wild Duck pattern, 1950s, 7in (18cm) wide.
£140–160
$200–240 ⊞ HO

A Derek Clarke studio pottery vase, with blue crystaline effect decoration, 1990s, 5½in (14cm) high.
£350–375
$500–550 ⊞ PGA

A Clarice Cliff Conical sugar shaker, decorated with Nasturtium pattern, c1930, 6in (15cm) high.
£500–600
$720–870 ⊞ BD

A Clarice Cliff Athens jug, decorated with Mondrian pattern, 1930s, 7½in (19cm) high.
£1,300–1,500
$1,900–2,200 ⊞ BD

A Clarice Cliff Inspiration charger, decorated with Caprice pattern, c1930, 18in (45.5cm) diam.
£3,700–4,000
$5,500–5,800 ⊞ BD

A pair of Clarice Cliff plates, decorated with Fragrance pattern, rim chips, 1930s, 9in (23cm) diam.
£120–150
$175–225 🔨 G(B)

A Clarice Cliff Conical sugar shaker, decorated with Orange Erin pattern, c1930, 6in (15cm) high.
£2,750–3,000
$4,000–4,500 ⊞ BD

A Clarice Cliff Bon Jour shape sugar shaker, decorated with Blue Crocus pattern, c1930, 5in (12.5cm) high.
£800–900
$1,150–1,300 ⊞ BD

◀ A Clarice Cliff coffee cup and saucer, decorated with Gayday pattern, c1930, cup 2½in (6.5cm) high.
£170–200
$250–300 ⊞ BD

A Clarice Cliff Wilkinson's bowl, decorated with Crocus pattern, printed mark, 1930s, 3½in (9cm) diam.
£110–130
$160–190 🔨 G(B)

▶ A Susie Cooper Paris shape jug, decorated with Nursery pattern, 1930s, 4in (10cm) high.
£450–500
$650–720 ⊞ BD

A Crown Devon musical jug, decorated with Daisy Daisy pattern, 1920s, 8in (20.5cm) high.
£300–325
$440–480 ⊞ AU

Butlin's

Sir William Heygate Edmund Colborne ('Billy') Butlin (1900–80) opened the first Butlin's at Skegness in 1936. Holiday camps had existed in Britain for 30 years, but it was Butlin who turned them into a mass attraction. 'All the jollity and comradeship of a camping holiday plus all the amenities of the first-class hotel' boasted the first advertisements, which promised cosy Elizabethan chalets, sport, concert parties and four good meals a day for £2 5s a week – 'a week's holiday for a week's pay'. More sites soon opened, and after WWII (when they were rented to the armed forces), Butlin's holiday camps boomed. Entertainment was provided by the famous Redcoats whose cry of 'Wakey Wakey' became a national catchphrase. Because of licensing laws, all campers had to wear a badge.

New patterns were introduced each season, different designs were produced for every camp, for specific events and clubs, and for all categories of staff. All in all, thousands of badges were manufactured which are collectable today, along with other Butlin's memorabilia.

A Butlin's soft-centre sweets tin, 1960s, 5½in (14cm) high.
£8–9
$10–12 ⊞ HUX

▶ **A Butlin's Holiday Worlds ashtray,** 1960s, 5½in square.
£4–6
$6–9 ✎ FLD

A Butlin's Xmas 1962 glass mug, with red lettering, 3in (7.5cm) high.
£5–6
$7–9 ⊞ HUX

A Butlin's jigsaw, red and blue on a yellow ground, 1960s, 9½ x 12in (24 x 30.5cm), in original box.
£12–15
$16–20 ⊞ HUX

A Butlin's Skegness badge, in red, blue and yellow, 1965, 1in (2.5cm) high.
£3–5
$4–7 ⊞ HUX

A Butlin's advertising mirror, 1960s, 3 x 2½in (7.5 x 6.5cm).
£3–5
$4–7 ⊞ HUX

◀ **A Butlin's Beaver Club badge,** in red, white and blue, 1960s, 2in (5cm) diam.
£2–4
$3–4 ⊞ HUX

Buttons

Eleven Victorian silver lustre glass buttons, with four- and two-hole metal shanks, largest 1in (2.5cm) diam.
£6–9
$10–15 each ⊞ **EV**
These silver glass buttons are often confused with cut-steel buttons. If unsure when buying, use a magnet.

A glazed ceramic button, with transfer-printed design of a mythological head wearing a helmet depicting a bird, set in a darkened brass border, mid-19thC, 1¼in (3cm) diam.
£60–100
$85–150 ⊞ **TB**

Nine pearl buttons, one hand-painted, c1850–1960, largest 2in (5cm) high.
£6–8
$8–12 each ⊞ **EV**

Two gilded copper and silver-plated sporting buttons, depicting boars within a belt, French, 19thC, 1in (2.5cm) diam.
£25–35
$40–50 ⊞ **TB**

A Victorian brass button, depicting St George and the Dragon, c1860, 1½in (4cm) diam.
£10–15
$15–20 ⊞ **EV**

▶ **A brass and wood button,** the stamped brass moon and falling star applied to a wood background, French, 1880–90, 1¼in (3cm) diam.
£30–35
$45–50 ⊞ **TB**

A set of four Victorian black glass buttons, with four-hole metal shanks, 1in (5cm) diam.
£24–30
$35–45 ⊞ **EV**
These black glass buttons, popular in the Victorian period and used for mourning wear, are sometimes mistaken for jet. The fossilized wood, however, was very rarely used for buttons, as it was too fragile and prone to chipping. Black glass such as this is also referred to as French jet.

A set of six dyed horn buttons, 19thC, ½in (1cm) diam.
£3–5
$5–8 ⊞ **EV**

A set of six .925 silver butterfly buttons, French, c1880, in red leather case.
£110–120
$160–175 ⊞ **JBB**

A set of nine buttons, bearing the lithographed portraits of famous French ladies, mounted under celluloid, marked Paris, c1890, ½in (1cm) diam, in a shaped box.
£110–130
$160–190 ⊞ JBB

Ten pearl-backed buttons, Austrian, c1890–1920, largest ½in (1cm) diam.
£2–3
$3–5 each ⊞ EV

A stamped brass button, depicting the arrival of Lohengrin, 1890–1900, 1½in (4cm) diam.
£10–15
$15–20 ⊞ TB

A set of five Ruskin glazed earthenware buttons, c1880, ½in (1cm) diam.
£40–50
$60–75 ⊞ SLL

◄ **An Art Nouveau silver button,** in the form of a female head with flowing hair, hallmarked, c1901, 1½in (4cm) diam.
£40–50
$60–75 ⊞ TB

A set of six tin-backed brass buttons, each depicting an open car, 1920–30, 2in (5cm) diam.
£25–40
$35–60 ⊞ JBB

A set of six ivory buttons, modelled as prowling lions, Tanzanian, 1920–30, 1in (2.5cm) long.
£10–12
$15–18 each ⊞ JBB

A set of six Art Deco plastic buttons and a matching buckle, in red, grey and silver, the buttons with self-shanks, centre fastening, 1in (2.5cm) diam.
£40–45
$60–65 ⊞ EV

A set of six Art Deco buttons, in deep pink celluloid with silvery metal overlay, ½in (1cm) diam.
£18–24
$25–35 ⊞ EV

A Bimini glass and metal button, 1940–50, 2in (5cm) diam.
£10–12
$15–18 ⊞ JBB

Cameras

A mahogany and brass magic lantern, professionally converted to electrical operation, complete with chimney and slide carrier, c1895, 19¾in (50cm) long.
£250–300
$360–440 ⊞ APC

An Otto Berning & Co Dusseldorf Robot Star 25 camera, with spring motor, capable of 25 exposures, 1969, 4¼in (11cm) wide.
£150–175
$220–255 ⊞ HEG

A Coronet Midget Bakelite novelty camera, in red, c1935, 2½in (6.5cm) high, in black stud-fastening case.
£60–80
$90–115 ⊞ HEG
This novelty camera was made in five different colours, and prices vary according to colour.
Black £50–60 ($75–90).
Brown and red £60–80 ($90–115).
Green £100–130 ($145–190).
Blue £120–180 ($175–260).

◄ **An Expo pocket watch camera,** in silver-coloured base metal, the winding knob forming the lens cap, 1905–35, 2¼in (5.5cm) diam.
£120–140
$175–200 ⊞ HEG

► **A Kodak Brownie folding pocket camera,** with No. 2 metal lensboard and black bellows, 1907–15, 7in (18cm) wide.
£25–30
$35–45 ⊞ HEG
This model was also made with red bellows, valued at £30–35 ($45–50).

A Hasselblad 500C camera, 1985, 8in (20.5cm) long.
£850–950
$1,250–1,400 ⊞ VCL

An Eastman Kodak Jiffy Kodak V.P. camera, made in the US, 1930, 6in (15cm) wide, in original cardboard box.
£40–50
$60–75 ⊞ HUX

Three Kodak Brownie box cameras, a Six-20 Model D, a Flash II and a Flash IV, 1950s, 4in (10cm) high.
£5–10
$8–15 each ⊞ VCL

A Kodak Signet 35 compact 35mm camera, with Ektor lens and Synchro 300 shutter, 1951–58, 4in (10cm) wide.
£70–80
$100–115 ⊞ HEG

A Kodak 930 Kodamatic Instant Camera, 1975, 6½in (16.5cm) wide, in original box.
£8–10
$12–15 ⊞ VCL

A Jaeger le Coultre Compass camera, with stereoscopic head, complete with accessories, Swiss, c1938, 3in (7.5cm) high.
£1,000–1,200
$1,500–1,750 ⚒ RBB

An Ernst Leitz Leica M3 camera, chrome-finished, with Elmar f1.8 5cm lens, c1955, 5¾in (14.5cm) wide.
£500–700
$720–1,000 ⊞ VCL

◄ **A Minolta 16 sub-miniature 16mm cassette-loading camera,** silver, 1957–60, 3in (7.5cm) wide.
£25–35
$35–50 ⊞ HEG
Minolta produced this camera in six different colours: black, chrome, blue, green, red and gold. Prices vary according to colour from £25–90 ($35–130).

A Paillard Bolex H16 16mm cine camera, with triple lens turret, Switar lenses, filters, instructions, and original receipts, 9¾in (25cm) high, in original carrying case.
£250–300
$350–450 ⊞ APC

► **A Polaroid SX-70 folding Land camera,** with auto-focus, c1970, 7in (18cm) wide.
£30–40
$45–60 ⊞ VCL

A Carl Zeiss Jena Rolleicord Art Deco-style camera, Germany, c1934, 8½in (21.5cm) high.
£150–200
$225–280 ⊞ VCL

A Carl Zeiss Jena Rolleiflex camera, with Tessar f3.5 75mm lens, for 120 roll film, 1932–38, 8in (20.5cm) high.
£70–80
$100–115 ⊞ HEG

A Carl Zeiss Jena Rolleiflex SLX camera, with Planar lens, c1980, 5½in (14cm) high.
£220–250
$320–360 ⊞ VCL

▶ **A Sanderson hand-and-stand camera,** with polished wood interior and leather exterior, c1900–20, 6½in (16.5cm).
£180–200
$260–300 ⊞ HEG

A Carl Zeiss Jena Rolleiflex SL66 camera, single lens reflex, c1975, 7in (18cm) long.
£500–600
$720–850 ⊞ VCL

A Carl Zeiss Jena Rolleiflex Sl35E camera, with Planar f1.8/80 lens, c1980, 6in (15cm) wide.
£125–150
$180–220 ⊞ VCL

A Tessina 16mm sub-miniature camera, Swiss, c1960, 2½in (6.5cm) wide.
£300–400
$440–580 ⊞ VCL

A Tasco binocular camera, 110 film cassette, c1975, 5in (12.5cm) deep.
£40–45
$60–65 ⊞ VCL

A W. Watson & Sons quarter-plate field camera outfit, in mahogany and brass, with Waterhouse stops and photographic plates, camera and lens marked, c1895, in manufacturer's original leather case.
£250–350
$375–500 ⊞ APC

▶ **A Zorki 2C Leica copy camera,** with green body, Russian, 1955–60, 5½in (14cm) wide, in original leather case.
£80–100
$115–145 ⊞ HEG
This example is green, but the Zorki 2C was also made in black, valued at £40–60 ($60–80) and grey, valued at £80–100 ($115–145).

A Universal Camera Corporation Univex AF Deluxe Folding Camera, with bellows, for 00 film, in green cast metal, 1935–39, 4in (10cm) high, in original box.
£30–35
$45–50 ⊞ HEG
This model was produced in various colours.

A Zeiss Super Iconta C camera, with 105mm f3.5 Tessar lens, 120 roll film, 1950–55, 6in (15cm) wide.
£160–180
$230–260 ⊞ HEG

Ceramics
Animals

A porcelain model of a sitting dog, 1830–40, 2in (5cm) high.
£90–110
$130–160 ⊞ SER

► **A pottery model of a tiger cub,** Russian, c1930–40, 4in (10cm) high.
£40–50
$60–80 ⊞ MRW

◄ **A pottery model of birds on a trough,** by Jerome Massier, French, c1880, 6in (15cm) wide.
£140–160
$200–230 ⊞ MLL

A model of two bears, on a grassy base, indistinct signature, Russian, dated 1911, 11in (28cm) high.
£300–375
$450–550 ↗ Pott

◄ **A Fürstenburg porcelain model of two kittens,** black and white with green eyes, 1950–60, 5in (12.5cm) high.
£90–100
$130–150 ⊞ WAC

A Royal Crown Derby Imari cat paperweight, in yellow, red and blue, c1985, 5in (12.5cm) high.
£70–80
$100–120 ↗ Pott

A Winstanley pottery model of a cat, hand-painted in Tiger pattern No. 4, c1998, 10in (25.5cm) high.
£30–40
$40–60 ⊞ RIA

Bargeware

Bargeware, also known as Meashamware, is the name given to treacly-brown glazed earthenware, decorated with applied pieces of clay. These were moulded into various shapes including flowers, grapes, pheasants and even lizards and newts, and crudely painted in pinks, blues and greens.

Said to be used by the people who worked the barges along the inland waterways (hence its name), bargeware was a popular gift, often brought back from a journey. Typical shapes include large teapots (often with a smaller teapot on the lid), jugs, mugs and bowls. Many pieces have a cartouche applied to the side impressed with printer's block letters.

Inscriptions can include a date and the name of the recipient (if the piece was a specific commission), or more generalized phrases such as 'A Present to a Friend' or 'Home Sweet Home' if it was bought off the shelf. Bargeware was manufactured from the mid-19th century by small potteries in the Burton-on-Trent area, the Midlands and the Cotswolds. Although very few pieces are marked, known makers include William Mason who began making bargeware in the 1880s at Church Gresley, Derbyshire. In 1901, the went into partnership with Mr Cash and as Mason, Cash & Co, the firm continued to produce the pottery until c1939.

A bargeware double-spouted teapot, with small cherub between the spouts, cartouche inscribed 'a present from', decorated in pink and green, c1875, 8in (20.5cm) high.
£550–650
$800–950 ⊞ JBL

A bargeware sugar bowl, elaborately decorated with flowers and foliage in red, blue and green, c1880, 6in (15cm) diam.
£180–230
$260–330 ⊞ JBL

A bargeware teapot, probably from Church Gresley, with teapot knop to domed cover, decorated with coloured sprigs of flowers and birds, cartouche impressed 'A H Simpson Esqr. Royal Artillery 1882', 15in (38cm) high.
£450–550
$650–800 ⚒ DN

A bargeware teapot-on-stand, decorated with pink and blue flowers with green foliage, cartouche inscribed 'Mr A Johnson Bath 1882', 11in (28cm) high.
£300–350
$450–500 ⊞ JBL

A bargeware money box, with traditional applied decoration in blue and pink, cartouche inscribed 'Put A Penny In', slot at front for coins, c1900, 5in (12.5cm) high.
£200–250
$300–350 ⊞ JBL

A bargeware teapot, with applied mounts, cartouche inscribed 'God Bless Our Home', late 19thC, 12½in (32cm) high.
£120–140
$170–200 ⚒ G(B)

Beswick

A Beswick model of a **Dalmatian,** Arnoldene, No. 961, 1941–93, 5¾in (14.5cm) long.
£50–60
$75–100 ✗ MED

A Beswick model of a **cockerel,** No. 2059, 20thC, 10in (25.5cm) high.
£570–620
$800–900 ✗ GAK

Condition

The condition is absolutely vital when assessing the value of a collectable. Damaged pieces on the whole appreciate much less than perfect examples. However a rare desirable piece may command a high price even when damaged.

◀ A Beswick model of a brown **Scottish terrier,** No. HN965, 1928–46, 3¾in (9.5cm) high.
£300–400
$450–550 ✗ BBR

A Beswick model of **Little Pig Robinson,** designed by Arthur Gredington, wearing a blue striped dress and carrying a brown basket with yellow cauliflowers, 1948–74, 3¾in (9.5cm) high.
£80–100
$115–145 ✗ BBR

A set of three Beswick **wall-hanging seagulls,** No. 658, designed by Mr. Watkin, decorated in white, black and yellow gloss, printed mark, 1938–67, largest 12in (30.5cm) long.
£140–160
$200–230 ✗ BBR

◀ A Beswick model of a white **bull terrier,** No. 970, designed by Arthur Gredington, printed mark, 1942–75, 5½in (14cm) high.
£60–80
$90–110 ✗ BBR

A Beswick model of a **Shire horse,** No. 818, decorated in rocking horse grey, 1952, 8in (20.5cm) long.
£350–400
$500–600 ⊞ PAC

A Beswick model of a white **fantail pigeon,** on a green base, No. 1614, 1959–69, 6in (15cm) wide.
£450–550
$650–800 ✗ Pott

◀ A Beswick model of a sitting **fox,** No. 2348, decorated in brown, white and black, 1970–83, 12¼in (31cm) high.
£170–200
$250–300 ✗ MED

Blue & White

A blue and white platter, decorated with Pagoda pattern, 18thC, 21in (53.5cm) long.
£110–130
$160–190 ⊞ MCC

A blue and white leaf-shaped pickle dish, with stalk handle, decorated with Willow pattern, 18thC, 6in (15cm) long.
£120–140
$170–200 ➤ DA

A blue and white pearlware tankard, decorated with buildings, trees and a stream, early 19thC, restored, 7in (18cm) high.
£320–350
$450–500 ➤ GAK

◀ **A blue and white plate,** decorated with a castle pattern, c1820, 9in (23cm) diam.
£160–190
$230–270 ⊞ SCO

▶ **A Staffordshire blue and white half-pint mug,** 19thC, 4in (10cm) high.
£30–40
$40–60 ⊞ MCC

A Samuel Barker & Son Swinton blue and white meat dish with well, No. 20, decorated with Willow pattern, blue griffin and shield mark to base, damaged, c1850, 21in (53.5cm) long.
£100–120
$145–175 ⚘ **LF**

A Booths blue and white supper set, comprising a central oval dish and six shaped dishes, decorated with Real Old Willow pattern, with treen tray, 19thC, 16½in (42cm) diam.
£150–180
$220–260 ⚘ **GAK**

An early Victorian blue and white toothbrush holder, 7in (18cm) high.
£35–38
$50–55 ⊞ **CAL**

A blue and white platter, with moulded juice channels and reservoir, decorated in Gothic Ruins pattern, with foliate printed border and shaped rim, printed mark for Charles Meigh to base, 19thC, 21in (53.5cm) long.
£200–250
$300–350 ⚘ **Mit**

A blue and white plate, decorated with Willow pattern, 19thC, 10in (25.5cm) diam.
£12–15
$15–20 ⊞ **MCC**

A blue and white milk jug, c1920, 10in (25.5cm) high.
£225–250
$320–360 ⊞ **SMI**

A blue and white spongeware pottery bowl, 1890, 5¼in (13.5cm) diam.
£30–35
$40–50 ⊞ **OD**

> **Cross Reference**
> See Colour Review (page 78)

▶ **A Copeland Spode blue and white plate,** Blue Italian pattern, Spode mark, 20thC, 9in (23cm) diam.
£10–15
$15–25 ⊞ **OD**

◀ **A Dedham Pottery blue and white moulded plate,** decorated with Turkey pattern, with crackle glaze, American, 1896–1943, 8½in (21.5cm) diam.
£110–125
$160–180 ⚘ **JMW**

A Copeland Spode blue and white quail egg set with cruet, Blue Italian pattern, 1930s, 2½in (6.5cm) long.
£75–100
$115–145 ⊞ **BEV**

Burleigh Ware

A Burleigh Ware milk jug, decorated with Sunray pattern, c1930, 4in (10cm) high.
£25–40
$40–60 ⊞ BUR

A Burleigh Ware hors d'oeuvres dish, decorated with Meadowland pattern in orange and green, c1930, 8in (20.5cm) diam.
£25–30
$40–50 ⊞ HO

A Burleigh Ware set of six egg cups and stand, decorated with Golden Days pattern in yellow, green and red, c1930, egg cup 2in (5cm) high.
£80–100
$115–145 ⊞ BUR

A Burleigh Ware Dickens Series character jug, Pickwick, 1940s, 4in (10cm) high.
£50–65
$70–90 ⊞ BUR

A set of Burleigh Ware bird jugs, Kingfisher, Blue Tit, Budgerigar, Bullfinch and Wren, decorated in naturalistic colours, 1955, 4in (10cm) high.
£200–250
$300–350 each ⊞ ERC

◀ **A Burleigh Ware character jug,** of Rt. Hon. J. C. Smuts, hand-coloured in brown, red, yellow and green, 1941, 5in (12.5cm) high.
£440–480
$650–700 ↗ Pott

Burmantofts

◀ **A Burmantofts faïence stick stand,** No. 1860, moulded with a band of stylized leaves on a fluted ground, decorated in light to dark green, impressed marks, c.1900, 24in (61cm) high.
£275–325
$400–470 ↗ AH

LOCATE THE SOURCE
The source of each illustration in Miller's can be found by checking the code letters below each caption with the Key to Illustrations, pages 444–452.

A Burmantofts faïence vase, decorated in blue, green, turquoise and yellow, 1890–1910, 9in (23cm) high.
£300–400
$440–580 ⊞ ASA

A Burmantofts faïence frog group, No. 1995, modelled as two frogs cuddling on a mushroom, decorated with a green glaze, glass eyes, impressed marks to base, c1900, 5in (12.5cm) high.
£380–420
$560–620 ↗ Pott

Carlton Ware

A Carlton Ware teapot, decorated with Early Blush pattern, c1880–1900, 5in (12.5cm) high.
£270–300
$400–450 ⊞ BEV

A Carlton Ware pedestal bowl, decorated with Floribunda pattern, c1929, 5in (12.5cm) wide.
£430–470
$620–700 ⊞ MI

A Carlton Ware jug, decorated with Butterfly and Dahlia pattern, c1930, 5in (12.5cm) high.
£500–600
$720–870 ⊞ BD

Two Carlton Ware chocolate beakers with lids, decorated in red, yellow, cream and green, c1930, 5in (12.5cm) high.
£100–125
$145–175 ⊞ BD

A late Victorian Carlton Ware biscuit barrel, No. 246831, transfer-printed in flow-blue trailing flowers and gilt, the cover with knop finial, 5in (12.5cm) high.
£150–180
$200–250 ⚒ DA

A pair of Carlton Ware candlesticks, c1930, 4in (10cm) high.
£200–225
$300–330 ⊞ BEV

A pair of Carlton Ware candlesticks, decorated in blue and white, c1930, 4in (10cm) high.
£250–270
$350–400 ⊞ BEV

A Carlton Ware cameo box, decorated with Moonlight pattern, c1920, 6in (15cm) long.
£300–350
$450–500 ⊞ BEV

A Carlton Ware vase, decorated with Chinoiserie pattern, c1930, 8in (20.5cm) high.
£130–150
$200–220 ⊞ BD

A Carlton Ware Tulip sugar shaker, 1930–32, 6¼in (16cm) high.
£75–85
$115–125 ⊞ StC

◄ **A Carlton Ware tube-lined bowl,** decorated with Trees and Fields pattern, 1930s, 9in (23cm) wide.
£550–600
$800–900 ⊞ BEV

A Carlton Ware vase, decorated with Lacecap Hydrangea pattern, 1930s, 6¼in (16cm) high.
£750–850
$1,000–1,200 ⊞ StC

A Carlton Ware jug, decorated with High Oak pattern, 1930s, 5¼in (13.5cm) high.
£80–100
$115–145 ⊞ StC

A Carlton Ware basket, moulded with Foxglove pattern, late 1930s, 6½in (16.5cm) wide.
£100–120
$145–175 ⊞ StC

A Carlton Ware butter dish, decorated with Wild Rose pattern, 1948, 5in (12.5cm) wide.
£25–30
$35–45 ⊞ StC

A Carlton Ware tray, decorated with Blackberry pattern, 1937, 10in (25.5cm) wide.
£75–85
$115–125 ⊞ StC

A Carlton Ware breakfast set, moulded with Apple Blossom pattern, c1940.
£650–800
$950–1,200 ⊞ AOT
This green Apple Blossom piece is one of the most sought-after Carlton Ware breakfast sets from the moulded floral range.

A Carlton Ware Walking Ware teapot, with white glaze and yellow shoes, 1978, 9in (23cm) high.
£150–170
$200–250 ⊞ BEV
Walking Ware was developed by husband and wife team Roger Michell and Danka Napiorkowska, and manufactured by Carlton from 1973.

► **A Carlton Ware Hovis teapot,** 1970s, 6¼in (16cm) high.
£60–70
$90–100 ⊞ StC

A Carlton Ware Rouge Royale vase, hand-painted with Wild Duck pattern, 1950s, 6in (15cm) high.
£240–280
$350–400 ⊞ HO

Chintz Ware

A Barker Bros sugar shaker, with all-over multi-coloured floral pattern, c1930, 8in (20.5cm) high.
£80–100
$115–145 ⊞ BD

A Royal Winton dish, decorated with Hazel pattern, c1930, 7in (18cm) long.
£100–120
$145–175 ⊞ BD

Checking chintz

Hazel, with its distinctive black ground, is one of the most popular of all Royal Winton chintz patterns. For maximum value, patterns should be crisp and clean. With all chintz ware check pieces carefully for scratches, fading or restoration.

A Royal Winton butter dish, decorated with the Kinver pattern, c1930, 6in (15cm) long.
£100–120
$145–175 ⊞ BD

A Barker Bros biscuit barrel, with all-over multi-coloured floral pattern, c1930, 6in (15cm) high.
£80–100
$115–145 ⊞ BD

A Royal Winton bowl, decorated with Hazel pattern, c1930, 8in (20.5cm) square.
£225–250
$320–360 ⊞ BEV

A Royal Winton muffin dish, decorated with all-over multi-coloured floral pattern, with blue rim, c1936, 6½in (16.5cm) diam.
£110–130
$160–190 ⊞ AOT

▶ **A Royal Winton covered cheese dish,** decorated with all-over multi-coloured floral pattern, base marked 'AUS. RD 29775', dated 1952, 6½in (16.5cm) wide.
£100–120
$145–175 ⊞ FL

A James Kent bowl, 1930s, 6½in (16.5cm) diam.
£30–40
$50–60 ⊞ DBo

A Royal Winton vase, decorated with Cheadle pattern, c1930, 6in (15cm) high.
£180–200
$250–300 ⊞ BEV

A Royal Winton Marguerite teapot, decorated with all-over multi-coloured floral pattern, c1940, 8in (20.5cm) long.
£240–270
$350–400 ⊞ AOT

Clarice Cliff

A Clarice Cliff coffee can and saucer, decorated with Mondrian pattern, c1930, cup 2in (5cm) diam.
£700–800
$1,000–1,150 ⊞ BD

A Clarice Cliff Conical cup and saucer, decorated with Crocus pattern, c1930, cup 2½in (6.5cm) high.
£200–250
$300–350 ⊞ BD

Three Clarice Cliff side plates, decorated with Crocus pattern, c1930, 7in (18cm) diam.
£40–50
$60–80 ⚲ G(L)

A Clarice Cliff Conical tea cup and saucer, decorated with Red Sunrise pattern, c1930, cup 2½in (6.5cm) high.
£450–500
$650–720 ⊞ BD

A Clarice Cliff Circus plate, decorated by Dame Laura Knight, c1930, 8in (20.5cm) diam.
£800–900
$1,150–1,300 ⊞ BD

A Clarice Cliff Bon Jour shape jam pot, decorated with Honolulu pattern, c1930, 4in (10cm) wide.
£550–650
$800–950 ⊞ BD

A Clarice Cliff Pixie nursery mug, c1930, 4in (10cm) high.
£225–275
$320–400 ⊞ JEZ

A Clarice Cliff Bizarre Dover jardinière, decorated with triangular and diamond motifs in shades of brown, purple and blue with green outlines, 1930s, 6½in (16.5cm) high.
£400–500
$580–720 ⚲ GH

A Clarice Cliff bowl, decorated with Cabbage Flower pattern, 1930s, 6½in (16.5cm) diam.
£160–190
$225–275 ⚲ G(L)

◀ **A Clarice Cliff plate,** decorated with Orange Roof Cottage pattern, printed mark, 1930s, 8in (20.5cm) diam.
£320–360
$450–500 ⚲ GAK

▶ **A Clarice Cliff Bizarre ribbed ovoid vase,** decorated with Viscaria pattern, printed marks, 1930s, 4½in (11.5cm) high.
£200–250
$300–350
⚲ WW

Susie Cooper

A Susie Cooper box and cover, decorated with Pomeranian pattern, 1930s, 4in (10cm) wide.
£900–1,000
$1,300–1,500 ⊞ BD

A Susie Cooper Kestrel teapot, decorated with green Patricia Rose pattern, c1930, 7½in (19cm) high.
£120–150
$175–225 ⊞ BD

A Susie Cooper trio, decorated with pink Patricia Rose pattern, c1930, plate 7in (18cm) diam.
£100–125
$145–175 ⊞ BD

A Susie Cooper consommé dish and stand, decorated in green and red on a white ground, 1930s, stand 7in (18cm) diam.
£40–50
$60–80 ⊞ BD

A Susie Cooper Quadrapets cereal bowl, 1930s, 5½in (14cm) diam.
£120–150
$175–225 ⊞ BD

A Susie Cooper studio pottery vase, decorated with incised squirrels on a butterscotch glaze, signed, c1930, 11½in (29cm) high.
£300–330
$450–480 ⊞ RUSK

Copeland

Insurance values

Always insure your valuable collectables for the cost of replacing them with similar items, regardless of the original price paid. Both dealers and auctioneers will provide a valuation service for a fee.

A pair of Copeland square section vases, decorated with flowers and foliage in blue and gilt, 'WMP' monograms, seal marks containing 'C', 1878–83, 8½in (21.5cm) high.
£220–250
$320–360 ⚹ WW

A Copeland stoneware jug, decorated with rugby players in white relief on a brown ground, beneath a band of floral decoration, 1895, 2in (5cm) high.
£300–350
$450–500 ⚹ ANA

◀ **A Copeland Spode sucrier,** decorated with Cabbage Leaf pattern, c1860, 6in (15cm) wide.
£240–280
$350–400 ⊞ JP

Crown Devon

A Crown Devon Daisy Bell musical cigarette box, decorated in red, green and blue, 1920s, 8in (20.5cm) long.
£500–550
$700–800 ⊞ AU

A Crown Devon doorstop, modelled as a dog, decorated in brown, black and white, 1930s, 10in (25.5cm) long.
£80–100
$115–145 ⊞ BD

▶ **A Crown Devon Pixie four-piece cruet set,** c1940, 3½in (9cm) high.
£120–140
$175–225 ⊞ AOT

A Crown Devon model of a greyhound, painted in natural tones of beige, brown and black, on a black octagonal base, c1930, 6in (15cm) high.
£100–120
$145–175 ⋗ Pott

A Crown Devon vase, decorated with two pheasants and butterflies among flowers against a ruby lustre ground, gold printed mark, 1930s, 11½in (29cm) high.
£370–400
$500–600 ⋗ S(S)

A Crown Derby Auld Lang Syne musical jug, c1940, 6in (15cm) high.
£120–140
$175–225 ⊞ AOT

Crown Ducal

Cross Reference
See Rhead (page 132)

◀ **A Crown Ducal vase,** No. 121, decorated with running yellow, orange and blue glaze over a brown base, 1920s mark, 8¾in (22cm) high.
£40–50
$60–80 ⊞ DEC

A Crown Ducal flower holder, modelled as a tree trunk, decorated with yellow, blue, red and black running glaze, with holes for eight blooms, 1920s, 3½in (9cm) high.
£20–25
$30–40 ⊞ DEC

A pair of Crown Ducal salad servers, decorated with Poppy pattern, c1930, 9in (23cm) long.
£65–75
$95–115 ⊞ BD

Cups, Saucers & Mugs

A *Diana* Cargo tea bowl and saucer, decorated with Diving Birds pattern, c1817, saucer 5½in (14cm) diam.
£270–300
$400–440 ⊞ RBA
These items were rescued from the vessel *Diana* which foundered c1817.

Cross Reference
See Colour Review (page 148)

An alphabet mug, printed *en grisaille* with interior scenes, inscribed 'C C Cook Cat Clock, early 19thC, 5in (12.5cm) high.
£100–120
$145–175 ⚒ GAK

A Shelley mug, hand-painted with Harmony pattern, c1930, 4in (10cm) high.
£70–75
$100–110 ⊞ BEV

A Gaudy Welsh mug, No. 1104, decorated with Grape pattern, 1829–90, 2¾in (7cm) high.
£75–95
$110–140 ⊞ CoHA

A Gaudy Welsh frog mug, decorated with Wagon Wheel pattern, with serpent handle, the interior with a yellow and black frog, 19thC, 5in (12.5cm) high.
£300–330
$450–500 ⚒ TMA

A Shelley trio, in Mode shape, 1931, cup 3in (7.5cm) high.
£225–25
$320–360 ⊞ BEV

A Minton trio, 1912–50, plate 8in (20.5cm) diam.
£30–35
$40–50 ⊞ CAL

A Derbyshire salt-glazed mug, decorated with a hunting scene, 1840, 5½in (14cm) high.
£160–180
$230–260 ⊞ OD

A Shelley trio, in Queen Anne shape, decorated with Black Leafy Tree pattern, 1927–29, cup 3½in (9cm) high.
£140–160
$200–250 ⊞ BEV

A Tarot tea reading cup and saucer, 1930s, saucer 4in (10cm) diam.
£40–45
$60–70 ⊞ LBe

A Pink Panther mug, 1981, 5in (12.5cm) high.
£60–70
$90–100 ⊞ TAC

Denby

A blue Denby Art Pottery vase, with early hand-painted Danesby Ware mark, mid-1920s, 4½in (11.5cm) high.
£55–65
$80–90 ⊞ KES

▶ A Denby Byngo, with mottled blue/brown trial glaze, late 1930s, 3½in (9cm) high.
£100–130
$140–190 ⊞ KES

A Denby mushroom vase, with cream glaze, c1938, 6in (15cm) diam.
£35–45
$50–70 ⊞ KES

A green Denby squirrel bowl, with Gretna glaze, c1938, 12½in (32cm) diam.
£200–225
$300–330 ⊞ KES

A brown Denby Utility teapot, produced for H.M. Forces, late 1940s, 3½ pint size.
£25–30
$35–45 ⊞ KES

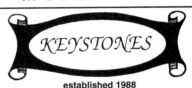

A Glyn Colledge plate, decorated in green, brown, blue and red, believed to be a Denby blank, c1948, 9in (23cm) diam.
£40–50
$60–80 ⊞ DSG

A Denby Greenwheat dinner service, comprising eight dinner plates, six salad plates, six soup bowls, six cereal bowls, four serving dishes, a coffee pot and 11 other matching items, 1950s.
£150–180
$220–260 ⏶ CAu
Greenwheat, designed by Albert Colledge in 1956, was one of the Denby's most successful lines.

Doulton

This year's Doulton section includes a selection of prototype figures from the Royal Doulton archives, sold through Phillips. Two hundred and sixty-three lots were offered, with an estimated value of some £250,000 ($360,000). The sale, however, totalled £423,570 ($615,000), proving the pulling power of these comparatively recent (post WWII) but genuinely unique items. Prototype figures are among the most desirable Royal Doulton products, including both one-off designs that never actually went into manufacture, as well as the original models that inspired the

mass-produced versions. Modern limited edition pieces are far more accessible. In some cases pieces have escalated in value, 'But what goes up does go down,' warns Philips expert Mark Oliver, 'and today's market is perhaps more cautious and more realistic than in recent years.' Oliver offers the following cautionary advice, 'If possible, don't buy from a large volume limited edition and allow a three to five year period before anticipating an appreciation in price. And finally buy because you like the object, not just as an investment.'

A Doulton stoneware commemorative jug, inscribed 'Emin Pasha Relief Expedition 1887–1890', chip to foot, 7½in (19cm) high.
£130–150
$200–220 ✠ SWO

A Doulton Lambeth stoneware teapot, c1890, 3½in (9cm) high.
£100–120
$145–175 ⊞ DSG

A Royal Doulton model of a bulldog, draped with a Union flag, No. 645658, green printed mark, early 20thC, 6in (15cm) high.
£180–200
$250–300 ✠ CDC

A pair of Royal Doulton Chine Ware baluster vases, the rough lace ground decorated with floral sprays and gilding, the neck and foot in deep blue glaze, circle, lion and crown and Doulton Slater patent marks, 1902–39, 10¾in (27.5cm) high.
£140–180
$200–250 ✠ MED

A Royal Doulton Pear's Soap dish, with deep blue glaze, butterfly-wing detail, 1914–18, 6in (15cm) wide.
£100–120
$145–175 ⊞ MURR

A Doulton Lambeth vase, by Emily E. Stormer, decorated with incised styled acanthus leaves, c1890, 6½in (16.5cm) high.
£250–300
$350–450 ✠ G(B)

A Royal Doulton stoneware jardinière, by Hannah Barlow, decorated in shades of brown and green, c1905, 10in (25.5cm) high.
£1,800–2,000
$2,600–2,900 ⊞ JE

◀ **A Royal Doulton Pear's Soap dish,** with deep blue glaze, butterfly-wing detail, 1914–18, 6in (15cm) wide.
£100–120
$145–175 ⊞ MURR

A Doulton Dickens ware vase, decorated in red, green and black, c1930, 6in (15cm) high.
£170–200
$250–300 ⊞ BD

A Doulton Farmer John character jug, designed by Charles Noke, decorated in shades of brown with a white collar, circle mark, lion and crown, 1938–60, 3¼in (8.5cm) high.
£40–50
$60–80 ⚒ BBR

A Doulton model of Ann Hathaway's cottage, with matt glaze, Royal Doulton circle mark, lion and crown, 7¼in (18.5cm) long.
£600–700
$870–1,000 ⚒ BBR

A Royal Doulton prototype figure of a seated woman, Reading the Tea Leaves, wearing a yellow dress, marked, 1960s, 5½in (14cm) high.
£3,300–3,600
$4,700–5,000 ⚒ P

A Royal Doulton Punch and Judy Man character jug, No. D6596, 1964–69, 2½in (6.5cm) high.
£200–225
$300–330 ⊞ ML

A Royal Doulton prototype group of a middle-aged couple seated in deck chairs, decorated in yellow, blue and green, marked, 1970, 6½in (16.5cm) high.
£6,000–6,500
$8,700–9,400 ⚒ P

▶ A Royal Doulton prototype figure of King of the Castle, wearing an orange jumper and blue trousers, marked, 1970s, 6in (15cm) high.
£3,500–3,800
$5,000–5,500 ⚒ P

◀ A Royal Doulton model of a West Highland terrier, a version of No. HN1048, in black basalt, marked, 1970s, 9in (23cm) long.
£1,200–1,400
$1,750–2,000 ⚒ P

▶ **A Royal Doulton prototype figure of Patience,**
wearing a turquoise dress
with a green shawl, marked,
1970s, 6¾in (17cm) high.
£3,000–3,250
$4,400–4,700 ✣ P

**A Doulton figure of
Statue of Liberty
Bunnykins,** No. DB198,
decorated in red, blue,
cream and green, 1970–80,
3in (7.5cm) high, boxed.
£60–70
$90–100 ✣ Pott

**A Royal Doulton proto-
type figure of Indian
Warrior,** decorated in
brown, yellow and
orange, marked, 1970s,
9in (23cm) high.
£3,500–4,000
$5,000–6,000 ✣ P

◀ **A Royal Doulton
figure of Morris Dancer
Bunnykins,** No. DB204,
marked, 1970–80, 4½in
(11.5cm) high, with box.
£25–28
$35–40 ✣ BBR

**A Royal Doulton model of
Snowman Savings Book,**
marked, 5¼in (13.5cm) high.
£70–80
$100–120 ✣ BBR

**A Doulton figure of
Jockey Bunnykins,** No.
DB169, decorated in yellow,
cream and green, No. 174
of a limited edition of 2,000,
1970–80, 3in (7.5cm) high,
boxed with certificate.
£130–150
$200–220 ✣ Pott

**A Royal Doulton figure
of Widdicombe Fair,**
marked, 1980s,
8¼in (21cm) high.
£3,000–3,400
$4,500–5,000 ✣ P

◀ **A Royal Doulton figure
of Welcome Home,**
No. HN3299, No. 3,398 of
a limited edition of 9,500,
1991, 8½in (21.5cm) high.
£120–140
$175–200 ✣ Pott

T. G. Green

Thomas Goodwin Green bought a pottery in Church Gresley, Derbyshire in 1864. The company specialized in utilitarian earthenware and affordable kitchenware and by the time of Green's death in 1905 it was a large concern. Under the management of his sons, the factory was modernized and produced an astonishing variety of ceramics including tableware. Their most famous line of all, introduced c1926, was a range of blue and white striped kitchen china: Cornish Ware.

According to legend, the name for this Derbyshire product was suggested by a south of England salesman, who claimed that the colours reminded him of 'the blue of the Cornish skies and the white crests of the waves'. True or not, there was certainly no doubt about Cornish Ware's success. In 1928 it received the Certificate of the Institute of Hygiene, the first of several awards. The clean and modern design appealed to a new generation of housewives,

many of whom were learning to do without the assistance of a full-time cook and, because they were spending more time in the kitchen, wanted objects that were attractive as well as functional. Cornish Ware became an instant classic.

T. G. Green experimented with other colours – Sunlit Yellow, Cornish Gold (a buff colour), red and black (both rare and very sought after today). However, blue and white remained the perennial favourite. A huge range of items was produced, ranging from plates and bowls to more unusual pieces, such as egg separators and rolling pins, which were not a success at the time since the striped design marked the pastry. Today however, these rarities are highly collectable. If shape is one indicator of value, another is simply a few printed letters. Cornish Ware became known for its named storage jars, and the more unusual inscriptions (Lux, Soap Flakes, Macaroni) can now command high sums.

◀ A T. G. Green **Ivanhoe vase,** decorated in green and red, 1890–1910, 6in (15cm) high.
£180–200
$250–300 ⊞ CAL

▶ A T. G. Green **blue and white jug,** 1900–10, 7in (18cm) high.
£125–150
$180–220 ⊞ CAL

A T. G. Green **mug,** hand-painted in yellow, green and red, with green-glazed interior, c1925, 5in (12.5cm) high.
£25–30
$35–45 ⊞ CAL

A T. G. Green **yellow and white globe teapot,** green shield mark, 1930–60, 5in (12.5cm) high.
£225–250
$320–360 ⊞ GeN

◀ A T. G. Green **Cornish Ware blue egg cup,** 1930–50, 4in (10cm) high.
£80–100
$115–145 ⊞ CAL

A T. G. Green **Streamline plate,** with green bands, 1930, 7in (18cm) diam.
£2–3
$5–8 ⊞ CAL

A T. G. Green cruet set, on a clover leaf base, decorated in blue with white spots, blue domino mark to base, 1930–50, base 5¾in (14.5cm) long.
£140–160
$200–230 ⚒ BBR

Ten T. G. Green plates, decorated in blue with white spots, 1930–50, four 9in (23cm) diam, six 7in (18cm) diam.
£35–45
$50–70 ⚒ BBR

A T. G. Green Cornish Ware flour shaker, decorated with blue and white bands, with handle, 1930–50, 5½in (14cm) high.
£120–160
$175–225 ⊞ CAL
The handled flour shaker is a rare item in Cornish Ware.

▶ **A T. G. Green Cornish Ware trio,** decorated with Morning Glory pattern, 1950s, plate 7in (18cm) diam.
£50–60
$75–90 ⊞ CAL

A T. G. Green Cube teapot, cream jug and sugar bowl, decorated in Dickens Days pattern, 1930.
£150–200
$220–300 ⊞ CAL

Backstamps

Over the years T. G. Green used a number of different marks. On Cornish Ware a shield-shaped mark, appearing in both black and green, was used from the late 1920s until the second half of the 1960s. From 1968 until the late 1970s this was replaced by a Target mark designed by Judith Onions. In the 1980s, a modern church mark was used. In 1987, T. G. Green was taken over by Cloverleaf, who introduced a cloverleaf backstamp.

▶ **A T. G. Green salt shaker,** with screw lid, decorated with blue and white bands, green shield mark to base, 1930–50, 5in (12.5cm) high.
£12–15
$15–20 ⚒ BBR

A T. G. Green biscuit barrel, decorated in blue with white spots, blue domino mark, 1930–50, 5in (12.5cm) high.
£350–450
$500–650 ⊞ CAL

◀ **A T. G. Green sugar bowl,** decorated with blue and white bands, 1940s, 5in (12.5cm) diam.
£15–20
$20–30 ⊞ TAC

A T. G. Green mug, decorated with yellow and white bands, 1940s, 4in (10cm) high.
£25–30
$35–45 ⊞ TAC

A T. G. Green Tally Ho teapot, decorated in blue and white, 1950s, 4½in (11.5cm) high.
£115–125
$160–180 ⊞ CAL
This pattern was made briefly in the 1950s for the Canadian market.

▶ A T. G. Green Cornish Ware pepper shaker, decorated with black and white bands, 1960, 5½in (14cm) high.
£100–120
$145–175 ⊞ CAL
Black Cornish Ware is very rare – it was only produced experimentally, not commercially.

A T. G. Green Cornish Ware egg separator, 1950s, 4in (10cm) high.
£95–110
$140–160 ⊞ CAL

◀ A T. G. Green coffee set, with four cups, designed by Judith Onions, decorated in Sark honey and black, 1968, coffee pot 8½in (21.5cm) high.
£70–80
$100–120 ⊞ CAL

A T. G. Green Cornish Ware Melior cafetière, decorated with blue and white bands, 1950, 6in (15cm) high.
£180–220
$260–320 ⊞ CAL

A T. G. Green Channel Isles cruet set, designed by Judith Onions, decorated in Jersey Green with a white glaze, 1968, 10in (25.5cm) long.
£30–40
$40–60 ⊞ CAL

A T. G. Green cup, decorated with blue and white bands, Judith Onions mark to base, 1970s, 2½in (6.5cm) high
£10–11
$15–18 ⊞ TAC

A T. G. Green measuring jug, decorated with blue and white bands, Judith Onions mark to base, 1970s, 5in (12.5cm) high.
£30–35
$40–60 ⊞ TAC

◀ **A Barley Sugar storage jar,** decorated with blue and white bands, Hygiene seal still attached, black shield mark to base, 1920–60, 5½in (14cm) high.
£300–350
$450–500 ⊞ GeN

A Cherries storage jar, decorated with blue and white bands, black shield mark to base, 1920–60, 3½in (9cm) high.
£90–120
$130–170 ⊞ GeN

A Cloves storage ja█ decorated with blue a█ white bands, no lid, b█ shield mark to base, 1920–60, 3¾in (9.5cm)█
£120–140
$170–200 ⚒ BBR

A Coffee storage jar, decorated with blue and white bands, 1930–50, 4½in (11.5cm) high.
£75–85
$115–125 ⊞ TAC

A T. G. Green Cornish Ware biscuit barrel, decorated with blue and white bands, with wicker handle, 1930–50, 5in (12.5cm) high.
£400–450
$580–650 ⊞ CAL

A Flour storage jar, decorated with blue and white bands, 1920–60, 6in (15cm) high.
£70–80
$100–120 ⊞ TAC

A Lux storage jar, decorated with blue █ white bands, lid miss█ black shield mark to █ 1930–50, 5½in (14cm)
£500–550
$700–800 ⚒ BBR
This jar is particularly█

A T. G. Green tea jar, decorated with blue and white bands, T. G. Green Church Gresley mark to base, 1980s, 6in (15cm) high.
£60–70
$90–100 ⊞ TAC
This mark replaced the Judith Onions Target mark in the 1980s.

A Parsley storage ja█ decorated with blue █ white bands, black sh█ mark to base, 1920–█ 3½in (9cm) high.
£100–110
$145–165 ⊞ GeN

Noritake

◀ A Noritake oval wall plaque, moulded with a dead duck and acorns, in naturalistic colours, printed mark, 20thC, 18in (45.5cm) wide.
£250–300
$360–440 ✗ GAK

A Noritake part tea set, decorated with blue and yellow flowers and a pale blue border, blue Komaru mark, cup 3in (7.5cm) high, c1915.
£140–160
$200–230 ⊞ DgC

A Noritake three-lobed dish, pale blue with black and gilt decoration and centre handle, green Komaru mark, c1920, 8in (20.5cm) wide.
£70–80
$100–115 ⊞ DgC

A Noritake comport, decorated with woodland cottages beside a lake, with gilt and blue border, on an EPNS pedestal, c1920, 9in (23cm) diam.
£100–120
$145–175 ✗ Pott

A Noritake shallow bowl, decorated with stylized flowers in blue and gilt on a cream ground, c1920, 6in (15cm) diam.
£110–130
$160–190 ✗ Pott

A Noritake oval dish, decorated with fruit and flowers and a pale green border with gilt bands, blue Komaru mark, c1920, 10½in (26.5cm) wide.
£80–90
$115–130 ⊞ DgC

A Noritake condiment set, with cruet and preserve pots decorated with red and gilt motifs on a matching tray, green Komaru mark, c1920, jam pot 4in (10cm) high.
£80–90
$115–130 ⊞ DgC

A Noritake trio, decorated with Howo Bird pattern in blue and white, blue Komaru mark, c1920, cup 4in (10cm) high.
£30–35
$45–65 ⊞ DgC

A Noritake lustre condiment set, decorated with a tropical scene on a peach ground, green Komaru mark, c1920, mustard pot 1½in (4cm) high.
£50–55
$75–80 ⊞ DgC

A Noritake bowl, decorated in blue with red and white flowers and green and yellow leaves, pierced rim, c1920, 7in (18cm) wide.
£30–40
$45–60 ⊞ DgC

A Noritake condiment set, with gilt decoration on red bands, c1925, 7in (18cm) wide.
£80–90
$115–130 ⊞ JACK

Pen Delfins

Pen Delfin was started in a garden shed on Coronation Day 1953 by freelance artist Jean Walmsley Heap and Jeannie Todd, both colleagues at Burnley Building Society. Their original intention was to produce clay models as Christmas gifts for friends. Since their shed was over-looked by Pendle, the legendary Lancashire Witch Hill, they called their little figures Pen Delfins, the second part of the name inspired by the 'elfin' quality of their creations. Early products included witches, pixies and elves and the mid-fifties saw the introduction of the popular Rabbit family, which helped to transform Pen Delfin from a part-time hobby into a full-time business.

The company continued to expand, moving to larger premises and exporting figures across the world. Today it attracts a large and enthusiastic collectors' club. In the 1950s you could have purchased a hand-crafted Pen Delfin figure for as little as 7s (35p). Today, rarities and early models can sell for hundreds of pounds.

◄ **A pair of Pen Delfin Rabbit bookends,** dressed in blue and pink, minor damage, 1958–65, 8in (20.5cm) high.
£650–700
$1,000–1,200 ✗ Pott

► **A Pen Delfin model,** Shiner, dressed in pink dungarees, 1960–67, 4in (10cm) high.
£350–400
$500–600 ⊞ AHJ

A Pen Delfin model of a pixie girl, Bod, dressed in orange, minor damage, 1965–67, 5in (12.5cm) high.
£220–250
$300–350 ✗ Pott

A Pen Delfin Model of the Year, Woody, dressed in turquoise trousers, 1997, 4¼in (11cm) high.
£60–70
$90–100 ⊞ AHJ

► **A Pen Delfin wall plaque,** modelled as a flying Pendle witch, finished in pewter, 1980, 7in (18cm) high.
£400–450
$580–650
✗ Pott

Plates & Dishes

A child's plate, black transfer-printed with cottage scene, 1820, 6½in (16.5cm) diam.
£45–50
$65–75 ⊞ OD

A James Green dish, with pink flowersprays on a white ground, blue and gilt border, c1873, 9in (23cm) diam.
£30–35
$45–50 ⊞ CAL

▶ **A Coalport Kingsware plate,** decorated in black with a Japanese design, 1900, 9in (23cm) diam.
£40–60
$60–90 ⊞ ES

A green-glazed plate, with realistic-looking Huntley & Palmer's biscuits, impressed marks to base 'RD 305509', 10¼in (26cm) wide.
£180–200
$250–300 ⚒ BBR

A child's plate, decorated with a girl with a basket, a cat and a dog, moulded floral border, c1830, 5in (12.5cm) diam.
£60–70
$90–100 ⊞ IW

An asparagus cradle, cream ground with moulded decoration in green and brown, c1880, 10 x 14in (25.5 x 35.5cm).
£225–245
$320–350 ⊞ MLL

▶ **A Brent Leigh dish,** with moulded decoration of leaves and flowers, c1935, 13in (33cm) wide.
£18–20
$20–30 ⊞ JACK

A nursery plate, the centre with inscription, the border moulded and enamelled with animals and flowers in shades of green and brown, c1835, 6¼in (16cm) wide.
£70–85
$100–130 ⚒ SAS

A Bo'ness wall plate, with floral decoration in autumn colours, c1880, 10¼in ((26cm) diam.
£40–45
$60–65 ⊞ JEB

An Old Bill dish, transfer-printed in brown with an illustration of Old Bill, the WWI solider created by artist Bruce Bairnsfather, 1917, 7in (18cm) wide.
£50–55
$75–80 ⊞ LeB

Poole Pottery

A Poole Pottery twin-handled vase, designed by Truda Carter, Yo pattern, painted by Gwen Haskins, c1950, 7in (18cm) high.
£300–340
$450–500 ⊞ **MI**

A Carter, Stabler & Adams pottery vase, inscribed 'EP', c1930, 10in (25.5cm) high.
£1,600–1,800
$2,300–2,600 ⊞ **BD**

A Poole Pottery vase, designed by Truda Adams, decorated with tulips by Pat Summers, impressed and painted marks, c1930, 9½in (24cm) high.
£625–700
$950–1,000 ⊞ **RUSK**

A Poole Pottery vase, designed by Truda Adams, decorated with harebells, impressed marks, c1930, 7in (18cm) high.
£240–270
$350–400 ⊞ **RUSK**

◀ **A Poole Pottery plate,** from designs by Tony Morris, with studio backstamp, 1963, 10in (25.5cm) diam.
£280–320
$400–450 ⊞ **HarC**

A Poole Pottery vase, impressed factory marks, c1960, 5½in (14cm) high.
£130–150
$200–220 ⚒ **SWO**

A Poole Pottery Aegean vase, decorated in shades of brown, 1970–75, 9in (23cm) high.
£70–80
£100–120 ⊞ **DSG**

▶ **A Poole Pottery Olympus bowl,** brown earthenware, 1977, 8in (20.5cm) diam.
£40–50
$60–75 ⊞ **DSG**

Three Poole Pottery Delphis vases, decorated in shades of red and yellow, 1970s, 4in (10cm) high.
£15–20
$20–30 each ⊞ **HarC**

Pot Lids & Prattware

Pot lids are the covers of the small domestic earthenware containers used to hold a wide range of 19th-century cosmetic and comestible products. As well as typographical pieces – advertising contents and manufacturer – pictorial pot lids were also produced. Felix Pratt (1813–94) was one of the pioneers of colour-transfer printing. From the late 1840s, F. & R. Pratt of Stoke-on-Trent produced thousands of decorative pot lids, the majority designed by resident artist Jesse Austin. Some of the earliest lids, decorated with ursine pictures, were for bear's grease: a Victorian pomade for the hair produced from Russian bears. Other popular subjects include contemporary celebrities (Duke of Wellington, Prince Albert), commemorative scenes (Crimean War, Great Exhibition) and

reproductions of paintings and landscapes. F. & R. Pratt remained in production until 1920, when the business was purchased by Cauldon Potteries Ltd, who reissued several Prattware pot lids on a creamier, more porcellaneous base. Other major pot lid producers include Ridgway and Co and T. J. & J. Mayer, active from 1843, and whose designs were again reissued in the 20th century.

While pictorial pot lids are sought after for their images, advertising pot lids can also be very collectable. Toothpaste lids have been commanding high prices in the current market, as this section shows. The majority of lids illustrated have no base, which generally makes little difference to their value. American buyers of advertising lids however like, if possible, to have the complete pot.

A pot lid, 'Polar Bears', by F. & R. Pratt, No. 18, polychrome-decorated, c1850, 3in (7.5cm) diam.
£200–270
$300–400 ⊞ JBL

A pot lid, 'Shakespeare's Birthplace', No. 227, with a leaf and scroll border, c1860, 5in (12.5cm) high.
£130–170
$200–220 ⊞ JBL

▶ **A pot lid, 'The Enthusiast',** by F. & R. Pratt, No. 245, c1860, 4in (10cm) diam.
£75–85
$100–125 ⊞ SER

A pot lid, 'Strasburg', by T. J. & J. Mayer, No. 331, polychrome-decorated, coloured border and base, c1850, 4¾in (12cm) diam.
£180–200
$260–300 ⋩ BBR

◀ **A pot lid,** by F. & R. Pratt, No. 19, depicting a bear, a lion and a cockerel, c1855, 3in (7.5cm) diam.
£70–90
$100–130 ⊞ JBL
This pot commemorates the Crimean War, with the English lion subduing the Russian bear.

A pot lid, 'The Late Prince Consort', by F. & R. Pratt, No. 153, c1862, 4in (10cm) diam.
£75–110
$100–160 ⊞ JBL
This portrait lid was made to commemorate the death of Albert, Queen Victoria's husband.

A pot lid, 'A Pretty Kettle of Fish', by F. & R. Pratt, No. 48, polychrome-decorated, c1875, 4in (10c) diam.
£50–80
$75–115 ⊞ JBL

A pot lid, 'Uncle Toby Courting the Widow Wadman', by F. & R. Pratt, No. 328, polychrome-decorated, c1880, 4in (10cm) diam.
£45–65
$65–100 ⊞ GRI
This scene comes from Laurence Sterne's novel *Tristram Shandy*. It is an engraving after a painting by C. R. Leslie.

A paste jar, 'Mending the Nets', by F. & R. Pratt, No. 70, 19thC, 4in (10cm) high.
£70–100
$100–150 ⊞ JBL

A pot and lid, by F. & R. Pratt, No. 62, polychrome illustration on lid, c1890, 3in (7.5cm) wide.
£110–120
$160–175 ⊞ GRI

A pot lid, 'Marbrero Toothpaste', 1890–1900, 3½in (9cm) wide.
£240–260
$350–380 ⚒ BBR
The picture of a toothbrush makes this lid desirable.

A pot lid, 'Valentine's Cherry Blossom Tooth Paste, with coloured overglaze transfer of a Chinese lady, 2¾in (7cm) square, with original base.
£320–350
$450–500 ⚒ BBR

A pot lid, 'American Dentrifice', blue transfer-printed, 3½in (9cm) diam.
£200–220
$300–320 ⚒ BBR

LOCATE THE SOURCE
The source of each illustration in Miller's can be found by checking the code letters below each caption with the Key to Illustrations, pages 444–452.

A pot lid and base, 'Rose Paste', black transfer-printed lettering on pink background, with gold band, damaged, 3½in (9cm) diam.
£120–140
$175–200 ⚒ BBR

Quimper

A Quimper faïence basket,
modelled as two swans with
outstetched necks forming the
handle, decorated in brown, blue
and yellow, c1920, 9in (23cm) high.
£160–175
$230–250 ⊞ MLL

A Quimper plate, decorated with
a man in blue, orange and green,
with yellow border, c1922,
7¼in (18.5cm) diam.
£35–40
$50–60 ⊞ SER

A pair of Quimper vases,
polychrome-decorated, c1930,
9in (23cm) high.
£180–200
$260–300 ⊞ MLL

A Quimper solitaire set, decorated with a
man and a woman in blue and orange, c1920,
platter 9in (23cm) wide.
£425–465
$620–680 ⊞ MLL

▶ **A Quimper cup and
saucer,** Broderie design,
1925–30, saucer
9½in (24cm) wide.
£40–45
$60–65 ⊞ SER

◀ **A pair of
Quimper plates,**
Corbeille design,
decorated in
red, green and
blue, c1930,
9in (23cm) diam.
£110–125
$160–180
⊞ MLL

▶ **A Quimper
fish dish,** Petit
Breton design,
c1930, 10½in
(26.5cm) wide.
£40–45
$60–65 ⊞ SER

A Quimper jug, decorated in
shades of brown and green, c1930,
4in (10cm) high.
£65–75
$95–110 ⊞ SER

A Quimper pin dish,
Butterfly/Bagpipe shape,
c1920, 7in (18cm) wide.
£75–95
$100–150 ⊞ MURR

A pair of Quimper clogs,
decorated with orange brown and
green, 20thC, 4in (10cm) long.
£15–20
$20–30 ⊞ SER

Radford

A Radford trio, decorated with swags of flowers and foliage on a cream ground, 1924, plate 7in (18cm) diam.
£12–14
$15–20 ⊞ DBo

A Radford milk jug, decorated with blue and pink flowers on a cream ground, c1930, 3in (7.5cm) high.
£45–50
$65–75 ⊞ BEV

A Radford Egyptian ware vase, decorated with yellow, green and blue geometric shapes on a beige ground, c1930, 10in (25.5cm) high.
£160–175
$230–250 ⊞ BEV

A Radford model of a hummingbird, in blue, yellow and brown, c1935, 6in (15cm) high.
£135–150
$200–220 ⊞ BEV

▶ **A Radford vase,** decorated in yellow, pink, blue and green, c1940, 9in (23cm) high.
£135–150
$195–220 ⊞ BEV

A Radford vase, decorated with red flowers on a cream ground, c1930, 3in (7.5cm) high.
£8–10
$10–15 ⊞ WAC

Charlotte Rhead

Two Bursley Ware dishes, designed by Charlotte Rhead, both decorated with stylized spring flower design on a beige mottled ground within a green border, both signed, 1930s, largest 12in (30.5cm) wide.
£170–210
$250–300 ⚲ GAK

A Crown Ducal vase, designed by Charlotte Rhead, stepped Art Deco shape, decorated in orange, buff, green and black on a cream ground, c1932, 6in (25.5cm) high.
£220–260
$320–380 ⊞ AOT

◀ **A Crown Ducal vase,** designed by Charlotte Rhead, No. 132, decorated with orange, yellow, black and gold on a light orange ground, printed and inscribed marks, 1930s, 10¼in (26cm) high.
£260–300
$380–450 ⚲ Mit

Staffordshire

A Staffordshire pastille burner, modelled as a house in naturalistic colours, c1850, 4in (10cm) high.
£140–150
$200–220 ⊞ SER

A Staffordshire Prattware figure of Bacchus, decorated in pink, brown and green glaze, 1780–1800, 5in (12.5cm) high.
£150–170
$220–250 ⊞ SER

A Staffordshire figure of a child, with red, blue and yellow robe and matching scarf, possibly by Enoch Wood, restored, 1820–30, 4½in (11.5cm) high.
£150–170
$220–250 ⊞ SER

A Staffordshire figure of a clergyman, preaching from a pulpit, with a verger at a reading desk below, wearing black robes, c1835, 10in (25.5cm) high.
£450–500
$650–720 ⊞ ML

▶ **A Staffordshire figure of a man,** with a turquoise frock coat and grey trousers, carrying a black hat, 1840–50, 7in (18cm) high.
£100–130
$145–190 ⊞ ML

▶ **A pair of Staffordshire dogs,** in brown and white, c1850, 7½in (19cm) high.
£450–500
$650–720 ⊞ TUN

A Staffordshire spill vase, modelled as a pair of foresters wearing turquoise jackets, c1850, 13in (33cm) high.
£350–400
$500–580 ⊞ ML

▶ **A Staffordshire biblical group,** depicting Rebecca at the well with Abraham, in pink, yellow, red and brown, c1855, 13in (33cm) high.
£150–200
$220–290 ⊞ TUN

A Staffordshire watch-holder group, the man in a blue coat with a musical instrument, the woman carrying an animal, the central pillar decorated with strawberries and leaves, 1855, 12½in (32cm) high.
£125–150
$180–220 ⊞ TUN

A Staffordshire figure of a sailor, in a pale blue shirt, red scarf and yellow hat, c1855, 12in (30.5cm) high.
£250–300
$360–440 ⊞ TUN

A Staffordshire figure, entitled 'The Wounded Soldier', in blue, red, pink and yellow, c1855, 10in (25.5cm) high.
£350–400
$500–580 ⊞ TUN

A Staffordshire group, entitled 'Auld Lang Syne', one man with a yellow tam-o-shanter, one with a red rug over his legs, and one in a red, white and green kilt and sash, c1855, 9in (23cm) high.
£250–300
$360–450 ⊞ TUN

▶ **A Staffordshire Parr figure,** depicting Garibaldi in a red shirt, 1863, 12½in (32cm) high.
£600–650
$900–1,000 ⊞ TUN

A Staffordshire spill vase, entitled 'Good Companions', depicting a brown horse and black and white cow drinking from a fountain, beneath a tree with birds, c1855, 10in (25.5cm) high.
£150–180
$220–250 ⊞ TUN

A Staffordshire Parr figure, depicting Hamlet wearing a black plumed hat, black cape trimmed in red, with red trousers and white hose, and holding a skull, c1860, 11in (28cm) high.
£350–400
£500–580 ⊞ TUN

LOCATE THE SOURCE
The source of each illustration in Miller's can be found by checking the code letters below each caption with the Key to Illustrations, pages 444–452.

◀ **A pair of Staffordshire models of cats,** with painted faces and blue collar bows, c1870, 8in (20.5cm) high.
£350–400
$500–600 ⊞ ML

A Staffordshire figure of a lady, wearing a green jacket and pink skirt, c1860, 4½in (11.5cm) high.
£30–35
$45–50 ⊞ IW

A Staffordshire stoop, depicting Christ crucified, with three angels, c1880, 8in (20.5cm) high.
£125–150
$180–220 ⊞ SER

Studio Pottery

A Michael Cardew Winchcombe stoneware teapot, decorated in brown with yellow slip, c1930, 5in (12.5cm) high.
£450–500
$650–725 ↗ **RBB**

► **An Isle of Wight basket pot,** cream and green mottled earthenware with woven cane handle, c1940, 7in (18cm) diam.
£30–40
$45–60 ⊞ **DSG**

A Derek Clarkson pottery bottle vase, yellow with crystalline decoration in shades of blue, c1990, 8¼in (21cm) high.
£250–300
$360–450 ⊞ **PGA**

A Holmegaard cast stoneware vase, designed by Arne Bang, model No. 6, with brown and grey glaze, marked AB, c1937, 5in (12.5cm) high.
£275–300
$400–450 ↗ **TREA**

A Bernard Leach stoneware pot and cover, probably made in Kyoto, the unglazed cover painted in blue and green with a well-head within concentric circles, the base with foliate motifs, cracks to cover, the base marked 'BL' in black enamel, c1934, 3½in (9cm) diam.
£350–400
$500–600 ↗ **Bon**

A slipware charger, in the style of Thomas Toft, decorated with the Royal arms, motto and inscription within a hatched border, slight restoration, 20thC, 17¾in (45cm) diam.
£90–100
$130–150 ↗ **Bon**
Although the maker of this particular charger is unknown, slipware examples of this type were potted by Bernard Leach at St Ives. Leach was interested in reviving traditional art forms that were being undermined by industry and was particularly inspired by the 17th-century slipware of Thomas Toft.

A Leach pottery Standard Ware bowl, with 'Z' design, impressed seal mark, c1960, 9in (23cm) diam.
£90–100
$130–150 ⊞ **RUSK**

A Yelland Pottery cup and saucer, by Michael Leach, with green glaze, 1960, saucer 5¾in (14.5cm) diam.
£15–20
$20–30 ⊞ **IW**

A Katherine Pleydell-Bouverie stoneware vase, decorated with sgraffito overlapping arch motif within Greek key border, impressed 'KBP' within a rectangle and 'Cole' within a triangle, 1925–28, 5in (12.5cm) high.
£350–400
$500–580 ↗ **CAu**

SylvaC

A SylvaC spring onion pot, decorated in green, cream and brown, No. 5042, 1930s, 5in (12.5cm) high.
£30–35
$45–50 ⊞ TAC

A SylvaC posy bowl, the border with three rabbits and leaves, in green and brown, No. 1312, 1930s, 9in (23cm) diam.
£45–55
$65–80 ⊞ TAC

A SylvaC duck, with white body and yellow beak and feet, No. 1499, 1930s, 4½in (11.5cm) high.
£40–45
$60–65 ⚹ BBR

A SylvaC Scottish terrier, with beige body and brown nose and collar, No. 1209, 1950s, 11in (28cm) high.
£70–80
$100–115 ⚹ BBR

A green SylvaC dog, 1950s, 4in (10cm) high.
£40–50
$60–75 ⊞ TAC

Three SylvaC comic rabbits, in graduated sizes, 1950s, largest 8in (20.5cm) high.
£30–50
$45–75 each ⊞ TAC

A SylvaC dog and basket, decorated in yellow and brown, No. 1996, 1950s, 5in (12.5cm) wide.
£30–35
$45–50 ⊞ TAC

A beige SylvaC long-eared dog, 1950s, 7in (18cm) high.
£40–45
$60–65 ⊞ TAC

A brown SylvaC chipmunk, 1960s, 7in (18cm) high.
£25–30
$35–45 ⊞ TAC

▶ **A SylvaC spaniel,** lying down, with a brown head and brown patches on body, 1950s, 3½in (9cm) long.
£30–35
$45–50 ⚹ BBR

Troika

A Troika River Thames plaque, signed 'Troika St Ives', with painted Trident mark, 1963–65, 10½in (26.5cm) high.
£650–750
$1,000–1,100 ⊞ TRO

A Troika charger, painted and incised dark blue and red, on a blue ground, impressed Trident mark, 1963–65, 10in (25.5cm) diam.
£250–300
$360–450 ⊞ TRO

A Troika ashtray, green with ochre dots, 1960s, 5in (12.5cm) square.
£50–70
$75–100 ⊞ MURR

▶ **A Troika ceramic drum,** by Ann Lewis, decorated with red circles and blue bands, 1967–70, 6½in (16.5cm) diam.
£275–325
$400–470
⊞ TRO

A Troika slab vase, probably by Benny Sirota, with oxide decoration, marked 'Troika St Ives BS', 1963–65, 7½in (19cm) high.
£200–250
$300–360 ⊞ TRO

A Troika cylinder vase, by Honor Curtis, decorated in beige and dark blue, signed 'Troika St Ives Cornwall HC', late 1960s, 6½in (16.5cm) high.
£170–190
$250–275 ⊞ TRO

> **Cross Reference**
> See Sixties & Seventies (page 354)

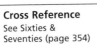

◀ **A Troika cylinder vase,** deep blue with light brown circles and bands on a brown and grey ground, signed 'Troika Cornwall AB', late 1970s, 14in (35.5cm) high.
£300–360
$450–520 ⊞ TRO

Wade

A Wadeheath Flaxman Pluto, decorated in yellow and black, 1937–38, 6½in (16.5cm) long.
£200–250
$300–360 ✦ Pott

Four Wade Disney Hat Box series animals, including Bambi, Lady and Scamp, 1950s–60s, largest 2½in (6.5cm) high.
£10–20
$15–30 each ⊞ PC

Two Wade gingerbread figures, an adult and two children, 1995, adult 4¼in (11cm) high.
£20–30
$30–45 each ⊞ PC

Four Wade animals, Bactrian Camel, Grizzly Cub, Grizzly Bear and Llama, in beige and white, 1950s, largest 2in (5cm) high.
£15–30
$20–45 each ⊞ PC

A Wadeheath panda, decorated in black and white enamels, 1950s, 7in (18cm) high.
£350–400
$500–600 ✦ Pott

◄ **Two Wade figures,** Yogi Bear and Mr Jinks, Yogi with red scarf, Mr Jinks with blue bow tie, 1962–63, largest 2½in (6.5cm) high.
£65–75
$100–110 ✦ BBR

A Wade Thomas the Tank Engine money box, decorated in blue, red, yellow and black, 1986, 6½in (16.5cm) long.
£100–120
$150–175 ✦ Pott

► **Three Wade Mr Men and Little Miss Figures,** Little Miss Giggles, Mr Happy and Mr Bump, for Robell Media Promotions, late 20thC, 3¾in (9.5cm) high.
£35–40
$50–60 ✦ BBR

A Wade Blow Up polar bear, 1962–63, 6in (15cm) high.
£80–100
$120–150 ✦ Pott

A Wade spaniel, brown, limited edition No. 0104 of 1,000, September 1994, 3¼in (8.5cm) high.
£15–20
$20–30 ✦ BBR

Wedgwood

A Wedgwood Drabware custard cup, modelled as a beige artichoke, with gilt outlines, c1790, 3½in (9cm) high.
£350–400
£500–600 ⊞ US

A pair of Wedgwood black basalt baluster vases, applied on either side with masks, with panel of dancing figures, integral socle, impressed marks, late 19thC, 8½in (21.5cm) high.
£100–120
$150–175 ♪ GAK

A Wedgwood lustre ware fluted bowl, decorated with four gilt dragons on a mottled lustre ground, slight crazing, pattern No. Z4831, printed mark, c1920, 7¼in (18.5cm) high.
£170–200
$250–300 ♪ WW

A Wedgwood black basalt bowl, designed by Keith Murray, 1930s–40s, 9in (23cm) diam.
£400–480
$600–700 ⊞ BEV

◄ **A Wedgwood grey vase,** designed by Keith Murray, c1930, 8in (20.5cm) high.
£800–850
$1,200–1,250 ⊞ BD

A Wedgwood vase, designed by Keith Murray, cream with horizontal ribbing, 1930s–40s, 6in (15cm) diam.
£300–350
$450–500 ⊞ BEV

► **A Wedgwood plate,** designed by Eric Ravilious with Garden pattern, 1950s, 7½in (19cm) diam.
£135–150
$200–225 ⊞ REN

Three Wedgwood pattern Russell Hobbs electrically-heated pots, a coffee percolator and milk warmer decorated in Glen Mist pattern, and a coffee percolator in Poppy pattern, 1970s, percolators 10in (25.5cm) high.
£8–10
$10–15 each ⊞ AND

Wemyss

A Wemyss spiral-moulded jardinière, painted with roses in pink and green, green rim, slight damage, c1900, 8¾in (22cm) diam.
£90–110
$130–160 ➶ WW

A Wemyss plate, painted with sweet peas in cerise, purple and green, blue rim, c1900, 5in (12.5cm) diam.
£150–200
$220–300 ⊞ RdeR

A Wemyss preserve pot, painted with hive and bees in brown, yellow, green and black, blue rim, c1900, 5in (12.5cm) high.
£270–300
$400–450 ⊞ RdeR

◄ **A Wemyss porridge bowl,** decorated with a black cockerel, inscribed in red 'Save yer braith tae cuil yer parritch', the rim with white leaves on a deep blue ground, c1920, 7in (18cm) diam.
£300–350
$450–500 ⊞ RdeR

A Wemyss pig, by Plichta, painted in pink and green with flowering clover, late 1930s, 12in (30.5cm) wide.
£500–700
$750–1,000 ⊞ RdeR

Worcester

A Worcester figure of a girl, with shoulder-length hair and flowing garments, painted in natural colours, impressed mark, c1862, 11¼in (28.5cm) high.
£330–360
$470–500 ➶ HYD

A Royal Worcester wall vase, modelled as an orchid in green and white with gilt highlights, printed mark in green, 1892, 7¾in (20cm) high.
£100–150
$150–220 ➶ L&E

A Royal Worcester figure, entitled 'The Loafer', by James Hadley, c1925, 5in (12.5cm) high.
£240–270
$350–400 ⊞ GRI

A Royal Worcester figure, entitled 'Friday's Child', depicting a boy in green trousers with red belt and sandals feeding a kitten from a red-rimmed bowl, 1950s, 7in (18cm) high.
£150–180
$220–260 ⊞ WAC

Colour Review

A Denby mug, by Glyn Colledge, 1948–55, 6in (15cm) high.
£45–60
$65–95 ⊞ DSG

A Doulton Lambeth faïence pilgrim flask, by Mary Butterton, assisted by Alice Campbell, No. L325, printed circular factory marks, painted artist's monograms, 1890s, 14¼in (36cm) high.
£700–800
$1,200–1,500 ⚒ S(NY)
Ex-Harriman Judd Collection.

► **A pair of Royal Doulton Tutankhamen vases,** 1923–29, 11in (28cm) high.
£1,300–1500
$1,900–2,200 ⊞ I&M

◄ **A Royal Doulton baseball player prototype character jug,** by David Briggs, No. D6624, printed factory mark, minor damage, 1970, 8½in (21.5cm) high.
£6,500–7,500
$9,500–11,000 ⚒ P

◄ **A Royal Doulton pottery vase,** by Frank Butler, incised with Art Nouveau-style flowers and trailing foliage, c1908, 13¾in (35cm) high.
£500–550
$700–800 ⚒ AH

◄ **A Goldscheider double dancing group,** c1930, 15in (38cm) high.
£2,750–3,000
$4,000–4,500 ⊞ BD

A Grafton china trio, 1930, plate 6in (15cm) square.
£10–12
$15–20 ⊞ CAL

A pair of Gray's Pottery coffee cans and saucers, designed by Susie Cooper, in bold geometric design, factory mark 8071, saucer 4½in (11.5cm) diam.
£250–275
$360–400 ⊁ RFA

A T. G. Green Mocha ware jug, 1910, 6¼in (16cm) high.
£100–120
$145–175 ⊞ WCa

◄ **A T. G. Green Pharos design biscuit barrel,** design No. 753176, registered 1930, 7in (18cm) high.
£450–500
$650–720 ⊞ CAL

► **A T. G. Green Streamline biscuit barrel,** 1930, 8in (20cm) high.
£180–200
$260–290 ⊞ CAL

A T. G. Green Cornish Ware jar, 1930s, 7in (18cm) high.
£60–65
$90–100 ⊞ CAL

A T. G. Green Cornish Ware sugar shaker, 1950, 7in (18cm) high.
£750–1,000
$1,100–1,500 ⊞ CAL
This rare red and white design was produced as a prototype only.

A T. G. Green Flair TV dinner plate, in the Patio shape, 1956, 9in (23cm) wide.
£25–30
$35–45 ⊞ CAL

A T. G. Green Cornish Ware marmalade pot, 1966, 4in (10cm) high.
£40–50
$60–75 ⊞ CAL
This is from the range designed by Judith Onions.

▶ **A Hancock's Cremorne vase,** c1930, 13in (33cm) high.
£270–300
$400–450 ⊞ BEV

◀ **A James Kent Apple Blossom chintz teapot,** c1930, 7in (18cm) high.
£175–200
$250–280 ⊞ BD

A Hummel Meditation figure, No. 13/0, TMK2, Bee trademark, 1950s, 6in (15cm) high.
£160–180
$230–260 ⊞ ATH

A Longchamps majolica cachepot, 1890, 9in (23cm) high.
£330–350
$470–500 ⊞ MLL

A Bernard Leach Standard ware dish with handle, St Ives Pottery, c1954, 6½in (16.5cm) wide.
£20–25
$30–35 ⊞ GRo

A Maling hand-painted lustre plate, 1930s, 11in (28cm) diam.
£170–200
$250–280 ⊞ TAC

◀ **A Midwinter Red Domino coffee cup and saucer,** 1950s, saucer 4¾in (12cm) diam.
£18–22
$25–35 ⋏ FLD

▶ **A Moorcroft Pomegranate vase,** c1930, 12in (30.5cm) high.
£1,600–1,800
$2,300–2,600 ⊞ BD

◀ **A Shelley vase,** decorated with Tulip pattern, 1930, 10in (25.5cm) high.
£225–250
$325–350 ⊞ BEV

A Shelley cup and saucer, in Vogue design, 1930, 3in (7.5cm) high.
£160–180
$230–260 ⊞ BEV

A Shelley Baby's Plate, decorated with a Red Riding Hood scene, 1940–60, 8in (20.5cm) diam.
£70–90
$100–130 ✎ G(L)

◀ **A Staffordshire spill vase,** modelled as a doe with young fawn, c1855, 12in (30.5cm) high.
£200–250
$300–350 ⊞ TUN

A Staffordshire group depicting the death of Nelson, c1850, 9in (23cm) high.
£250–300
$350–450 ⊞ ML

▶ **A Staffordshire jug,** modelled as a monkey playing a viola, c1870, 12in (30.5cm) high.
£450–500
$650–720 ⊞ ML

◄ A SylvaC rabbit, No. 1065, 1950s, 6in (15cm) high.
£55–65
$80–95 ⊞ TAC

A Troika storage jar, by Alison Brigden, decorated with Snakeskin pattern, signed 'Troika Cornwall AB', late 1970s, 8½in (21.5cm) high.
£170–190
$250–275 ⊞ TRO

A Sally Tuffin Double Dove plate, designed for Dennis China Works, 1996, 10in (25.5cm) diam.
£100–120
$145–175 ⊞ NP

A Wemyss preserve pot, painted with plums, c1900, 5in (12.5cm) high.
£180–200
$260–290 ⊞ RdeR

A Royal Worcester figure, 'Saturday's Child', depicting a child knitting watched by a cat, 1951, 6in (15cm) high.
£220–240
$320–350 ⊞ WAC

► A Winstanley hand-painted tabby cat, c1998, 12in (30.5cm) high.
£55–65
$80–95 ⊞ RIA

Cigarette & Trade Cards

▶ **Taddy & Co,** VC Heroes 81–100, 20 portraits of Victoria Cross winners from the Boer War, part of a continuous series of 125 VC winners issued between 1901–04, 1902.
£325–360
$470–560 ⊞ MUR

◀ **A set of 24 trade cards,** Occupations, with text to reverse, French, c1900.
£110–130
$160–190 ↗ VS

Lambert & Butler, World's Locomotives, set of 25, 1912.
£75–80
$110–115 ⊞ MUR

◀ **Taddy & Co,** Prominent Footballers, series of 600 pictures, 1907.
£14–16
$15–20 each ⊞ LCC

Smith's Pinewood Cigarettes, Cricketers series, set of 50, 1912.
£610–675
$870–1,000 ⊞ LCC

▶ **Gallaher Cigarettes,** The Great War, set of 100, 1915.
£180–200
$260–280 ⊞ MUR

Typhoo Tea, Ancient Annual Customs, 25 cards, 1922.
£35–40
$50–60 ⊞ MAr

Godfrey Phillips, Optical Illusions, set of 25 cards, 1925.
£45–50
$65–75 ⊞ MUR

W. D. & H. O. Wills, British Butterflies, 50 cards, 1927.
£45–50
$65–75 ⊞ MAr

W. D. & H. O. Wills, Radio Celebrities, cigarette cards in album, 1930.
£9–10
$12–15 ⊞ LCC

John Player & Sons, Tennis, cigarette cards in album, 1930s.
£9–10
$12–15 ⊞ LCC

W. D. & H. O. Wills, Military Aircraft, five uncut sheets comprising complete set of 50 cards, compiled late 1930s, date stamped 24 March 1966.
£80–120
$115–175 ⋗ VS

◀ **W. D. & H. O. Wills,** Safety First, cigarette cards in album, produced in conjunction with the government, 1934.
£9–10
$12–15 ⊞ LCC

John Player & Sons, Derby and Grand National Winners, set of 50 cards, 1933.
£70–80
$100–115 ⊞ MUR

▶ **John Player & Sons,** Motor Cars, set of 50 cards, 1935.
£50–60
$75–90 ⊞ MAr

Liebig trade cards, Symbols of Power, 1971.
£50–70
$75–100 ⊞ MAr

John Player & Sons,
Golf, complete set of
25, 1939.
£80–100
$115–150 ⚒ VS

Philadelphia Chewing Gum Corporation, War
Bulletin, 88 cards depicting
events from WWII, 1965.
£95–110
$150–160 ⊞ MUR

Brooke Bond, Magic World of Disney, set of 25
cards, 1989.
£5-6
$7–10 ⊞ LCC

◄ John Player & Sons, History of Motor Racing, set of
30 cards from Tom Thumb cigars, 1986.
£25–30
$35–45 ⊞ LCC

Brooke Bond, The Secret Diary of Kevin Tipps, set of 50
American-size cards from PG Tips tea, 1995.
£7–9
$10–15 ⊞ LCC

Brooke Bond, International
Footballers, set of 20 cards
from PG Tips tea, 1998.
£3–5
$5–7 ⊞ LCC

Topps Bubblegum, X Files,
set of 72 cards, 1997.
£8–10
$12–15 ⊞ LCC

Comics & Annuals

Action Comics, New Year cover, 1945.
£40–50
$60–75 ✗ CBP

The Beano Book, No. 1, 1940.
£2,800–3,000
$4,000–4,500 ✗ CBP

Fantastic Four 1 comic, 1961.
£350–400
$500–580 ✗ CBP

Adventure comic,
Nos. 27–52,
March–September, 1922.
£230–250
$330–380 ✗ CBP

The Dandy comic,
48 issues between 1,155 and 1,205, 1964.
£190–220
$275–320 ✗ CBP

Funny Wonder comics,
1893–1942.
£2–12
$5–15 each ⊞ DPO

▶ **The Beano Comic**,
No. 13, 1938.
£500–550
$720–800 ✗ CBP

The Beano Comic,
No. 5, 1938.
£600–700
$870–1,000 ✗ CBP

▶ **Champion The Wonder Horse** annual,
1958, 9 x 11in (23 x 28cm).
£4–6
$5–8 ⊞ YR

Two *Huckleberry Hound Television Story Book* annuals, 1961, 9 x 11in (23 x 28cm).
£5–7
$6–10 ⊞ YR

The Magic Comic, No. 1, 1939.
£1,200–1,500
$1,750–2,200 ⚒ CBP

Mickey Mouse Weekly comic, No. 1, 1936.
£250–280
$360–400 ⚒ CBP

Mickey Mouse Annual, 1948, 8 x 10in (20.5 x 25.5cm).
£45–50
$65–75 ⊞ SDP

Nipper's Magazine, 1921.
£2–3
$5–8 ⊞ J&S

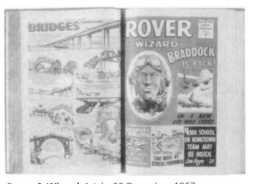

Rover & Wizard, 1 July–20 December, 1967.
£100–110
$150–160 ⚒ CBP

▶ *Superman* comic, No. 44, 1947.
£140–160
$200–230 ⚒ CBP

More Adventures of Rupert Bear, 1937, 4°.
£550–600
$800–870 ⚒ DW

New Triumph comics, Nos. 771–792, 1939.
£1,800–2,000
$2,500–3,000 ⚒ CBP

LOCATE THE SOURCE
The source of each illustration in Miller's can be found by checking the code letters below each caption with the Key to Illustrations, pages 444–452.

◀ *Amazing Spider-Man* comic, No. 20 issued with the cover of No. 21, January 1965.
£450–500
$650–720 ⚒ CBP

Commemorative Ware
Exhibitions

A polychrome pot lid, entitled 'The Grand International Building of 1851' and inscribed 'For the Exhibition of Art and Industry of all Nations', c1851, 5in (12.5cm) diam.
£90–120
$130–175 ⊞ JBL

An ivory comb, inscribed 'GREAT EXHIBITION OF 1862/THE EAST FRONT VIEW', decorated with a view of the exhibition building, 1862, 3¼in (8.5cm) long.
£50–60
$75–90 ⊞ TML

A wooden box, commemorating the Festival of Britain, made of wood from the old London Bridge, 1951, 7in (18cm) wide.
£50–60
$75–90 ⊞ MURR

A 7in record, commemorating the Festival of Britain, 'Make your own recording in music', by Pavilion, green and white, 1951.
£65–75
$95–110 ⊞ MURR

A light-green moulded pint glass, commemorating the Festival of Britain, 1951, 5in (12.5cm) high.
£38–45
$55–65 ⊞ MURR

A red plastic fold-away beaker, commemorating the Festival of Britain, 1951, 2in (5cm) high.
£30–35
$45–50 ⊞ MURR

> **Cross Reference**
> See Politics (page 301)

A Festival of Britain postcard, 1951.
£12–15
$15–20 ⊞ REN

LOCATE THE SOURCE
The source of each illustration in Miller's can be found by checking the code letters below each caption with the Key to Illustrations, pages 444–452.

Two glasses, commemorating the Festival of Britain, with red, white and blue emblems, 1951, largest 3in (7.5cm) high.
£3–6
$4–8 each ⊞ HUX

▶ **A Festival of Britain watermark on paper,** 1951, 7 x 5in (18 x 12.5cm).
£12–15
$15–20 ⊞ REN

Military

A brass box, containing 14 paper discs inscribed with the names and dates of the Duke of Wellington's Continental victories, the reverse inscribed with the legend in 11 lines within a wreath, 1815, discs 1¾in (4.5cm) diam.
£150–175
$220–255 ⊞ TML

A Staffordshire pot lid, with portrait of the Duke of Wellington and date 'Sept 14th 1852', with malachite border and gold line decoration, the base similarly decorated, restored, 1852, 4¾in (12cm) diam.
£300–360
$440–520 ⚶ SAS

A pink lustre jug, commemorating the Crimean War, printed in black and enamelled in red and blue, the reverse with the Sailor's Return, rim chip, 1856, 4¼in (11cm) high.
£80–100
$115–145 ⚶ SAS

A commemorative plate, with a portrait of Lord Baden Powell, 1914–18, 8in (20.5cm) diam.
£40–45
$60–65 ⊞ RCo

◀ **A Copeland tyg,** commemorating the Boer War, decorated in red, pink, yellow and green, c1900, 7in (18cm) high.
£1,000–1,200
£1,500–1,750 ⊞ RdV

A ceramic jug, in the form of President Wilson, wearing a grey jacket and red and white striped trousers, inscribed 'Welcome Uncle Sam', enamel flaking, c1917, 10½in (26.5cm) high.
£220–260
$320–380 ⚶ SAS

A ceramic jug, in the form of Marshall Joffre, wearing a dark blue jacket and red trousers, inscribed 'Ce que J'Offre', c1917, 10¼in (26cm) high.
£350–420
$500–600 ⚶ SAS

A ceramic jug, in the form of Marshall Foch, wearing a light blue jacket and trousers with brown boots, enamel flaking, c1917, 11¾in (30cm) high.
£100–120
$145–175 ⚶ SAS

A ceramic jug, in the form of Sir John French, wearing a green jacket and trousers with brown boots, inscribed 'French pour les Français', c1917, 9¾in (25cm) high.
£250–300
$350–450 ⚶ SAS

A ceramic jug, in the form of Admiral Beatty, wearing a dark blue jacket and trousers, inscribed 'Dread nought', c1917, 9¾in (25cm) high.
£250–300
$350–450 ⚲ SAS

A ceramic jug, in the form of Lord Kitchener, wearing a dark blue jacket and trousers, inscribed 'Bitter for the Kaiser', c1917 10¼in (26cm) high.
£350–420
$500–600 ⚲ SAS

A ceramic jug, depicting the Allies, George V, the Czar of Russia, King Albert of Belgium and President Poincaré, 1914–18, 8in (20.5cm) high.
£65–75
$95–110 ⊞ RCo

A T. G. Green commemorative mug, inscribed 'To Commemorate Peace The Great European War', 1919, 4in (10cm) high.
£70–80
$100–120 ⊞ CAL

> Items in the Commemorative Ware section have been arranged in date order within each sub-section.

Royalty

A pressed boxwood plaque, probably by Westwood, inscribed 'HRH George Prince of Wales Installed Regent of the British Dominions 5 Feb. 1811', 3¼in (8.5cm) diam.
£130–150
$200–220 ⊞ TML

A blue and white ceramic plate, inscribed 'Her Majesty Caroline Queen of England', with impressed border, 1820, 5¾in (14.5cm) diam.
£450–550
$650–800 ⚲ SAS

◀ **A Coronation mug,** printed in black with portraits of King William IV and Queen Adelaide, rim restored, 1831, 3½in (9cm) high.
£250–300
$350–450 ⚲ SAS

▶ **A Swansea pottery plate,** commemorating Queen Victoria's Coronation, printed in purple with named and dated portrait, impressed mark, 1838, 6¼in (16cm) diam.
£280–330
$400–480 ⚲ SAS

A brown stoneware spirit flask, impressed 'William IVths Reform Cordial', c1832, 7½in (19cm) high.
£210–250
$300–360 ⚲ SAS

A copy of *The Court Journal: Gazette of the Fashionable World*, celebrating Queen Victoria's 18th birthday, 1837, 11 x 9in (28 x 23cm).
£15–20
$20–30 ⊞ J&S

A Swansea pottery mug, commemorating Queen Victoria's Coronation, printed in purple with portraits centred by a crown, name and dates inscribed, 1838, 3¼in (8.5cm) high.
£600–700
$870–1,000 ⚲ SAS

A Copeland pottery comport, Albert in Memoriam, for the Art Union of London, printed in black, brown and green with central inscribed portrait and three cartouches depicting his achievements, within a border inscribed with an extract from his 1848 speech, gilt rim, printed marks, 1861, 16¼in (41.5cm) diam.
£1,700–2,000
$2,500–3,000 ⚲ SAS

Two ceramic figures, commemorating the wedding of Prince Edward and Princess Alexandra, French, 1863, 15in (38cm) high.
£1,700–2,000
$2,500–3,000 ⊞ BRT

A pottery mug, commemorating the wedding of George and Mary, 6th July 1893, 3½in (9cm) high.
£150–180
$220–260 ⊞ BRT

LOCATE THE SOURCE
The source of each illustration in Miller's can be found by checking the code letters below each caption with the Key to Illustrations, pages 444–452.

A W. H. Goss pin dish, commemorating Queen Victoria's Diamond Jubilee, with crinkle edge, 1897, 3½in (9cm) diam.
£50–75
$75–115 ⊞ MURR

A Doulton Lambert brown stoneware jug, commemorating Queen Victoria's Diamond Jubilee, moulded with young and old portrait ovals, inscribed in white, unmarked, 1897, 7¼in (18.5cm) high.
£25–30
$35–45 ⚲ SAS

A programme of the Royal Procession to St Paul's Cathedral, and thanksgiving service, celebrating Queen Victoria's Diamond Jubilee, 22nd June 1897, 9 x 6in (23 x 15cm).
£25–30
$35–40 ⊞ J&S

A Queen's Day programme,
1897, 14 x 5in (35.5 x 12.5cm).
£18–20
$20–30 ⊞ J&S

A chocolate tin, commemorating
the Coronation of King Edward VII
and Queen Alexandra, decorated in
pink, green and yellow on a blue
ground, June 1902, 5in (12.5cm) wide.
£20–35
$30–50 ⊞ MURR

A Crown Ducal tyg, designed by
Charlotte Rhead, commemorating
Edward VIII's Coronation, decorated
in blue, orange and gilt, 1937,
7in (18cm) high.
£280–330
$400–480 ⏚ SAS

**An Edward VII and Alexandra Royal
menu,** embossed and appliquéd,
1902, 7 x 4½in (18 x 11.5cm).
£20–25
$30–35 ⊞ J&S

**Two Royal Doulton porcelain
mugs,** commemorating the
Coronation of King Edward VII and
Queen Alexandra, 1902, largest
3¼in (8.5cm) high.
£60–85
$100–120 each ⊞ GWR

A T. G. Green beaker, commemorating King George and Queen
Mary's Silver Jubilee, 1936,
5in (12.5cm) high.
£30–40
$40–60 ⊞ CAL

A silk, commemorating the
Coronation of King Edward VII and
Queen Alexandra, 1902, 14 x 8in
(35.5 x 20.5cm).
£300–350
$450–500 ⊞ AEL

A Rowntree & Co chocolate tin,
commemorating the Coronation
Fête, Crystal Palace, with full
contents, 1911, 5½in (14cm) long.
£100–120
$145–175 ⊞ RUSS

A copy of *The Illustrated London
News,* Record of the Lying-in-State
and Funeral of his Late Majesty
King George V, 1936, 14 x 10in
(35.5 x 25.5cm).
£10–12
$15–18 ⊞ J&S

A terracotta jug, by Longpark of Torquay, commemorating Edward VIII's Coronation, the rim and foot coloured mauve, painted with floral sprays, incised inscription, 1937, 6in (15cm) high.
£150–180
$220–260 ⚒ SAS

An Aynsley plate, No. 6743, commemorating Queen Elizabeth II's Coronation, the central portrait within a gilt floral border, gilt rim, 1953, 8in (20.5cm) diam.
£55–65
$80–100 ⊞ MGC

A T. G. Green Mocha Ware mug, commemorating the marriage of Prince Charles and Lady Diana Spencer, decorated in blue, orange and black on a yellow ground, limited edition, 1981, 4½in (11.5cm) high.
£50–70
$70–100 ⊞ CAL

A mug, commemorating Edward VIII's Coronation, 1937, 5in (12.5cm) high.
£30–35
$45–50 ⊞ AnS

An Oxo tin, commemorating Queen Elizabeth II's Coronation, 1953, 4in (10cm) wide.
£4–5
$5–8 ⊞ ES

A Royal Worcester urn and cover, commemorating the marriage of Prince Charles and Lady Diana Spencer, with twin Prince of Wales feather handles, decorated in colours with coats-of-arms and inscription, banded in puce and gilt, 1981, 8¼in (21cm) high.
£170–200
$250–300 ⚒ SAS

A copy of The Illustrated London News, Special Number, featuring the Death of King George VI, 1952, 14 x 10in (35.5 x 25.5cm).
£10–12
$15–18 ⊞ J&S

A Charbonnel & Walker chocolate box, commemorating the engagement of Prince Charles and Lady Diana Spencer, 1981, 4in (10cm) diam.
£3–5
$5–8 ⊞ RTT

A Royal wedding programme, commemorating the marriage of Prince Andrew and Sarah Ferguson, 1986, 11 x 9in (28 x 23cm).
£10–15
$15–20 ⊞ COB

Corkscrews

A silver pocket corkscrew, with double scroll swivel handle, white metal sheath, restored, re-threaded shaft, silver seal marked 'HC', early 18thC, 3in (7.5cm) long.
£450–500
$650–700 ⚒ P(B)

A silver pocket corkscrew, with banded mother-of-pearl handle, the plain tapering sheath with base marked 'SP' for Samuel Pemberton, and 'ME', late 18th/early 19thC, 3in (7.5cm) long.
£300–350
$450–500 ⚒ P(B)

A folding pocket corkscrew and hoof pick, 19thC, 3in (7.5cm) long.
£30–40
$40–60 ⊞ JOL

A Henshall-style corkscrew, c1850, 5in (12.5cm) long.
£75–85
$115–125 ⊞ CAL
In 1795, Rev Samuel Henshall patented a design for a corkscrew with a button or disc that prevented the screw or 'worm' from entering too far into the cork. The brush at the end of the handle was used for cleaning the neck of the bottle and for removing traces of sealing wax.

A Farrow & Jackson-type brass butterfly wing-nut corkscrew, marked 'Wilson & Co' to both wings, 19thC, 5½in (14cm) long.
£160–190
$225–275 ⚒ P(B)

A four-pillar 'King's Screw' corkscrew, with nickel body and side-winder handle, the turned bone handle with brush and hanging ring, 19thC, 9in (23cm) long.
£650–750
$900–1,100 ⚒ P(B)

A wide rack 'King's Screw' corkscrew, with turned bone handle with brush and side-winder handle, the bronze barrel with tablet marked 'Dowler Patents, Ne Plus Ultra', replacement brush, 19thC, 7in (18cm) long.
£360–400
$500–600 ⚒ P(B)

l. A Wiers concertina corkscrew, by James Heeley & Sons, Birmingham, with traces of gilt/bronze finish, patented 1884, 5¼in (13.5cm) long.
£45–50
$65–75
r. A Wiers double concertina corkscrew, by James Heeley & Sons, Birmingham, marked 'Double No. 4283', patented 1884, 4¼in (11cm) long.
£600–650
$850–950 ⊞ CS
The double concertina corkscrew is very rare, hence its value.

◀ An engine-turned silver roundlet corkscrew, with initials, London 1879, 3in (7.5cm) long.
£440–480
$650–700 ⊞ CAL

A Chambers bar corkscrew, named 'The Merritt', marked 'Chambers Patent', replacement worm, patented 1888, 17in (43cm) long.
£170–200
$250–300 ✦ P(B)

l. A steel corkscrew, named 'The Challenge, c1880, 5½in (14cm) long.
£25–30
$35–45 ⊞ CS
r. A steel corkscrew, named 'The Surprise', registered by George Willets in 1884, 5in (12.5cm) long.
£12–15
$15–20 ⊞ CS

A Heeley's patent double lever corkscrew, named 'The Empire', marked 'J. heeley & Sons patent', lacks nickel-bronze plating, action loose, 1890, 6in (15cm) long.
£900–1,000
$1,300–1,500 ✦ P(B)

A 'Hercules' corkscrew, with a Dorset wine merchant's advertisement, German, 1890, 7in (18cm) long.
£60–70
$90–100 ⊞ CAL

A brass 'Waiter's Friend' folding corkscrew and bottle opener, with Italian advertisement, German, c1890, 4in (10cm) long.
£90–110
$130–160 ⊞ CAL

A Berkeley registered straight pull corkscrew, with nickel-capped rosewood handle and banded rosewood shank with flat button, top of band marked 'Rd 202169', 1896, 5½in (14cm) long.
£160–190
$225–275 ✦ P(B)

▶ **An Art Nouveau bronze straight pull corkscrew,** the crescent-shaped handle decorated with a grapevine, marked 'Miault', French, 6in (15cm) long.
£200–240
$300–350 ✦ P(B)

A continuous action corkscrew, named 'Monopol', German, c1900, 5½in (14cm) long, with original cardboard box.
£20–25
$30–40 ⊞ CS

A Thomason corkscrew, with ringed bronze barrel, tablet marked 'Brookes & Son, Sheffield', replacement wooden handle, late 19thC, 6in (15cm) long.
£140–170
$200–250 ✦ P(B)

A bell cap wire cutter corkscrew, the wooden handle with a beer advertisement, American, c1900, 5½in (14cm) long.
£40–45
$60–65 ⊞ CAL

A William & Son medicine spoon and corkscrew, American, c1900, 3½in (9cm) long.
£85–95
$125–145 ⊞ CAL

A silver combination corkscrew and cigar cutter, by William Frederick Wright, engraved with leaves, hallmarked London 1903, 5½in (14cm) long.
£260–300
$380–440 ⚒ P(B)

► **A steel champagne tap,** with pull ring, early 20thC, 7in (18cm) long.
£90–100
$125–145 ⊞ JOL

A spring cage bell cork-screw, by Gotlieb Geibler Hallenberg, DRGM No. 596751, with wooden handle, German, c1920, 7in (18cm) long.
£20–25
$30–35 ⊞ BSA

An Edwardian brass bar corkscrew, named 'The Swift', with ebony handle, 16in (40.5cm) long.
£120–140
$170–200 ⊞ JOL

A silver penknife with corkscrew, hallmarked Sheffield 1911, 2in (5cm) long.
£50–60
$75–100 ⊞ JOL

A silver-plated corkscrew, modelled as a Highland terrier, 1930, 4in (10cm) long.
£50–60
$70–90 ⊞ BEV

A corkscrew, with wooden handle and wire breaker, c1920, 6in (15cm) long.
£24–28
$35–45 ⊞ CAL

A bronze figure corkscrew and bottle opener, Scandinavian, mid-20thC, 6in (15cm) high.
£75–85
$115–125 ⊞ CAL

► **A brass corkscrew and bottle opener,** modelled as Andy Cap and Flo, 1950s, 5in (12.5cm) high.
£40–50
$60–80 ⊞ JOL

Cosmetics & Hairdressing

In the Victorian period cosmetics were not greatly used. Generally speaking, ladies restricted themselves to soap and water and cold cream, which was supplied in similar ceramic pots to those containing potted meats and anchovy paste. A dusting of powder, a smear of lip salve and possibly a little bit of rouge were all permissible, as long as they were applied with restraint and in private. Not until after WWI did it become commonplace for ladies to flaunt both made-up faces and make-up containers in public.

The 1920s saw the birth of the compact which, with its compartments for powder, rouge, lipstick, and even cigarettes, reflected a new age of female liberation. The 1920s and '30s were a golden age in terms of design, with styles ranging from simple circular powder compacts to multi-sectioned vanity cases in a wide range of patterns.

Production of compacts (and cosmetics) ceased during the war, but with peace came a renewed desire for luxury and femininity and the compact industry flourished. As the '50s progressed, however, new technology not only brought new cosmetics (such as cream as opposed to loose powder) but also plastic disposable packaging. With the development of throwaway containers and changing fashions in the 1960s, the personal powder compact fell from popularity. Today vintage examples are sought after and there are collectors' societies both in the United Kingdom and America.

Two early Victorian wig powderers, the largest 10½in (26.5cm) long.
£15–20
$20–30 each ⊞ VB
Powdering wigs became fashionable in the early 18th century to conceal faded or discoloured hair. The wig was first greased with pomade and then dusted with ground starch or wheat flour, scented with essential oils and sometimes coloured. In 1795, however, the government introduced a powder tax of one guinea a year, and wigs eventually went out of fashion for all but liveried servants.

A Guerlain ointment pot, in white glaze with blue transfer lettering, base chips, French, 1900–20, 2¼in (5.5cm) high.
£40–50
$60–75 ⚲ BBR

A W. S. Park & Son Cold Cream pot, Australian, 1900–20, 2¾in (7cm) diam.
£125–150
$180–220 ⚲ BBR

A manicure set, with yellow Bakelite handles, in a yellow and black Bakelite holder set with rhinestones, original yellow tassel, 1920, 3in (7.5cm) long.
£250–280
$360–400 ⊞ LaF

> **Cross Reference**
> See Pot Lids (page 129)

◄ **A Lip Salve pot,** with flower and leaf transfer-decoration, slight damage, 1920–30, 2in (5cm) diam.
£35–40
$50–60 ⚲ BBR

A hairdresser's brass washbasin, on a turned wooden stand, c1920, 41in (104cm) high.
£350–400
$500–600 ⊞ MLL

A silver miniature brush set, comprising mirror, brush, comb and clothes brush, Birmingham 1922, brush 5in (12.5cm) long, in original box.
£150–175
$220–260 ⊞ GLa

A Ferd Mülhens 4711 talcum powder tin, decorated in turquoise and gold, German, c1925, 5in (12.5cm) high.
£15–20
$20–30 ⊞ HUX

A silver and enamel six-piece dressing table set, for Mappin & Webb, Birmingham 1930, in original box 14¼in (37cm) wide.
£245–285
$350–400 ⊞ GLa

A Bourjois Evening in Paris talcum powder tin, 1950s, 4½in (11.5cm) high.
£13–15
$20–22 ⊞ HUX

A Yardley Old English Lavender talcum powder tin, c1930, 5in (12.5cm) high.
£12–15
$18–22 ⊞ HUX

A Cuticura talcum powder tin, 1930s, 5in (12.5cm) high.
£12–14
$18–20 ⊞ HUX

A bottle of Saturday Night Lotion, 1930s, 5in (12.5cm) high.
£12–14
$18–20 ⊞ HUX

A wash and travel bag, decorated with hotel labels in pink, black and gold, with original contents, unused, American, 1950s, 9in (23cm) wide.
£40–45
$60–65 ⊞ HSt

A Boots Drug Co Solidified Tonair Brilliantine tin, 1950s, 3½in (9cm) wide.
£10–12
$15–18 ⊞ HUX
While the Victorians used bear's grease to slick down and moisturize their hair, the 20thC saw the development of non-animal based products such as brilliantine, made from vegetable and mineral oils.

A Coty Talc for Men tin, c1960, 5in (12.5cm) high.
£7–8
$10–12 ⊞ HUX

Compacts

A celluloid compact, in *faux* marble, the lid surmounted by a deep pink rose, 1920s, 1½in (4cm) high.
£100–125
$150–180 ⊞ LBe

Two powder tins, unbranded, one blue with wet weather silhouettes, one green with children's silhouettes, c1920, 2½in (6.5cm) diam.
£18–20
$27–30 each ⊞ TMa

▶ **A gilt compact,** with original rouge and swans-down puff, original cord and tassel, c1930, 3in (7.5cm) diam.
£130–150
$190–220 ⊞ LaF

A brass dressing table compact, on three legs, 1940s, 2½in (6.5cm) diam.
£175–195
$250–280 ⊞ LBe

A locket compact, with silhouette motif, American, 1940s, 1½in (4cm) diam.
£65–75
$100–110 ⊞ LBe

A brass compact with chain, with a theatrical mask in pink enamel, 1940s, 3in (7.5cm) high.
£150–175
$225–255 ⊞ LBe

An Evans carry-all, in gold, a compartment for cosmetics to one side, the other side for coins, cigarettes and lighter, American, c1950, 3in (7.5cm) square.
£100–120
$145–175 ⊞ LaF

A silver and enamel compact, inscribed 'With love from Maurice, 16.1.44', 1944, 2½in (6.5cm) square.
£120–180
$175–260 ⊞ ASA

A Deva Dassy bracelet compact, in gold coloured metal and jade green plastic, 1940s, 2½in (6.5cm) wide.
£265–300
$380–440 ⊞ LBe

A silver powder compact, made for Fiat's 50th anniversary, decorated with red, blue, green and white cars, 1940s, 3in (7.5cm) diam.
£345–385
$500–570 ⊞ SSM

A basket-shaped compact, by Kigu, decorated in gold basketweave, the lid with jewelled flower motif, two stones missing, c1950, 2in (5cm) diam.
£90–100
$125–145 ⊞ LaF

A Yardley's English Lavender powder compact, decorated with a rustic scene in shades of brown, yellow and blue, 1950s, 3in (7.5cm) diam.
£20–25
$30–40 ⊞ LBe

A Stratton gilt compact, the lid set with diamantes, c1960, 3in (7.5cm) diam.
£35–40
$50–60 ⊞ SBL

Shaving

A Rasoir Star tin, razor and blades, the tin decorated in orange and cream on a green ground, French, c1920, 2½in (6.5cm) wide.
£30–35
$45–50 ⊞ HUX

The Dime safety razor, with original tin, 1920s, 3in (7.5cm) high.
£32–35
$45–50 ⊞ HUX

A tin of Vinolia shaving soap, with brown transfer decoration, 1930–40, 3¼in (8.5cm) diam.
£18–20
$25–30 ↗ BBR

◀ **A moustache cup and saucer,** with green, pink and white floral decoration and gilt rim, probably German, 1930, cup 3in (7.5cm) high.
£120–140
$170–200
⊞ MLa

A tin of Thibaud Gibbs & Co shaving soap, with gold lettering on a black ground, 1925–35, 3½in (9cm) high.
£12–15
$15–20 ⊞ HUX

A Pears Jif shaving stick, in a tin decorated with blue and cream stripes, 1925–35, 3½in (9cm) high.
£12–14
$15–20 ⊞ HUX

▶ **Hai Karate Body Talc and After Shave Lotion,** c1970, largest 6in (15cm) high.
£8–10
$10–15 ⊞ HUX

Crime

Fascination with real-life crime is no new phenomenon. In the 19th century, the Staffordshire potters made a killing themselves from producing models of famous highwaymen and murderers; in our own age interest is reflected in the plethora of crime-related TV programmes, films, books, articles etc.

This section looks at memorabilia associated with celebrated criminals. Whilst many might find the idea of buying Charles Manson's signature ghoulish to say the least, collectors of the genre claim that there is little difference between watching a documentary or reading a biography of a killer and buying an autographed letter by the same person. Whatever one's personal moral convictions, however, there is no denying that these objects have a market value and that, with the passage of time, even the most horrific killer can somehow be transformed into an interesting and collectable historical figure.

The Impartial Protestant Mercury, Friday, March 10th to Tuesday, March 14th 1684, covering the executions of the three murderers of Thomas Thynn, 11 x 7in (28 x 18cm).
£60–80
$95–115 ⊞ HaR

Two Staffordshire figures of Tom King and Dick Turpin, decorated in black, yellow, red and green, c1850, 8in (20.5cm) high.
£450–500
$650–720 ⊞ TUN

Le Petit Journal, the back cover depicting an electrocution scene in America, French, 1899, 18 x 12in (45.5 x 30.5cm).
£35–40
$50–60 ⊞ IQ

Henry Mayhew and John Binny, *The Criminal Prisons of London and Scenes of Prison Life,* first edition, with wood engravings, original blind-stamped cloth gilt, new endpapers, 1862, 8°.
£200–220
$300–330 ⚒ DW

▶ **Ethel Le Neve,** *Her Life Story with the True Account of Their Flight and Her Friendship for Dr. Crippen,* c1910, 7 x 5in (18 x 12.5cm).
£50–60
$70–90 ⊞ IQ

A Staffordshire model of Potash Farm, rented by the murderer James Rush, decorated in blue, yellow red and green on a cream ground, c1860, 9in (23cm) high.
£345–385
$500–550 ⊞ TUN
James Rush was hanged in 1849 for shooting dead Isaac Jermy and his son, and wounding his wife and servant. Rush had mortgaged his home, Potash Farm, to Jermy for £5,000 but then forged a document which gave him complete ownership of the farm.

A Post Office 'Wanted' poster of Bonnie and Clyde, by US Department of Justice, Washington DC, 1934, 8in (20.5cm) square, framed.
£450–500
$650–720 ⊞ IQ

John R. H. Christie, an envelope forged to his sister-in-law, two days after he murdered his wife, 1952, 4 x 7in (10 x 18cm).
£1,000–1,200
$1,500–1,800 ⊞ IQ

Robert Stroud, the Birdman of Alcatraz, an autograph letter with two signatures, written to a family member from Alcatraz, 1954, 10 x 8in (25.5 x 20.5cm).
£600–650
$870–950 ⊞ IQ

Docteur Marcel Petiot, famous French murderer and one of the last people to be guillotined, a prescription on his headed notepaper, 1939, 7 x 5in (18 x 12.5cm).
£550–600
$800–870 ⊞ IQ

Ethel Christie, a hand-written letter from 10 Rillington Place mentioning her concern at the death of a woman and baby living in the top flat, 1949, 9 x 7in (23 x 18cm).
£1,800–2,000
$2,600–2,900 ⊞ IQ

Charles Manson, the 1960s' murderer, a two-sided letter on Manson's personal stationery, 1970s, 10 x 8in (25.5 x 20.5cm).
£250–275
$350–400 ⊞ IQ

Patty Hearst, an FBI 'Wanted' poster, c1974, 15 x 10in (38 x 25.5cm).
£180–200
$250–300 ⊞ IQ

Piers Paul Read, *The Train Robbers, Their Story*, signed by Buster Edwards, Bruce Reynolds, Tommy Wisbey, Roger Cordrey, Jimmy White, Charles Wilson and Jimmy Hussey, paperback, published by Coronet, 1979, 7 x 4½in (18 x 11.5cm).
£225–255
$320–360 ⊞ IQ

Reg & Ron Kray, Our Story, with Fred Dinenage, 1988, 10 x 6in (25.5 x 15cm).
£130–150
$200–220 ⊞ IQ

The Killer Autograph, a *Daily Mail* illustration of John Lennon signing his last autograph to Mark Chapman, 1990, 18 x 12in (45.5 x 30.5cm).
£30–40
$40–60 ⊞ IQ

▶ **A plastic electric chair,** battery-operated, gives a shock, 1995, 7½in (19cm) high.
£40–50
$60–80 ⊞ IQ
This is sold in America as a tourist souvenir item.

Doctor Who

Doctor Who was first aired on 23 November 1963. The BBC had commissioned an educational programme in which the Doctor's travels were meant to provide information on science and history. 'No cheap-jack bug-eyed monsters', warned the head of drama. Thankfully, producer Verity Lambert ignored these instructions. The second story saw the introduction of the Daleks (devised by Terry Nation), and a TV legend was born. Until the final story in December 1989, generations of children hid behind the sofa on Saturdays to watch the adventures of the time-travelling doctor, his glamorous assistants and his monstrous opponents. From William Hartnell in the first episode to Sylvester McCoy in the last, seven different Doctors took control of the Tardis. Tom Baker is often regarded as the definitive Time Lord. 'Exterminate! Exterminate!', became a national catchphrase and the word Dalek entered the Oxford English Dictionary. TV merchandising was still in its infancy in the early sixties. The first item produced was *The Dalek Book* in June 1964, toys and games were introduced by Christmas the following year, and since then, production of Doctor Who merchandise has never stopped. During the 1980s the show gained a large fan base in the USA, and thanks to video and TV repeats the programme continues to attract new viewers and collectors.

A photograph and autograph of William Hartnell, the first Doctor Who, 1960s, 10 x 8in (25.5 x 20.5cm).
£200–225
$300–325 ⊞ WHO

A set of 50 *Doctor Who and the Daleks* **cigarette cards,** mint, 1965.
£110–125
$160–180 ⊞ WHO

▶ *The Dalek Pocketbook and Space-Travellers' Guide,* published by Panther Books, 1965, 7 x 5in (18 x 12.5cm).
£40–50
$60–75 ⊞ WHO

Miller's is a price GUIDE not a price LIST

◀ **An original *Doctor Who* Dalek,** wood, canvas, metal and plastic, the domed top with orange lights, the structure painted in blue, silver and grey, mounted on casters with articulated plunger, ray gun and sensor, the interior signed in green felt-tip pen 'John Pertwee, the Doctor', 1973, 75in (190.5cm) high.
£4,500–5,000
$6,500–7,250 ⚹ RFA
The Daleks were created by Terry Nation in the Doctor's second adventure, *The Red Planet*. They were designed by Raymond Cusick and remain to this day one of the most popular monsters in television history, with the name appearing in the Oxford English Dictionary. This Dalek is one of five built for the 1973 stage show the *Ultimate Adventure*, with John Pertwee as the Doctor.

An original *Doctor Who* Ice Warrior costume, worn by Bernard Bresslaw in the 1965 series *The Ice Warriors,* with green-painted fibreglass body, mounted on a wood and metal armature, on a wheeled rectangular plinth painted to resemble ice, the interior bearing the signature of Debbie Watling, who played the Doctor's assistant Victoria during Patrick Troughton's period as Dr Who, and signed on the shoulder by Nicola Bryant who played the Doctor's assistant, Peri, during Colin Baker's period as the Doctor, c1965, 75in (190.5cm) high.
£800–1,000
$1,150–1,500 ⚹ RFA

A *Doctor Who* flyer and signed photograph of Trevor Martin, who played Doctor Who in the play *The Seven Keys to Doomsday* at the Adelphi Theatre in 1974, mounted and framed, frame 14 x 16in (35.5 x 40.5cm).
£300–350
$450–500 ⊞ WHO

A BBC Talking Dalek, by Palitoy, red and black plastic, 1975, 6in (15cm) high, in original box.
£100–125
$150–180 ⊞ WHO

A *Doctor Who* giant robot, by Denys Fisher, 1976, 10in (25.5cm) high, in original box.
£90–100
$130–150 ⊞ WHO

◄ **Two *Doctor Who* magazines,** with original fold-out posters, 1975 and 1976, 11 x 8in (28 x 20.5cm).
£20–25
$30–35 each ⊞ WHO

Cross Reference
See Colour Review (page 192)

A *Doctor Who* head-piece, warn by Martin Clunes in *Snake Dance*, 1983, 14in (35.5cm) high.
£550–600
$800–1,000 ⊞ WHO

A *Doctor Who* Tetrap gun, a wood and fibreglass prop used in *Time in the Rani*, 1987, 20in (51cm) long.
£550–600
$800–870 ⊞ WHO

A *Doctor Who* Dalek, manufactured by This Planet Earth, black, silver and blue, with detachable claw, with plaque inscribed 'This Planet Earth Limited', 'The Dalek from *Remembrance Of The Dalek*, taken from the original BBC mouldings, Serial No. 15497A', and signed in black marker 'I Clarke', late 1980s, 67in (170cm) high.
£2,000–2,500
$2,900–3,600 ⚒ Bon(C)
This was made from the original mould for a 1988 television Dalek and modified to look like a Dalek from the 1966 film *Dalek Invasion Earth, 2150 AD*.

A page of original artwork for *Doctor Who* magazine, originally in black and white, with later colouring for *Voyager* book, 1985, 12½ x 9½in (32 x 24cm).
£300–350
$450–500 ⊞ BRG

A part set of *Doctor Who* pewter chess pieces, by Danbury Mint, 38 pieces including 7 different kings, part of a larger boxed set, 1992, 3in (7.5cm) high.
£20–25
$30–35 each piece ⊞ WHO

Dolls

A china pincushion doll, c1930s, 4in (10cm) high.
£85–120
$125–175 ⊞ MURR

A cut-out male doll, with 62 pieces of clothes and accessories, contained in 12 folded paper pockets, doll and costumes all hand-coloured aquatint, the sections bound but now lacking boards, early 19thC, doll 8¼in (21cm) high.
£230–260
$330–380 ⊞ F&C

A wax-over-composition doll, with blonde curly wig, weighted brown glass eyes, cloth body with wax over lower arms and legs, wearing original blue silk dress with lace, blue bonnet, stockings and leather marked shoes, slight damage, c1870, 22in (60cm) high.
£350–400
$500–580 ⚲ Bon(C)

A wooden peg-top doll, wearing Welsh traditional dress, 19thC, 7in (18cm) high excluding hat.
£150–180
$220–260 ⚲ G(L)

A Chad Valley Mabel Lucie Attwell Bambino doll, with black curly hair, brown velvet body and wearing orange felt dungarees, c1932, 16in (40.5)cm high.
£350–450
$500–650 ⊞ MEM

A Lenci felt-headed doll, with painted facial features, wearing an embroidered hat and costume, wooden clogs, with paper label 'No. 82-B', 1930s, 9½in (24cm) high.
£150–200
$220–300 ⊞ ES

▶ **A Mattel talking Beany doll,** with yellow hair, wearing a red jumper and turquoise cord dungarees, 1967, 11in (28cm) high.
£40–45
$60–65 ⊞ HarC

Bisque

A bisque-headed needlecase doll, wearing a cream and red dress, 19thC, 7½in (19cm) high.
£60–70
$90–100 ⊞ PSA

▶ **A Madame Barrois bisque-headed fashion doll,** with mohair wig, fixed blue glass eyes, leather body with bisque lower arms, wearing a brown dress and red leather boots, body incorrect, French, c1880, 16in (40.5cm) high.
£700–800
$1,000–1,200 ➶ Bon

A DEP bisque-headed doll, mould 289, with blonde wig, weighted brown glass eyes and pierced ears, on a fully-jointed wooden body, wearing a cream dress and cape with lace bonnet and leather shoes, German, c1905, 15in (38cm) high.
£200–250
$300–360 ➶ Bon

> **Cross Reference**
> See Colour Review
> (page 189)

◀ **An Alt, Beck & Gottschalk bisque shoulder-headed doll,** with long blonde hair, fixed blue glass eyes, cloth body with bisque lower arms and composition lower legs, wearing original white knitted clothes, German, c1900, 12in (30.5cm) high.
£200–250
$300–360
➶ Bon(C)

A Kestner 192 bisque-headed doll, with mohair wig, weighted blue glass eyes and pierced ears, on a five-piece composition body with fixed wrists and painted socks and shoes, wearing a white dress, German, c1905, 10½in (26.5cm) high.
£700–800
$1,000–1,200 ➶ Bon

An Armand Marseille bisque-headed doll, with brown wig and blue sleep eyes, on a five-piece baby body, wearing contemporary white clothes, some damage, French, early 20thC, 21in (53.5cm) high.
£140–180
$200–260 ➶ G(L)

◀ **An S.F.B.J. bisque-headed doll,** with brown wig and eyes, on a jointed composition body, wearing original brown velvet coat and hat and cream dress, socks and shoes, French, early 20thC, 21in (53.5cm) high.
£400–450
$580–650 ⊞ BaN

A Heubach Koppelsdorf bisque-headed doll, mould 321, with short blonde wig and weighted blue eyes, on a composition baby body, wearing a white dress and pink knitted jacket and bonnet, German, c1910, 15in (38cm) high.
£130–150
$190–220 ↗ Bon(C)

A Shoenau & Hoffmeister bisque-headed doll, with long brown wig and blue eyes, on a jointed composition body, wearing a cream dress and cap, together with a fabric covered trunk containing a collection of clothes for a small doll, impressed '4½' and '1901', German, 22¾in (58cm) high.
$300–350
$450–500 ↗ DN

▶ **A DEP bisque-headed doll,** with brown mohair wig, weighted blue glass eyes and pierced ears, on a fully-jointed composition body, wearing original pink frilled organza dress and matching bonnet, German, c1910, 25in (63.5cm) high.
£450–550
$650–800 ↗ Bon(C)

A Simon & Halbig bisque-headed Oriental doll, mould 1129, with black mohair wig, slanted and weighted brown glass eyes and pierced ears, on a fully jointed composition body, wearing a pink jacket and trousers, German, c1910, 13½in (34.5cm) high.
£350–450
$500–650 ↗ Bon(C)

Items in the Dolls section have been arranged in date order within each sub-section.

▶ **An S.F.B.J. bisque-headed doll,** with brown wig and blue sleep eyes, on a jointed composition body, wearing original pink silk and lace-trimmed dress, the head impressed '301', French, early 20thC, 18¼in (46cm) high, in original cardboard box marked 'Mon Amour de Poupée'.
£230–270
$330–400 ↗ DN

A Rose O'Neill bisque Kewpie doll, with moulded top-knot and painted eyes, jointed at shoulders, with star-fish hands, incised 'Germany', c1910, 7in (18cm) high.
£250–300
$360–440 ↗ Bon

An Armand Marseille bisque-headed doll, mould 290, with brown wig and blue sleep eyes, on a jointed composition body, wearing a blue checked shirt, French, early 20thC, 24in (61cm) high.
£150–180
$220–260 ↗ G(L)

Plastic

This section, devoted to plastic dolls, includes a selection of Barbie products. Created by Mattel in 1959, Barbie has been through innumerable permutations and has acquired legions of friends and an extensive family. The examples shown below all come from what is known as the Vintage Era (1959–72). Collectors often subdivide this into two major categories: the Ponytail Era (1959–66) and the Mod Era (1967–72). In addition to Barbie herself, characters shown include boyfriend Ken; friends Jamie, Stacey and Midge; Midge's boyfriend Alan, and Barbie's cousin Francie. Mattel created a whole range of celebrity

friends for their best-selling doll, including Truly Scrumptious, from the 1968 film *Chitty Chitty Bang Bang*.

Mattel was also among the first companies to produce Afro-American dolls in the 1960s, such as Brad (friend of Alan) and Julia. Julia was based on a popular US TV character played by Diahann Carroll, and the actress herself voiced the talking doll.

As these examples show, prices for Vintage Barbie material (both dolls and outfits) can be extremely high, but whilst age and rarity are always important, values are also critically affected by condition.

A British National Doll Co hard plastic toddler doll, wearing original white and blue dress and white shoes, 1950, 13in (33cm) high.
£30–40
$45–60 ⊞ A&J

A Polyflex plastic doll, with a brown wig, wearing a blue and white spotted dress, French, c1950, 16in (40.5cm) high.
£60–70
$70–100 ⊞ T&D

> **Miller's is a price GUIDE not a price LIST**

▶ **A Rosebud plastic doll,** with blonde wig and blue eyes, wearing a pink knitted jumper, red trousers and white plastic shoes, c1960, 11in (29cm) high.
£40–45
$60–65 ⊞ PAR

▶ **A Miss Rosebud plastic doll,** with blonde wig, wearing original peach knitted dress, blue cape and shoes, c1960, 7½in (19cm) high.
£35–40
$50–60 ⊞ PAR

A Pedigree plastic black doll, wearing a white dress, red jacket and white plastic shoes, c1960, 20in (51cm) high.
£70–80
$100–115 ⊞ PAR

A plastic bride doll, with plastic moulded hair, wearing a white net-covered wedding gown trimmed with rosebuds, and white net veil on a band of rosebuds, 1960s, 8½in (21.5cm) high.
£10–15
$15–20 ⊞ GRa

A Palitoy plastic doll, wearing a short yellow dress and white plastic shoes, c1960, in original box, 11 x 7in (28 x 18cm).
£140–165
$200–240 ⊞ T&D

A Mattel Freckles Midge doll, with auburn wig and blue eyes, wearing the 'Country Club Dance' outfit of white dress with gold-striped bodice and trim, long white gloves and white shoes, American, c1962, 11½in (29cm) high.
£450–500
$650–720 ⊞ T&D

A Mattel Ken doll, wearing the 'Play Ball' outfit of red cap, grey shirt and trousers with red stripe trim, red socks, baseball glove and carrying a bat, American, c1962, 12in (30.5cm) high.
£135–165
$200–240 ⊞ T&D

A Mattel Alan doll, wearing the 'Dream Boat' outfit of hat with red band, grey patterned shirt, olive green jacket and brown trousers, American, c1962, 12in (30.5cm) high.
£130–150
$200–225 ⊞ T&D

A Mattel Midge doll, straight-leg version, wearing a lime green crop-top and red shorts, American, c1963, 12in (30.5cm) high, in original box.
£240–270
$350–400 ⊞ T&D
This doll has never been removed from its original box.

A Mattel Barbie doll, with blonde ponytail and white lips, wearing a red swimsuit, American, c1965, 12in (30.5cm) high, in original box.
£540–600
$800–870 ⊞ T&D

◄ A Mattel 'long-haired American girl' Barbie doll, wearing the 'Saturday Matinée' outfit of fur-trimmed tweed suit and matching hat, brown gloves and peep-toe shoes, American, c1966, 11½in (29cm) high.
£1,200–1,400
$1,750–2,000 ⊞ T&D
This model of 'American girl' doll is valued at £700–800 ($1,000–1,150) without the outfit. The outfit, available separately, is valued at £500–600 ($720–870).

◄ A Mattel Francie doll, straight-leg version, wearing a red on white polka dot crop-top and matching reverse polka dot shorts, American, c1966, 12in (30.5cm) high, in original box.
£350–400
$500–580 ⊞ T&D

A Mattel Stacey 'Twist and Turn' doll, wearing a multicoloured print top, American, c1967, 12in (30.5cm) high, in original box.
£600–700
$870–1,000 ⊞ T&D
This doll has never been removed from its original box.

A Mattel Truly Scrumptious doll, from the film *Chitty Chitty Bang Bang*, in a pink dress with lace overlay, American, c1968, in original box 15 x 6in (38 x 15cm).
£450–500
$650–720 ⊞ T&D
This doll has never been removed from its original box.

A Mattel Talking Stacey doll, in a pink, green and blue beach outfit, American, c1968, in original box, 13 x 4½in (33 x 11.5cm).
£380–425
$560–620 ⊞ T&D
This doll has never been removed from its original box.

A Mattel Walking Jamie doll, wearing 'Pepsi' outfit of red and white shirt with matching headband, white trousers and eye-shield, American, c1968, 11½in (29cm) high.
£250–285
$360–420 ⊞ T&D

Dolls' Houses & Dolls' House Furniture

Ten pewter dolls' house plates, with moulded pewter food including fish, fruit, bread and a blancmange, German, late 18thC, largest 2½in (6.5cm) diam.
£380–430
$560–620 ↗ Bon(C)

A tinplate dolls' house mirror-on-stand, painted in wood-grain effect, the wing mirror on scroll supports, probably by Evans & Cartwright, 1810–50, 4½in (11.4cm) high.
£280–330
$420–480 ↗ Bon

A late Victorian dolls' house, designed as a pair of semi-detached houses, with double opening front, cream exterior walls with green details, four rooms, decorated and with carpet and curtains, some restoration required, 24 x 15in (61 x 38cm).
£320–360
$470–540 ↗ WAL

▶ **A dolls' house porcelain coffee set and tray,** decorated with green, yellow and blue roses, French, c1890, tray 3in (7.5cm) wide, together with a Coalport trinket and glass ware.
£100–120
$145–175 ↗ Bon

A dolls' house pram, with cream and gold scroll decoration, with yellow silk seats and silk hood, 1890s, 3¼in (8.5cm) long.
£550–650
$800–950 ✗ Bon

► **A Moritz Gottschalk dolls' house,** with lithographed brick paper exterior and green tiled roof, with original wallpaper and flooring, containing fittings and furniture, German, c1900, 30in (76cm) wide.
£1,200–1,500
$1,750–2,200
✗ Bon(C)

A dolls' house fire screen, with lithophane picture of a young girl with a dog, in an ornate gilt frame with candle holder to back, late 19thC, 4¾in (12cm) high.
£750–850
$1,100–1,250 ✗ Bon

A dolls' school house, 'Boston House, Miss Pinkerton's Academy', with Victorian-style double opening front giving access to classroom, library, dormitory, dining room, gymnasium, cloakroom and bathroom, with all furniture and fittings, 1933, the front 25 x 37in (63.5 x 94cm).
£230–260
$330–380 ✗ WAL
This was made by the girls of Eastbourne High School.

A pair of Simon & Halbig dolls' house dolls, each with weighted blue glass eyes and five-piece composition bodies, the girl with long blonde mohair wig, wearing a cream cotton dress with lace collar, the boy with curly brown wig, wearing red knitted shorts, jumper and bobble hat, German, c1910, 4¾in (12cm) high.
£450–500
$650–720 ✗ Bon

A painted wooden dolls' house, with cream exterior, glazed windows with etched top panels, four rooms and wooden staircase, side opening giving access to rear bathroom, with fittings, furniture and furnishings, 1920s, 39½in (100.5cm) wide.
£900–1,200
$1,300–1,750 ✗ Bon(C)

A Silber Fleming dolls' house, with brick-effect papered front, orange sides and green front door, four rooms, each with papered walls, fireplace, rugs and curtains, some refurbishment needed, c1890, 21in (53.5cm) wide.
£260–300
$380–440 WAL

► **A John Mitchell Victorian-style doll's house,** painted in pale green with white woodwork, with three rooms, complete with furniture and furnishings, 1970s, 12in (30.5cm) wide.
£170–220
$250–320 ✗ WAL

A Duncan Mirylees Victorian-style dolls' shop, 'The Antique Shop', made from a Camp Coffee packing case with brick-effect paper over, square bay shop window with display, two rooms and staircase, c1978, 15in (38cm) wide.
£160–200
$230–300 ✗ WAL

Miller's is a price GUIDE not a price LIST

A woodentop peg doll, with jointed legs, in floral print long dress, German, doll 19thC, dress 20thC, 11¾in (30cm) high.
£60–70
$90–100 ⚒ G(L)

A Simon & Halbig bisque-headed doll, with weighted blue glass eyes, open mouth and upper teeth, long mohair wig, on a fully-jointed composition body, wearing striped dress, underclothes and leather boots, c1910, 25½in (65cm) high.
£900–1,100
$1,300–1,600 ⚒ Bon

A Jumeau bisque-headed doll, for S.F.B.J., with sleep eyes and long wig, on a composition and wooden jointed body, French, 1915–20, 29in (74cm) high.
£1,100–1,250
$1,600–1,800 ⊞ DOL

A Limoges bisque-headed doll, with fixed blue eyes, open mouth, teeth and wig, on a jointed composition body, wearing bonnet, dress and shoes, French, 1920s, 19in (48cm) high.
£90–110
$130–160 ⚒ G(L)

A Tri-ang Ultra Modern Series Art Deco-style detached dolls' house, with integral garage, glass windows, balconies and removeable sun room, with three fitted fireplaces, decorated rooms and curtains, on simulated crazy paving base, No. 53, 1930s, 40in (101.5cm) wide.
£650–750
$950–1,100 ⚒ WAL

A Bisque button-hole Kewpie doll, in fisherman's creel, slight damage, 1920s, 2in (5cm) high.
£55–65
$80–90 ⊞ DOL

A Tudor-style suburban detached dolls' house, with fixed front bay window and opening front door, with four rooms, complete with electric lighting and period furniture and fittings, with access by removeable rear panel, late 1920s, 16½in (42cm) high.
£275–325
$400–470 ⚒ WAL

Three sailor dolls, with hatbands for Queen Mary, Mauretania and Viking III, 1960s, 9in (23cm) high.
£15–45
$20–65 each ⊞ COB

▶ **A B. N. D. plastic doll,** original, c1960, 9in (23cm) high.
£40–45
$60–100 ⊞ PAR

◀ **A plastic doll,** with sleep eyes, wearing a knitted dress with a doll in the pocket, 1950s, 12in (30.5cm) high.
£20–25
$30–35 ⊞ GRa

A Victorian scrap book, containing a number of Louis Wain cats, 17 x 13in (43 x 33cm).
£270–300
$390–440   ⊞ MRW

A block of six Victorian chromo-lithograph cut-out scraps of angels, c1880, 10in (25.5cm) wide.
£35–40
$50–60   ⊞ SDP

A paper fan, with eye slits, advertising cream products, 1920s, 8½in (21.5cm) wide.
£120–150
$175–220   ⊞ LBe

A pack of calling cards, bound with original red ribbon, 1930s, 2 x 3½in (5 x 9cm).
£30–35
$45–50   ⊞ LBe

A set of 50 Wills' Association Footballers cigarette cards, including Stanley Matthews, 1935.
£60–65
$90–95   ⊞ LCC

A theatre programme, for the Hippodrome theatre, Coventry, 1948, 9 x 5in (23 x 13cm).
£1–2
$2–3   ⊞ MRW

A set of 25 Taddy's Royalty Series No. 25 cigarette cards, including Princess Victoria, the Duke of Cambridge and Princess Louise, Duchess of Fife, 1904.
£400–430
$580–625   ⊞ LCC

A set of 90 Star Trek Topps Bubblegum cards, American, 1997.
£9–10
$13–15   ⊞ LCC

A set of 50 Wills' Speed Series cigarette cards, including the Bristolian Express, Coronation Express, Coronation Scot Express and Princess Elizabeth, 1938.
£15–18
$20–27   ⊞ LCC

A set of 50 A&BC Gum *Outer Limits* cards, based on the TV series, 1966.
£140–160
$200–230   ⊞ MUR

A vinyl stool, on wooden legs, late 1950s, 17in (43cm) high.
£34–45
$50–65 ⊞ ZOOM

A Piero Fornasetti newspaper rack, 1950s, 16in (40.5cm) wide.
£250–280
$360–410 ⊞ ZOOM

A Verner Panton cone chair, in covered fabric, 1958.
£650–700
$950–1,000 ⊞ ZOOM

A Formica cocktail table, 1950s, 24in (61cm) high.
£55–65
$80–95 ⊞ FLD

A Jens Quistgaard enamel Koben ware water pitcher, in Dansk design, late 1950s, 10in (25.5cm) high.
£70–80
$100–115 ⊞ ORI

A Herbert Krenchel enamel salad bowl, in Krenit design, 1955, 10in (25.5cm) diam.
£60–70
$90–100 ⊞ ORI

A glazed ceramic vase, hand-decorated, West German, c1950, 28¼in (72cm) high.
£20–25
$30–35 ⊞ V&S

A ceramic dish, Austrian, mid-1950s, 10in (25.5cm) diam.
£15–20
$20–30 ⊞ HSt

An ornamental vase, modelled as a fish, 1950s, 4in (10cm) high.
£20–25
$30–35 ⊞ LBe

A pair of Vari-vue novelty plastic sunglasses, featuring a pin-up girl, late 1950s.
£38–42
$55–65 ⊞ SpM

▶ **Four** *Practical Wireless* **magazines,** 1950s.
£0.50–1
$1–1.50 ⊞ GM

A Shirley Temple glass cereal bowl, 1940s, 6½in (16.5cm) diam.
£18–20
$27–30 ⊞ HUX

A James Bond magazine, c1966, 13in (33cm) high.
£5–8
$8–10 ⊞ CTO

A knife used by Leonardo DiCaprio, in the film *The Beach*, mounted with descriptive plaque, colour still of DiCaprio from the film and Fox Archives certificate of authenticity, framed and glazed, with holster attached to back of frame, 2000, frame 20in (51cm) square.
£600–700
$875–1,000 ⚲ FO

A Clark Gable Lyon's toffee tin, 1940s, 6½in (16.5cm) high.
£18–20
$27–30 ⊞ HUX

A ceramic model of the Pink Panther, UAC marked on base, 1980s, 8in (20.5cm) high.
£60–70
$90–100 ⊞ TAC

Three fibreglass Jack O'Lanterns, used as dressing on the set of *Sleepy Hollow*, 1999, largest 12in (30.5cm) high.
£300–350
$440–500 ⚲ FO

▶ **A Spanish poster for Dr Who and the Daleks,** 1986, 40 x 32in (101.5 x 81.5cm).
£180–200
$260–290 ⊞ WHO

An original studio model of Stingray, in wood and plastic, made by Reg Hill, Associate Producer of the TV series, the prototype for other studio models, 1963, 22in (56cm) long.
£9,000–10,000
$13,000–14,500 ⚲ FO
Ex-Philip Rae collection.

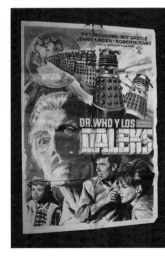

A *Nightmare Before Christmas* plastic figure, of Mayor Loose, 1993, 7in (18cm) high.
£45–55
$65–80 ⊞ TB

A mahogany solitaire board, with coloured spiral marbles, 19thC, 14in (35.5cm) diam.
£800–900
$1,150–1,300 ♠ G(B)

A hand-made glass marble, with basket-weave incisions, c1880, 1in (2.5cm) diam.
£25–30
$35–45 ⊞ MRW

A pack of Royal National Patriotic playing cards, c1900, 3½ x 2in (9 x 5cm).
£120–150
$175–220 ⊞ MURR

A ball bearing puzzle, of a mounted soldier, German, c1910, 2½in (5cm) diam.
£10–12
$15–18 ⊞ HUX

▶ A Humpty Dumpty game, by Parker Brothers, USA, 1920s, in original box, 7 x 13in (18 x 33cm).
£50–55
$75–80 ⊞ J&J

A Radio Questionaire game, by the Durable Toy and Novelty Corp, USA, 1928, in original box, 9in (23cm) square.
£18–20
$27–30 ⊞ J&J

A Chad Valley Stumpy Joe quoits game, complete, c1930, in original box, 8in (20.5cm) high.
£18–20
$27–30 ⊞ J&J

A Superman Speed Game, by Milton Bradley Co, USA, complete with four painted wooden pieces, wooden die and oval board, early 1940s, in original box, 16 x 9in (60.5 x 23cm).
£700–750
$1,000–1,100 ♠ CBP

An Enid Blyton stencil and painting set, c1950, in original box, 13in (33cm) wide.
£18–22
$27–32 ⊞ J&J

An 'Art Studies' pack of playing cards, plastic coated, featuring pin-up girls, American, 1950s, in original box, 3½in (9cm) high.
£32–36
$48–55 ⊞ SpM

A War of the Daleks board game, by Denys Fisher, 1975, in original box, 18in (45.5cm) wide.
£100–125
$145–180 ⊞ WHO

A Victorian cranberry glass bell, c1860, 9in (23cm) high.
£135–150
$195–220 ⊞ AOY

A facet-cut cranberry/ ruby glass decanter, c1880, 11in (28cm) high.
£200–230
$300–330 ⊞ GRI

A late Victorian opaline glass biscuit barrel, with plated mounts, swing handle and applied butterfly and floral beadwork, 10in (25.5cm) high.
£70–80
$100–115 ⚒ DD

A Victorian cranberry glass baluster jug, with frilled rim, clear handle and jewelled decorations, 10½in (26.5cm) high.
£100–120
$145–175 ⚒ WBH

An Art Nouveau glass vase, 7in (18cm) high.
£170–190
$250–275 ⊞ BEV

A gilt-metal inkstand, with cranberry glass trays and clear bottles, c1880, 8in (20.5cm) wide.
£150–165
$220–240 ⊞ GRI

A pair of Jack-in-the-Pulpit cranberry glass vases, c1900, 13in (33cm) high.
£380–425
$570–625 ⊞ AOY

A Carnival glass bowl, by Imperial Glass Co, with open rose pattern inside and panelled rose outside, American, c1910, 9in (23cm) diam.
£175–195
$250–280 ⊞ CAL

◀ **A Fenton Carnival glass vase,** in diamond and rib pattern, 1910, 10in (25.5cm) high.
£110–130
$160–190 ⊞ CAL

An amethyst glass specimen vase, with gilt and enamel decoration, c1910, 6in (15cm) high.
£55–60
$80–90 ⊞ GRI

An Art Deco-style jug, moulded, 1907–40, 7in (18cm) high.
£18–22
$27–33 ⊞ TWAC

◄ **A cut-glass scent bottle,** with amethyst colouring, c1920, 5in (12.5cm) high.
£125–140
$180–200 ⊞ GRI

A Bohemian cut-glass goblet, overlaid with painted flowers and enamel, c1920, 5in (12.5cm) high.
£45–55
$65–80 ⊞ BRU

A George Davidson cloud glass vase, 1922–39, 9in (23cm) high.
£70–80
$100–115 ⊞ BEV

► **A George Davidson cloud glass vase,** c1922–39, 7in (18cm) high.
£80–90
$115–130 ⊞ BEV

◄ **A George Davidson glass candlestick,** in rare orange colour, 1922–39, 2in (5cm) high.
£60–70
$90–100 ⊞ BEV

A George Davidson glass bowl, with down-turned rim and matching flower block, c1930, 12in (30.5cm) diam.
£130–150
$190–220 ⊞ BEV

A Venetian glass millefiori figure, 1930s, 9in (23cm) high.
£190–220
$275–320 ⊞ BRU

► **A Monart jade glass bowl,** the rim flecked with mica, 1924–61, 6in (15cm) diam.
£45–55
$65–80 ⊞ TCG

Ephemera

The last will and testament of
James Green, with the seal of
Edward Cook, Chancellor of the
County of Gloucester, embossed
with the Royal coat-of-arms,
dated 9 September 1811,
9½ x 11½in (23 x 29cm).
£30–35
$45–50 ⊞ **ES**

A Victorian cut-out chromolithograph scrap of a Punch and Judy
show, c1880, 7 x 5in (18 x 13cm).
£50–55
$75–80 ⊞ **SDP**

A Victorian cut-out chromolithograph scrap, 'Pigs at School',
c1880, 7 x 11in (18 x 28cm).
£60–65
$90–95 ⊞ **SDP**
Compiling scrap albums was a
popular Victorian hobby. In
addition to pictures taken from
newspapers, magazines and
other miscellaneous ephemera,
manufacturers also produced
sheets of glossy, brightly-coloured
chromolithographic scraps
specifically designed to be cut out
and stuck into books and greeting
cards, and on to screens etc. Major
printers included Louis Prang in
the USA, Raphael Tuck in the UK,
and Zoecke & Mittmeyer and
Mamelok & Soehne in Germany.

A strip of Victorian cut-out chromolithograph scraps,
'The Three Little Kittens', c1880, 5 x 18in (12.5 x 45.5cm).
£50–55
$75–80 ⊞ **SDP**

A copy of the Freedom of the City of London,
awarded by the Goldsmiths' Company, 1919, in original
red wallet, 3 x 4in (7.5 x 10cm).
£20–25
$30–35 ⊞ **WAB**

A Barclays Bank cheque book, in original plastic
cover, 1960s, 8½in (21.5cm) wide.
£4–6
$6–9 ⊞ **Mo**

Erotica

▶ **A WWII pin-up girl tin silhouette,** on a wooden stand, c1940, 6in (15cm) high.
£30–35
$45–50 ⊞ SpM

A Time for Bed Vaudoscope drop-card viewer, with one-penny slot, 1904, 69in (175.5cm) high.
£800–850
$1,150–1,250
⊞ JUN

A Tabarin Theatre programme, illustrating show girls, French, 1939, 9in (23cm) square.
£15–20
$20–30 ⊞J&S

Miller's is a price GUIDE not a price LIST

An Esquire calendar, with decorated envelope, 1953, 11 x 9in (29 x 23cm).
£135–150
$200–220 ⊞ SpM

A pin-up poster, after Jean d'Ylen, c1950, 18¾ x 12¼in (47.5 x 31cm).
£110–130
$160–190 ➴ VSP

An erotic glass tumbler, the exterior painted with a bride, the reverse undressed, 1950s, 5½in (14cm) high.
£10–15
$15–20 ⊞ SpM

***Men Only* magazine,** featuring a Marilyn Monroe pin-up inside, 1956, 7 x 5in (18 x 12.5cm).
£8–12
$12–18 ⊞ RTT

Four erotic match books, late 1940s, 2½in (6.5cm) high.
£8–10
$12–15 ⊞ SpM

An erotic handkerchief, featuring a dog looking up a woman's skirt, 1940–50, 11in (28cm) square.
£85–95
$125–140 ⊞ LBe

An International Exotic Glamourwear catalogue, 1970s, 11 x 8in (28 x 18cm).
£15–20
$20–30 ⊞ PLB

Furniture

A Formica-topped table, with metal legs, decorated with fruit, 1950s, 36in (91.5cm) wide.
£65–75
$100–110 ⊞ HSt

A George Nelson oval soft-edge dining table, by Herman Miller, No. 5259, the putty-coloured plastic top with white rubber trim to edge, on satin chrome crossed legs, American, 1950s, 78in (198cm) wide.
£350–400
$500–600 ⋀ TREA

A Kandya plywood stacking chair, designed by Carl Jacobs, 1950.
£160–180
$230–260 ⊞ ORI

A kidney-bean table, on three legs, 1950s, 16in (40.5cm) wide.
£14–16
$20–25 ⊞ FLD

A conical wicker chair, on metal supports, 1950s.
£35–40
$50–60 ⊞ FLD

A wire chair, by Harry Bertoia, 1950s.
£150–200
$220–290 ⊞ ZOOM

▶ **A child's vinyl-covered chair,** with blue seat, 1950s.
£50–60
$75–90 ⊞ FLD

◀ **A white moulded chair,** by Eero Saarinen, 1957.
£500–600
$720–870 ⊞ ZOOM

A Fritz Hansen Ant three-legged chair, designed by Arne Jacobsen, model No. 3100, 1952.
£200–220
$300–330 ⊞ ORI

▶ **A Formica-topped cocktail table,** the black surface with party design, 1950s, 19in (48.5cm) high.
£20–25
$30–35 ⊞ FLD

A diner chrome bar stool, with vinyl seat, 1950s, 24in (61cm) high.
£60–70
$90–100 ⊞ TRA

Pottery & Porcelain

A pair of Bristol Longline storage jars, with yellow lids, decorated with cutlery, c1950, 6in (15cm) high.
£34–38
$50–55 each ⊞ B&R

A black fish ashtray, with green fins and tail, orange mouth and coloured spots, foreign, 1950s, 3in (7.5cm) high.
£20–25
$30–35 ⊞ LBe

▶ **A Beswick vase,** the shape designed by Arthur Hallam, the zebra stripe pattern created by Jim Hayward, 1950s, 8in (20.5cm) high.
£45–50
$65–75 ⊞ BEV

A Paragon Festival of Britain bone china mug, decorated in white and gilt on a turquoise ground, 1951, 4in (10cm) high.
£250–300
$360–440 ⊞ BRT

A Crown Clarence Autumn 15-piece coffee set, made for the C. W. S. and the Pioneer Society, 1950s, coffee pot 9¾in (25cm) high.
£100–120
$150–175 ⊞ ES

A pottery string holder, modelled as a cat's head, black with blue bow, 1950s, 6in (15cm) wide.
£40–45
$60–65 ⊞ LBe

◀ **A glazed ashtray,** hand-painted in black, white and turquoise on a red ground, Italian, 1950s, 5in (12.5cm) wide.
£15–18
$20–27 ⊞ V&S

A pair of black and white textured vases, with flower decoration in red, yellow and blue, Italian, 1950s, 7in (18cm) high.
£30–35
$45–50 ⊞ V&S

A black vase, hand painted with white stripes and red, orange, blue and green squares, Austrian, 1950s, 4in (10cm) high.
£18–20
$27–30 ⊞ HSt

A Rye Pottery vinegar bottle, in white, with black stripes, 1955, 4¼in (11cm) high.
£30–40
$45–60 ⊞ DSG

Film & TV

A Shirley Temple glass water jug, 1940s, 4½in (11.4cm) high.
£18–20
$27–30 ⊞ HUX

A grey woollen cardigan worn by Marlon Brando in *The Godfather,* with original label for Western Costume Co, Hollywood, with 'Marlon Brando # 1' typed in, and two colour pictures from the film showing Brando wearing a similar cardigan, slight damage, 1972.
£1,800–2,000
$2,600–3,000 ✗ FO

◀ **A** *Blade Runner* **crew jacket,** in black bomber style, with Blade Runner embroidered on the back in red and white, 1982.
£750–850
$1,100–1,250 ✗ FO

A spacecraft/spacesuit joystick from *2001: A Space Odyssey,* Bakelite and metal, 1959, 10in (25.5cm) long.
£350–400
$500–600 ✗ FO
This unused joystick was one of a batch manufactured in 1959 and supplied for the 1968 film *2001: A Space Odyssey* and for Gerry Anderson's *UFO,* for spacecraft interiors and spacesuit chest-packs.

A fibreglass Kryat dragon-bone from *Star Wars,* part of the Kryat dragon skeleton, mounted with photograph and plaque, framed and glazed, 1977, 13 x 18in (33 x 45.5cm).
£800–1,000
$1,150–1,500 ✗ FO
This item was accompanied by a description by the original owner, detailing how he came across the 'bones' in the Tunisian desert.

***ABC Film Review* magazine,** with Sean Connery on the cover, July 1965, 9 x 7in (23 x 18cm).
£4–6
$6–9 ⊞ CTO

**A Shirley... **

A *Some Like it Hot* **metal thermometer,** showing Marilyn Monroe in a classic pose from the film, 1960s, 12½in (32cm) high, in original packaging.
£90–100
$130–145 ✗ VS

◀ **Three promotional items for** *Clockwork Orange,* a press booklet, a set of front-of-house stills, and an advertisement folder, c1971, booklet 11 x 9in (28 x 23cm).
£225–250
$325–360 ⊞ CTO

Cross Reference

See Autographs (page 34)
See Doctor Who (page 176)
See Toys (page 403)

A Nostromo Perspex and plastic airlock from *Alien,* made by Bill Pearson, with sliding outer door and fully detailed interior, and original miniature body used in filming the ejection sequence, 1979, 12in (30.5cm) wide.
£1,000–1,200
$1,500–1,750 ✗ FO

A moulded latex prototype *E.T.* hand, with internal metal rods for manipulation, with lighting apparatus including titanium bulb and power pack for forefinger, and four original four-fold publicity posters for the Spielberg film.
£650–750
$950–1,100 FO

Items in the Film & TV section have been arranged in date order within each sub-section.

◀ **A model of Roger Moore as James Bond in *A View to a Kill*,** with fibreglass head and body, latex hands, and etched aluminium Rolex watch, used in filming the Golden Gate Bridge sequence, in a display case with plaque and invitation to film premiere, and an additional film still of the model in use, 1985, case 36in (91.5cm) high.
£8,000–10,000
$11,500–14,500 FO

Six Prop casino chips from *Licence to Kill*, each marked 'Casino de Isthmus City', mounted with a still featuring Timothy Dalton as Bond at the casino, framed and glazed, 1989, 10 x 12in (25.5 x 20.5cm).
£240–280
$350–410 FO

A blue cotton polo shirt worn by Tom Cruise in *Rain Man*, by Carroll & Co, Beverly Hills, with original label reading 'Tom Cruise "Charlie" Sc #64 thru 78 No Coat same pants from Sc #61', with colour still of Tom Cruise and Dustin Hoffman, signed by both, framed and glazed, 1988, photo 16 x 13in (40.5 x 33cm).
£1,000–1,200
$1,500–1,750 FO

A model gateway to Hallowe'en Town from *The Nightmare before Christmas*, foam and wood, with working light, 1993, 31in (78.5cm) high.
£1,500–2,000
$2,200–3,200 FO

A star pendant worn by Christina Ricci in *Sleepy Hollow*, mounted with a still of Ricci wearing the pendant, together with a descriptive plaque, framed and glazed, 1999, 27½ x 18in (80 x 45.5cm).
£450–500
$650–720 FO

A 007 *Tomorrow Never Dies* calculator, 1997, 4in (10cm) wide.
£30–35
$45–50 GRa

◀ **A Thai Police form from *The Beach*,** signed on screen by Leonardo DiCaprio as Richard Fischer, mounted with certificate of authenticity from Fox Archives, together with descriptive plaque, framed and glazed, 2000, 16 x 19½in (40.5 x 49.5cm).
£420–470
$600–680 FO

Games

Three miniature bone dice, 1850–70, 4mm square.
£10–15
$15–20 ⊞ MRW

◀ **A handmade glass marble,** with basket-weave incisions, c1880, 1in (2.5cm) diam.
£25–30
$35–45 ⊞ MRW

A Victorian leather dice shaker, 4½in (11.5cm) high.
£12–15
$18–20 ⊞ HO

A Staunton ebony and boxwood weighted chess set, by The British Chess Company, with original box and label, c1900, king 4¼in (11cm) high.
£650–800
$1,000–1,150 ⊞ TMi

Howard Staunton (1810–74) was regarded as perhaps the world's leading chess player in the 1840s. In 1851 he organized the first modern international chess tournament, and the chess pieces that he designed in 1849 were adopted as the standard model, preferred over all other types for use in serious tournaments and matches. In the best quality sets, ebony was used for the black pieces and boxwood for the white. In cheaper sets, all pieces were made from boxwood and coloured accordingly.

◀ **A Ping Pong or Gossima table game,** by J. Jaques & Son and Hamley Bros, c1900, in original box, 9 x 32in (23 x 81.5cm).
£90–100
$130–145 ⊞ J&J

Two rosewood and bone whist markers, c1910, 1½in (4cm) diam.
£50–55
$75–80 ⊞ HO

Cross Reference
See Colour Review (page 193)

A pack of Goodall's Bystander Fragments playing cards, Fragments from France, by Capt Bruce Bairnsfather, featuring his 'Old Bill' character, 1917–19, 3½ x 2in (9 x 5cm).
£45–60
$65–90 ⊞ MURR

A pack of Schneider Trophy playing cards, by Waddingtons, featuring Flying Boat Supermarine S6, c1929, 2 x 3½in (5 x 9cm).
£25–35
$35–50 ⊞ MURR

An Old Maid card game, by Chad Valley, 1920, 4in (10cm) square.
£18–20
$27–30 ⊞ J&J

A Puzzle Drive with Anchor Stone puzzles, 1920s,
3¾in (9.5cm) square.
£20–25
$30–35 ⊞ HUX

A Dover Patrol or Naval Tactics game, by H. P.
Gibson & Sons, instructions missing, 1930s, 8 x 15in
(20.5 x 38cm).
£25–30
$35–45 ⊞ J&J

**A Bounce-O table basket ball
game,** by Sa-Vu, c1930, in original
box, 6 x 7in (15 x 18cm).
£20–25
$30–35 ⊞ J&J

A Jack of All Trades card game,
by Kum-Bak of London, 1930s,
4 x 3in (10 x 7.5cm).
£15–18
$20–25 ⊞ J&J

An Air Raid Puzzle game, 1940s,
4 x 5in (10 x 12.5cm).
£25–30
$35–45 ⊞ HUX

A Game of Commando board game, by Chad Valley,
c1940, 9 x 14in (23 x 35.5cm).
£15–20
$20–30 ⊞ J&J

A Race to Toy Town game, by Chad Valley, 1950s,
7 x 12in (18 x 30.5cm).
£18–20
$25–30 ⊞ J&J

**A Shredded Wheat circular ball
bearing puzzle game,** illustrated
with Rin Tin Tin and Rusty, 1950s,
1¼in (3cm) diam.
£22–24
$32–36 ⊞ HUX

A Motorist puzzle game, 1950s,
4 x 5in (10 x 12.5cm).
£15–18
$20–25 ⊞ HUX

The Army Game board game,
by Bell, based on the Granada
TV comedy show, 1959,
14in (35.5cm) square.
£15–20
$20–30 ⊞ J&J

A Bugs Bunny Tiddley Winks game, by Berwick, 1963, 8 x 11in (20.5 x 28cm).
£8–10
$12–15 ⊞ J&J

> **Cross Reference**
> See Toys (page 403)

A Waddington's Succession game, some damage, 1976, 4½ x 6in (11.5 x 15cm).
£2–3
$3–5 ⊞ CMF

◀ **A Mastermind logic game,** by Vic-Toy, with Design Centre logo, 1972, 12½ x 5in (32 x 12.5cm).
£8–10
$12–15 ⊞ HUX

Jigsaws

A Boyhood of Raleigh wooden jigsaw puzzle, by Zig Zag Puzzles, 1910, 5 x 7in (12.5 x 18cm).
£30–35
$45–50 ⊞ J&J

A Heart of London jigsaw puzzle, by Chichester Jig-Saw Map Puzzles, 1930s, 6 x 8in (15 x 20.5cm)
£10–15
$15–20 ⊞ COB

A Last of the Mohicans jigsaw puzzle, by Waddington's, 1930s, 11 x 9in (28 x 23cm).
£12–15
$18–20 ⊞ J&J

▶ **An Imperial Empire Flying Boat wooden puzzle,** by Victory, c1930, 16in (40.5cm) wide.
£180–220
$260–320 ⚲ P(WM)

A Royal Navy 3-D Battleship wooden jigsaw puzzle, 1930s, 14 x 12in (35.5 x 30.5cm).
£10–20
$15–30 ⊞ COB

◀ **A Joyful Mystery birthday card jigsaw puzzle,** 1950s, in original envelope, 4 x 5in (10 x 12.5cm).
£12–15
$18–20 ⊞ J&J

Garden & Farm Collectables

A limestone garden roller, with wrought-iron handle, early 19thC, 30in (76cm) wide.
£235–265
$330–380 ⊞ DOR

A watering can, c1900, 13in (33cm) long.
£18–25
$30–35 ⊞ HOP

A Citadol brass garden syringe, c1910, 25in (63.5cm) long.
£20–25
$30–40 ⊞ GaB

An iron and wood drain spade, c1920, 80in (203cm) long.
£10–15
$15–20 ⊞ AL

▶ **A brass garden sprayer,** c1920, 18in (45.5cm) high.
£70–80
$100–120 ⊞ AL

A wooden cart wheel, with original paint, c1850, 54in (137cm) diam.
£125–150
$180–220 ⊞ HOP

A selection of steel and iron spades, with elm handles, 1900s, largest 43in (109cm) long.
£20–40
$30–60 each ⊞ HOP

A copper garden sprayer, with wooden handle, c1920, 30in (76cm) high.
£80–100
$115–145 ⊞ AL

A pair of Shaker woven splint basket oxen muzzles, American, mid-19thC, 14in (35.5cm) diam.
£2,000–2,400
$3,000–3,500 ⤢ SK(B)

Two Victorian elm potato dibbers, with metal ends, original green paint, largest 38in (96.5cm) long.
£40–45
$60–70 each ⊞ HOP

A selection of painted cast-iron cattle drinkers, c1920, 14in (35.5cm) wide.
£15–20
$20–30 each ⊞ HOP

A pressed clear glass bowl with four dishes, signed 'André Delatte', French, c1928, bowl 9in (23cm) diam.
£120–150
$175–225 ⊞ CAL

A Monart glass bowl, decorated with lemon, amber, turquoise and gold aventurine, c1930, 9½in (24cm) diam.
£150–180
$220–260 ⊞ RUSK

A Stombelt pale blue glass vase, etched mark 'Stromberg-Shyttan', c1930, 8in (20.5cm) high.
£75–85
$115–125 ⊞ RUSK

A Lalique blue-stained and opalescent Coupe Muguet glass bowl, signed, 1930–31, 9½in (24cm) diam.
£900–1,100
$1,300–1,600 ⊞ RUSK

A Gray-Stan flattened globular-shaped vase, decorated with apricot marble swirls, engraved mark 'Gray-Stan', c1930, 6½in (16.5cm) high.
£230–260
$330–390 ⊞ RUSK

A Venetian glass millefiori figure, 1930s, 9in (23cm) high.
£190–220
$275–325 ⊞ BRU

A Murano white and gold glass bowl, by Barovier, Italian, 1930s, 11in (28cm) diam.
£150–180
$220–260 ⊞ BRU

A Jobling jade glass bowl, with flower block, on a black glass stand, c1934, 5in (12.5cm) wide.
£45–55
$60–80 ⊞ CAL

▶ **A Nuutajarvi Notsjo vase,** designed by Gunnel Nyman, free-blown clear crystal with spike-mould controlled bubbles, marked, 1947–58, 12¾in (32.5cm) high.
£125–145
$180–220 ⊞ RUSK

A Steuben clear glass bowl American, 1950s, 7in (18cm) wide.
£25–30
$35–40 ⊞ MCC

A Royal Brierley cut-glass jug, commemorating the Coronation of Queen Elizabeth, c1953, 12in (30.5cm) high.
£125–145
$180–220 ⊞ RUSK

A Stella Polaris Orrefors clear glass vase, Swedish, 1950s, 7in (18cm) high.
£140–160
$200–250 ⊞ BRU

A Murano red-cased glass vase, with original label, 1950s, 9½in (24cm) high.
£25–30
$35–40 ⊞ MCC

A Val St Lambert blue and clear glass vase, 1950s, 10in (25.5cm) high.
£250–275
$350–400 ⊞ MCC

An Orrefors Kraka-style blue glass vase, by Sven Palmqvist, 1950s, 7in (18cm) high.
£400–500
$650–720 ⊞ MCC

▶ **A Stromberg pink-and-yellow cased glass ashtray,** 1950s, 5in (12.5cm) wide.
£25–30
$35–45 ⊞ MCC

An Orrefors glass plate, designed by Sven Palmqvist, blown yellow and steel-blue crystal with controlled bubbles, marked 'Orrefors Kraka Nr.486 Sven Palmqvist', c1955, 2in (5cm) high.
£225–275
$330–400 ↗ TREA

A glass bird, designed by Oiva Toikka Nuutajarvi, Finnish, 1950s, 8in (20.5cm) wide.
£300–400
$440–580 ⊞ MCC

A Kosta amethyst-coloured glass bowl, by Elis Berg, Swedish, 1950s, 8½in (21.5cm) high.
£90–100
$125–145 ⊞ MCC

◀ **A white opaque glass vase,** by Tapio Wirkkala, Finish, c1950, 6in (15cm) high.
£68–75
$100–110 ⊞ BRU

▶ **A Holmegaard freeform clear glass bowl,** by Per Lutken, signed, 1950s–60s, 8in (20.5cm) wide.
£50–60
$70–90 ⊞ ORI

A Holmegaard glass candlestick,
by Per Lutken, 1950s–60s,
4in (10cm) high.
£45–50
$65–75 ⊞ ORI

Per Lutken

Danish designer Per Lutken (1916–98)
is regarded as one of Scandinavia's
leading 20th-century glassmakers.
From 1942, he was chief designer at the
Kastrup and Holmegaard Glassworks,
where during the '40s and '50s he
created fluid, organic shapes in a subtle
range of colours. Lutken produced
domestic tableware as well as art
glass. In the 1960s he pioneered the
development of strong and practical
pedestal drinking glasses and during
the '70s he experimented with streaked
and textured studio ware. Today his
works attract many collectors.

**A Holmegaard beak
glass vase,** by Per
Lutken, 1950s–60s,
10in (25.5cm) high.
£60–70
$90–100 ⊞ ORI

An Elme black glass vase, by
Edvin Oiles, Swedish, early 1960s,
8in (20.5cm) high.
£75–85
$115–125 ⊞ MCC

> **Cross Reference**
> See Colour Review (page 194)

A pair of glass figures, by
G. Toffolo, Murano, decorated in
red, black and gold, signed, Italian,
c1960, 16in (40.5cm) high.
£350–400
$500–600 ⊞ BRU

▶ **A Mdina blue and yellow
glass bowl,** Maltese, 1960s,
6in (15cm) diam.
£18–22
$20–30 ⊞ HSt

**A Holmegaard Herveze glass heart
vase,** by Per Lutken, signed, designed
1950s, 1961, 5¾in (14.5cm) high.
£100–120
$145–175 ⊞ ORI

A blue glass vase,
by Lucciano Gaspari,
Murano, Italian, c1960,
13in (33cm) high.
£145–160
$200–230 ⊞ BRU

A green and clear glass fish, possibly
Murano, Italian, 1960s, 5in (12.5cm) high.
£50–60
$70–90 ⊞ REN

▶ **A Strömberg glass ice bucket,** Swedish,
with sterling silver mount by Aage Dragsted,
Danish, 1960s, 9½in (24cm) wide.
£50–60
$75–90 ⊞ DID

A Holmegaard amber glass Gulvase, by Otto Breuer, Danish, 1960s, 12in (30.5cm) high.
£50–60
$75–90 ⊞ ORI

A James Powell & Sons, Whitefriars, smoky-grey glass bark vase, by Geoffrey Baxter, 1960s, 8in (20.5cm) high.
£40–45
$60–70 ⊞ MCC

A Holmegaard set of smoky-grey glass vases, by Per Lutken, 1970s, 12in (30.5cm) high.
£100–120
$145–175 ⊞ MCC

A Venini black-and-white glass VVV vase, one of seven designs by Gianni Versace for Venini, with random red and yellow squares, Italian, 1999, 10in (25.5cm) high.
£700–780
$1,000–1,200 ⊞ HaG

A hand-made Maiori glass bowl, by Bebe Facente, Memphis, American, c1986, 13in (33cm) diam.
£500–550
$720–800 ⊞ FMa

A Capo Nord flat glass vase, by Seguso Viro, Murano, the black-and-white spiral of canes encased in blue, aquamarine and clear glass, Italian, 1999, 10in (25.5cm) high.
£650–700
$900–1,000 ⊞ HaG

A Baccarat lead crystal vase, by Nicholas Triboulot, French, designed 1996, 9½in (24cm) high.
£680–750
$1,000–1,100 ⊞ HaG

Carnival Glass

A Carnival glass bowl, orange with a marigold pattern, c1900, 8in (20.5cm) diam.
£25–30
$35–45 ⊞ SER

A Carnival glass fruit bowl, decorated with roses pattern, c1920, 9in (23cm) diam.
£45–50
$70–80 ⊞ ML

A Carnival glass spatula-footed plate, by Northwood Glass Co, Ohio, decorated with grape and cable pattern to the centre, American, c1910, 9in (23cm) diam.
£110–130
$150–200 ⊞ CAL

Cranberry Glass

A cranberry glass jug, with clear glass reeded looped handle, foot, 19thC, 8in (20.5cm) high.
£140–160
$200–230 GAK

A cranberry glass two-branch candelabrum, with wrythen stem and spreading circular foot, 19thC, 4½in (11.5cm) high.
£180–200
$250–300 GAK

▶ **A Victorian part-cranberry glass vase,** 12in (30.5cm) high.
£200–225
$300–330 AOY

A Victorian cranberry and clear glass posy vase, formed as a hanging basket, 9½in (24cm) high.
£150–170
$220–250
 DD

A cranberry glass bell, with folded-over foot and original handle, 1890, 10in (25.5cm) high.
£120–140
$170–200 GRI

A Stourbridge cranberry glass cream jug and sugar bowl, the rims decorated with white threaded and clear crystal applied decoration, on frilled feet, c1895, bowl 5in (12.5cm) diam.
£260–300
$380–440 GRI

A single coronet cut top cranberry glass lustre, c1900, 8in (20.5cm) high.
£300–320
$440–480 GRI

A cranberry glass sugar or preserve bowl, with applied crystal frilled decoration, c1910, 5in (12.5cm) diam.
£80–100
$115–145 GRI

A cranberry glass decanter, with clear glass stopper and reeded handle, c1900, 11in (28cm) high.
£190–220
$275–325 GRI

A cross-cut cranberry and clear glass decanter, probably Stourbridge, c1930, 12in (30.5cm) high.
£150–170
$220–250 GRI

A cranberry glass powder bowl, with clear glass rustic knop and frilled feet, 1910, 5in (12.5cm) diam.
£110–120
$160–180 GRI

Davidson & Chippendale Glass

George Davidson (1822–91) founded the Teams Flint Glass Works in Gateshead near Newcastle in 1866. Initially the firm made chimney lamps, but soon moved on to producing tableware. After his father's death, Thomas Davidson (1860–1937) took control and introduced many new designs. He pioneered the glass flower block (registered 1910) and in the 1920s developed a new line of cloud glass. 'The latest addition is a unique purple cloud or alabaster effect,' reported the *Pottery Gazette and Glass Trades Review* in October 1923. 'This new treatment is offered in bowls with. . .flower blocks to match.' Cloud glass, made by trailing dark glass into lighter glass, was a popular line and came in various colours. In 1933 Davidson began to manufacture Chippendale glass – a range of pressed glass with broad facets. The design was first registered in the USA in 1907 and was produced under licence from Charles Pratt's National Glass Company. Initially it was imported to the UK, but Davidson bought the rights and the moulds and manufactured the glass until WWII.

A pair of George Davidson tazza clear glass compotes, 1885, 8in (20.5cm) diam.
£65–75
$90–110 ⊞ CAL

◀ **A George Davidson green cloud glass vase,** c1922–39, 7½in (19cm) high.
£70–80
$100–120
⊞ BEV

▶ **A George Davidson amber cloud glass vase,** c1922–39, 5½in (14cm) high.
£35–40
$50–60 ⊞ BEV

A George Davidson topaz glass fan vase, c1922–39, 5in (12.5cm) high.
£70–80
$100–120 ⊞ BEV

▶ **A Chippendale clear glass preserve pot,** 1907–40, 3in (7.5cm) high.
£9–11
$12–15 ⊞ TWAC

Two George Davidson green glass frogs/flower blocks, c1930, largest 7in (18cm) wide.
£36–40
$50–60 ⊞ BEV

A Chippendale green glass candlestick, 1907–40, 7½in (19cm) high.
£9–11
$12–15 ⊞ TWAC

▶ **A Chippendale clear glass mayonnaise bowl,** 1907–40, 5in (12.5cm) diam.
£6–8
$7–10 ⊞ TWAC

A Chippendale clear glass celery tray, 1907–40, 11in (28cm) wide.
£10–12
$15–18 ⊞ TWAC

Miller's is a price GUIDE not a price LIST

▶ **A Chippendale clear glass sugar bowl,** 1907–40, 4¾in (12cm) high.
£6–8
$7–10 ⊞ TWAC

A Chippendale clear glass oil flask and stopper, 1907–40, 8½in (21.5cm) high.
£10–12
$15–18 ⊞ TWAC

Decanters

◀ **An oak tantalus,** with three square cut-glass decanters, 19thC, 13in (33cm) wide.
£350–400
$500–600 ⊞ MCC

A yellow glass decanter and six shot glasses, by Moser, c1930, decanter 10in (25.5cm) high.
£300–350
$450–500 ⊞ JEZ

A claret decanter, with fluted clear glass body and silver-plated mounts, c1910, 11in (28cm) high.
£350–400
$500–580 ⊞ DAD

◀ **A clear Iittala Glass decanter,** by Tapio Wirkkala, Finnish, 1970s, 11in (28cm) high.
£90–110
$130–160 ⊞ MCC

Condition

The condition is absolutely vital when assessing the value of a collectable. Damaged pieces on the whole appreciate much less than perfect examples. However, a rare desirable piece may command a high price even when damaged.

Drinking Glasses

A cut-glass tumbler, with moulded base, c1810, 6in (15cm) high.
£50–60
$70–90 ⊞ JHa

A wine glass, with drawn trumpet bowl, multi-spiral air-twist stem, on a conical foot, c1750, 6½in (16.5cm) high.
£200–250
$300–350 ⊞ JHa

A wine glass, with ogee bowl engraved with two figures in a chinoiserie landscape, on a double series opaque twist stem with a conical foot, c1770, 5½in (14cm) high.
£340–400
$500–600 ➤ S(S)

A liqueur glass, the ovoid bowl with swag engraving, c1780, 3¾in (9.5cm) high.
£35–40
$50–60 ⊞ TWAC

▶ **A diamond-cut port glass,** c1810, 3½in (9cm) high.
£20–30
$30–50 ⊞ JHa

A slice-cut Champagne flute, c1830, 6¼in (16cm) high.
£35–40
$50–60 ⊞ JHa

A thistle-cut sherry glass, c1820, 5in (12.5cm) high.
£20–25
$30–35 ⊞ JHa

◀ **A gram or gin glass,** with ball knop stem, c1840, 4in (10cm) high.
£25–35
$30–50 ⊞ JHa

▶ **A Continental port glass,** with engraved and moulded bowl, c1840, 4½in (11.5cm) high.
£25–30
$35–40 ⊞ JHa

A blaze- and feather-cut Champagne glass, c1820, 5in (12.5cm) high.
£30–40
$45–60 ⊞ JHa

A liqueur glass, with panel cut bowl and flattened knop, c1840, 3¼in (8.5cm) high.
£18–22
$25–35 ⊞ **TWAC**

A press-moulded rummer, c1850, 6in (15cm) high.
£24–28
$35–40 ⊞ **TWAC**

A turquoise wine glass, probably James Powell & Sons, Whitefriars, c1860, 5in (12.5cm) high.
£30–35
$40–50 ⊞ **JHa**

A Champagne glass, the bowl engraved with Greek key and star pattern, c1870, 5in (12.5cm) high.
£15–20
$20–30 ⊞ **JHa**

► **A pressed moulded beer tankard,** by Henry Greener, c1890, 4¼in (11cm) high.
£20–25
$30–35 ⊞ **JHa**

A set of six James Powell & Sons, Whitefriars flint wine glasses, c1880, 4½in (11.5cm) high.
£145–165
$200–250 ⊞ **RUSK**

A James Powell & Sons, Whitefriars sherry glass, with wrythen bowl and twisted stem, c1880, 4in (10cm) high.
£20–25
$30–40 ⊞ **JHa**

> Items in the Glass section have been arranged in date order within each sub-section.

A Thomas Webb dimpled beer glass, c1900, 5½in (14cm) high.
£18–22
$25–35 ⊞ **JHa**

A Holmegaard neck-glass, Danish, 1970s, 4½in (11.5cm) high, boxed.
£20–25
$30–35 ⊞ **PLB**

◄ **A pair of slice-cut pub rummers** c1900, 6in (15cm) high.
£65–75
$90–110 ⊞ **RUSK**

A pair of Champagne tumblers, engraved with butterflies, c1910, 4in (10cm) high.
£63–70
$90–100 ⊞ **JHa**

Dumps & Paperweights

Dumps were made from waste glass, that would otherwise be dumped, hence their name. They were often produced by apprentices at bottle glassworks that produced green glass. Centres of manufacture include Sunderland, Stourbridge and Waterford. Depending on size, dumps can be used as either paperweights or doorstops. They are decorated with air bubbles, tears and sometimes contain sulphide images of figures or portrait medallions.

A green glass dump,
the centre with cream and red bubbles, c1860, 5in (12.5cm) high.
£160–200
$230–300 ⊞ JBL

A Victorian green glass dump, with internal floral decoration, 5in (12.5cm) high.
£110–130
$150–200 ⊞ OCAC

A green glass dump,
filled with effervescing bubbles, late 19thC, 3½in (9cm) high.
£130–160
$200–230 ⊞ JBL

A green glass dump,
enclosing a sulphide portrait of Sir William Gladstone, late 19thC, 5in (12.5cm) high.
£130–150
$200–220 ⊞ RWA

A green glass dump,
enclosing a sulphide figure of a child and parasol, late 19thC, 4in (10cm) high.
£170–190
$250–275 ⊞ RWA

◄ **A pair of pedestal paperweights,** one enclosing a motif of crossed machine guns below a coronet, the other inscribed 'Cambridgeshire Regiment', early 20thC, 3½in (9cm) high.
£230–250
$330–360 ⤢ GAK

A Lalique amethyst-tinted glass paperweight, decorated with St Christopher, impressed mark, French, c1930, 4½in (11.5cm) high.
£600–700
$870–1,000 ⊞ RUSK

A Sabino glass paperweight,
enclosing a nude figure, 1930s, 4½in (11.5cm) diam.
£200–250
$300–350 ⊞ JEZ

A Bohemian glass paperweight,
enclosing a portrait, c1920, 4in (10cm) high.
£55–65
$80–100 ⊞ SWB

A Paul Ysart paperweight, with multicoloured millefiori floral decoration, signed, 1950–60, 3in (7.5cm) diam.
£480–530
$700–750 ⊞ SWB

A Baccarat paperweight, with multicoloured close-pack millefiori, c1970, 3in (7.5cm) diam.
£300–400
$440–580 ⊞ DLP

◄ **A Baccarat paperweight,** with a blue butterfly, limited edition, No. 33 of 125, 1978, 3in (7.5cm) diam.
£350–390
$500–580 ⊞ SWB

► **A St Louis paperweight,** green, cream and red, 1986, 2½in (6.5cm) diam.
£570–620
$850–900 ⊞ MLa

A Whitefriars blue-and-clear glass millefiori paperweight, limited edition, No. 28 of 487, 1975, 3½in (9cm) diam.
£450–500
$650–720 ⊞ SWB

A Chris Buzzini Bouquet paperweight, yellow, red, green and purple, limited edition, No. 23 of 25, American, 1991, 3in (7.5cm) diam.
£600–650
$870–970 ⊞ SWB

A Caithness Double Salamander paperweight, red, green and cream, limited edition, No. 17 of 25, 1993, 3in (7.5cm) diam.
£350–400
$500–600 ⊞ SWB

A Correia paperweight, decorated with black cats on a red ground, American, 1999, 3in (7.5cm) diam.
£85–95
$125–145 ⊞ SWB

A Ferro & Lazzarini Murano paperweight, red and cream, Italian, 2000, 3in (7.5cm) high.
£28–33
$35–45 ⊞ SWB

Guinness

A Guinness razor, 1935, 4in (10cm) long.
£60–70
$90–100 ⊞ HUX

A set of Guinness Canasta playing cards, with rules and score sheet, made by Waddington's, 1951, 7 x 5in (18 x 12.5cm), in original box.
£40–50
$60–75 ⊞ MURR

A Guinness advertising mirror, with gold and black lettering on green background, 1920s–30s, 53½ x 38½in (136 x 99cm), in a wooden frame.
£2,200–2,500
$3,200–3,600 ➶ BBR

A Guinness Celluloid advertising sign, depicting red Cheshire and English farmhouse cheeses with a pint of Guinness, 1950s–60s, 10 x 18in (25.5 x 45.5cm).
£150–175
$220–250 ⊞ MURR

◀ A Guinness laminated card stand-up advertisement, depicting golfers searching for a golf ball on a pebble beach, multicoloured, 1950s–60s, 10¼ x 7¼in (26 x 18.5cm).
£750–850
$1,000—1,250 ➶ BBR

A Guinness metal crate omnibus, red with yellow, white and black colouring, slight rusting, 1950s–60s, 18in (45.5cm) long.
£130–150
$190–220 ➶ BBR

A Huntley & Palmer's Guinness biscuit tin, 1950s–60s, 10in (25.5cm) wide.
£140–150
$200–220 ⊞ MURR

A Guinness gnome, with red hat and blue coat, sitting on a wooden stool, 1950s, 5in (12.5cm) high.
£230–260
$330–380 ➶ BBR

▶ A Guinness barometer, the wooden frame inscribed 'Lovely Day for a Guinness', slight damage, 1950s, 8¼in (21cm) diam.
£40–50
$60–75 ➶ DN

A Carlton Ware Guinness advertising model, shaped as a tortoise with a pint of Guinness on its back, painted in naturalistic colours, on a cream base inscribed 'My Goodness – My Guinness' in red lettering, red-printed maker's mark and impressed reference number, 1960–70, 3½in (9cm) high.
£75–90
$100–130 ➶ DN

A Guinness silver-plated pocket watch, the face decorated with a smiling face glass of Guinness, a nodding toucan and 'Guinness Time' in red lettering, 1950s–60s.
£420–480
$580–700 ➶ **BBR**

A Guinness tin tray, in naturalistic colours, inscribed 'Toucans in their nest agree, Guinness is good for you, Open some today and see, What one or Toucan do', 1950s, 12in (30.5cm) diam.
£60–75
$90–110 ⊞ **MURR**

A Guinness mains-operated illuminated clock, with Perspex face and chrome top, green and red lettering to face, 1950s–60s, 16in (40.5cm) high.
£300–350
$450–500 ➶ **BBR**

A Guinness enamel badge, in the shape of a penguin and a glass of Guinness, embossed 'Draught Guinness' and 'Guinness is Good for You', 1950s–60s, 1½in (4cm) high.
£40–50
$60–75 ➶ **BBR**

A pair of Guinness enamel cufflinks, 1950s–60s.
£40–45
$60–65 ➶ **BBR**

◀ **A Guinness extra stout bottle,** to celebrate the company's bicentenary, 1759–1959, 1959, 9in (23cm) high.
£25–30
$35–45 ⊞ **HUX**

A Carlton Ware Guinness tea set, by James Blackmore, comprising teapot, jug, sugar bowl, black and white with gold harp and lettering, 1960, teapot 5¾in (14.5cm) high.
£500–550
$720–800 ➶ **BBR**

A Guinness stand-up advertisment, plastic-covered tin, red, black and cream, 'Guinness is Good For You, Enjoy it with Meals When Tired, Before Retiring', 6¼ x 9¼in (16 x 23.5cm).
£150–175
$220–255 ➶ **BBR**

▶ **A Carlton Ware Guinness advertising simulated stoneware bottle,** with wire-bound cork stopper, 'Guinness Extra Stout' red seal label, inscribed 'Guinness is Good For You', around base, black-printed maker's mark and impressed reference number, 1960–70, 7in (17.5cm) high.
£20–25
$30–35 ➶ **DN**

A Guinness cigarette lighter, with a coloured image of a Native American chief holding a canoe full of braves above his head, inscribed 'Guinness – Him Strong!' to one side and 'Good Health from Ireland' to the other, 1950s–60s, 1¾in (4.5cm) high, in original box.
£90–110
$130–160 ➶ **BBR**

Handbags & Luggage

A late Victorian wooden chest, with domed top and lift-out tray, 37in (94cm) wide.
£250–300
$350–450 ⊞ TPC

◀ A beaded bag, with silver and gold-coloured beads and brass clasp, 1920, 6in (15cm) high.
£65–75
$90–110 ⊞ Ech

A beaded bag, with plastic tortoiseshell-effect clasp, 1900, 9in (23cm) high.
£75–85
$100–125 ⊞ Ech

A metal-beaded purse, with moonstone decoration, French, 1920–30, 8in (20.5cm) long.
£225–250
$320–360 ⊞ CRIS

A hessian steamer trunk, with wooden bands, leather corners, brass locks and reproduction labels, c1930, 36in (91.5cm) wide.
£85–95
$125–150 ⊞ HO

A chrome-framed snakeskin handbag, with integral purse, c1930, 11in (28cm) wide.
£45–50
$65–75 ⊞ SBL

A Biene & Davis embroidered chenille bag, with red, peach and lilac flowers and green foliage, with original purse, American, c1930, 8in (20.5cm) wide.
£100–120
$150–175 ⊞ LaF

A leather hat box, silk-lined, made for Harrods, c1930, 16in (40.5cm) wide.
£150–175
$220–250 ⊞ HO

A black crepe evening bag, with Austrian crystal decoration, c1940, 4in (10cm) wide.
£90–100
$130–150 ⊞ LaF

A wicker bag, with blue and black appliquéd butterflies and Lucite handle and frame, American, c1950, 11½in (29cm) wide.
£70–80
$100–115 ⊞ SBL

A Perspex handbag, white marble effect, mid-1950s, 8in (20.5cm) wide.
£160–180
$230–260 ⊞ HSt

A Perspex and rhinestone handbag, by Midas of Miami, American, 1950s, 9in (23cm) wide.
£220–240
$320–350 ⊞ SpM

A plastic laminated bag, with Lucite handle, decorated with a picture of a Japanese lady wearing a red kimono, American, 1950s, 9½in (24cm) high.
£100–120
$150–175 ⊞ LBe

A gilt chainmail bag, by Whiting & Davis, American, 1950s, 6in (15cm) wide.
£120–140
$175–200 ⊞ SBT

A picnic hamper, by Brexton, blue case with white fittings, 1950s, 30in (76cm) wide.
£120–140
$175–200 ⊞ PPH

A black patent vinyl weekend bag, c1950s, 10in (25.5cm) high.
£45–50
$65–75 ⊞ LaF

A leather suitcase, with chrome locks, 1960s, 22in (56cm) wide.
£55–65
$80–100 ⊞ HO

LOCATE THE SOURCE

The source of each illustration in Miller's can be found by checking the code letters below each caption with the Key to Illustrations, pages 444–452.

A box handbag, by Pucci, multi-coloured, 1960s, 7in (18cm) high.
£350–400
$500–580 ⊞ SBT

▶ **A gilt-frame black silk evening bag,** decorated with gilt appliqué, c1970, 7in (18cm) wide.
£50–60
$75–100 ⊞ SBL

A plastic vanity case, by Antler, grey snakeskin effect with red lining, fitted, c1970, 12in (30.5)cm wide.
£50–60
$75–100 ⊞ SBL

Horse Brasses

A Victorian camel brass, with owner's penknife and seal, 5in (12.5cm) wide.
£40–50
$60–75 ⊞ PJo

A brass swinger, single crescent, c1890, 3½in (9cm) diam.
£20–25
$30–35 ⊞ HBr

A miller's horse brass, c1920, 5in (12.5cm) high.
£5–10
$10–15 ⊞ PJo

► **A commemorative horse brass,** for King George V's Silver Jubilee, 1935, 3½in (9cm) diam.
£30–35
$45–50 ⊞ HBr

A commemorative cast-brass shield, for Queen Victoria's Golden Jubilee, 1887, 4in (10cm) high.
£100–120
$150–175 ⊞ HBr

A commemorative cast-brass horse brass, for Queen Victoria's Diamond Jubilee, 1897, 4in (10cm) high.
£110–125
$160–180 ⊞ HBr

A Victorian horse brass, 4in (10cm) diam.
£20–25
$30–450 ⊞ PJo

A John Edgington advertising brass, c1900, 4in (10cm) high.
£30–35
$45–50 ⊞ PJo

A horse brass, commemorating Ealing Victory Horse Parade, 1946, 5in (12.5cm) high.
£30–40
$45–60 ⊞ PJo

A phenolic cruet set, 1930s,
4in (10cm) long.
£160–190
$230–280 ⊞ BEV

**An Edbar International Corp VP
Twin plastic novelty camera,** made
for Woolworths, takes 127mm roll
film, c1938, 3in (7.5cm) wide.
£30–35
$45–50 ⊞ HEG
These cameras came in various
colours, of which blue is the
rarest. The most common colour,
black, is valued at £5–10 ($8–15).

A phenolic box, c1930s,
3in (7.5cm) diam.
£80–90
$120–130 ⊞ BEV

**A Bakelite Michelin Man money
box,** late 1930s, 6in (15cm) high.
£160–190
$230–275 ⊞ BEV

▶ **A urea formaldehyde bowl,** by
Beatl, 1940s, 8in (20.5cm) diam.
£120–150
$175–220 ⊞ GAD

**A Perspex pen stand and card
stand,** American, 1950s,
3in (7.5cm) wide.
£20–25
$30–50 pair ⊞ LBe

A pair of plastic sunglasses, with batwing-style
frames, Italian, c1950.
£30–35
$45–50 ⊞ SBL

▶ **Three plastic
Tupperware
containers,**
with ribbed lids,
1960s, 5in
(12.5cm) diam.
£6–8
$9–12 each
⊞ Mo

Two plastic necklaces, with faceted beads,
c1960, 20in (51cm) long.
£15–20
$20–30 each ⊞ SBL

A plastic juice set, with six tumblers,
two stirrers and a jug, French, 1970,
10¼in (26cm) high, in original box.
£55–65
$80–100 ⊞ PLB

**An ABS plastic umbrella
stand,** Dedalo design
by Emma Gismondi
Schweinberger for Artemide
of Milan, Italian, 1970s,
14in (35.5cm) high.
£80–90
$120–140 ⊞ PLB

A pottery mug, commemorating the 1845 Corn Law repeal, enamelled with flowers and a sheaf of corn, star crack to base, c1846, 4in (10cm) high.
£130–150
$200–225 ✕ SAS

A commemorative plate, by Wallis Gimson, with a portrait of Benjamin Disraeli and a verse, c1881, 11in (28cm) wide.
£135–165
$200–240 ⊞ POL

A commemorative plate, by Wallis Gimson, with a portrait of the Marquis of Salisbury, c1887, 11in (28cm) wide.
£30–40
$45–60 ✕ SAS

A commemorative plaque, by Burgess & Leigh, with a portrait of Gladstone, 1898, 14¼in (36cm) diam.
£85–100
$125–150 ✕ SAS

A commemorative plate, by Meakin, with reversible portraits of Balfour and Asquith, inscribed 'Rule Britannia' and 'Britannia Rues', hairline crack, c1906, 4in (10cm) diam.
£45–55
$65–80 ✕ SAS

A commemorative Carnival glass bottle, embossed with President Dwight Eisenhower, first edition, c1969, 8in (20.5cm) high.
£60–70
$90–100 ⊞ CAL

◀ **A biscuit tin,** the lid with an illustration of Sir Winston Churchill, c1955, 10 x 8¼in (25.5 x 21cm).
£15–20
$20–30 ⊞ HUX

A car-bumper sticker, produced by Massachusetts Democrats, unused, signed by John F. Kennedy, American, c1960, 6in (15cm) wide.
£1,350–1,500
$2,000–2,200 ⊞ IQ

▶ **A collection of presidential campaign metal badges,** American, 20thC, largest 1½in (4cm) diam.
£40–50
$60–75 ⊞ IE

A biscuit tin, featuring Presidents of the USA with John F. Kennedy in the centre, American, 1961, 8½ x 9½in (21.5 x 24cm).
£25–30
$35–45 ⊞ HUX

A Royal Doulton bust of Margaret Thatcher, printed factory mark, signed 'M. Woodhouse', c1982, 4¾in (12cm) high.
£400–480
$600–700 ⚲ P

A ceramic character jug, modelled as the *Spitting Image* character of Neil Kinnock, limited edition, No. 169 of 650, 1980s, 5in (12.5cm) high.
£30–50
$45–75 ⚲ Pott

An Aynsley plate, with a portrait of Margaret Thatcher against a background of the Houses of Parliament, 1987, 10½in (26.5cm) diam.
£20–25
$30–35 ⊞ HUX

A pottery character jug, by Kevin Francis, depicting Mikhail Gorbachov, limited edition, No. 438 of 1,000, 9½in (23.5cm) high.
£40–50
$60–75 ⚲ SAS

Harold Wilson, by Ben Pimlott, a political biography, published by HarperCollins, 1993, 8 x 5¼in (20.5 x 13.5cm).
£13–15
$20–25 ⊞ POL

A photograph of Sir Winston Churchill, signed by his grandson and granddaughter, 1990s, 30 x 23in (76 x 58.5cm).
£175–195
$250–280 ⊞ POL

A concrete garden gnome, modelled as Tony Blair, entitled 'The Urban Gardener', 2001, 16in (40.5cm) high.
£50–60
$75–90 ⊞ POL

▶ **A political cartoon,** by Martin Rowson, entitled 'Mad Cow', 1999, 9 x 11in (23 x 28cm).
£225–250
$320–360 ⊞ POL

A political badge, featuring Peter Mandelson, inscribed 'Bring Back Mandy', 2001, 1½in (4cm) diam.
£1–2
$2–3 ⊞ POL

◀ **An electoral campaign poster,** on behalf of the Labour Party, featuring William Hague as Margaret Thatcher, 2001, 7½ x 15½in (19 x 37cm).
£1–2
$2–3 ⊞ POL

A lithographic poster, 'Théâtre National de L'Opéra Carnaval 1892', by Jules Chéret, printed by Chaix, Paris, 47¼ x 33¾in (120 x 85.5cm).
£1,000–1,200
$1,500–1,800 ⚘ S

Miller's is a price GUIDE not a price LIST

A poster, 'P&O Cruises', by Greig, printed by Lamson Agency, c1930, 39¾ x 24¾in (101 x 63cm).
£750–800
$1,000–1,200 ⚘ Bea(E)

A Compagnies de l'Ouest & de Brighton poster, 'Paris a Londres l'Angleterre & l'Ecosse', by G. Fraipont, detailing routes between Paris and London, 1894, 40 x 25in (101.5 x 63.5cm), glazed and framed.
£200–300
$300–450 ⚘ P(WM)

◄ **A lithographic poster,** 'Philips', by Hans Oertle, printed by Emrik & Binger, Haarlem, c1924, 60 x 40in (152.5 x 101.5cm).
£1,150–1,250
$1,600–1,800 ⊞ VSP

A lithographic poster, 'Invest in the Victory Liberty Loan', by L. A. Shafer, printed by The W. F. Powers Co, New York, American, c1917, 29¼ x 39½in (74.5 x 100.5cm).
£330–370
$470–550 ⊞ VSP

◄ **A poster,** 'Miss England III Réalise La Plus Grand Vitesse sur l'Eau', advertising Castrol, mounted on linen, 1929, 30¾ x 23¾in (78 x 60.5cm).
£200–240
$300–350 ⚘ ONS

◄ **A poster,** 'Shell', by A. Stewart-Hill, featuring Mousehole, Cornwall, c1934, 25 x 40in (63.5 x 101.5cm).
£2,700–3,000
$4,000–4,500 ⊞ REN

A poster, 'Redcar – It's Quicker by Rail', by Leonard Cusden, for LNER, printed by Jarrold & Sons, c1935, 39¾ x 50¾in (101 x 129cm).
£800–900
$1,200–1,300 ⚘ Bea(E)

◄ **A poster,** 'Cruises Around Africa', by O. Anton, for German African Lines, 1936, 46 x 24in (117 x 61cm).
£550–600
$700–850 ⊞ REN

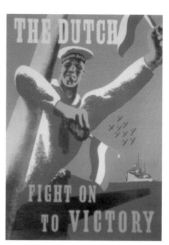

◀ **A poster,** 'North Wales for Holidays – Dolbadarn Castle, Llanberis', by John Mace, for London, Midland and Scottish Railway, c1936, 39 x 24¾in (99 x 63cm).
£550–600
$800–900 ⤳ Bea(E)
Dolbadarn Castle was built by Llewelyn the Great before 1230 and is now in the Snowdonia National Park.

A poster, 'Southport – for a Holiday in Wintertime', by Fortunino Matania, for London, Midland and Scottish Railway, printed by Waterlow & Sons, c1936, 39¾ x 50¾in (101 x 126cm).
£4,600–5,000
$6,500–7,300 ⤳ Bea(E)

A WWII poster, 'The Dutch Fight on to Victory', 1942, 32 x 23¾in (81.5 x 60cm).
£420–470
$600–700 ⊞ VSP

A poster, 'New York Exposition Universelle 1939', by A. M. Cassandre, for Cie Gle Transatlantique, printed by Alliance Graphique L. Danel, Paris, 39½ x 24½in (100.5 x 61.5cm).
£4,750–5,250
$7,000–7,500 ⊞ VSP

A poster, 'Fishguard– Rosslare', by Arthur G. Mills, published by RWER, printed by Waterlow & Sons, c1950, 40¼ x 26in (102 x 66cm).
£600–700
$870–1,000 ⤳ ONS

A poster, 'The Royal Air Force covers the World, Volunteer for Regular Service', 1950, 40¼ x 24½in (102 x 62cm).
£60–70
$90–100 ⤳ ONS

A poster, 'Fly Aer Lingus', by Bainbridge, c1950, 40¼ x 25½in (102 x 65cm).
£90–100
$130–150 ⤳ ONS

A poster, by John Minton, for London Transport, 1951, 40 x 25in (101.5 x 63.5cm).
£3,600–4,000
$5,000–6,000 ⊞ REN

An American poster, 'Teamwork Wins', by C. P. Benton, for United States Maritime Commission, c1943, 40¼ x 30in (102 x 76cm).
£200–240
$300–350 ⤳ ONS

▶ **A poster,** 'Wills's Cut Golden Bar', by Abram Games, c1950, 10 x 8in (25.5 x 20.5cm).
£270–300
$400–450 ⊞ REN

A Universal film poster, *'Twilight for the Gods'*, 1958, 25 x 40in (63.5 x 101.5cm), with six colour lobby cards.
£25–30
$35–45 ♪ **DN**

A United Artists film poster, *'Thunderbird 6'*, 1960s, 30 x 40in (76 x 101.5cm).
£150–180
$220–260 ⊞ **SDP**

A United Artists film poster,
'Goldfinger', Belgium, 1964,
20 x 22in (51 x 56cm).
£225–250
$330–360 ⊞ **SDP**

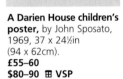

A British Lion film poster, *'Girl on a Motorcycle'*, 1968, 30 x 40in (76 x 101.5cm).
£260–300
$380–440 ⊞ **SDP**

A Darien House children's poster, by John Sposato, 1969, 37 x 24½in (94 x 62cm).
£55–60
$80–90 ⊞ **VSP**

◄ **A Rank Organisation poster,** *'Carry On Girls'*, 1973, 40 x 30in (101.5 x 76cm).
£30–35
$40–50 ⊞ **SDP**

A Peter Max poster, 'Pan Am 747', October 1969, 42¼ x 28in (107.5 x 71cm).
£150–180
$220–260 ♪ **ONS**

► **A double feature poster,** *'Carquake'* and *'The Giant Spider Invasion'*, c1977, 30 x 40in (76 x 101.5cm).
£40–50
$60–80 ⊞ **Dri**

A Bally poster, by Bernard Villemot, 1989, 60 x 40in (152.5 x 101.5cm).
£270–300
$400–450 ⊞ **VSP**

◀ **Five cylinders for phonographs,** 1900–10, 5in (12.5cm) high.
£5–10
$10–15 ⊞ **GM**

An HMV Model 2 wind-up gramophone, 1920, 27in (68.5cm) high.
£800–900
$1,200–1,300 ⋏ **CBGR**

An HMV 101 portable gramophone, 1928, 16in (40.5cm) long.
£130–160
$200–230 ⋏ **CBGR**

A Burgoyne Midget 5 portable wireless, with 5 valves, moving iron speaker, later case clips, 1930, 11in (28cm) wide.
£80–100
$115–145 ⊞ **GM**

A Pye Model P Classic radio, in a walnut cabinet with sunrise design, 1933, 18in (45.5cm) high.
£100–150
$145–225 ⊞ **GM**

▶ **An Emor globe mains radio,** three wavebands, globe turns for tuning, c1948, 43in (109cm) high.
£300–400
$450–550 ⊞ **OTA**

An Ekco Model AD36 Bakelite 'sad face' radio, designed by Wells Coates, limited production, case cracked, 1934, 16in (40.5cm) high.
£5,000–6,000
$7,250–8,750 ⊞ **OTA**

A French Ocean Cadre radio, with illuminated compartments at each end, 1955, 23in (58.5cm) wide.
£150–200
$220–300 ⊞ **GM**

An EMI Model TR52 professional tape recorder, 1962, 13in (33cm) wide.
£70–100
$100–150 ⊞ **GM**
This portable stereo recorder was widely used by the BBC and other broadcasting companies.

A Kolster Brander model RB10 Gavotte radio, long and medium wave, in a plastic cabinet, 1960, 12in (30.5cm) wide.
£30–35
$40–50 ⊞ **GM**

A Philips battery record player, 1960s, 16in (40.5cm) wide.
£65–75
$95–115 ⊞ **PPH**

A set of six plastic Beatles clothes tags, used in Apple's stores, 1960s, 2½in (6.5cm) wide.
£45–50
$65–80 ✦ SAF

A bar of ABBA soap, 1970s, 4in (10cm) long.
£10–12
$15–20 ✦ SAF

▶ A Yellow Submarine thermos flask, American, 1968, 6½in (16.5cm) high.
£155–185
$225–275 ✦ SAF

The Beatles Scrap Book, by Walt Howarth, unused, 1966, 12 x 10in (30.5 x 25.5cm).
£35–40
$50–60 ✦ CBP

A Beatles hair spray can, 1960s, 8in (20.5cm) high.
£20–25
$30–35 ✦ SAF

A Beatles Cellophane tape display card, with 12 reels of tape, 1960s, 11in (28cm) high.
£125–150
$180–220 ✦ SAF

A set of four Royal Doulton porcelain character jugs, depicting the Beatles, marked, 1984, 6in (15cm) high.
£500–600
$720–870 ✦ FO

A Ray Charles LP record, by ABC Paramount, Dutch, 1961.
£15–20
$20–30 ⊞ TOT

A Jimi Hendrix electric toy guitar and amplifier, 1968, guitar 29in (73.5cm) long.
£150–180
$220–260 ✦ SAF

▶ A Jimi Hendrix stars and stripes stage shirt, labelled 'Head Ease Los Angeles', with photographs of Jimi Hendrix wearing the shirt on stage at Temple Stadium, Philadelphia, 16th May 1970.
£16,000–18,000
$23,000–26,000 ✦ Bon

A Jimmy Cliff single record, 'Wonderful World Beautiful People', by Island Records, Belgium, 1970.
£10–12
$15–20 ⊞ TOT

From Jimi Hendrix to Jimmy Somerville...
whatever you're into, it's on eBay!

Buy

Sell

You can buy and sell
practically anything on eBay.

ebaY™ .CO.UK

◀ **A singles record case,** featuring Donny and Marie Osmond on both sides, 1970, 8in (20.5cm) high.
£16–19
$20–30 ⚹ SAF

A Mick Jagger Sticky Fingers promotional standee, 1971, 69in (175.5cm) high.
£650–700
$900–1,000 ⚹ FO

A set of six Monkee pin badges, with original card advertisement, 1967, 3¼in (8.5cm) diam.
£18–20
$20–30 ⚹ SAF

Three Pink Floyd concert tickets, from the 1994 World Tour, 7in (18cm) wide.
£18–20
$20–30 ⚹ SAF

Two Elvis Presley film posters, 'Frankie and Johnny', by United Artists, Sweden, 1966, and 'A Plein Tube Volle Gas' (Speedway), by MGM, Belgium, 1968, largest 40 x 27in (101.5 x 68.5cm).
£100–120
$145–175 ⚹ FO

An embroidered jacket, designed by Granny Takes a Trip, worn by Gram Parsons and later given to Keith Richard, c1970.
£11,000–12,000
$16,000–17,500 ⚹ FO

A Sex Pistols Rock and Roll Swindle promotional standee, given to HMV shops, 1978, 33in (84cm) wide.
£225–250
$320–360 ⊞ IQ

A Tyrannosaurus Rex LP record, by EMI Records, mono, 1968.
£35–40
$50–60 ⊞ TOT

The Wind in the Willows LP record, with Debbie Harry, by EMI Records, mono, 1968.
£15–20
$20–30 ⊞ TOT

A Seeburg 148 Trash Can jukebox, playing 78rpm records, 1948, 60in (152.5cm) high.
£3,200–3,500
$4,500–5,000 ⊞ KA

Hot Water Bottles

As we at Miller's know, anything can be collectable and hot water bottles are no exception. The majority of examples shown dates from the early part of the 20th century. In the era before central heating, hot water bottles came in every style. There were miniature muff warmers for the hands, larger bottles for the feet and novelty designs to decorate as well as heat the bed. Bottles were produced by many major potteries such as Denby, Doulton, and Old Fulham Pottery.

Many hot water bottles cost pennies when they were made, today rare examples can fetch three-figure sums. Values depend on shape (novelty designs are the most collectable), decoration (look out for interesting transfers) and condition. Examples are often excavated by bottle collectors and can become damaged. A bottle will be worth more if it retains its original stopper and other features, such as labels or the leather handle on the Gladstone bag bottle shown below.

A Bourne Denby miniature muff warmer, c1910–20, 5½in (13.5cm) wide.
£225–275
$320–390 ⊞ MURR

A Handy muff warmer, transfer-printed in black on an off-white glaze, 1910–20, 4¾in (12cm) high.
£270–320
$400–450 ⚹ BBR

A Maws radium muff warmer, c1910–20, 6½in (13.5cm) wide.
£100–120
$145–175 ⊞ MURR

A Bourne Gladstone bag foot warmer, decorated with a blue glaze with brown top and stopper, with leather carrying handle, 1910–20, 9¾in (25cm) wide.
£400–450
$580–650 ⚹ BBR

A Denby Stoneware 'The Bungalow' foot warmer, transfer-printed in blue on an off-white glaze, 1910–20, 10½in (26.5cm) high.
£90–110
$130–160 ⚹ BBR

A bed warmer, with carrying handle, the front decorated with a cat and mouse in relief, the base printed 'Velray, Made in England', 1910–20, 7in (18cm) high.
£370–420
$550–620 ⚹ BBR

A fish foot warmer, with stopper, decorated with a bright yellow glaze, 1910–20, 14in (35.5cm) long.
£430–480
$620–700 ⚹ BBR

Condition

The condition is absolutely vital when assessing the value of a collectable. Damaged pieces on the whole appreciate much less than perfect examples. However a rare desirable piece may command a high price even when damaged.

A Bourne Denby Little Folks Foot warmer, transfer-printed in blue on an off-white glaze, restored, 1910–20, 6½in (16.5cm) high.
£100–120
$145–175 ➤ BBR

A clock foot warmer, the face with raised numerals, decorated with a brown and tan glaze, with chain carrying handle, original paper label to side, 1910–20, 6¾in (17cm) high.
£320–360
$450–500 ➤ BBR

An Old Fulham Pottery Adaptable hot water bottle, transfer-printed in black on an off-white glaze, 1910–20, 8½in (21.5cm) high.
£12–16
$15–20 ➤ BBR

A Winton & Grimwades Mecca foot warmer, transfer-printed in green on a white glaze, 1910–20, 11in (28cm) high.
£180–220
$260–320 ➤ BBR

A Nolon foot warmer, transfer-printed in black on an off-white glaze, 1910–20, 9¾in (25cm) high.
£5–10
$10–15 ➤ BBR

A King Sol hot water bottle, transfer-printed in black on an off-white glaze, 1910–20, 8in (20.5cm) high.
£70–90
$100–130 ➤ BBR

A pair of chrome shoe warmers, c1930, 10in (25.5cm) long.
£55–65
$80–100 ⊞ HO

A Doultons Reliable foot warmer, transfer-printed in brown on a white glaze, 1910–20, 8¾in (22cm) high.
£10–15
$15–20 ➤ BBR

A Lawleys foot warmer, transfer-printed in black on an off-white glaze, with brown top, 1921, 10¼in (26cm) high.
£5–10
$10–15 ➤ BBR

A rubber hot water bottle, modelled as a clown, by Roger Hargreaves, 1970, 12in (30.5cm) high.
£10–12
$15–18 ⊞ HarC

Jewellery
Bracelets

A **Victorian silver and paste bracelet,** 5in (12.5cm) long.
£100–120
$145–175 ⊞ Ma

A **vulcanite bangle,** 1875,
1¾in (4.5cm) wide.
£40–45
$60–70 ⊞ AM

◀ An **Art Deco chrome
and red Bakelite
bracelet,** Germany,
1930s, 8in (20.5cm) long.
£60–70
$90–100 ⊞ LaF

▶ A **Schiaparelli grey rhinestone bracelet,** 1950s,
7½in (19cm) long.
£450–500
$650–720 ⊞ CRIS

A **Kramer blue stone bracelet,** American, c1960,
1½in (4cm) wide.
£90–100
$130–150 ⊞ SBL

▶ A **Joachim
rock crystal and
hand-beaten
silver bracelet,**
Finnish, c1970,
2½in (6.5cm) wide.
£200–250
$300–350 ⊞ DID

◀ A **Chanel
bracelet,** set
with *faux* rubies,
diamonds and
pearls, 1980s,
2½in (6.5cm) wide.
£450–500
$650–720 ⊞ SBT

Brooches

◀ **A Tunbridge ware brooch,** 1830, 1½in (4cm) long.
£24–28
$35–45 ⊞ VBo

An 18ct gold commemorative brooch, set with black onyx and pearls, inscribed 'In memory of', the reverse with a locket, 1850, 2½in (6.5cm) wide.
£320–400
$450–550 ⊞ Ma

An 18ct gold 'target' brooch, the centre set with amethyst and gold balls, the reverse with a locket, c1860, 1¼in (3cm) diam.
£450–500
$650–720 ⊞ AMC

A hair brooch, set in a gold mount designed as a knot, the reverse with a locket, c1880, 1½in (4cm) wide.
£175–195
$250–300 ⊞ AMC

A Victorian Scottish silver buckle brooch, set with semi-precious stones, 2in (5cm) diam.
£120–140
$170–200 ⚲ WBH

◀ **An Edwardian silver paste star brooch,** 1½in (4cm) high.
£60–100
$100–150 ⊞ Ma

A Scottish silver and agate brooch, the centre set with amber glass, c1890, 1in (2.5cm) diam.
£30–40
$40–60 ⊞ BWA

Three silver name brooches, Maggie, Agnes and Clara in gold inlay, 1900–20, 1½in (4cm) wide.
£40–50
$60–80 each ⊞ EXC

Cross Reference
See Colour Review (page 233–234)

A paste and glass brooch, 1920s, 1¼in (3cm) wide.
£5–6
$7–10 ⊞ STP

▶ **An Art Deco marcasite 'fruit salad' baguette pin,** set with red, blue and green stones, French, 1920s, 3½in (9cm) long.
£450–500
$650–720 ⊞ CRIS

A diamanté brooch, modelled as a car with a lady alighting, 1920, 3in (7.5cm) wide.
£245–285
$350–400 ⊞ SSM

An Art Deco gold metal and red glass brooch, modelled as flowers and buds, Czechoslovakian, c1930, 3in (7.5cm) wide.
£45–50
$65–75 ⊞ LaF

A winged Sphinx brooch, set with white, red, green and blue paste stones, 1940s, 2½in (6.5cm) wide.
£135–150
$200–220 ⊞ LBe

A brown enamel on sterling silver abstract brooch, designed by Henning Koppel for Georg Jensen, c1947, 1¼in (3cm) wide.
£600–700
$870–1,000 ⊞ DID

A Trifari blue Jelly Belly swordfish, set with white paste stones, 1940s, 3in (7.5cm) wide.
£360–450
$500–650 ⊞ CRIS

A Trifari gold-coloured leopard brooch, with *faux* ruby eyes, 1950s, 2in (5cm) wide.
£75–85
$115–125 ⊞ FMa

Two Trifari gold- and silver-coloured fruit pins, modelled as apples, 1950s, 1in (2.5cm) high.
£18–20
$25–30 ⊞ CRIS

A Coro silver tone and crystal floral brooch, American, c1950, 4in (10cm) high.
£35–40
$50–60 ⊞ LaF

A Sybil Dunlop silver and gold brooch, the centre set with a citrine, c1964, 2in (5cm) diam.
£600–700
$870–1,000 ⊞ DID

◀ **A gold-coloured diamanté brooch,** 1950s–60s, 2in (5cm) wide.
£4–5
$6–8 ⊞ STP

A Christian Dior diamanté brooch, modelled as the head of a circus horse, set with *faux* pearls, 1966, 4in (10cm) high.
£275–300
$400–440 ⊞ LBe

Cameos

Cameos became extremely popular from the beginning of the 19th century. 'A fashionable lady wears cameos at her girdle, cameos in her necklace, cameos on each of her bracelets, a cameo on her tiara,' noted the *Journal des Dames* in 1805. During the Victorian period, cameos were produced for every level of the market. They ranged from finely-carved precious stones to more affordable examples made from shell or lava stone (produced in Italy from the lava of Mount Vesuvius). Whatever the medium, however, classical subjects were a favourite theme.

◀ **A conch shell cameo brooch,** carved with a neoclassical lady's head and shoulders, 19thC, 2in (5cm) high.
£60–70
$90–100 ➹ WilP

A pair of gilt-metal-mounted cameo bracelets, each classical portrait within an acanthus frame on an eight-bar bracelet, one converted to a brooch, c1840, 2¼in (5.5cm) high.
£700–750
$1,000–1,100 ➹ Bea(E)

▶ **A silver-mounted cameo brooch,** carved with a she-wolf suckling Romulus and Remus, with rope-twist border, c1900, 2¼in (5.5cm) high.
£300–350
$450–500 ⊞ AMC

A gold-mounted cameo brooch, carved with a Roman soldier, c1900, 1¼in (3cm) high.
£200–225
$300–330 ⊞ AMC

Earrings

A pair of Christian Dior entremblant crystal earrings, by Mitchell Mayer, Austrian, 1951–54, 1in (2.5cm) high.
£160–190
$230–280 ⊞ LaF

A pair of Miriam Haskell earrings, modelled as gold-coloured flowers with silver-coloured balls, 1940s, 1¼in (3cm) diam.
£225–250
$320–360 ⊞ SBT

◀ **A pair of diamanté drop earrings,** Austrian, c1950, 3in (7.5cm) long.
£7–8
$10–12 ⊞ STP

▶ **A pair of yellow-painted metal and coloured glass earrings,** Austrian, 1960, 1in (2.5cm) high.
£5–6
$8–10 ⊞ STP

A pair of Butler & Wilson diamanté earrings, c1970, 4½in (11.5cm) long.
£130–150
$200–220 ⊞ SBL

Hat Pins

Hat pins were an essential part of a lady's wardrobe from the late 19th century until WWI. The crinolined skirts and close-fitting bonnets of the Victorian period were replaced by slim-line dresses and large picture hats, supported by piled-up hair and secured with a pair of hat pins. Pins came in many different designs and materials and numerous patents were taken out for point protectors. Edwardian hat pins could be 12in (30.5cm) in length and were viciously sharp. In many public places, particularly on public transport, hat pins with uncovered points were banned for fear of accidents. Prominent makers include Charles Horner and values depend on medium and style. Pairs of hat pins are worth more than single examples.

A pair of jet and cameo hat pins, c1875, 4in (10cm) long.
£165–185
$250–280 ⊞ AM

A silver bicycle hat pin, Birmingham 1898, 10in (25.5cm) long.
£175–195
$250–280 ⊞ SSM

A Charles Horner silver hat pin, set with a red semi-precious stone, 1910, 10in (25.5cm) long.
£60–65
$90–100 ⊞ VB

Two Norene gold-coloured hat pins, 1911, 10in (25.5cm) long.
£30–40
$40–60 each ⊞ VB

Jet

A horn brooch, decorated with acorns and oak leaves, c1860, 1½in (4cm) high.
£15–20
$20–30 ⊞ EMP

A horn bracelet, with plain overlapping discs, c1860, 1¼in (3cm) wide.
£20–25
$30–35 ⊞ EMP

A pair of Whitby jet drop earrings, with swing bob, c1860, 3in (7.5cm) long.
£115–125
$170–180 ⊞ EMP

▶ **A Whitby jet locket,** with deep carving to both sides, c1860, 1½in (4cm) high.
£100–115
$145–165 ⊞ EMP

▶ **A pair of French jet earrings,** c1860, 2in (5cm) long.
£225–250
$320–360 ⊞ AM

Different types of Jet

Whitby Jet, made from fossilized wood, has been used for jewellery since ancient times but it was not until the mid-19th century that it became highly fashionable. It is hand-carved, lightweight and warm to the touch. As the industry flourished, various man-made alternatives were developed, which are described below.

- **Vulcanite** is a compound of rubber and sulphur invented by Goodyear (tyres) in 1846. It is moulded and tends to have a brownish tinge, sometimes even khaki coloured, due to exposure to light.
- **French jet** is a black glass with a heavy, cold feel. The beads are generally shiny and black in appearance but some display a dull crêpe or satinized finish that is very attractive to the eye.
- **Vauxhall glass** is a black glass mounted on metal with a surprising lightness in design and weight, but cold to the touch as would be expected.
- **Bog oak jet** is a fossilized wood that has been compressed in Irish peat bogs and has a dull finish. Lightweight and warm to the touch, it is not as finely carved as Whitby jet.
- **Bois Durci** is a 19th-century compound of compressed wood powder painted black, sometimes with paste decoration.
- **Horn,** used by prehistoric man for essentials, survived to the Victorian age when fashion dyed it black. It can be distinguished by observing compacted hair showing through minor cracks on the backs of objects. It is dull in appearance.

A Whitby jet carved knot brooch, c1860, 3in (7.5cm) wide.
£135–150
$200–220 ⊞ EMP

A Whitby jet faceted bar bracelet, on elastic, c1870, 1½in (4cm) wide.
£50–60
$80–90 ⊞ EMP

A Whitby jet cameo, carved with a Grecian female head within a floral ribbon border, c1870, 2½in (6.5cm) diam.
£115–125
$170–180 ⊞ EMP

A jet bracelet, c1875, 1in (2.5cm) wide.
£145–165
$200–240 ⊞ AM

▶ **A jet crucifix,** late 19thC, 2½in (6.5cm) long.
£50–55
$70–80 ⊞ AM

A jet necklace with locket, c1880, 16in (40.5cm) long.
£270–300
$400–440 ⊞ AM

A French jet brooch, c1880, 4¾in (12cm) long.
£80–90
$115–135 ⊞ AM

A Whitby jet chain necklace, with floral pendant, c1880, 18in (45.5cm) long.
£225–250
$320–360 ⊞ EMP

A Whitby jet carved floral brooch, c1880, 2in (5cm) diam.
£160–175
$230–260 ⊞ EMP

A Whitby jet box, carved with a bird among ivy leaves, c1880, 2in (5cm) wide.
£130–145
$200–220 ⊞ EMP

A Whitby jet faceted graduated bead necklace, restrung, modern fastening, c1880, 32in (81.5cm) long.
£160–175
$230–260 ⊞ EMP

A pair of Vauxhall glass faceted bracelets, forming a choker necklace when linked, c1880, 1in (2.5cm) wide.
£90–100
$130–150 ⊞ EMP

▶ **A French jet black glass necklace,** with tassel, c1880, 32in (81.5cm) long.
£70–75
$100–110 ⊞ EMP

A **vulcanite bracelet,** carved with a rose, c1880, 2in (5cm) wide.
£35–40
$50–60 ⊞ EMP

A **Bois Durci brooch,** set with paste stones, c1880, 2in (5cm) wide.
£35–40
$50–60 ⊞ EMP

A **bog oak brooch,** carved with a rose, thistle, leek and shamrock to represent England, Scotland, Wales and Ireland, c1880, 3in (7.5cm) wide.
£90–100
$130–150 ⊞ EMP

A **French jet choker,** c1890, 17in (43cm) long.
£100–125
$145–175 ⊞ AM

A **pair of French jet beaded epaulettes,** c1890, 7in (18cm) wide.
£70–90
$100–130 ⊞ AM

◀ A **vulcanite pendant,** carved with a female head and shoulders, 1900s, 2½in (6.5cm) high.
£100–125
$145–175 ⊞ LBe

Jewellery Sets

An **18ct gold brooch and earrings set,** with rope and ball applied decoration and tassel drop, the brooch reverse with a locket, c1850, brooch 1½in (4cm) high.
£750–800
$1,000–1,200 ⊞ AMC

A **Miriam Haskell tassel lariat necklace and earrings set,** the necklace designed to be knotted or hung around the neck, 1950s, necklace 40in (101.5cm) long.
£250–275
$350–400 ⊞ CRIS

A **Weiss black and white *faux* diamond brooch and earrings set,** American, c1950, brooch 2in (5cm) high.
£160–180
$230–260 ⊞ LaF

A **plastic and gilt pendant and bracelet set,** 1950s–60s, pendant 3in (7.5cm) long.
£45–50
$65–75 ⊞ SBL

▶ A **sterling silver necklace and earrings set,** Danish, c1960.
£300–350
$450–500 ⊞ DID

Men's Accessories

Cufflinks are a relatively recent addition to the average male wardrobe. In the 1600s, sleeves were tied with a piece of ribbon. The late 17th century saw the introduction of the 'sleeve button': matching jewelled buttons, attached by a small chain. These were the preserve of the rich and only in the Victorian period, with the combination of an expanding middle class, cheaper production methods, and the evolution of the modern shirt cuff, did cufflinks become more available.

Whilst Victorian designs were comparatively restrained, the 20th century saw a wealth of shapes and patterns. Fashion leaders such as Edward VII and his grandson Edward VIII helped popularize this form of male jewellery and cufflinks were produced in every style. While some links will be marked with the name of a maker, unless this is a jeweller of some significance, value tends to depend above all on shape and medium. Not just the front, but the backs of cufflinks came in different designs. Some are linked by chains or loops, other have a solid baton designed for pushing through the shirt cuff with one hand. Before buying, the condition of both sides should be checked.

A Victorian 9ct rose gold watch chain, 16in (40.5cm) long.
£480–520
$700–750 ⊞ AnS

A set of six ruby and faceted glass dress studs, each with a circular-cut ruby, 19thC.
£250–300
$350–450 ⋟ Bea(E)

A pair of Art Deco ruby and diamond mounted cufflinks, with matching stud and a set of three ruby and diamond mounted studs.
£650–700
$900–1,000 ⋟ Bea(E)

◀ **A pair of sterling silver cufflinks,** modelled as American TV cameras, made for the TV industry, 1950s.
£85–95
$125–145 ⊞ SpM

▶ **A metal tie pin,** modelled as a sword, 1950s, 3in (7.5cm) long.
£5–6
$8–12 ⊞ Mo

◀ **A 9ct gold tie clip,** with safety chain, 1985, 2in (5cm) long.
£70–80
$100–120 ⊞ BND

A pair of Courage Brewery gilded brass advertising cufflinks, modelled as cockerels, 1950–60.
£30–40
$40–60 ⊞ JBB

▶ **A pair of rolled gold on base metal working watch cufflinks,** German, 1950s–60s, 1¼in (3cm) wide.
£85–95
$125–145 ⊞ SpM

Necklaces

An Art Nouveau 15ct gold pendant/brooch, set with amethysts and pearls, 1890–1910, 1½in (4cm) high.
£325–350
$450–500 ⊞ AMC

A Victorian faceted amber necklace, Baltic, 17in (43cm) long.
£50–60
$70–90 ⊞ Ma

An Art Nouveau silver and moonstone pendant, c1900.
£280–330
$400–480 ⊞ ASA

An Art Nouveau silver and enamelled pendant, turquoise, blue, red and yellow, stamped 'M.B.', Birmingham 1908, 1in (2.5cm) high.
£170–200
$250–300 ⋊ DD

A dark blue glass and aventurine bead necklace, with two pendant beads and barrel fastening, 1920s–30s, 17in (43cm) long.
£30–35
$40–50 ⊞ DEC

An Art Deco chrome and red Bakelite necklace, Germany, c1930, 15in (38cm) long.
£110–130
$160–190 ⊞ LaF

▶ **A marble and crackle-style green glass necklace,** 1940s, 14in (35.5cm) long.
£10–12
$15–18 ⊞ STP

◀ **A diamanté necklace,** set with four rectangular blue paste stones, 1950s, 14in (35.5cm) long.
£10–15
$15–20 ⊞ STP

A Christian Dior starburst crystal and pearl necklace, by Mitchell Mayer, 1951–54, 5in (12.5cm) wide.
£650–750
$900–1,000 ⊞ LaF

A red enamel and gilt necklace, 1950s, 2½in (6.5cm) wide.
£35–40
$50–60 ⊞ SBL

▶ **A Gloria Vanderbilt gilt choker,** with central paste inset, American, 1980s, 15in (38cm) long.
£40–50
$60–80 ⊞ SBL

Kitchenware

A bronze skillet, by Warner, c1840, 5in (12.5cm) long.
£300–350
$450–500 ⊞ **SEA**

A set of three copper saucepans, with steel handles, 19thC, 14in (35.5cm) long.
£130–150
$200–220 ↗ **WBH**

A wire potato basket, early 19thC, 18in (45.5cm) diam.
£45–50
$65–75 ⊞ **SMI**

◀ **A green glass fly-trap,** 19thC, 7in (18cm) high.
£250–275
$350–400 ⊞ **SEA**

▶ **A brass jam-making pan,** c1870, 11in (28cm) diam.
£85–95
$125–140 ⊞ **AL**

A metal cafetière, c1900, 14in (35.5cm) high.
£80–90
$115–130 ⊞ **B&R**

A set of tin pastry cutters, in a conical tin, c1890, 6½in (16.5cm) long.
£25–30
$35–50 ⊞ **AL**

▶ **A cast-iron Family Scale weighing machine,** with enamel face, 1920, 13in (33cm) high.
£140–170
$200–250 ⊞ **SMI**

A wooden egg box, c1920, 14in (35.5cm) wide.
£70–80
$100–115 ⊞ SMI

A Matador brass and green enamel paraffin cooker, c1930, 17in (43cm) wide.
£45–55
$65–80 ⊞ AL

► A collection of bisque cake decoration figures, c1930, largest 3in (7.5cm) high.
£40–60
$60–90 each
⊞ AL

A blue enamelled tin cafetière, decorated with hand-painted flowers, Belgian, 1930, 10in (25.5cm) high.
£80–90
$115–130 ⊞ B&R

An Eagle cast-iron and enamel range, 1936, 63in (160cm) high.
£2,000–2,250
$3,000–3,300 ⊞ WRe

A Tala blue plastic vegetable rack, with white baskets, c1960, 30in (76cm) high.
£30–35
$45–50 ⊞ AL

Ceramics

A slipware baking dish, decorated in brown and yellow, Welsh, 19thC, 15in (38cm) wide.
£180–200
$260–300 ⊞ CoA

A pottery colander, decorated in beige and white, c1890, 11in (28cm) diam.
£35–40
$50–60 ⊞ AL

◄ A pottery sugar jar, decorated in greens and browns, Scottish, late 19thC, 10in (25.5cm) high.
£90–100
$130–145 ⊞ B&R

► A Lord Mayor's Pudding Basin, white with black inscription, early 20thC, 8½in (21.5cm) diam.
£70–80
$100–115 ⊞ B&R

A Kent's Improved Monroes Patent Egg Beater and Batter Mixer, with blue inscription on the reverse, repaired, late 19thC, 9in (23cm) high.
£150–170
$220–250 ⊞ B&R

A Bretby blue and white Cream of Tartar jar, c1900, 4in (10cm) high.
£30–35
$45–50 ⊞ B&R

A brown salt-glazed soup jar, decorated with a turtle, c1920, 8in (20.5cm) high.
£90–100
$130–145 ⊞ SMI

A Pyrita red pottery egg separator, c1920, 4in (10cm) diam.
£8–10
$12–15 ⊞ AL

Three ceramic storage jars, with wooden lids, decorated in blue with black lettering, 1930s, 7in (18cm) high.
£25–30
$35–45 each ⊞ AL

A T. G. Green Easi-mix white pottery bowl, with blue interior, 1950, 10in (25.5cm) diam.
£20–25
$30–35 ⊞ AL

A Homepride 'Fred' ceramic condiment set, the salt and pepper pots modelled as flour bags, 1970s, 4½in (11.5cm) high.
£55–60
$80–90 🔨 BBR

Choppers

A steel herb chopper, with wooden handle, late 19thC, 5½in (14cm) wide.
£40–45
$60–65 ⊞ B&R

A steel herb chopper, with a wooden handle, late 19thC, 11in (28cm) wide.
£25–30
$35–45 ⊞ B&R

A steel herb chopper, by S. C. J. Clark, with a wooden handle and heart and star design, c1880, 8in (20.5cm) wide.
£120–140
$175–200 ⊞ SMI

> **Cross Reference**
> See Colour Review (page 235)

A steel herb chopper, with a brass and wood handle, c1880, 5in (12.5cm) wide.
£70–80
$100–115 ⊞ SMI
Although much 19th-century kitchen metalware and cutlery were mass-produced in large industrial centres such as Sheffield, herb choppers were often handmade by local craftsmen. Designs therefore could be idiosyncratic and today the more decorative the piece the higher the value.

◀ **A steel herb chopper,** with a wooden handle and birds design, c1880, 9in (23cm) wide.
£90–100
$130–145 ⊞ SMI

Dairying

This section shows the huge wealth of products developed for dairying, from 19th-century yokes and wooden bowls, to 1960s aluminium milk churns. The majority of objects, however, dates from the Victorian and Edwardian periods. Many are connected with the manufacture of butter. Milk would first be cooled in a setting dish.

The cream would be taken off with a metal skimmer and left to mature for 48 hours. It would then be churned – examples illustrated include a plunger churn and a box churn operated by a crank handle – the butter would then be washed in cold water, squeezed and beaten to get rid of excess moisture, and worked with butter pats. The correct amount of butter would be weighed on butter scales (often wooden) and the pats were marked with stamps, both for decoration and to distinguish the produce of a specific dairy.

A brass cream skimmer, with steel handle, mid-19thC, 23in (58.5cm) long.
£150–170
$220–250 ⊞ NEW

A wooden butter moulding box, with floral carving to interior base, Scandinavian, mid-19thC, 7in (18cm) square.
£110–130
$160–200 ⊞ NEW

▶ **A wooden dairy yoke,** 1890–1900, 31in (78.5cm) long.
£40–45
$60–65 ⊞ AL

A pair of green cast-iron butter/cheese scales, with ceramic platter, c1900, 18in (45.5cm) wide.
£90–100
$130–145 ⊞ B&R

A sycamore dairy bowl, c1880, 17in (43cm) diam.
£250–300
$360–440 ⊞ SMI

A pair of sycamore dairy scales, from the Gower peninsula, Welsh, 19thC, 20in (51cm) high.
£250–280
$360–400 ⊞ CoA

A set of three sycamore butter prints, with bird designs, c1900, largest 5in (12.5cm) diam.
£70–80
$100–115 ⊞ SMI

▶ **A steel and brass cream can,** Scottish, c1900, 6in (15cm) high.
£175–200
$250–290 ⊞ SMI

A steel milk bucket, with brass label, c1900, 20in (51cm) high.
£150–175
$220–250 ⊞ B&R

Miller's is a price GUIDE not a price LIST

A ceramic butter dish, with wooden surround, transfer-printed with the verse 'The Trusty Servant', 1900–25, 6in (15cm) diam.
£25–30
$35–45 ⊞ MGC

A clear pressed glass butter dish, decorated with a cow, c1930, 5in (12.5cm) wide.
£50–60
$75–90 ⊞ MRW

A wooden and tin butter box, by the Dairy Supply Co, marked 'The Iceberg', c1900, 7½in (19cm) wide.
£170–185
$250–270 ⊞ B&R

A wooden rounded box butter churn, with crank handle, bound with iron, c1910, 20in (51cm) high.
£70–80
$100–115 ⊞ DFA

Two white ceramic milk beakers, inscribed 'New Milk', c1920, 4in (10cm) high.
£45–50
$65–75 ⊞ SMI

A tin cheese mould, French, c1930, 3½in (9cm) diam.
£8–10
$12–15 ⊞ AL

A wooden plunger butter churn, bound with iron, c1900, 23in (58.5cm) high.
£100–120
$145–175 ⊞ DFA

A white ceramic butter slab, inscribed 'Bartlett & Son, Limited, Bristol', early 20thC, 12½in (32cm) diam.
£220–250
$320–360 ⊞ B&R

▶ A white ceramic dairy thermometer, c1920, 14in (35.5cm) long.
£180–200
$260–290 ⊞ SMI

Three aluminium milk churns, 1960s, 38in (96.5cm) high.
£30–40
$45–60 ⊞ A&H

Enamel Bins & Tins

Two white enamel Flour and Meal bins, with red lettering, c1900, 11½in (29cm) high.
£30–40
$45–60 each ⊞ B&R

A white enamel Cakes bin, with black lettering, early 20thC, 14½in (37cm) wide.
£40–50
$60–75 ⊞ B&R

A white enamel Scribbans's Purity Bread bin, with black lettering, early 20thC, 12in (30.5cm) high.
£50–70
$75–100 ⊞ B&R

A tin Demerara barrel, decorated in brown combed paint, with black lettering, early 20thC, 15in (38cm) high.
£100–125
$145–180 ⊞ B&R

A green Tapioca tin, with gold lettering, c1910, 6in (15cm) high.
£8–10
$12–15 ⊞ AL

A tin Flour barrel, with original brown paint and black lettering, c1920, 24in (61cm) high.
£225–250
$325–360 ⊞ SMI

A Rice tin, light green with yellow lettering, c1930, 6in (15cm) high.
£10–12
$15–20 ⊞ AL

Kettles

A brass toddy kettle, with a ceramic handle, Scottish, c1850, 9in (23cm) high.
£220–240
$320–350 ⊞ SEA

A copper kettle, c1780, 9in (23cm) high.
£240–280
$350–410 ⊞ SEA

A Victorian copper kettle, 17in (43cm) high.
£220–250
$320–360 ➚ WBH

> Items in the Kitchenware section have been arranged in date order within each sub-section.

A brass kettle, with a wooden handle, on a filigree stand with paw feet, c1820, 17in (43cm) high.
£400–450
$580–650 ⊞ SEA

▶ **Two cast-iron kettles,** one with a brass handle, c1890, largest 6in (15cm) high.
£110–125
$160–180 each ⊞ SMI

Laundry & Housework

A maid's brass can, c1890, 10½in (26.5cm) high.
£65–75
$95–110 ⊞ AL

A Beetall cast-iron gas steam iron, with wooden handle, c1880, 11in (28cm) long.
£125–150
$180–220 ⊞ SMI

A Waine wood and steel clothes mangle, c1910, 24in (61cm) wide.
£130–150
$190–200 ⊞ FST

A W. C. Nixey's Black Lead wooden box, c1920s, 10in (25.5cm) wide.
£18–22
$26–32 ⊞ B&R

A wicker washing basket, with wooden pegs, 1920s, 9in (23cm) diam.
£35–45
$50–65 ⊞ SMI

▶ **A Lloyd Loom linen basket,** with original green and gold paint, dated June 1934, 27in (69cm) high.
£75–95
$110–140 ⊞ NET

Moulds

A tin and copper mould, late 19thC, 6in (15cm) wide.
£70–80
$100–115 ⊞ **B&R**

A tin chocolate mould, in the shape of a skier, c1900, 5½in (14cm) high.
£80–90
$115–130 ⊞ **B&R**

▶ **A tin chocolate mould,** in the shape of a fish, by Anton Reich, German, c1910, 10¼in (26cm) wide.
£90–100
$130–150
⊞ **MSB**

◀ **A tin chocolate mould,** in the shape of six lobsters, by Anton Reich, German, c1930, 6¾in (17cm) wide.
£120–135
$175–195
⊞ **MSB**

A copper castellated jelly mould, 19thC, 4½in (11.5cm) diam.
£220–250
$320–360 ⊞ **SEA**

A pewter ice-cream mould, in the shape of a pear, c1900, 7¾in (19.5cm) high.
£520–580
$760–850 ⊞ **MSB**

A Copeland ceramic mould, in the shape of a pineapple, 1890, slight damage, 7in (18cm) wide.
£50–55
$75–80 ⊞ **B&R**

A Mrs Olive's Plum Pudding ceramic mould, c1900, 7in (18cm) diam.
£90–100
$130–145 ⊞ **SMI**

A pale yellow ceramic jelly mould, c1910, 3in (7.5cm) high.
£20–25
$30–35 ⊞ **AL**

A pewter ice-cream mould, in the shape of a bunch of asparagus, c1930s, 3in (7.5cm) high.
£90–100
$130–150 ⊞ **MSB**

Utensils

A brass fish slice, early 18thC, 17in (43cm) long.
£270–300
$400–440 ⊞ SEA

A wrought-iron toasting fork, 1780, 20in (51cm) long.
£160–190
$230–275 ⊞ SEA

A brass clockwork bottle jack,
c1850, 25in (63.5cm) long.
£110–125
$160–180 ⊞ FST

A cast-iron apple peeling machine,
with table clamp mounting, the cast
top cover with detailed inscription
'Made only by the Reading
Hardware Co., Reading Pa...' 1869,
12½in (36cm) high.
£60–70
$90–100 ⋏ DN
Numerous patented mechanical
kitchen devices were developed
in the 19th century.

A steel whisk,
c1880, 10½in
(26.5cm) long.
£25–30
$35–45 ⊞ SMI

A wrought-iron roasting fork, c1770, 22in (56cm) long.
£160–190
$230–275 ⊞ SEA

A steel cheese scope,
c1780, 7in (18cm) long.
£250–275
$350–400 ⊞ SEA

◀ **A brass ladle,** 19thC,
14in (35.5cm) long.
£130–150
$190–220 ⊞ SEA

▶ **A copper ale muller,**
c1850, 11in (28cm) high.
£150–175
$220–255 ⊞ SEA

A cast-iron sugar cutter, the arm with foliate decoration
and turned wooden handle, the base with brass maker's
plaque for 'W. Bullock & Co Patent', registration
diamond for 15 July 1869, 14¼in (36cm) long.
£30–40
$45–60 ⋏ DN

A Victorian metal can opener, in the shape of a bull,
with kite mark, 6in (15cm) long.
£15–18
$20–25 ⊞ JOL

A cast-iron coffee mill, by W. Bullock & Co, c1880, 6in (15cm) high.
£125–150
$180–220 ⊞ SMI

▶ **A tin nutmeg grater,** early 1920s, 7in (18cm) long.
£55–65
$80–95 ⊞ SMI

A Holborn cast-iron lemon squeezer, with ceramic jug, c1880, 10in (25.5cm) high.
£175–200
$255–290 ⊞ SMI

A tin folding grater, c1930, 9½in (24cm) high.
£6–8
$8–10 ⊞ AL

Miller's is a price GUIDE not a price LIST

Wood

A wooden galette turner, French, c1800, 21in (53.5cm) long.
£18–22
$25–30 ⊞ B&R

A bentwood box, probably for food storage, with stamped circular decoration, Swedish, early 19thC, 9in (23cm) wide.
£110–130
$160–190 ⊞ NEW

An elm pie peel, Welsh, 19thC, 30in (76cm) long.
£135–155
$195–225 ⊞ MFB
A peel is a long-handled shovel used by bakers.

A fruitwood apple rack, c1880, 33in (84cm) wide.
£110–125
$160–180 ⊞ MLL

A lignum vitae pestle, c1900, 19in (48.5cm) long.
£60–65
$90–95 ⊞ AL

A boxwood rolling pin, c1900, 18in (45.5cm) long.
£50–60
$75–90 ⊞ SMI

A wooden oatmeal roller, early 1920s, 19in (48.5cm) long.
£40–50
$60–75 ⊞ SMI

A sycamore biscuit roller, Scottish, c1900, 5in (12.5cm) diam.
£70–80
$100–115 ⊞ SMI

A carved sycamore breadboard, c1920, 6in (15cm) diam.
£70–80
$100–115 ⊞ SMI

A wooden one gallon grain measure, with steel banding, early 20thC, 8in (20.5cm) high.
£50–60
$75–90 ⊞ NEW

Prices

The price ranges quoted in this book reflect the average price a purchaser might expect to pay for a similar item from a similar source. The price will vary according to the condition, rarity, size, popularity, provenance, colour and restoration of the item, and this must be taken into account when assessing values. Don't forget that if you are selling it is quite likely that you will be offered less than the price range.

◄ A wooden egg rack, early 1920s, 12in (30.5cm) wide.
£60–70
$90–100 ⊞ SMI

A set of four silver-plated knives and forks, with carved wooden handles, c1920.
£45–50
$65–75 ⊞ SMI

► A wood and chrome biscuit barrel, 1940s, 9¾in (25cm) high.
£8–10
$12–15 ⊞ UTP

Lighting

A brass Corinthian column and Burmese glass oil lamp, with crimped domed shade and wrythen font, 19thC, 18in (45.5cm) high.
£160–200
$230–300 ✦ GAK

A Benson brass and copper oil lamp, with original lacquer finish, contemporary Powell spiral shade, original Hinks oil burner and Benson sump, c1900, 30in (75.2cm) high.
£850–950
$1,250–1,400 ⊞ HUN

A Victorian Staffordshire pottery oil lamp, with glass chimney and etched frosted glass shade, the reservoir decorated with chrysanthemums in red and blue on a white ground, the fittings made by Hinks & Sons, 22½in (57cm) high.
£320–360
$450–550 ✦ RTo

An opalescent glass hanging light, with brass chains, 1890–1910, 11in (28cm) diam.
£300–400
$450–580 ⊞ ASA

An Art Nouveau copper lamp, with domed quatrefoil above the circular base and a broad loop handle, unmarked, c1890, 14¼in (36cm) high.
£250–280
$350–400 ✦ P(B)

A copper lantern, with original crackle glass liner, c1910, 20in (51cm) high.
£450–500
$650–720 ⊞ CHA

An Art Nouveau brass and copper table lamp, c1900, 26in (66cm) high.
£150–250
$220–360 ⊞ ASA

A hanging brass gas lamp, with cranberry glass shade, 1890–1910, 31in (78.5cm) high.
£140–160
$200–230 ⊞ JW

A pair of hanging lights, shaped as bunches of grapes, Italian, c1910, 11in (28cm) high.
£1,100–1,200
$1,600–1,750 ⊞ OLA

A pair of brass two-arm wall sconces, c1910, 10in (25.5cm) high.
£140–160
$200–230 ⊞ JW

A desk lamp, with shell-shaped brass shade, flexible arm and black cast-iron base, 1920s, 13in (33cm) high.
£90–110
$130–160 ⊞ LIB

An Art Deco spelter table lamp, with marble-effect fan-shaped glass shade supported by a nude figure of a woman, 15in (38cm) high.
£300–350
$450–500 ⚒ SWO

► **An Art Deco bronze lamp,** modelled as a Chinese pheasant, painted in naturalistic colours, c1925, 22in (56cm).
£225–245
$320–350 ⊞ KA

LOCATE THE SOURCE

The source of each illustration in Miller's can be found by checking the code letters below each caption with the Key to Illustrations, pages 444–452.

► **A Bakelite desk lamp,** 1930s, 12in (30.5cm) high.
£125–145
$180–200 ⊞ ZOOM

A hanging lamp, with brass gallery, chain and ceiling rose and pink-frosted glass shade, 1920s, 15in (38cm) long
£130–150
$200–220 ⊞ LIB

A Lorraine glass lamp, designed by Pierre Davesn, with cream fabric shade, 1929–33, 13in (33cm) high.
£115–130
$160–180 ⊞ KA

A ceramic lamp, modelled as a dog in shades of brown, with glass eyes, 1930s, 7½in (19cm) high.
£165–185
$250–270 ⊞ LBe

An Art Deco chrome table lamp, with dancing nude support, 19in (48cm) high.
£90–100
$130–150 ⊞ ZOOM

◄ **A chandelier,** by Gino Sarfatti for Arteluce, Italian, 1953, 26in (66cm) high.
£400–500
$580–720 ⊞ MARK

The Italian designer Gino Sarfatti (1912–85) trained as an aeronautical engineer and founded Arteluce in 1939. Sarfatti won major awards for his lamp designs in the 1950s and his company made an important contribution to the development of post-war lighting in Italy.

An extendable desk lamp, by Ferdinand Solère, with chrome shade and stem, French, 1950s, 23in (58.5cm) high.
£125–150
$180–220 ⊞ ZOOM

A pair of chrome wall lights, by Castiglioni for Flos, Italian, 1960s, 15in (38cm) wide.
£300–350
$450–500 ⊞ ZOOM

◄ **A Perspex and glass Plastacrush Dream lamp,** 1970s, 19½in (49.5cm) high.
£35–45
$50–65 ⊞ FLD

Candlesticks

A brass chamberstick, with snuffer and wick trimmer, c1800, 5in (12.5cm) high.
£425–475
$620–700 ⊞ SEA

► **A tin candle mould,** c1900, 10½in (26.5cm) high.
£100–125
$145–180 ⊞ B&R

► **An adjustable cast-iron candlestick,** French, early 19thC, 8in (20.5cm) high.
£80–90
$115–130 ⊞ B&R

A pair of brass piano sconces, c1910, 9½in (24cm) wide.
£130–150
$190–220 ⊞ MURR

A pair of copper-mounted wooden candlesticks, by A. E. Jones, c1900, 8½in (21cm) high.
£325–375
$470–550 ⊞ SHA

A pair of Benson brass tripod candlesticks, with trefid toes and six-point copper leaf drip pans, unmarked, 1902, 7in (18cm) high.
£650–750
$950–1,100 ⊞ HUN

◄ **A pair of brass candlesticks,** modelled as Felix the Cat, c1920, 8in (20.5cm) high.
£200–250
$300–360 ⊞ MURR

Lanterns

▶ **A miner's brass and polished steel lamp,** made by The Protector Lamp & Lighting Co for the Ministry of Power, c1890–1900, 10in (25.5cm) high.
£90–100
$130–150 ⊞ MRW

A pottery lantern, with reeded loop handle, the body pierced with small holes, probably Iranian, 11th–12thC, 9in (23cm) high.
£165–185
$240–270 ⊞ CrF

A lady's brass extending reading lantern, Dutch, c1770, 7in (18cm) high.
£600–675
$870–1,000 ⊞ SEA

A bull's eye lamp, 1920s, 4in (10cm) high.
£30–35
$45–50 ⊞ GAC

▶ **A Lucas self-generating brass carbide lamp,** 1910, 10in (25.5cm) wide.
£500–600
$720–870
⊞ JUN

▶ **A pair of brass and copper mast-head lights,** c1930s, 19in (48.5cm) high.
£550–600
$800–870 ⊞ AOY

Nightlights & Fairylights

A glass nightlight, the monk's head in green satin glass on a clear satin glass base, 19thC, 4¼in (11cm) high.
£375–425
$550–620 ⚒ BBR

A Pearline fairylight, the blue shade on a matching petalled Pearline No. 24 base, registered number 176239, 1891, 4¼in (11cm) high.
£30–40
$45–60 ⚒ BBR

An amethyst glass nightlight, in the form of Edward VII, with ground top, registered number 298585, damaged, 1897, 4¼in (11cm) high.
£30–40
$45–60 ⚒ BBR

Medals
Commemorative

A silver medal, awarded by the Royal Humane Society to John Dymond for restoring the health of Sarah Binder, with contemporary suspension loop, 1777, 2¾in (7cm) diam.
£400–500
$580–720 ✦ DNW

<table>
<tr><td>Cross Reference
See Crime
(page 174–175)</td></tr>
</table>

A white metal medal, commemorating the price riot at Covent Garden Opera House, 1809, 1¾in (45mm) diam.
£40–50
$60–75 ⊞ TML
The riots started with the opening of the New Covent Garden Theatre by J. P. Kemble, who increased prices of admission. This lasted about three months until the old prices were restored.

A white metal medal, by T. Wyon, commemorating the Battle of the Nile, 1798.
£100–125
$145–180 ⊞ TML

An engraved cartwheel penny, depicting Henry Fauntleroy, inscribed 'Fauntleroy, the Robber of Widows and Orphans, Executed at Newgate' and 'Such be the Fate of all Insolvent Bilking Bankers and Agents', the reverse a cartwheel penny, 1824, 1½in (36mm) diam.
£225–250
$320–360 ⊞ TML
Banker Henry Fauntleroy (1785–1824) was found guilty of forging signatures over a ten year period, and according to the contemporary press, misappropriated trust funds worth c£25,000 ($36,250) much of which he spent on gambling and mistresses. Though Fauntleroy pleaded his innocence, he was sentenced to execution and a crowd of 100,000 people were reported to have attended his hanging at Newgate. These engraved pennies were produced as souvenirs.

A bronze medal, by T. Wyon, commemorating Joseph Hanson, the industrial reformer, with a head of Hanson and the inscription 'The Weaver's Friend, Strangeways Manchester 1810', the reverse with loom, spinning wheel and printing machine within a wreath, 1810, 1¾in (42mm) diam.
£40–50
$60–75 ⊞ TML
Hanson was imprisoned and fined for acts on behalf of the Luddites. About forty thousand subscribers each contributed one penny to a fund set up to help him.

A silver medal, commemorating the great flood, depicting a swollen river and broken bridge, the reverse inscribed 'Presented by the Central Committee for the Flood Fund to Hugh Wright, Findhorn as an Honorary Reward for the Courage and Humanity shewn at the Great Flood, August 4th 1829', with claw and double loop suspension, 1829, 1¼in (3cm) diam.
£300–350
$450–500 ✦ DNW

Cross Reference
See Militaria &
Emergency Services
(page 280–288)

A Society for the Protection of Life from Fire silver medal, depicting an eye within a sunburst with a banner inscribed 'Vigilo', the reverse inscribed 'To Edd. P.C. A65, who at the risk of his own life saved from Death by Fire a person at Marylebone St., May 14th 1840'.
£800–900
$1,200–1,300 ➶ DNW

A silver-gilt and enamel Masonic medal, with past Masters' Jewel, presented to Professor Mohammed Fadel al Jamali, a former Premier of Iraq, presented by the Dar es Salam Lodge, Baghdad, the reverse with engraving, with riband and suspender, 1940–41.
£420–500
$580–720 ➶ Gle

A Brighton and Hove Motor Club medal, for the Brighton Bees Trial, 1933, 1in (25mm) diam, in original box.
£75–85
$110–125 ⊞ BiR

Two medals, awarded to Ronnie O'Hara for rescuing a dog at Middlesbrough docks, one the PDSA Gallantry Cross, gilt-metal and white enamel, the other the RSPCA Life Saving Medal, silver, both cased, together with their named presentation certificates, several newspaper cuttings and the recipient's National Registration Identity Card, 1949.
£600–700
$850–1,000 ➶ DNW

◀ **A prize silver medal,** awarded by the Worcestershire Bull Terrier Club, inscribed on reverse 'to commemorate win of Sporting Parson Cup by Mr Thompson's Dauntless Duchess at Worcester Ch. Show, 21.8.24', 1924, 1¾in (45mcm) diam.
£75–85
$110–125 ⊞ TML

Two May Day badges, one brass, 1934, the other aluminium, German, 1936, 1½in (38mm) diam.
£30–35
$45–50 each ⊞ AnS

▶ **A silvered-bronze medal,** by J. Fray, commemorating the visit of Joseph Chamberlain to South Africa, with a bust of Chamberlain, the reverse with an inscription, 1903, 2in (50mm) diam.
£65–75
$95–110 ⊞ TML

Military

A Military General Service Medal, awarded to J. Hall, 38th Foot, with six bars for Busaco, Badajoz, Salamanca, Vittoria, St Sebastian, Nive, minor repair, 1793–1814.
£700–800
$1,000–1,200 ⚒ Gle

An army medal, awarded to 4815 Pte M. Geoghegan of the King's Own Scottish Borderers, with two bars inscribed 'Cape Colony' and 'Paardeberg', for the Queen's Campaign South Africa, 1900.
£135–150
$200–220 ⊞ RMC

A pair of Queen's South Africa medals, with four bars for Cape Colony, Tugela Heights, Relief of Ladysmith and Transvaal, and King's South Africa with two bars for South Africa 1901 and 1902, re-named to 9258 PO J. Hay, HMS *Powerful.*
£100–120
$150–175 ⚒ PFK
Only three members of the crew of this ship were present at the relief of Ladysmith.

A Queen's South Africa medal, with three bars for Transvaal, Orange Free State and Cape Colony, awarded to J. Donnelly, Royal Fusiliers, 1899–1902.
£100–120
$150–175 ⚒ PFK

A Royal Navy Medal, awarded to M18354 ERAI W. J. R. Vosper of HMS *Pembroke* for long service and good conduct, 1914–18.
£45–50
$65–75 ⊞ RMC

Three Royal Marines medals, the Star, the War Medal and the Victory Medal, awarded to 14843 Pte. S. A. Carpenter of Royal Marine Light Infantry, who survived the sinking of HMS *Louvain* in 1918, 1914–18.
£110–125
$160–180 ⊞ RMC

A group of six WWI medals, Distinguished Service, British War and Victory, Royal Navy Long Service and Good Conduct, awarded to Gunner H. C. E. Callaway, Royal Marines Artillery, 1914–18.
£1,100–1,300
$1,600–1,900 ⚒ Gle

A group of five WWII medals, Distinguished Flying, 1939–45 Star, Air Crew Europe Star, Defence Medal, War Medal, awarded to Sgt A. Massey, Royal Air Force, 1939–45.
£850–950
$1,250–1,400 ⚒ Gle

A group of four WWII medals, 1939–45 Star, Atlantic Star Bar, War medal, French Medal of Honour, awarded to G. Billett, mounted as worn, 1939–45.
£120–135
$175–200 ⊞ RMC

A group of five WWII medals, the India General Service, General Service, Long Service, Good Conduct, Defence and War and British Empire, awarded to Warrant Officer Albert Kirman, with Warrant dated November 1962, his certificate of service and copies of photographs.
£300–340
$450–500 ⚒ HOLL

Militaria & Emergency Services

A teak military chest, with two short and three long drawers and recessed brass handles, 19thC, 35¾in (91cm) wide.
£1,000–1,200
$1,500–1,750 ⚲ WilP

▶ A WWI Trench Art miniature coal scuttle, made from a shell case, 1914–18, 6in (15cm) wide.
£40–50
$60–75 ⊞ AnS

▶ An iron-bound water barrel, with two wooden plugs and iron carrying handle, as used by soldiers, 19thC, 10in (25.5cm) wide.
£160–180
$230–260
⊞ ASB

▶ A Mississippi 41st Army bandsman's mace, silver-mounted, marked London, c1950s, 56in (142cm) long.
£1,200–1,500
$1,750–2,150
⊞ Q&C

Badges, Plates & Uniforms

A Victorian 2nd East Riding of Yorkshire Royal Garrison of Artillery Volunteers officer's sable bearskin, together with an Edwardian home-pattern service helmet in blue cloth and case, formerly the property of Capt H. Hall.
£1,300–1,400
$1,900–2,000 ⊞ Q&C

Items in the Militaria & Emergency Services section have been arranged in date order within each sub-section.

A Victorian Queensland Scottish Regiment other ranks' white metal helmet plate, Australian, mid- to late 19thC.
£160–200
$230–300 ⚲ WAL

A Victorian Middlesex Regiment officer's helmet, 1880, 11in (28cm) high.
£350–450
$500–650 ⊞ CYA

◀ A 3rd (Prince of Wales) Dragoon Guards NCO's silver arm badge, hollow construction, some wear, 1887.
£160–200
$230–300 ⚲ WAL

A 95th Saskatchewan Rifles officer's silver-plated pouch belt badge, by J. R. Gaunt, Montreal, pre-1914.
£220–250
$320–360 ✗ WAL

A manufacturer's pattern for a 2nd Battalion The Lincolnshire Regiment pouch belt badge, with WW1 battle honours on a silver-plated backplate, possibly by Ludlows.
£330–360
$470–520 ✗ WAL

An 11th (Lonsdale) Battalion The Border Regiment other ranks' brass cap badge, 1914–18.
£110–130
$160–190 ✗ WAL

A Life Guards officer's uniform, all named or initialled to R. L. Loyd, Lt 16th Lancers 1914, Capt 1st Life Guards 1919, c1925.
£600–700
$870–1,000 ✗ WAL

An Egyptian Port Said pith helmet, 1939–45.
£75–85
$110–125 ⊞ UCO

A German military tropical helmet, 1939–45.
£175–195
$255–275 ⊞ UCO

A German despatch rider's helmet, 1937.
£250–280
$360–400 ⊞ UCO

▶ **A black ostrich-feather bonnet of the Black Watch Regiment,** with red cockade, 1945–95.
£250–300
$360–440 ⊞ UCO

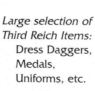

A bearskin of the Welsh Guards, of bamboo basket construction, with white and green cockade, 1950–60.
£250–300
$360–440 ⊞ UCO

Four Home Service helmets, with regional badges, 1960s.
£175–225
$255–325 each ⊞ Q&C

Edged Weapons

A broad-bladed hand-and-a-half sword, with wooden leather-covered grip, c1450–1500, blade 29½in (75cm) long.
£3,200–3,500
$4,500–5,000 ⊞ GV

An American officer's spontoon head, stamped with maker's name 'Marsh', from the period of the American War of Independence, c1775–80, 10in (25.5cm) long.
£500–560
$725–825 ⊞ ASB

A Victorian 2nd Cinque Ports Artillery Volunteers officer's 1821 pattern sword, the blade by Ravenscroft of London, in original steel scabbard c1875.
£300–350
$450–500 ⚔ WAL

A Victorian 1857 pattern cavalry trooper's sword and scabbard, the three-bar hilt with compressed leather grips, blade 35½in (90cm) long.
£250–275
$360–400 ⊞ GV

A Royal Horse Guards basket-hilt sword, engraved with crown, 'GR', and 'Harvey', with original fishskin grip, slight damage, dated 1759, blade 38in (96.5cm) long.
£2,000–2,400
$3,000–3,500 ⊞ WSA

A Victorian Royal Horse Guards officer's 1874 pattern sword, in original brass-mounted scabbard with leather cover, blade 38½in (98cm) long.
£600–700
$870–1,000 ⚔ WAL

◀ **A 2nd Dragoon Guards 1912 pattern officer's sword,** the blade etched with crowned GVR, Royal arms, regimental badge, 'BAYS' and owner's initial 'F M W-S, c1918, blade 34in (86.5cm).
£650–750
$950–1,100 ⚔ WAL

An Irish officer's single-edged sword, retailed by J. Reed of Dublin, with gilt-brass hilt, original black leather scabbard with gilt-brass mounts, early 19thC, blade 32in (81.5cm) long.
£1,100–1,250
$1,600–1,800 ⊞ ASB
This sword is typical of those carried by infantry officers in Wellington's army.

A Coorg sword Ayda-Katti, with partly chequered horn grip, the single-edged blade stamped 'G F Watson Indian Staff Corps 1896', Malabar, blade 17in (43cm) long.
£270–300
$400–450 ⚔ WAL

Firearms

A gunsmith's brass ladle, with turned wooden handle and stem, c1750, 28in (71cm) long.
£220–250
$320–360 ⊞ SEA
This item was used in the making of lead musket balls.

A brass-mounted powder horn, the brass top with inverted swivel adjustable charger, spring broken, c1810, 11in (28cm) long.
£150–180
$220–260 ⋏ WD

A flintlock blunderbuss, with walnut stock and brass barrel, trigger guard and butt cap, engraved lock inscribed 'Carter', early 19thC, 30in (76cm) long.
£550–650
$800–950 ⋏ CDC

A pistol flask, from a pair of French pistols, with measure cap, c1840, 5in (12.5cm) long.
£350–400
$500–600 ⊞ ARB

A .120 pocket revolver mould, 1850s, 7in (18cm) long.
£85–95
$125–140 ⊞ SPA

A flintlock Sea Service pistol, with walnut fullstock, regulation brass furniture, the 12in (30.5cm) barrel with ordnance marks and sold out of service mark, 1806.
£1,100–1,200
$1,600–1,750 ⊞ WSA

An 80-bore air gun, by Goodwin & Co, London, with walnut butt, the barrel with ram-rod rib beneath, engraved with trophies of flags and maker's name, iron ball reservoir beneath, early 19thC, 47½in (121cm) long.
£500–600
$720–870 ⋏ WAL

A pair of turn-off barrel boxlock percussion pistols, signed 'C. Adams & Son, London', the walnut grips inlaid with nickel silver wire and leaves, one replacement hammer, c1825, 2¾in (7cm) barrels.
£550–600
$800–900 ⊞ ASB

A percussion pistol, by Bentley of London, with powder flask and accessories, concealed in a leather-bound book, 1850–60, 8 x 5in (20.5 x 12.5cm).
£300–350
$450–500 ⊞ HEG

Firefighting

This year *Miller's Collectables Price Guide* includes a new section devoted to the history of firefighting.

The terrorist destruction of the World Trade Centre in New York brought both the role and the courage of firefighters to world attention. The objects illustrated below commemorate the story of brave men and tragic events, beginning in the 18th century and ending with an American fireman's helmet from the 1940s.

Many come from an American sale of fire-fighting memorabilia, held shortly after the attack on 11 September 2001. 'The perspectives and priorities of all Americans and the vast majority of the world changed that day', noted a special introduction in the catalogue.

The objects fetched high prices, perhaps reflecting not only their rarity but also the embattled mood of the moment. 'The preservation and appreciation of historic fire-fighting artefacts is a worthy reminder of just how important our nation's fire-fighters, rescue workers and police are to us and how eternally grateful we are to them', concluded the catalogue. A portion of the proceeds of the sale was devoted to the Uniformed Fire-fighter's Association Widows' and Children's Fund in New York City.

A City of Boston Fire Department certificate, presented to Thomas D. Quincy, signed by Mayor James Armstrong, American, 1836, 16½in (42cm) high.
£200–230
$300–330 ✗ SK(B)

A fireman's black wool parade top hat, inscribed in gilt 'Friendship Fire Co 5 Inst. March 4th 1848', with owner's initial 'H.J.' on top, red brim liner, American, 6½in (16.5cm) high.
£2,100–2,500
$3,000–3,600 ✗ SK(B)

A Baltimore Equitable Society cast-iron firemark, painted red, green and black on a black ground, American, mid-19thC, 9½in (24cm) wide.
£950–1,000
$1,380–1500 ✗ SK(B)

A half-plate Daguerro-type of three members of The Union No. 2 Fire Company, in parade dress, with original mount, in later frame, American, c1850, 9 x 6in (23 x 15cm).
£6,300–7,000
$9,000–10,000 ✗ SK(B)
The men's helmets depict their rank – one star, two star, and clerk.

A red-painted leather fire bucket and cotton salvage bag, the bag labelled 'Daniel Sheaffer 1853', American, bucket 12½in (32cm) high.
£620–700
$900–1,000 ✗ SK(B)

A membership certificate of the Philadelphia Association for the Relief of Disabled Firemen, incorporating a coloured print by J. R. Smith, signed by the Association's President, Vice President and Secretary, framed and glazed, dated 1861, American, 19½in (49.5cm) square.
£630–700
$920–1,000 ✗ SK(B)

◄ **A leather-covered brass steamer composition nozzle,** stamped 'Button & Blake, Waterford N.Y. Patented June 7, Jan 10 1853 1860', American, 38in (96.5cm) long.
£700–800
$1,000–1,100 ✗ SK(B)

LOCATE THE SOURCE
The source of each illustration in Miller's can be found by checking the code letters below each caption with the Key to Illustrations, pages 444–452.

A photograph of the members of the Insurance Protective Department, Boston, Mass, framed and glazed, American, 1873, 18 x 22in (45.5 x 56cm).
£140–160
$200–230 ⚒ SK(B)

A fireman's brass parade helmet, by Merryweather, with brass-edged visor, chin-strap and ear rosettes, c1880, 10in (25.5cm) high.
£650–700
$950–1,100 ⊞ UCO

A pair of late Victorian leather fire buckets, with painted cream shields, red crosses and swords, on a black ground, dated 1886, 12in (30.5cm) high.
£550–650
$800–950 ⚒ RTo

A membership certificate of the Veteran Volunteer Firemen's Association of Baltimore, for Alexander Ramsey, with coloured chromolithograph of fire tender, signed by the President and Secretary, American, 1885, 10½ x 13¾in (26.5 x 35cm) high.
£250–300
$360–440 ⚒ SK(B)

A German fireman's steel and brass helmet, late 19thC.
£120–160
$175–230 ⊞ ET

A Plainfield Fire Department certificate, declaring that 'Dan'l Hogan, Jr. has served as a Fireman', illustrated with firemen, cherubs and scrollwork, American, 1888, 17 x 22½in (43 x 56cm).
£210–250
$300–360 ⚒ SK(B)

A shield-shaped souvenir booklet, for the Veteran Fireman's Association of New York excursion to Troy, Watertown and Buffalo, August 19–25, 1890, with six pages in Celluloid covers, American, 5¼ x 4in (13.5 x 10cm).
£140–160
$200–230 ⚒ SK(B)

▶ **An oak tool box of the Latrobe Fire Dept. No. 5,** by Seagrave, with metal latch, American, 19thC, 24in (61cm) wide.
£350–400
$500–580 ⚒ SK(B)

A photograph of the Barnicoat Fire Association, the men in dress uniform with soft hats and helmets, some damage, American, 1890, 17 x 21¾in (43 x 55.5cm).
£160–180
$230–260 ⚒ SK(B)

▶ **A chief engineer's lantern,** by White Mfg. Co, the engraved bevelled glass front lens inscribed 'Chief Engineer' and 'A' surrounded by a wreath, patented 'Feb & Aug 1874, Bridgeport, Conn.', late 19thC, 13in (33cm) high.
£1,100–1,200
$1,600–1,750 ⚒ SK(B)

An Empire Apparatus fire extinguisher, inscribed with patent date 3 September 1898, American, 21in (53.5cm) high.
£230–260
$330–380 ⚡ SK(B)

A Veteran Firemen's Association aluminium presentation shield, inscribed 'VFA Testimonial to Veteran Firemen's Association Hartford, Conn. Oct. 1st 2nd 1900, from Veteran Firemen's Association Poughkeepsie, N.Y.', in original stained wood display frame, American, 20½in (52cm) high.
£1,450–1,650
$2,100–2,400 ⚡ SK(B)

A scratch-built wooden model of a front-wheel drive ladder wagon, with six ground and two side ladders, American, c1900, 26in (66cm) long.
£140–160
$200–230 ⚡ SK(B)

A Vulcan cast-iron and brass high-pressure Baltimore Apparatus Hydrant, by the Ross Valve Mfg. Co, with five 2½in steamer cups, American, c1900, 20in (53.5cm) high.
£550–650
$800–950 ⚡ SK(B)

An Amoskeag Xtra Size 1 steam fire engine, by the American Locomotive Works, New Hampshire, with double crane-neck frame, American, 1905, 297in (754.5cm) long.
£15,500–16,500
$22,500–24,000 ⚡ SK(B)
Built in 1905 for the Lynn, Massachusetts fire brigade, this engine was originally horse-drawn, was motorized at some point and then returned to being horse-drawn.

◄ **A Tientsin Volunteer Fire Brigade Long Service Medal,** with silver Maltese cross, the reverse inscribed 'Tientsin 1902 to 1907 presented by the British Municipal Councils for Long Service to W. A. Forbes', with four silver ribbon bars for 8, 11, 14 and 16 years, and top suspension brooch inscribed 'T.V.F.B 1902–1918', marked Birmingham 1909, c1918.
£470–520
$670–750 ⚡ DNW

A Latvian fireman's helmet, with brass plate and trim, early 1900s.
£125–145
$180–220 ⊞ UCO

A Czechoslovakian fireman's leather-coated metal helmet, with a brass plate, early 1900s.
£160–180
$230–260 ⊞ UCO

A Society for the Protection of Life from Fire silver medal, 5th type (from 1902), depicting a man rescuing a woman with two children, on a red ribbon, c1916.
£420–460
$600–660 ⚡ DNW
This medal was awarded to Dr. D. R. Thomas, of Taffs Well, for rescuing three people from a fire caused by an exploding lamp, on 13 March 1916 at Radyr, near Cardiff.

A German fireman's metal helmet, with brass trim, Stuttgart, 1928.
£125–145
$180–210 ⊞ UCO

A model of the Friendship 1774 Hand Pumper, by Colark Ship Model Builders of Philadelphia, with red cast-iron handles and wheels, aluminium air chamber, brass pistons and rubber hoses, American, 1930s, 15½in (39.5cm) long.
£700–800
$1,000–1,150 ⤢ SK(B)

A Haley fireman's black leather helmet, with gold lettering on a red ground, American, 1940s.
£150–175
$220–255 ⊞ UCO

Police

A pottery nursery plate commemorating Sir Robert Peel, printed in green within a moulded border enamelled in green, blue and yellow, 19thC, 6½in (16.5cm) diameter.
£50–60
$75–90 ⤢ SAS
In 1829, Home Secretary Sir Robert Peel established the Metropolitan Police in London, hence the slang terms 'Peeler' and 'Bobby' for policemen.

A Georgian wooden tipstaff, by Hugh Laughton of Keighley, with brass tips, dated 1812, 18¼in (46.5cm) long.
£400–450
$580–650 ⊞ CCB

A police truncheon, 1830, 15in (38cm) long.
£175–200
$250–300 ⊞ MB

A Metropolitan policeman's helmet, blue serge cloth over cork base, 1953–60.
£85–95
$125–140 ⊞ UCO

◄ **A German policeman's helmet,** with white metal plate, mid-20thC.
£125–145
$180–210 ⊞ UCO

A collection of 42 police helmet badges, from British borough and county forces, mid-20thC, largest 4in (10cm) high.
£15–25
$20–35 each ⊞ Q&C

Money Boxes

A Tartan ware money box, with a transfer print of Glasgow University, 19thC, 3in (7.5cm) high.
£75–85
$115–125 ⊞ Fai

A cast-iron 'city bank' money box, slight damage, c1900, 4in (10cm) high.
£25–35
$30–50 ⊞ HAL

A tin post-box money box, decorated in red, black, and cream, c1916–20, 7in (18cm) high.
£45–65
$65–95 ⊞ MURR

A Bakelite cat money box, with gold eyes, Japanese, 1930s, 4in (10cm) high.
£85–95
$125–145 ⊞ LBe

Miller's is a price GUIDE not a price LIST

A Midland Bank Limited metal money box, 1930s, 3¼in (8.5cm) diam.
£12–15
$17–20 ⊞ HUX

A Queen Elizabeth II Coronation metal money box, c1953, 3in (7.5cm) high.
£15–20
$20–30 ⊞ FST

▶ **A steel partitioned money box,** painted red, 1960, 8in (20.5cm) long.
£10–12
$15–18 ⊞ Mo

A ceramic guitarist money box, inscribed 'One For The Record', 1960s, 7in (18cm) high.
£20–25
$30–35 ⋗ SAF

A TSB plastic rocket money box, red and white, 1960s, 11in (28cm) high.
£12–15
$17–20 ⊞ HUX

Newspapers & Magazines

The London Gazette,
dated 31 August to
4 September 1682,
11 x 7in (28 x 18cm).
£40–50
$60–75 ⊞ **HaR**

The New Observator,
dated Saturday 10 January
1691, 11 x 8in (28 x 20.5cm).
£65–80
$95–115 ⊞ **HaR**

The Norwich Gazette,
dated 17 to 24 February
1728, with early engravings,
10 x 9in (25.5 x 23cm).
£100–150
$145–225 ⊞ **HaR**

**Bonner and Middleton
Bristol Journal,** dated
Saturday 1 July 1781,
21 x 13in (53.5 x 33cm).
£30–40
$45–60 ⊞ **J&S**

The Courier, featuring
articles about Wellington
and Robert Peel, 1813,
19 x 13in (48.5 x 33cm).
£20–25
$30–35 ⊞ **J&S**

The Times, dated 20 July
1863, bound, 23½ x 17¾in
(59.5 x 45cm).
£10–20
$15–25 ⊞ **HaR**

The Citizen, No. 1,
marked 'Specimen', 1876,
16 x 12in (40.5 x 30.5cm).
£60–65
$95–100 ⊞ **J&S**

▶ **Isle of Wight
Advertiser,** dated
Saturday 12 May
1888, 26 x 18in
(66 x 45.5cm).
£15–20
$20–30 ⊞ **MRW**

Army and Navy Gazette,
dated Saturday 25 May
1888, 15 x 11in (38 x 28cm).
£15–20
$20–30 ⊞ **MRW**

◀ **Daily Mail,** No. 1,
1896, 24 x 17in
(61 x 43cm).
£25–30
$35–45 ⊞ **J&S**

Condition

The condition is
absolutely vital
when assessing
the value of a
collectable. Damaged
pieces on the whole
appreciate much
less than perfect
examples. However
a rare desirable
piece may command
a high price even
when damaged.

Black & White Budget,
dated February 1900,
reporting on the Boer War,
11 x 8in (28 x 20.5cm).
£8–10
$10–15 ⊞ J&S

The Graphic, dated
Saturday 13 November
1880, the front cover
depicting scenes of
agitation in Ireland,
16 x 12in (40.5 x 30.5cm).
£6–8
$8–10 ⊞ HaR

The Play, the front cover
depicting Forbes Robertson
as Hamlet, 1913, 12 x 9in
(30.5 x 23cm).
£5–6
$7–8 ⊞ J&S

**Le Petit Echo de la
Mode,** French, 1930,
14 x 11in (35.5 x 28cm).
£5–6
$7–10 ⊞ J&S

**Marine Engineer
Officers' Magazine,**
dated May/June 1930,
9 x 6in (23 x 15cm).
£35–40
$50–60 ⊞ J&S

**News Of The World
promotional miniature
newspaper,** 1933,
5½ x 4in (14 x 10cm).
£18–22
$25–35 ⊞ RUSS

Bristol Evening Post,
No. 1, 1932, 16 x 12in
(40.5 x 30.5cm).
£45–50
$65–75 ⊞ J&S

Woman and Home,
dated June 1940, 12 x 9in
(30.5 x 23cm).
£2–3
$3–5 ⊞ MRW

LOCATE THE SOURCE
The source of each illustration in Miller's can be
found by checking the code letters below each
caption with the Key to Illustrations, pages
444–452.

Woman's Day, dated
Friday 13 June 1959,
13 x 10in (33 x 25.5cm).
£3–4
$5–6 ⚒ FLD

News Chronicle, dated
Thursday 10 July 1947,
reporting on the
engagement of Princess
Elizabeth and Lieutenant
Philip Mountbatten,
23 x 17in (58.5 x 43cm).
£2–4
$3–6 ⊞ HaR

Two copies of Ideal Home, 1949–50, 12 x 9in
(30.5 x 23cm).
£2–3
$3–5 each ⊞ MRW

Osbornes

An Osborne plaque, entitled 'Dover Castle', green, brown and cream, 1917, 3in (7.5cm) wide.
£20–30
$30–45 ⊞ Rac

An Osborne plaque, entitled 'Bath Abbey', brown and orange, 1918, 3in (7.5cm) wide.
£20–30
$30–45 ⊞ Rac

An Osborne plaque, entitled 'Western Towers, Westminster Abbey', brown and cream, 1923, 3¼in (8.5cm) wide.
£18–22
$30–40 ⊞ JMC

An Osborne plaque, entitled 'Burns' Cottage Interior', brown, cream and blue, 1920s, 4½in (11.5cm) wide.
£25–30
$35–45 ⊞ JMC

An Osborne plaque, entitled 'Temple Bar in Dr Johnson's Time', brown, cream and blue, 1920s, 8in (20.5cm) wide.
£55–60
$80–90 ⊞ JMC

An Osborne plaque, entitled 'The Old Folks at Home', 1930s, 9¼in (23.5cm) wide.
£25–30
$35–45 ⊞ JMC

An Osborne plaque, entitled 'RMS Queen Mary', cream, black, red and blue, c1936, 7in (18cm) wide.
£25–35
$30–50 ⊞ MURR

An Osborne plaque, entitled 'Coventry, City of Three Spires', 1940, 5in (12.5cm) wide.
£20–25
$30–35 ⊞ JMC

◀ **An Osborne plaque,** entitled 'Going to Market', brown, green, grey and cream, 1940s, 3¾ x 5¼in (9.5 x 13.5cm).
£25–30
$35–45 ⊞ JMC

Two Osborne figures of Mr Micawber and David Copperfield, from a set of eight Dickens characters, 1940s, largest 5in (12.5cm) high.
£55–65
$80–100 each ⊞ JMC

Owls

Throughout history, the owl has been both feared and venerated. In Ancient Greece, the owl was the symbol of Athena and is found on the back of coins bearing her image and other decorative objects such as ceramics. As well as being goddess of war, Athena was also goddess of wisdom, hence the persistent idea of the 'wise old owl' and the association of the bird with education.

The owl – which belongs to the order of birds called strigiformes – is carniverous, nocturnal and unlike other birds of prey has an almost noiseless flight. Its hearing and vision are acute. Possibly for these reasons the Romans called the owl 'strix' (plural: striges, hence strigiformes), the same word as used for a witch. Owls are traditionally connected with sorcery and Halloween. In some cultures they signify bad luck, in others, good.

Famous owls in literature include *The Owl and the Pussycat* (Edward Lear) and Owl in A. A. Milne's *Winnie the Pooh*. Hedwig, the owl in J. K. Rowling's *Harry Potter* stories, has stimulated a new range of soft toys and other merchandise and carries on the tradition of owls being associated with witchcraft, wizardry and seats of learning.

◄ A red figure skyphos, the sides decorated with an owl flanked by laurel leaves, Italian, 4thC BC, 3½in (9cm) diam.
£450–550
$650–800 ➤ P

A hand-coloured lithograph of a tawny or wood owl, by John & Elizabeth Gould, printed by Charles Hullmandel, in a maple veneered frame, 1832–37, 20 x 13¾in (51 x 35cm).
£360–420
$500–600 ➤ Bon

A Victorian silver novelty owl pepper pot, the pull-off lid pierced and set with two glass eyes, the body engraved with feathers, maker's mark of Edward Charles Brown, London 1873, 3in (7.5cm) high.
£420–480
$620–700 ➤ Bon

◄ A pair of Continental green-glazed pottery owl spill vases, 10in (25.5cm) high.
£400–450
$600–650 ⊞ KA

A Victorian ceramic owl oil lamp, with green glass shade, 30in (76cm) high.
£450–500
$650–720 ⊞ BSa

A Victorian nursery oil lamp, with six-line Kosmos burner, the ceramic base decorated with owls among foliage, 24in (61cm) high.
£275–325
$400–480 ⊞ BSa

◄ An Arts and Crafts hand-beaten copper wall-hanging clock, set with a lapis lazuli-style stone, the original pendulum with hand-hammered owl decoration, 'Improve time in time while time lasts for sometimes no time when times past' in relief, late 19thC, 17in (43cm) high.
£1,800–2,200
$2,600–3,200 ➤ TF

Edward Lear, *Nonsense Songs,* illustrated by L. Leslie Brooke, first edition, published by F. Warne & Co, the front cover depicting Owl from *The Owl and the Pussycat,* c1900, 9 x 7in (23 x 18cm).
£80–90
$115–135 ⊞ BIB

A terracotta owl, Italian, 1910–20, 24in (61cm) high.
£450–500
$650–720 ⊞ KA

A pottery figure of an owl, perched upon three books, painted in naturalistic colours, 1930s, 23in (58.5cm) high.
£400–450
$580–650 🔨 HYD

A pair of ceramic owls, decorated in brown and cream, inscribed 'ENS voltstadt', German, 1930s–40s, 10in (25.5cm) high.
£250–300
$360–440 ⊞ KA

Two wooden owl inkwells, with red-painted ears, beaks and feet and glass bead eyes, with ceramic liners, German, 1930s–50s, 4in (10cm) high.
£35–40
$50–60 each ⊞ RUSS

A Steiff mohair owl hand puppet, brown and cream with green glass bead eyes, 1950–60.
£20–25
$30–40 ⊞ DMG

A Wedgwood glass owl paperweight, decorated in brown, with gold eyes, 1970, 3in (7.5cm) high.
£20–25
$30–40 ⊞ DMG

A wooden owl clock, German, 20thC, 10in (25.5cm) high.
£70–80
$100–120 ⊞ DCA

A set of five Poole Pottery plates, by John Gould, decorated with owls in green, brown and cream, 1980s, 6in (15cm) diam.
£10–12
$15–17 each ⊞ DCA

Paper Money

An Alton Bank one pound note, 'payable at Alton or through Messrs. Austen, Maunde, Tilson, Bankers, London', October 1815.
£270–300
$400–440 ✗ P
The Austen in this partnership was the brother of Jane Austen.

A Bank of England one pound note, signed by Jacob Perkins, with vignette of Britannia seated with Scotia, Hibernia and cherubs flanked by portraits of George IV, c1819.
£200–250
$300–350 ✗ P

A Bank of England five pound note, c1820, 8in (20.5cm) wide.
£120–150
$175–225 ✗ P

A 10 shilling Treasury note, signed by John Bradbury, August 1914.
£300–350
$450–500 ✗ P

A United Kingdom of Great Britain and Ireland ten shilling note, with Dardanelles overprint, 1915, 5¼in (13.5cm) wide.
£475–525
$700–750 ✗ P

A Deutsch-Ostafrikanische Bank 200 rupien note, German East African, 1915.
£275–300
$400–440 ✗ P

A one pound Treasury note, signed by John Bradbury, part of first issue, the reverse with light pencil graffiti, August 1914.
£475–525
$700–750 ✗ P
The declaration of WWI on 4 August 1914 nearly caused a financial crisis. Gold full and half sovereigns were instantly withdrawn and replaced by paper money – one pound notes in black and ten shilling notes in red. These emergency notes were nicknamed 'Bradburys' after the signature of John Bradbury, Secretary to the Treasury, which appeared on the bottom. They are also known as Treasury notes.

LOCATE THE SOURCE
The source of each illustration in Miller's can be found by checking the code letters below each caption with the Key to Illustrations, pages 444–452.

A United Kingdom of Great Britain and Ireland 10 shilling Treasury note, signed by John Bradbury, 1918.
£725–775
$1,000–1,200 🔨 P

A United Kington of Great Britain and Ireland 10 shilling Treasury note, signed by Warren Fisher, 2nd issue, 1922, 5½in (14cm) wide.
£60–70
$90–100 ⊞ ML

A United Kingdom of Great Britain and Ireland one pound note, signed by John Bradbury, 1923, 6in (15cm) wide.
£27–30
$35–45 ⊞ ML

A Bank of England 50 pound note, dated 20 May 1932.
£625–675
$900–1,000 🔨 P

A Banca D'Italia 1000 lire note, Italian East African, 1938.
£250–300
$360–440 🔨 P

A Bank of England emergency issue blue one pound note, 1940, 6in (15cm) wide.
£12–14
$15–18 ⊞ ML
In 1940, the colour of one pound notes was changed from green to blue, and 10 shilling notes went from brown to mauve. Wartime banknotes were produced by offset lithography rather than recess printing and only in 1948 were the original pre-war colours restored.

A Bank of England mauve 10 pound note, signed by K. O. Peppiat, 1940–48.
£30–35
$40–50 ⊞ ML

A Commercial Bank of Scotland blue five pound note, signed by J. M. Erskine, dated 5 January 1943, 8in (20.5cm) wide.
£70–80
$100–120 ⊞ ML

A Provincial Bank of Ireland 20 pound note, dated 20 November 1944.
£125–140
$180–200 ⊞ WP

A Bank of England white five pound note, signed by P. S. Beale, dated 17 September 1949, 8½in (21.5cm) wide.
£80–90
$115–135 ⊞ ML

A Bank of England green one pound note, signed by P. S. Beale, 1950, 6in (15cm) wide.
£20–25
$30–40 ⊞ ML

A Clydesdale & North of Scotland Bank 100 pound note, signed by J. J. Campbell, part of a 5,000 print run for this date, dated 2 May 1951.
£420–470
$600–700 🔨 P

A Bank of England blue five pound note, signed by L. K. O'Brien, 1957, 6in (15cm) wide.
£12–15
$15–20 ⊞ ML

A Central Bank of Ireland orange 10 shilling note, 1968.
£14–16
$18–22 ⊞ WP

Photography

A *carte de visite*, depicting a coach and horses, c1870, 3 x 4in (7.5 x 10cm).
£14–16
$18–22 ⊞ J&S

A *carte de visite*, depicting tram transportation in Bristol, c1895, 3 x 4in (7.5 x 10cm).
£16–18
$22–28 ⊞ J&S

A photograph of two Native American infants, signed 'Elliott', copyrighted in 1898, 7 x 5in (18 x 12.5cm), in an Arts & Crafts oak frame.
£350–420
$500–600 ↗ TREA

▶ A WWI military wedding photograph, 1915, 4½ x 6½in (11.5 x 16.5cm).
£8–10
$12–15 ⊞ J&S

An album of photographs of Queen Victoria, with an original photograph of Queen Victoria laying the foundation stone to Mar Lodge, a hitherto unknown photograph of Queen Victoria and a large quantity of original photographs of Victorian Royalty and nobility, some signed, 1880–1920.
£850–950
$1,250–1,400 ↗ DW
These images provide hitherto unknown snapshots of Queen Victoria and her family as well as many leading Victorian courtiers and a record of a way of life long gone. This album was once in the possession of Lord 'Lucky' Lucan, who is still officially at large and sought for the murder of his children's nanny.

Three photographic portraits, mounted on card, c1900, 6 x 4in (15 x 10cm).
£0.50–1
$1–3 each ↗ DW

A photograph album, with 71 black and white photographs of high-ranking Victorians and four hitherto unknown photographs of Mrs Alice Keppel, 1889–92.
£500–600
$720–870 ↗ DW
Alice Keppel was Edward VII's most celebrated mistress. Ironically, she was also Camilla Parker-Bowles grandmother.

A photograph album, with 24 photographs showing Queen Alexandra and other members of the Royal family relaxing, including the future Edward VIII and George VI, image size approx 3 x 3in (7.5 x 7.5cm), in original Kodak album, small 4°.
£400–500
£580–720 ↗ DW
Queen Alexandra, a keen photographer, published a volume entitled 'Photographs from my Camera' in association with *The Daily Telegraph*, in order to raise money for charity in 1908 (copies of this book can be found in many second-hand bookshops). This album contains hitherto unknown images, including the Queen seated outside at a tea table, with a cigarette in her left hand.

A Victorian leather-bound photograph album, the pages with floral decoration and central cut-out, 12 x 9in (30.5 x 23cm).
£130–150
$190–220 ⊞ TAC

A Mauchlin ware sycamore photograph album, decorated with floral design and verse, c1880, 4 x 3in (10 x 7.5cm).
£50–60
£75–90 ⊞ MB

An onyx photograph album, with hardstone and gilt-metal decoration, late 19thC, 12 x 8in (30.5 x 20.5cm), with original fitted case.
£450–500
$650–720 ⚒ Mit

Miller's is a price GUIDE not a price LIST

A tooled-leather photograph album, with illustrations of historical scenes, c1880, 12 x 9½in (30.5 x 24cm).
£75–85
$110–125 ⊞ HEG

A Victorian velvet photograph frame, 8 x 7in (20.5 x 18cm).
£20–30
$30–45 ⊞ CAL

A Victorian red velvet double photograph frame, with gilt-metal corner decoration, 7 x 4½in (18 x 11.5cm).
£40–50
$60–75 ⊞ CAL

A silver photograph frame, the arched surmount with ribbon and reed borders, Chester 1908, 10¼ x 7½in (26 x 19cm).
£300–350
$450–500 ⚒ RTo

A silver photograph frame, Chester 1903, 6in (15cm) diam.
£280–320
$400–450 ⊞ HCA

A carved wood hanging photograph frame, with gilt decoration, 1920s, 12 x 9in (30.5 x 23cm).
£60–70
$90–100 ⊞ AMR

Plastic

This section on plastic includes a collection of Tupperware. This light and unbreakable polythene kitchenware was invented by American plastics chemist Earl S. Tupper (1908–83). After wartime restrictions were over, he launched his new product on to the market in 1946. He was particularly proud of the patented airtight seal, (inspired by the lids of paint cans) which was designed to keep the contents fresh for longer than in other containers.

Consumers, however, didn't know how to open these lids and Tupperware sold poorly in the shops until 1948 when the company introduced home demonstrations. One of their earliest demonstrators, a lady called Brownie Wise, came up with the idea of the Tupperware party and a marketing legend was born. These now celebrated get-togethers were an instant success. For the company they offered direct access to the housewife. For women they provided not just home shopping and affordable plastics, but a social occasion and a job opportunity that they could combine with family life.

Beginning in the USA, Tupperware parties came to Britain in 1960 and today they still take place across the world. The Tupperware Corporation is now a $1.1 billion multinational company trading in over 100 countries. While new products include such esoteric creations as the Kimchi keeper and the Kimono keeper, there are collectors who focus on vintage products – the humble cereal containers and pudding bowls that made Tupperware a household name.

A Bakelite cheroot or cigarette holder, in the form of a hockey player's leg, c1890, 4in (10cm) high.
£65–75
$95–110 ⊞ WAB

▶ **A Bakelite Tiemaster,** 1930s–40s, 5in (12.5cm) high.
£18–22
$30–35 ⚒ MED

A Bakelite vesta case, 1915, 2¼in (5.5cm) wide.
£14–16
$18–22 ⊞ VB

A Bakelite coffee grinder, Italian, 1930s, 6in (15cm) high.
£70–80
$100–115 ⊞ GAD

> **Cross Reference**
> See Colour Review
> (page 239)

A Bakelite pipe rack, 1940s, 5¼in (13cm) high.
£15–20
$20–30 ⊞ DHAR

A Bakelite ashtray, featuring a drunken man leaning against a lampost, with inscription 'Oh What a Beautiful Evenin'!!', 1940s, 5in (12.5cm) high.
£20–25
$30–45 ⊞ HarC

A Bakelite tobacco jar, with decorative leaf borders, c1940, 5in (12.5cm) high.
£15–20
$20–30 ⊞ DHAR

An orange Perspex basket, 1950s, 12in (30.5cm) wide.
£12–15
$17–20 ⊞ HSt

A Tupperware Wonderlier green plastic pudding bowl, with white lid for steaming, 1960, 7½in (19cm) diam.
£10–12
$15–18 ⊞ Mo

A set of six Tupperware plastic beakers, various colours, 1960, 6in (15cm) high.
£30–35
$45–50 ⊞ Mo

Two ribbed Tupperware orange plastic containers, with flower motifs, 1962, largest 8in (20.5cm) diam.
£20–25
$30–35 ⊞ Mo
Very few of these containers were produced with a floral motif.

A pink Bakelite perpetual calendar, with floral decoration and inscription 'A Present from Weston-Super-Mare', 1950s, 5in (12.5cm) high.
£20–25
$30–35 ⊞ DHAR

Two Tupperware clear plastic containers, one for bran the other flour, with lids and scoops, 1960, largest 7in (18cm) high.
£12–15
$18–20 each ⊞ Mo

▶ **A set of six Tupperware clear plastic sundae vases,** 1960s, 6in (12.5cm) high.
£20–25
$30–35 ⊞ Mo

A Tupperware green plastic container, with a clear lid, 1960s, 3in (7.5cm) high.
£3–5
$5–7 ⊞ Mo

A Tupperware white plastic cereal container, with flip top, c1960, 9in (23cm) high.
£10–12
$15–18 ⊞ Mo
This was one of the first to be produced in the UK.

A Tupperware brown plastic spice container, with clear lid, 1960, 3in (7.5cm) high.
£8–10
$12–15 ⊞ Mo

A Tupperware green plastic colander, with clear lid, 1960s, 8in (20.5cm) diam.
£8–10
$12–15 ⊞ Mo

Politics

Politics and politicians have inspired a wealth of decorative arts and commemorative material over the centuries. This section opens with an admission ticket to the trial of Warren Hastings, a famous political scandal in the 18th century, and closes with a Conservative mousemat from the 2001 British election campaign. 'Political memorabilia has been described as the small change of history,' says Andrew Hilton, from Special Auction Services, a saleroom that specializes in commemoratives. 'In many instances, the objects are not great works of art in themselves. A potter would turn something out quickly and cheaply to commemorate a current event. It didn't have to be a thing of beauty, it was there to make its point. And today, what attracts people to these items is that sense of holding history in your hands.'

Popular subjects include major political happenings such as the Reform Act of 1832 and great political figures. According to Hilton, the top five collectable British Prime Ministers are (in no particular ranking order) Wellington, Gladstone, Disraeli, Churchill and Margaret Thatcher. Items connected with less successful politicians can also be sought after because of their rarity value – so perhaps William Hague will one day prove desirable in the auction room! Objects illustrated range from the serious to the satirical. Again from more recent times, Hilton recommends material inspired by the *Spitting Image* TV show (such as the Margaret Thatcher teapot), as being among the most significant political commemoratives of the 1980s. This section also includes commemoratives relating to American and other foreign politicians.

An engraved admission ticket for the trial of Warren Hastings, admitting the bearer to the 23rd day of the trials, with a small piece torn from the top left-hand corner, which was a method of cancellation indicating entry to the trial, c1738, 8°.
£130–160
$190–220 ⚚ DW
Warren Hastings, 1732–1818, a former Governor General of India, was impeached for financial irregularities by Parliament and put on trial, which was held sporadically over seven years between 1788 and 1795, thus making it one of the longest trials in British legal history.

A bronze medal commemorating the death of Charles James Fox, the reverse with an inscription 'Born Jany 13 1749, Died Sept 13 1806, Revered for Talent Fortitute & Patriotism', 1806, 1½in (4cm) diam.
£40–50
$60–75 ⊞ TML

A pottery plate commemorating Lord John Russell, printed in black with a portrait, 1832, 4in (10cm) diam.
£120–140
$175–200 ⚚ SAS

A white stoneware jug, applied with a moulded cartouche of a deer and trees beneath the inscription 'Burdett & Liberty', with blue neck and handle, c1810, 4½in (11.5cm) high.
£200–240
$300–350 ⚚ SAS

▶ **A three-volume set of books,** by Adam Smith, Edinburgh, an inquiry into the nature and causes of the Wealth of Nations, contemporary calf binding, 1819, 8½ x 5in (21.5 x 12.5cm).
£500–600
$720–870 ⊞ BAY

A London Pitt Club silver-gilt medal, by James Tassie, with a cameo glass bust of William Pitt, the reverse with inscription 'Henry Morgan Godwin Esqre', c1815, 1¾in (4.5cm) high.
£150–175
$220–255 ⊞ TML

◀ **A salt-glazed stoneware Reform flask,** modelled as Lord John Russell holding a scroll impressed 'The True Spirit of Reform', with 'Lord John Russell' impressed below, 'Preece, 72 High Holborn impressed to rear, c1832, 7in (18cm) high.
£300–350
$450–500 ⚖ BBR
Produced during the passing of the Reform Bill in 1832, Reform flasks were decorated with moulded portraits of the champions of parliamentary reform including Lord John Russell and Lord Brougham.

A salt-glazed stoneware Reform flask, modelled as Lord Brougham holding a scroll impressed 'The True Spirit of Reform', with 'Brougham Reform Cordial' impressed below, marked Doulton & Watts, c1832, 7in (18cm) high.
£190–230
$275–330 ⚖ BBR

A Minton bisque figure of the Duke of Wellington, c1846, 11in (28cm) high.
£500–550
$720–800 ⊞ JAK

▶ **A ceramic jug commemorating the Duke of Wellington,** black transfer-printed on a white body, 1850s, 5in (12.5cm) high.
£100–115
$145–170
⚖ RCo

A ceramic jug commemorating the Duke of Wellington, decorated with a hand-coloured print, with silver lustre decoration to top, slight damage, 1850s, 6in (15cm) high.
£125–150
$180–220 ⚖ RCo
If undamaged this price range would be £425–475 ($620–700).

◀ **A Parian bust of Lord Palmerston,** on a named socle base, 1864, 10¾in (27.5cm) high.
£160–190
$230–275 ⚖ SAS

A Staffordshire pottery figure of Lord Palmerston, 1860, 3½in (9cm) high.
£90–110
$130–150 ⚖ RCo

▶ **A Parian bust of Richard Cobden,** by Adams & Co, published by John Stark, the reverse with impressed marks, lacking socle base, c1865, 13in (33cm) high.
£85–100
$125–150 ⚖ SAS

◀ **A Staffordshire pottery figure of Garibaldi,** with orange shirt, holding a rolled banner 'Liberte', 19thC, 13in (33cm) high.
£120–150
$175–220 ⚖ L&E

A pottery tankard commemorating Earl Russell and Lord Derby, black transfer-printed with named portraits, with decoration to handle and interior, c1865, 5¼in (13cm) high.
£260–300
$380–440 ⚒ SAS

A Parian bust of John Bright, by Adams & Co, by John Stark, the reverse with impressed marks, lacking socle base, c1868, 14in (35.5cm) high.
£90–110
$130–160 ⚒ SAS

A plate commemorating the Marquis of Salisbury, black transfer-printed, bordered by dog roses, c1880, 11in (28cm) wide.
£150–165
$220–250 ⊞ POL

A carte de visite depicting Abraham Lincoln, c1880, 4 x 3in (10 x 7.5cm).
£6–10
$8–15 ⊞ J&S

A plate commemorating William Gladstone, black transfer-printed with his commercial and political achievements bordered by roses, c1886, 11in (28cm) wide.
£85–95
$125–150 ⊞ POL

A loving cup commemorating Benjamin Disraeli, transfer-printed in black with a portrait, late 1880s, 5in (12.5cm) high.
£165–185
$250–270 ⚒ RCo

A cast-iron bust of Randolph Churchill, bronze-finished, c1886, 5½in (14cm) high.
£90–110
$130–160 ⚒ RCo

A bronze medal commemorating William Gladstone, the reverse with a 59-line inscription listing the Members of the House for the year, 1894, 3¾in (9.5cm) diam.
£130–150
$190–220 ⊞ TML

A base metal and enamel William Gladstone memorial badge, with a photographic portrait of Gladstone within an enamel heart, mounted on original printed card with inscription 'In Memoriam, W. E. Gladstone, Christian, Patriot, Statesman', 1898, 24 x 28¾in (61 x 73cm).
£55–65
$80–100 ⊞ TML

A National Union of Women's Suffrage Society leaflet, entitled 'White Slave Traffic', printed both sides, slightly creased, c1900, 8½ x 5½in (21.5 x 14cm).
£260–320
$380–450 ✵ VS

▶ Winston Churchill's autograph, signed in black fountain pen, on an album page, 1931, 3¼ x 4in (8 x 10cm).
£800–1,000
$1,200–1,500 ✵ Bon(C)

Charles de Gaulle, a signed letter written in French to Miss Eardley-Wilmot thanking her for her letter of encouragement and offering her services to the Free French, 1940.
£400–450
$580–650 ✵ VS

▶ **The Daily News**, front cover story reporting the assassination of Lee Harvey Oswald by Jack Ruby, together with a cheque signed by Ruby dated 17 July 1956, 14 x 7in (35.5 x 18cm) .
£375–425
$560–620 ⊞ IQ
Two days after his arrest on suspicion of shooting President John F. Kennedy, Lee Harvey Oswald (1939–63) was shot down by local Dallas strip-club owner Jack Ruby in full view of TV cameras. Ruby was sentenced to death but died of cancer in 1967 while appealing for a retrial. Uncertainty and conspiracy theories continue to surround the Kennedy assassination.

A pottery jug commemorating Beville Stanier, elected Member of Parliament for Shropshire, 1908, 6½in (16.5cm) high.
£75–85
$110–125 ⊞ POL

A political cartoon, 'The Man at the Wheel', taken from *Punch* magazine, c1929, 11 x 9in (28 x 23cm).
£14–16
$18–22 ⊞ POL

SOVIET
COMMUNISM
–A NEW CIVILISATION
by
SIDNEY & BEATRICE WEBB

LEFT BOOK CLUB EDITION
NOT FOR SALE TO THE PUBLIC

◀ Sidney & Beatrice Webb, *Soviet Communism – A New Civilisation*, Left Book Club edition, published by Gollancz, 1937, 8¾ x 5¾in (22 x 14.5cm).
£40–50
$60–75 ⊞ BIB

An Ashtead Pottery cream-glazed caricature jug of Stanley Baldwin, impressed to base 'The Right Hon Stanley Baldwin M.P', No. 509 of a limited edition of 1,000, 1924–37, 7¾in (19.5cm) high.
£120–150
$175–220 ✵ BBR

William Beveridge, *Full Employment in a Free Society*, published by Allen & Unwin, 1944, 8¾ x 6in (22 x 15cm).
£30–35
$45–50 ⊞ BIB
In 1942, economist William Beveridge (1879–1963) produced his Report on Social Insurance and Allied Services (the Beveridge Report), which led to the creation of the Welfare State. Although the Labour Government implemented many of his suggestions, Beveridge himself was a member of the Liberal Party.

The Daily Telegraph,
reporting the assassination of President John F. Kennedy, 23 November 1963, 24 x 17in (61 x 43cm).
£8–10
$10–15 ⊞ IQ

A papier mâché bust of President John F. Kennedy, 1963, 6in (15cm) high.
£20–25
$30–35 ⊞ HUX

The Evening News & Star,
reporting the assassination of President John F. Kennedy, 23 November 1963, 23 x 17in (58.5 x 43cm).
£8–10
$12–15 ⊞ IQ

Margaret Thatcher, a signed black and white photograph, 1970s, 10 x 8in (25.5 x 20.5cm).
£150–175
$220–250 ⊞ POL

► **A set of ten cardboard drinks mats,** with cartoons of Harold Wilson, 1960s–70s, 3½in (9cm) square.
£10–12
$15–18 ⁄ RCo

A political poster, 'Proletarians of all Nations get United', 1973, 24 x 45¾in (61 x 115.5cm).
£70–80
$100–115 ⁄ VSP

A ceramic plate, commemorating Edward Heath's term as Prime Minister, designed by A. Kitson Towler, 1975, 10in (25.5cm) diam.
£75–85
$110–125 ⊞ POL

A Labour Party pottery mug, black transfer-printed with portraits of Harold Wilson and Jim Callaghan, 1976, 4½in (11.5cm) high.
£30–40
$45–60 ⊞ POL

A 1979 General Election Mug, with photographic portraits of the Conservative, Labour and Liberal Party candidates, 1979, 3½in (9cm) high.
£28–32
$45–50 ⁄ RCo

► **A white pottery *Spitting Image* Mrs Thatcher teapot,** by Luck and Flaw, slight damage, 1981, 8¼in (21cm) high.
£90–120
$130–175 ⁄ SAS

Condition

The condition is absolutely vital when assessing the value of a collectable. Damaged pieces on the whole appreciate much less than perfect examples. However a rare desirable piece may command a high price even when damaged.

Margaret Thatcher, *The Downing Street Years,* limited edition, 1993, 10 x 6¾in (25.5 x 17cm).
£35–40
$50–60 ⊞ POL

A Royal Crown Derby dish, commemorating Margaret Thatcher, with a cobalt blue border and gilt inscription, 1990, 4½in (11.5cm) diam.
£30–40
$45–60 ⚲ SAS

A ceramic plate, commemorating the 50th anniversary of the East Midlands Labour Party, by the Edwardian Fine China Co, No. 1 of a limited edition of 250, 1992, 11in (28cm) diam.
£30–40
$45–6 ⚲ RCo

A Conservative Party video, 'No! No! No! Margaret Thatcher's Last Year in the House of Commons', presented by Lord Tebbit, 1994.
£10–13
$15–18 ⊞ POL

A video of the 1997 General Election, produced by the BBC, 1997.
£14–16
$18–22 ⊞ POL

▶ **A Blair and Hague salt and pepper set,** by Ventnor Ceramics, Blair in a grey suit and red tie, Hague in a blue suit and blue tie, 2001, 5in (12.5cm) high.
£25–30
$35–45 ⊞ POL

A Toby jug, modelled as John Major, 1990s, 9in (23cm) high.
£125–145
$180–200 ⊞ POL

A Bill Clinton Meanie Toy, 'Bull Clinton', dressed in Stars and Stripes shorts, white shirt and red tie, American, c1998, 8in (20.5cm) high.
£12–15
$18–20 ⊞ TBoy

A Labour Party campaign poster, 'The Repossessed', 2001, 12 x 17in (30.5 x 43cm).
£0.50–1
$1–3 ⊞ POL

▶ **A Conservative Party mouse mat,** 'Four years of Labour and he still hasn't delivered', red lettering on a black and white ground, 2001, 8 x 10in (20.5 x 25.5cm).
£4–5
$5–7 ⊞ POL

Postcards

A topographical postcard, depicting black and white vignettes of Mumbles linked by garlands of flowers, 1890.
£4–5
$5–7 ⊞ JMC
At this period, one side of the postcard had to be left free for the stamp, name and address. The picture and message had to share the other side.

A topographical postcard, depicting coloured vignettes of Windsor, 1897.
£15–20
$20–30 ⊞ JMC

A London & South-Western Railway postcard, depicting St Paul's Cathedral in muted colours, published by Pictorial Post-Card Syndicate, 1900.
£35–40
$50–60 ⊞ JMC

▶ **A postcard,** depicting Shakespeare's House, Stratford-on-Avon in brown, green and cream, 1901.
£15–20
$20–30 ⊞ JMC

◀ **A Boer War postcard,** depicting an equestrian portrait of Colonel Baden-Powell, c1900.
£12–15
$17–20 ⊞ JMC

A set of seven Raphael Kirchner postcards,
Les Péchés Capitaux.
£120–150
$175–225 ⚒ VS

A bas-relief postcard of HRH Princess of Wales, with jewelled effect, 1900–10.
£10–15
$15–20 ⊞ ES

◀ **A photographic postcard,** depicting the Old Post Office, Lee, published by Twiss Bros, Ilfracombe, 1908.
£15–20
$20–30 ⊞ JMC

An RMS advertising postcard, with vignette in gold, blue, red and green, published by David MacBrayne, 1908.
£10–15
$15–20 ⊞ JMC

A postcard, depicting The University and Kelvingrove Park, in brown, red, green and blue, published by H. Cassiers, c1910.
£6–8
$10–15 ⊞ JMC

A comic postcard, depicting a banknote, c1910
£8–10
$10–15 ⊞ WP

A comic postcard, red, blue and brown on a white ground, c1940.
£3–4
$5–6 ⊞ WP

A postcard, 'Just found a pebble on the beach at Perranporth', Wildt & Kray Series No. 2438, 1930–40.
£1–2
$3–5 ⊞ ES

A postcard, 'Mr Bruins is surprised', G. G. Series No. 310, 1930–40.
£1–2
$3–5 ⊞ ES

A WWI Royal Flying Corps coloured silk embroidered postcard, c1916.
£25–30
$35–45 ⊞ GAA

A WWI Royal Engineers coloured silk embroidered postcard, 1915–18.
£12–15
$17–20 ⊞ GAA

A Boy Scouts perfumed card, in aid of charity funds, 1916.
£15–20
$20–30 ⊞ MURR

> **Cross Reference**
> See Mabel Lucie
> Attwell (page 31–33)

▶ **Three Mabel Lucie Attwell postcards,** 1930s.
£5–10
$10–15 each
⊞ MEM

Posters

A London Brighton and South Coast Railway poster, by Charles Pears, printed in blue, white and red, 1924, 39½ x 60¼in (100 x 153cm).
£400–480
$600–700 ⚒ ONS

A XXVII Internationaal Eucharistisch Congres poster, by Jan Th. Toorop, printed in red, gold and blue by N. V. J. Smulders & Co, Dutch, 1924, 13 x 8¼in (33 x 21cm).
£200–230
$300–330 ⚒ VSP

FIRTH OF CLYDE CRUISES BY THE LUXURIOUS NEW LMS STEAMERS 'CALEDONIA & MERCURY' CHEAP RAIL TICKETS FROM THIS STATION

A London, Midland & Scottish Railway poster, by Norman Wilkinson, printed in blue, green, white and grey by John Harn, c1925, 39½ x 25¼in (100.5 x 64cm).
£600–650
$850–950 ⚒ Bea(E)

Cross Reference
See Colour Review
(page 242–244)

A coloured lithographic Clear Light newspaper poster, printed by Karl Koch, German, c1930, 36¾ x 25½in (93.5 x 65cm).
£160–200
$230–300 ⚒ VSP

A Castrol Golden Arrow World Land Speed Record poster, by Jean Pilod, printed in yellow, red, black and blue, French, 1929, 31½ x 23¾in (80 x 60.5cm).
£350–400
$500–600 ⚒ BKS

◄ An American Overseas Airlines poster, by Lewitt Him, printed in blue, yellow, pink and white, 1940s, 40 x 25in (101.5 x 63.5cm).
£700–800
$1,000–1,200 ⊞ REN

An Olivetti Lettera 22 poster, by Raymond Savignac, printed in red and purple on a green ground by Alfieri e Lacrois, Milan, Italian, c1950, 27¾ x 39¼in (70.5 x 99.5cm).
£350–430
$500–600 ⚒ VSP

A GPO poster, '4d minimum foreign rate', by Tom Elkasley, 1950, 27 x 36in (68.5 x 91.5cm).
£1,300–1,500
$2,000–2,200 ⊞ REN

A United Nations Fight For Freedom poster, printed in blue, white, red and yellow, c1943, 40½ x 28¼in (103 x 72cm).
£15–20
$20–30 ⚒ ONS

◀ **A Triumph TR4 showroom advertising poster,** dated December 1962, 29½ x 39½in (75 x 100.5cm).
£230–270
$330–400 ♪ BKS

Miller's is a price GUIDE not a price LIST

A Philips Television poster, by A. M. Cassandre, printed in red, blue, black and brown by Smeets Weert, Dutch, 1951, 16¾ x 12½in (42.5 x 32cm).
£420–500
$600–700 ♪ VSP

A Vermouth Linherr poster, by Athur Zegler, printed in cream, green, blue and red, by W. U. B. Innsbruck, c1955, 46½ x 32¼in (118 x 82cm).
£160–200
$230–300 ♪ VSP

▶ **An Amerikansk Pop-konst poster,** by Roy Lichtenstein, Swedish, 1967, 39 x 28in (99 x 71cm).
£200–300
$300–450 ⊞ CJP

Film Posters

▶ **A Universal film poster,** *Man of a Thousand Faces,* 1957, 30 x 40in (76 x 101.5cm).
£100–120
$145–175 ♪ DN

▶ **A Rank film poster,** *Carry on Henry,* 1960s, 40 x 27in (101.5 x 68.5cm).
£55–65
$80–100 ⊞ SDP

A Goya Films poster, *La Caravana de la Ilusion,* by Enzo Nistri, printed in blue, purple, red and yellow, by Graficas Valencia, c1955, 39½ x 27½in (100 x 70cm).
£80–100
$115–145 ♪ VSP

A 20th Century-Fox film poster, *Bus Stop,* American, 1956, 41 x 27in (104 x 68.5cm).
£200–250
$300–350 ♪ Bon(C)

▶ **A Mirsch Company film poster,** *The Great Escape,* American, 1963, 41 x 27in (104 x 68.5cm).
£350–390
$500–580 ⊞ SDP

A 20th Century-Fox film poster, *Batman,* 1966, 30 x 40in (76 x 101.5cm).
£600–700
$800–1,000 ♪ Bon(C)

A United Artists film poster, *Bons Baisers de Russie,* French, 1963, 60 x 40in (152.5 x 101.5cm).
£500–600
$720–870 ♪ FO

A 20th Century-Fox film poster, *Two For The Road*, 1966, 30 x 40in (76 x 101.5cm).
£80–100
$115–145 ⊞ SEY

A British Lion film poster, *The Man Who Fell To Earth*, printed in blue, red and white on a black ground, 1977, 30 x 40in (76 x 101.5cm).
£80–100
$115–145 ⊞ CTO

A United Artists film poster, *Never Say Never Again*, printed in red on a black and white ground, 1983, 30 x 40in (76 x 101.5cm).
£250–300
$360–440 ⚒ FO

Tretchikoff Prints

Vladimir Tretchikoff has been described as the most genuinely popular artist of the 20th century. Born in Siberia in 1913, he lived in China and Singapore before settling in South Africa in 1946. The self-taught painter became famous in the post-war period not for his original canvases but for reproductions, which appeared in department stores around the world. Typical subjects include exotic ladies, bathed in a distinctive luminous glow. Art critics scoffed and serious accounts of period painting ignored him, but these affordable prints sold in their thousands, making Tretchikoff a fortune.

Hugely popular in the 1950s, in later years works by the artist were considered the epitome of bad taste. Today fashion has turned full circle. Tretchikoff is now seen as an icon of kitsch and his works are once again sought after.

A Water and Glass, Weeping Rose print, by Tretchikoff, the cream rose on a blue and green ground, 1948, 22 x 21in (56 x 53.5cm).
£15–18
$20–25 ⚒ FLD

An Orchid on the Stairs print, by Tretchikoff, printed in white, pink, blue and green, 1948, 22 x 21in (56 x 53.5cm).
£20–25
$30–35 ⚒ FLD

A Chinese Girl print, by Tretchikoff, printed in yellow, red, black and blue, 1950s, 25 x 21in (63.5 x 53.5cm).
£35–45
$50–60 ⚒ FLD

A Balinese Girl print, by Tretchikoff, printed in green, yellow, pink and blue, 1950s, 24 x 19in (61 x 48.5cm).
£40–45
$60–70 ⚒ HSt

▶ **A Zulu Girl print,** by Tretchikoff, printed in blue, brown, red, black and gold, 1955, 24 x 30in (61 x 76cm), framed.
£75–95
$110–140 ⊞ PLB

◀ **A Miss Wong print,** by Tretchikoff, printed in green, gold, pink and black, 1950s, 25 x 21in (63.5 x 53.5cm).
£35–45
$50–70 ⚒ FLD

Puppets

Two Pelham Walt Disney Character string puppets, with carved head, hands and feet, Jiminy Cricket wearing black tails, grey trousers and brown felt hat, and carrying a carved umbrella, and Pinocchio wearing black waistcoat, red shorts, shirt with bowtie and yellow felt hat, 1950s, 8in (20.5cm) high, in original boxes with blue printed labels.
£270–300
$400–440 ➤ Bon(C)

A Pelham donkey string puppet, with carrot, early 1950s, 8in (20.5cm) high, in original box.
£90–110
$130–160 ⊞ J&J

A Pelham sailor string puppet, 1950s, 12in (30.5cm) high.
£42–48
$60–70 ⊞ J&J

◄ **A Pelham wooden string puppet,** Bengo, 1960s, 6in (15cm) high, in original yellow box.
£10–15
$15–20 ⊞ ARo

A Pelham schoolmaster string puppet, 1960s, 14in (35.5cm) high.
£25–35
$30–50 ⊞ ARo

A Womble string puppet, Great Uncle Bulgaria, wearing a blue, red and yellow tartan hat, poncho and slippers, 1970s, 9in (23cm) high, in original window box.
£20–25
$30–35 ⊞ ARo

► **A Pelham golly string puppet,** 1980s, 9in (23cm) high.
£35–45
$50–70 ⊞ ARo

Colour Review

An abalone thimble case, c1800, 2in (5cm) high.
£75–85
$100–125 ⊞ DHA

Three Victorian lacemaker's bobbins, bone with glass spangles, engraved, largest 4in (10cm) long.
£15–25
$20–35 each ⊞ WAB

◀ **Two pin-cushions,** one set in a fir cone, 1880–1920, tomato 1½in (4cm) diam.
£15–30
$20–45 each ⊞ VB

Three pincushion dolls, c1920, 2in (5cm) high.
£10–30
$15–45 each ⊞ VB

A cast-iron novelty sewing machine, by Steinfeldt Blasberg, German, 1868, 8in (20.5cm) high.
£8,500–9,000
$12,300–13,000 ⊞ WSM

A Victorian embroidered card needle book, 2in (5cm) wide.
£35–45
$50–65 ⊞ VB

A Bakelite sewing box, decorated with a cat, 1920s, 3in (7.5cm) wide.
£165–185
$240–270 ⊞ LBe

◀ **A WWII pamphlet,** *Make Do and Mend,* prepared for the Board of Trade by the Ministry of Information, 8½ x 5½in (21.5 x 14cm).
£2–3
$3–5 ⊞ HUX

A Victorian glass thimble holder, modelled as a shoe, 2¼in (5.5cm) long.
£55–65
$80–95 ⊞ VB

A Victorian Tunbridge ware pincushion, 2in (5cm) diam.
£45–50
$65–75 ⊞ VBo

A brass sextant, by W. F. Sannon, London, 1840, 10 x 12in (25.5 x 30.5cm), in original mahogany case.
£650–700
$950–1,100 ⊞ **BoC**

A White Star Line postcard, from RMS *Oceanic*, 1903.
£15–20
$20–30 ⊞ **JMC**

A tin box, decorated with an illustration of HMS *Dreadnought*, 1906, 6in (15cm) square.
£75–90
$100–130 ⊞ **COB**

A plastic egg timer, modelled as a yacht, 1930s, 5in (12.5cm) high.
£60–70
$90–100 ⊞ **REG**

A Cunard Christmas annual, 1931, 6 x 4in (15 x 10cm).
£15–20
$20–30 ⊞ **COB**

A White Star Line Cruising Programme, 1934, 6 x 4in (15 x 10cm).
£15–20
$20–30 ⊞ **COB**

A Cunard White Star advertising brochure, for RMS *Queen Mary*, late 1930s, 10 x 12in (25.5 x 30.5cm).
£90–100
$130–150 ⊞ **MRW**

A Blue Star Line badge, 1950s, 1½in (4cm) diam.
£10–15
$15–20 ⊞ **COB**

A biscuit tin, decorated with an illustration of *Pride of the Clyde,* 1960s, 9in (23cm) wide.
£20–35
$30–50 ⊞ **COB**

A set of playing cards, featuring the *Stirling Castle*, 1960s, 2½ x 4in (6.5 x 10cm).
£5–10
$10–15 ⊞ **COB**

***Paris Match* magazine,** Special France edition, 1961, 15 x 10in (38 x 25.5cm).
£30–35
$45–50 ⊞ **COB**

A Mecca Cigarettes baseball card, Johnny Evers of the Chicago Nationals, 1911.
£100–110
$145–165 ⊞ HALL

A Press Steward badge, for the 1933 FA Cup Final, Everton v Manchester City, 3in (7.5cm) high.
£220–250
$320–360 ↗ P(NW)

A golfing playing card holder, for two packs of cards, 1940s, 5in (12.5cm) high.
£60–70
$90–100 ⊞ BEV

A set of croquet balls, in a pine box, c1920, 16in (40.5cm) long.
£55–65
$80–100 ⊞ SA

Two mahogany and brass Nottingham reels, with star-backed Slater catches, c1920, largest 3½in (9cm) diam.
£35–65
$50–100 each ⊞ SA

A stuffed and mounted Chub, by Cooper, in a bowfronted case, inscription reads 'Avon Chub, 4lbs 8oz, Caught by S. De'Courcy, Royalty Water, Christchurch 14th Nov: 1948', case 26in (66cm) wide.
£1,000–1,200
$1,500–1,800 ⊞ SA

A set of Roehampton composition croquet balls, c1920, 8in (20.5cm) wide, in original box.
£55–65
$80–100 ⊞ SA

A Press Steward badge, for the 1934 FA Cup Final, Manchester City v Portsmouth, 1½in (4cm) diam.
£130–150
$200–220 ↗ P(NW)

An Amateur Cup football programme, Pegasus v Harwich & Parkeston, 1953, 9 x 6in (23 x 15cm).
£8–10
$10–15 ⊞ MRW

◄ **Two autographed luncheon menus,** for the 1957 and 1958 FA Cup Finals, Aston Villa v Manchester United and Bolton Wanderers v Manchester United, largest 10in (25.5cm) high.
£620–720
$900–1,000 ↗ P(NW)

An All England Women's Hockey Association programme, England v Belgium, 1953, 9 x 5in (23 x 12.5cm).
£8–10
$10–15 ⊞ MRW

An FA Steward's badge, for the 1963 centenary year, 2in (5cm) long.
£45–55
$60–80 ⋩ P(NW)

A signed photograph of Jean Alesi, mid-1990s, 6 x 4in (15 x 10cm).
£45–50
$65–75 ⊞ SSL

A boxing glove, signed by Jake La Motta, with a signed photographic print, 1950s, 12in (30.5cm) long.
£160–190
$225–275 ⋩ P(NW)

A Superintendent lapel badge, for the 1966 World Cup, Wembley, 1½in (4cm) square.
£220–250
$320–360 ⋩ P(NW)

▶ **A cricket bat,** signed by Sir Richard Hadlee, with details of his career record, 1987.
£300–400
$450–550 ⊞ SMW

◀ **A signed photograph of Ryan Giggs,** 1990s, 11½ x 15½in (29 x 39.5cm).
£100–110
$140–160 ⋩ SWO

An Avon plastic aftershave bottle, modelled as a golf ball, 1960s, 3in (7.5cm) high.
£20–25
$30–40 ⊞ LBe

A Heuer Trackmaster mechanical stopwatch, c1970.
£60–80
$90–120 ⊞ HARP

A Vodafone Manchester United replica shirt, signed, c2000.
£325–350
$470–500 ⊞ SSL

Three signed photographs of David Beckham, mounted and framed, c2000, 15 x 25in (38 x 63.5cm).
£200–220
$300–320 ⊞ SSL

Radios, Gramophones & Tape Recorders

▶ **Three early wireless valves,** 1922–25, 5in (12.5cm) high.
£15–25
$20–35 each
⊞ GM

A Gecophone crystal radio set, with headphones, 1923, 9in (23cm) wide.
£100–120
$150–175 ⊞ OTA
The term radio 'ham' comes from the word 'amateur'. Many enthusiasts put together their own crystal sets which, equipped with a single pair of head-phones, could be listened to by only one person at a time. Britain's first sustained, regular broadcasting service was started by the Marconi station in February 1922, and consisted of only one half-hour programme every Tuesday evening. But November that year saw the launch of the British Broadcasting Service (two short news bulletins and a weather report made up the first day's programming) and soon radio became central to people's lives and living rooms.

A Cosmos Metro-Vick Radiophone, with five original valves, in original oak cabinet with retailer's plate for 'Walker & Hutton, Mechanical and Electrical Engineers, Scarboro', 1924, 17in (43cm) wide.
£900–1,100
$1,300–1,600 ⊞ OTA
When new, this Radio-phone cost over £30 ($45), the equivalent of about three months' salary for an office worker in 1924.

Three Igranic coils, labelled 'What are the wild waves saying?', 1920s, 3½in (9cm) wide.
£4–5
$6–8 ⊞ GM
These coils were plug-in units used to determine the frequency range of a wireless.

A Philips 830C Bakelite and Arbolite radio, in a simulated walnut cabinet, 1932, 19in (48.5cm) high.
£400–450
$580–650 ⊞ GM

◀ **A Rolls-Caydon Rondo five-valve battery-operated portable wireless,** with moveable tuning figures within the central aperture of the main tuning knob, in a wood and cardboard cabinet, 1929, 15in (38cm) wide.
£80–100
$115–145 ⊞ GM

A Murphy B4 radio, designed by E. J. Power, in a walnut cabinet, 1932, 17in (43cm) high.
£100–120
$145–175 ⊞ OTA

A Pye Model S radio, with rising sun fret motif in front of speaker, 1933, 19in (48.5cm) high.
£120–150
$175–220 ⊞ OTA

In 1929 Pye & Co adopted the classic rising sun motif on their wooden radio cabinets, inspired by a design the sales manager had seen on a colleague's cigarette case. It remained in use until 1948, when a new version of the radio was released without the usual clouds among its fretwork sun rays. The new image resembled the flag of Japan, Britain's war-time enemy. There was a public outcry and the wireless was rapidly withdrawn.

A Colonial New World Globe Bakelite radio, American, 1934, 17in (43cm) high.
£800–900
$1,150–1,300 ⊞ GAD

An Ekco AC86 black and chrome Bakelite radio, designed by Serge Chermayeff, 1935–36, 22in (56cm) wide.
£300–350
$450–500 ⊞ OTA

▶ **A Philco 'People's Set' Model 444 radio,** 1936, 16in (40.5cm) high.
£250–300
$360–440 ⊞ OTA

A CWS Defiant Model MSH 948 radio, with motor-driven tuning and switchable tone filters, 1938, 31in (78.5cm) wide.
£180–220
$260–320 ⊞ OTA
In the 1930s, signatories of the Radio Wholesale Trading Agreement refused to supply Co-operative stores with receivers, because they saw the Co-op dividend as unfair price cutting. The Co-operative Wholesale Society defiantly organized the manufacture of its own brand of receivers, hence the name of this radio.

A Murphy A30C console radio, designed by R. D. Russell, with 12-inch speaker mounted in acoustically treated cabinet, unrestored, 1936, 35in (89cm) high.
£80–100
$115–145 ⊞ GM

A Philco car radio, with tuner and amplifier/power pack as separate units, unrestored, 1937, 6in (15cm) wide.
£75–100
$110–145 ⊞ GM

A Silvertone Bullet sprayed Bakelite radio, with push-button controls, American, 1938, 12in (30.5cm) wide.
£900–1,000
$1,300–1,500 ⊞ GAD

A Radio Acoustics Products three-valve superhet radio, in a walnut-veneered cabinet, unrestored, 1947, 21in (53.5cm) wide.
£80–100
$115–145 ⊞ GM

A GEC BC4750 three wave-band radio, with push-button wave-change, in a solid mahogany cabinet, c1947, 22in (56cm) wide.
£130–150
$190–220 ⊞ OTA

An Etronic RA640 AC mains radio, in wooden cabinet, c1948, 19in (48.5cm) wide.
£20–30
$30–45 ⊞ OTA

A Murphy 146 Baffleboard radio receiver, long and medium waves, with separate amplifier, unrestored, 1948, 33in (84cm) high.
£80–100
$115–145 ⊞ GM

An Ardente Type 309 hearing-aid booster amplifier, in dark green Bakelite cabinet, unrestored, 1950, 12in (30.5cm) wide.
£35–50
$50–75 ⊞ GM

A Bush DAC 90A AC/DC brown Bakelite radio, with two wavebands, 1950–51, 12in (30.5cm) wide.
£120–140
$175–200 ⊞ CORD
This model was also available in ivory and green Bakelite, rare.

A KB Toaster Model FB10 cream Bakelite radio, two wavebands, AC only, 1951, 10in (25.5cm) wide.
£150–180
$220–260 ⊞ CORD
This model was also available in red and green Bakelite.

A Rambler portable radio, in a carrying case, 1950s, 9in (23cm) wide.
£5–8
$8–12 ⋟ SAF

Miller's is a price GUIDE not a price LIST

◄ **A Philips 353A Bakelite radio,** with three wavebands including VHF, 1957, 16in (40.5cm) wide.
£70–80
$100–115 ⊞ CORD

A Bush DAC70C Bakelite and chrome table radio, with long and medium wave, unrestored, 1959, 13in (33cm) wide.
£30–40
$45–60 ⊞ GM

A Sony Model TR 650 pocket transistor radio, with six transistors, in a black and silver-coloured finish, Japanese, 1963, 4in (10cm) high.
£35–55
$50–80 ⊞ OVE

A Columbia two-minute cylinder graphophone, in a wooden case, 1906, 22in (56cm) high.
£375–425
$560–620 ⊞ CBGR

A Roberts RT7 transistor portable radio, with push-button wave-change and concentric volume and tone controls, cased in simulated leather finish, c1960, 11in (28cm) wide.
£40–50
$60–75 ⊞ GM

▶ **A Heathkit transistor radio,** in a brown leather case, 1970, 8in (20.5cm) high.
£15–20
$20–30 ↗ SAF

A Heathkit Mohican portable communication receiver, by Daystrom, originally supplied either in kit form or ready-assembled, 1965, 12in (30.5cm) wide.
£45–60
$65–90 ⊞ GM

An HMV Model 1 hornless gramophone, in oak, c1920, 15in (38cm) wide.
£100–130
$145–190 ⊞ CBGR

◀ **A Peter Pan box camera-style miniature portable gramophone,** 1920s, 6in (15cm) high.
£160–180
$230–260 ⊞ CBGR

A Silvertone Model 1209 Medalist pocket transistor radio, with seven transistors, in an ice-blue and chrome-finish case, American, 1961, 7in (18cm) wide.
£25–35
$35–50 ⊞ OVE

A Roberts RM33 mains transistor table radio, in a wooden cabinet, 1980, 12in (30.5cm) wide.
£20–30
$30–45 ⊞ GM
Many of these tiny but practical radios are still in use.

An HMV Model VI gramophone, with painted steel flower horn, c1912, 32in (81.5cm) wide.
£825–925
$1,200–1,350 ⊞ CBGR

A Columbia brown leatherette and chrome wind-up gramophone, 1920s, 17in (43cm) wide.
£30–40
$45–60 ⟋ SAF

An Amplion oak flower-horn speaker, with nickel-plated base, c1924, 20in (51cm) high.
£180–200
$260–290 ⊞ OTA

An HMV fibre-needle cutter, in original packaging, 1930s, 5in (12.5cm) wide.
£35–50
$50–75 ⊞ MURR

◄ **An IM Pointmaster needle sharpener,** in original packaging, 1930s, 6in (15cm) wide.
£10–15
$15–20 ⊞ CBGR

► **A turntable speed tester,** paper, labelled for W. E. Salisbury of Marlborough, c1950, 5in (12.5cm) diam.
£1–2
$2–3 ⊞ CBGR

A Kudelski Nagra III tape deck, Swiss, 1968, 12in (30.5cm) wide.
£220–250
$320–360 ⊞ GM
This model became a world standard, and was used by many broadcasting companies.

A Dansette record player, in red and cream case, in working order, 1960s, 15in (38cm) wide.
£20–25
$30–35 ⟋ SAF

A National portable record player and radio, with speakers integral to case lid, late 1960s, 13in (33cm) wide.
£50–60
$75–90 ⊞ PPH

Railwayana

A tin and brass railway lamp, in working order, 19thC, 15in (38cm) high.
£325–375
$470–560 ⊞ SEA

A photograph of the London Transport Southern Region Royal Train locomotive, framed, c1910, 13 x 14in (33 x 35.5cm).
£55–65
$80–95 ⊞ HO

A presentation silver spanner, marking the opening of the Jagersfontein Railway, South African, marked 'Fine silver', maker's mark 'A.F&Co', 9¼in (23.5cm) long.
£120–140
$175–200 ↗ P(B)
The shaft of this spanner is inscribed on one side 'Jagersfontein' and 'Jany 31. 1905' on the other. The closed end is inscribed on one side 'Facsimilie of the Excelsior Diamond weight 971 carats found in the Jagersfontein Mine' and 'Presented to His Excellency Sir R.H.J. Goold Adam K.C.M.G.C.B. Lieut Governor O.P.C. on opening Railway Jagersfontein'.

◀ **A brass locomotive shield,** face polished, German, 19½in (49.5cm) high.
£1,700–1,900
$2,500–2,750 ↗ SRA
This was fitted to one of the few Orenstein & Koppel 2–8–0Ts exported to Africa between 1905 and 1907.

An LBSCR brass nameplate, 'St Catherine's Point', 1906, 57in (145cm) wide.
£13,500–16,000
$19,500–23,500 ↗ SRA
This plate was carried by the Class H1 4–4–2 LBSCR 40, built by Kitson as Works No. 4354 in February 1906. It was finally withdrawn in January 1944, the nameplates being fortunate to survive during the wartime scrap drive.

◀ **A Southern Railway poster of Canterbury,** in brown with red roofs and bright green trees, 1920s, 40 x 50in (101.5 x 127cm).
£2,700–3,000
$4,000–4,500
⊞ REN

▶ **An L&SWR cast-iron sign,** white with red lettering and border, 1923, 16in (40.5cm) high.
£55–65
$80–95 ↗ RAR

A CK&P cast-iron bridgeplate, painted in white with black lettering, 1864–1923, 12in (30.5cm) wide.
£320–360
$460–520 SRA

A pair of mahogany signal box block instruments, one an SWR East Putney box Sykes lock and block from Mount Pleasant, the other a No. 4 Treadle lock and block to 'B' instrument, both with single circular enamel dials, c1920s, 13½in (34.5cm) high.
£130–160
$190–230 P(C)

A railway nameplate and works-plate, for Bristol, the worksplate for Peckett & Sons, 1923, nameplate 28in (71cm) wide.
£2,000–2,200
$3,000–3,200 SRA
This set of plates was carried by a Peckett Type R2 0–4–0ST with outside cylinders that left the Works in October 1923. In December 1963 it went to the Brooklyn Engineering Company at Chandler's Ford, presumably for scrap.

An LMS cast-brass nameplate crest, 'Royal Scot', 1927, 11in (28cm) diam.
£12,000–13,000
$17,500–18,850 SRA
This plate was carried by the class 6P 4–6–0 LMS 6132 locomotive 'King's Regiment Liverpool'. Built at the North British Locomotive's Hyde Park Works as Works No. 23627 in September 1927, it was withdrawn in February 1964 to be cut up by the West of Scotland Shipbreaking Company of Troon in April 1965.

◄ **Two railway service brass badges,** one for LNER, one for LMS, 1930s, 1½in (4cm) wide.
£12–15
$18–22 each COB

A GWR inner signal lamp, c1930, 11in (28cm) high.
£40–45
$60–65 FST

A BR(M) guard's whistle and railway ashtray, the whistle with chain, the ashtray with 'Southampton Dock Centenary 1838–1938 Southern Railways' engraved around central company seal.
£25–30
$35–45 P(C)

An LNER B1 cast brass nameplate, 'Springbok', 1942, face restored, 43in (109cm) wide.
£16,500–18,000
$24,000–26,000 SRA
This plate was for the first of the class 4–6–0 locomotives, LNER 8301, built at Darlington in December 1942. It was withdrawn from Colwick on 5 March 1962.

An LNER cast brass nameplate, 'Steady Aim', with three of its original six bolts, face restored, 1946, 58in (147.5cm) wide.
£19,000–21,000
$27,500–30,500 ✗ SRA
This plate, named for the horse that won the 1946 Oaks, was carried by the LNER Class A2/3 4–6–2 Pacific, LNER 512, built at Doncaster in 1946 as Works No. 2003, and was initially in service at Gateshead. It was withdrawn on 19 June 1965.

A Great Northern Railway of Ireland Class U engraved brass nameplate, 'Louth', 1948, 15in (38cm) wide.
£3,000–3,500
$4,400–5,000 ✗ SRA
This plate was carried by the Great Northern Railway of Ireland Class U 5ft 3in gauge 4–4–0 No. 202, built by Beyer Peacock as Works No. 7245 in January 1948. It became UTA No. 67 in 1958 and was withdrawn in May 1965.

A railway ticket-stamping machine, by Waterlow & Sons, London, 1950, 10in (25.5cm) high.
£85–95
$125–140 ⊞ FST

A Vic Welch BR colour poster, publicizing the electrification of the Manchester–Sheffield line, c1955, 39¾ x 49½in (101 x 126cm).
£300–350
$440–500 ✗ Bea(E)
Vic Welch worked in the BR (LMR) design department.

▶ An LMS Tyer's signal box, two-needle absolute with F-type block, complete with bell-plunger and rotary commutator, side meshes and Tyer's transfer, in wooden housing, late 1940s, 18in (45.5cm) high.
£220–250
$320–360 ✗ SRA

A BR enamel station sign, 'Trent Station', red with white lettering, 1960s, 160in (406.5cm) wide.
£300–350
$440–500 ⊞ TRA

▶ A BR alloy works plate, grey letters on a blue ground, face restored, 1965, 8½in (21.5cm) wide.
£50–80
$75–115 ⊞ SOL

◀ A London Underground red, white and blue enamel station sign, 'Balham', 1970s, 28in (71cm) wide.
£55–65
$80–95 ⊞ COB

Rock & Pop

A charcoal sketch of George Harrison, by Stuart Sutcliffe, the 'fifth Beatle', c1959, 14½ x 11¼in (37 x 28.5cm).
£1,300–1,500
$1,900–2,150 ⊞ IQ

Stuart Sutcliffe, a hand-written letter from Hamburg, on six sides, with original envelope, c1960.
£800–900
$1,150–1,300 ✗ FO
This extremely candid letter, written over several days and addressed to 'Dear Susan', an ex-girlfriend, tellingly expresses Sutcliffe's artistic frustrations.

A Beatles song sheet, for 'Why', written by Bill Crompton and Tony Sheridan, published by Pan-Musik of Denmark Street, London, 1960s, 10 x 8in (25.5 x 20.5cm).
£20–25
$30–35 ✗ SAF

Miller's is a price GUIDE not a price LIST

◀ **George Harrison,** a black and white photograph signed 'George Harrison x x', and inscribed on the reverse, in a different hand 'George Harrison, Maclatts [sic] lane, Woolton, 25', c1963, 5½ x 3½in (14 x 9cm).
£200–240
$300–350 ✗ FO
Mackets Lane was George Harrison's home address.

Two torn Beatles tickets, for a concert at Birkenhead, 10 February 1962.
£600–700
$870–1,000 ✗ FO

▶ **The Beatles,** a black and white photograph taken during a recording of their performance in the *Morecambe and Wise Show*, on Monday 2nd December 1963, 72 x 36in (183 x 91.5cm).
£160–200
$230–300 ✗ FO

A black and white Beatles beach hat, American, 1964, 12in (30.5cm) wide.
£30–40
$45–60 ♣ SAF

A copy of 'The Beatles Christmas Album' LP, issued for the US market, 1963.
£80–100
$115–145 ♣ SAF

A Beatles yellow plastic wallet, by Standard Plastic Products, with sepia images of the Beatles, American, 1964, 4½in (11cm) wide.
£60–70
$90–100 ♣ SAF

A Beatles concert programme, for Brighton Hippodrome, Sunday 12 July 1964, with notes by original owner on the performance and the audience, 10 x 8in (25.5 x 20.5cm).
£150–180
$220–260 ♣ FO

◀ **A Beatles white three-ring binder,** with sepia images of the Beatles and facsimile signatures, American, 1964, 11¾in (30cm) high.
£50–60
$75–90 ♣ SAF

▶ **A Beatles pottery bowl,** by Washington Pottery, with images of the Beatles and fac-simile signatures, American, 1964, 6in (15cm) diam.
£20–25
$30–35 ⊞ BTC

A set of four Beatles plastic dolls, with twisting heads, 1960, 4in (10cm) high.
£10–15
$15–20 ♣ SAF

▶ **A Beatles Burrite mug and plastic cup,** American, 1960s, mug 6in (15cm) high.
£10–15
$15–20 ♣ SAF

► **A Beatles** *Help!* **film poster,** some damage, 1965, 30 x 40in (76 x 101.5cm).
£120–140
$175–200 ⚏ **CBP**

A Beatles calendar, by Beat Publications, complete, one page loose, 1964, 11 x 9in (28 x 23cm).
£30–40
$45–60 ⚏ **SAF**

Two Beatles tickets, for Another Beatles Christmas Show, one ticket over-stamped 'Guest', Thursday 7th January 1965, 2½in (6.5cm) square.
£120–140
$175–200 ⚏ **FO**

A set of four Beatles badges, 1965, 1¼in (3cm) diam.
£8–12
$12–18 ⚏ **SAF**

A Beatles blue vinyl brunch bag, American, 1965, 8in (20.5cm) high.
£320–380
$470–570 ⚏ **SAF**
It is unusual to find this item in such good condition.

A Beatles *Yellow Submarine* **film poster,** *Le Sous-marin Jaune,* with images of the Beatles and other characters from the film, Belgian, 1968, 21 x 13in (53.5 x 33cm).
£100–120
$145–175 ⚏ **Bon(C)**

A Beatles cream record-carrying case, with individual and group images and facsimile signatures, Dutch, 1960s, 8½in (21.5cm) high.
£80–100
$115–145 ⚏ **SAF**

Items in the Rock & Pop section have been arranged in alphabetical order.

A shop display stand-up cardboard cut-out of Paul McCartney, with a Rome concert poster, 1989, 33in (84cm) high.
£10–15
$15–20 ⚏ **SAF**

► **A signed concert programme for Paul McCartney's Liverpool Oratorio,** 1990.
£100–120
$145–175 ⊞ **BTC**

A 'Blues Fell This Morning' LP,
released by Philips, including rare
recordings of Southern blues
singers, 1960.
£50–60
$75–90 ⊞ TOT

**A copy of the 'Catch A Wave'
10in LP double album,** including
tracks by Blondie, Motorhead and
Ultravox, very good condition, 1978.
£15–20
$20–30 ⊞ TOT

A 'Kings of the Blues' 10in LP,
issued by RCA as Volume 3 in their
'Backgrounds of Jazz' series,
excellent condition, American, 1961.
£40–45
$60–65 ⊞ TOT

**A Marc Bolan vinyl picture disc
collection,** featuring interviews in
America, 1972, 7 x 4in (18 x 10cm).
£20–25
$30–35 ⋰ SAF

**A Grateful Dead white metal
buckle,** modelled as a skull, in box
signed by Jerry Garcia, 1988, buckle
3in (7.5cm) high.
£180–220
$260–320 ⋰ FO

The Corrs, a signed colour
photograph, signed first names only,
c2000, 10 x 8in (25.5 x 20.5cm).
£120–140
$175–200 ⋰ VS

An Embrace promotional CD,
'Drawn from Memory', in moulded
gilt tin, 2000, 5in (12.5cm) diam.
£12–15
$18–20 ⊞ TOT

Cross Reference
See Colour Review (page 246)

A copy of the first Jimi Hendrix single, 'Hey Joe!', signed by Noel Redding, inscribed 'Best Wishes to Tony', issued by Polydor, 1966.
£80–100
$115–145 ✦ Bon

A black and white photograph of Buddy Holly, by Lew Allen, at the Auditorium Theater, Rochester, New York, limited edition, signed and titled by Allen, sold without copyright, 19 January 1958, 11 x 14in (28 x 35.5cm).
£220–250
$320–360 ✦ FO
Lew Allen was the only photographer to document this event.

A Manic Street Preachers concert ticket, for a concert at Bournemouth Academy, signed and inscribed, together with a colour photograph taken by the drummer, Sean Moore, 19 October 1992, ticket 2¾ x 3½in (7 x 9cm).
£25–35
$35–50 ✦ Bon(C)

Jimi Hendrix's lucky silver dollar, dated 1889, 1½in (4cm) diam.
£1,600–1,900
$2,300–2,750 ✦ Bon
In 1966, Jimi Hendrix was stranded without any money when he missed the bus to a gig. Thereafter, he always carried a silver dollar, usually in his shoe, but sometimes in his hat-band. This coin was the one he carried from late 1966 through to the early 1970s.

A copy of the 'Elmore James memorial album' 12in LP, issued by Sue Records, 1965.
£40–50
$60–75 ⊞ TOT

A Led Zeppelin 'Remasters' promotional CD, four tracks, boxed, American, 1990.
£25–30
$35–45 ⊞ TOT

A Jimi Hendrix cardboard coat hanger, by Saunders Enterprises, with a cut-out slot to hang a pair of trousers, 1967, 17in (43cm) high.
£100–120
$145–175 ✦ Bon

An Elton John silkscreen concert poster, for a concert arranged by Entecom, with Noir as a supporting act, purple and black on a white ground, January 1971, 30 x 20in (76 x 51cm).
£180–220
$260–320 ✦ FO
Entecom was the Entertainment Committee of Southampton University Students Union, and concerts were held in the Old Union Refectory. These posters were produced by the Southampton University Students Union, and designed by John Liverton, then Publicity Officer.

◀ **A Bank of England one pound note signed by Annie Lennox,** 1990s, 2½ x 5½in (6.5 x 13.5cm).
£60–80
$90–115 ✦ Bon

A black leather biker jacket, by T/T Leathers, worn by Freddie Mercury on the promo for 'Crazy Little Thing Called Love' in 1979, and the 'Crazy' European Tour in 1980, with an image of Mercury wearing a similar jacket on stage.
£1,000–1,200
$1,500–1,750 ⚲ FO
This jacket was originally purchased at a Queen Fan Club convention. Many years later the new owner met Mercury in Greece and jokingly asked if he would like to buy the jacket back, to which the response was 'I never buy anything second-hand, my dear!'

A copy of 'Negativeland' 12in LP, issued by Seeland Records, American, 1980.
£40–50
$60–75 ⊞ TOT

An Oasis singles collection '(What's the Story) Morning Glory', in a gold cigarette pack box with black and green lettering, early 1990s, 6in (15cm) high.
£20–25
$30–35 ⚲ SAF

> **Cross Reference**
> See Colour Review
> (page 246–248)

◄ **An Oasis one-sided 'I am the Walrus' 12in promotional single,** limited edition of 250, mint condition, 1994.
£250–350
$360–500 ⊞ TOT

An Ozzy Osbourne 'Blizzard of Oz' flightcase and Marshall bass amp, the flightcase with white stencilled lettering, containing a Marshall JCM 800 Bass Series amplifier, 1980s, flightcase 58in (147.5cm) wide.
£250–300
$360–440 ⚲ Bon(C)

► **An Elvis Presley lady's handbag mirror,** with facsimile inscription, surrounded by a pale green rim, c1957, 3in (7.5cm) diam.
£40–50
$60–75 ⊞ MURR

A signed Elvis Presley mono album, from the soundtrack of the film *Clambake*, issued by RCA Victor, inscribed and signed in black ballpoint on the front cover 'My best to you Elvis Presley' 1968.
£400–450
$580–650 ↗ FO

A Billy Preston 'Greazee Soul' 12in mono LP, mint condition, 1969.
£18–22
$27–33 ⊞ TOT

A Cliff Richard concert flyer and booking form, for a gig at City Hall, Sheffield on 14 April 1964, printed in red and yellow, mounted and framed, 11½ x 5½in (29 x 14cm).
£25–35
$35–50 ⊞ BTC

A Las Vegas postcard signed by Elvis Presley, with inscription in red fibre pen 'To Charline, Elvis Presley August 70' on the reverse, 3½ x 11in (9 x 28cm).
£250–300
$360–440 ↗ Bon(C)

A white silk shirt worn by Prince, during his 'Lovesexy' tour and in the tour programme photographs, together with a copy of the programme, 1988.
£400–500
$580–720 ↗ FO

A photograph of the Rolling Stones, taken by the River Thames, signed by Mick Jagger, Brian Jones, Keith Richards, Bill Wyman and Charlie Watts, 1960s, 10 x 8in (25.5 x 20.5cm).
£420–500
$600–720 ↗ VS

An Elvis Presley memorial plate, the rim with blue lettering, red and yellow star motifs and a gilt edge, 1978, 10in (25.5cm) diam.
£15–20
$20–30 ↗ SAF

A black and white promotional photograph of R.E.M., with Michael Stipe's initials and Pete Buck's and Mike Mills' signatures, and 'Hi – Bill Berry' in blue marker, framed and glazed, 1990s, 16 x 14in (40.5 x 35.5cm).
£120–140
$175–200 ↗ FO

A Rolling Stones stereo 12in LP with 3-D cover, 'Their Satanic Majesties Request', issued by Decca, 1967.
£70–80
$100–115 ⊞ TOT

A Sex Pistols 'Pretty Vacant' promotional poster, 1978, 28 x 39in (71 x 99cm).
£350–400
$500–580 ⊞ IQ

A signed colour photograph of Britney Spears, c2000, 10 x 8in (25.5 x 20.5cm).
£60–70
$90–100 ⤢ VS

A Sex Pistols 'Holidays in the Sun' poster, promoting the LP issued by Virgin Records, 1977, 28in (71cm) square.
£250–300
$360–440 ⊞ IQ

Seven Throbbing Gristle cassettes, recorded at live concerts, issued by Industrial Records, 1976–81.
£10–15
$15–20 each ⊞ MVX

A Rod Stewart recording tape, recorded at the Abbey Road studio, featuring 'Baby Jane' and 'Ready Now', 1983, in original box, 7in (18cm) square.
£20–25
$30–35 ⤢ SAF

A cream plastic part scratch plate signed by Frank Zappa, with a doodle of a man smoking, 7in (18cm) wide.
£120–140
$175–200 ⤢ FO

A 'Velvet Underground & Nico' 12in LP, issued by Verve, the sleeve with original peel-off banana, 1960.
£60–70
$90–100 ⤢ SAF

A Wurlitzer 1800 jukebox, holds 52 records, in perfect working order, 1956, 56in (142cm) high.
£4,750–5,250
$7,000–7,500 ⊞ MARK

A Rock-Ola 120 Hi-Fi jukebox, holds 120 records, 1957, 54in (137cm) high.
£2,500–3,000
$3,600–4,400 ⤢ GAZE

A Rock-Ola 744 jukebox, holds 100 records, in working order, with keys and records, 1970s, 45in (114.5cm) high.
£400–500
$580–720 ⤢ SAF

Scent Bottles

A Webb cameo glass scent bottle, red glass with fuchsia design in white, and 'Remember the giver' engraved on the silver collar, 1883, 2½in (6.5cm) high.
£600–800
$870–1,150 ⊞ ALiN

A Webb cameo glass scent bottle, dark green glass with poppy and butterfly design in white, marked 'Stakenasa', 1885, 3¼in (8.5cm) high.
£700–900
$1,000–1,300 ⊞ ALiN

A silver-mounted cut-glass scent bottle, Birmingham 1906, 5in (12.5cm) high.
£100–150
$145–220 ⊞ CoHA

A clear and frosted glass scent bottle, decorated with a silhouette of a dancing female nude below a border of roses, with copper mount and stand, c1920, 8in (20.5cm) high.
£55–65
$80–95 ⊞ TWAC

A Blue Lagoon talcum powder bottle, by Dubarry, with Art Deco-style blue frosted glass, original labels, c1930, 6in (15cm) high.
£16–18
£24–27 ⊞ HUX

An Art Nouveau perfume bottle, decorated with moulded flowers, stained black, with matching stopper, French, 5½in (14cm) high.
£300–350
$440–500 ⊞ LBe

▶ **A Joy de Jean Patou plastic display bottle,** black with gold lettering and neck string, red domed top, French, 1950s, 7in (18cm) high.
£85–95
$125–140 ⊞ LBe

An Adorée perfume bottle, by E. Roy, with a frosted glass stopper in the form of a kneeling female nude, French, 1930s, 4in (10cm) high, with original box.
£300–350
$440–500 ⊞ LBe

JOY
DE
JEAN PATOU
PARIS

An Elizabeth Arden gift set, each clear glass bottle with a brass top and set with a coloured stone, in a grey pouch and original box, 1950s, 3in (7.5cm) high.
£85–95
$125–140 ⊞ LBe

A Potter & Moore's Mitcham Lavender green glass bottle, with screw top, 1935, 5½in (14cm) high.
£14–17
$21–25 ⊞ HUX

Science & Technology

A bronze sundial, by Benjamin Scott, the engraved compass, months and hours dissected with indicators to London, Constantinople, Babylon and other place names and a coat-of-arms, 18thC, base 15½in (39.5cm) diam.
£700–800
$1,000–1,200 ⚹ EH

A lacquered-brass micrometer, with bevelled glass, for measuring paper, c1850–60, 2½in (6.5cm) diam.
£80–100
$115–145 ⊞ TOM

A brass sextant, by W. F. Cannon, London, in a mahogany case, 19thC, 9¾in (25cm) wide.
£320–370
$450–550 ⚹ TRM

► **An engine-turned ivory thermometer,** with original glass dome, c1860, 10in (25.5cm) high.
£400–450
$550–650 ⊞ RAY

An Excise Office boxwood and brass barrel dipping rule, by Loftus, London, in five sections, c1870, 50in (127cm) long extended, in original leather case.
£70–80
$100–120 ⊞ TOM

A Victorian dip circle, in a mahogany case, 11in (28cm) high.
£450–500
$650–720 ⊞ ETO
A magnetic needle, mounted in a vertical graduated circle, indicates by its dip the direction of the earth's magnetism and measures the amount of the dip.

► **A lacquered-brass carbon arc lamp,** by F. J. Cox, London, on a mahogany base, c1870, 16in (40.5cm) high.
£250–300
$360–440 ⊞ TOM

A hydrometer, by Brown & Brothers, Edinburgh, c1890, 11in (28cm) long, in a wooden case.
£38–42
$50–60 ⊞ FST
This instrument was used to determine the gravity of liquids.

A surveyor's cross, by H. Morin, with original lacquer, c1890, 10in (25.5cm) long, in original wooden box.
£340–380
$500–550 ⊞ ETO

Two brass three-draw telescopes,
top. c1890–1910, 19in (48.5cm) extended.
£35–45
$50–60
bottom. c1890–1910, 24in (61cm) extended.
£65–75
$90–110 ⊞ HEG

An ivory sector, by Elliot, London, c1900, 6in (15cm) long.
£20–30
$30–45 ⊞ TOM

A boxwood cavalry map/paper holder, the reverse with protractor and compass, 1909, 10in (25.5cm) high.
£100–120
$145–175 ⊞ FST

▶ **A brass monocular microscope,** in a fitted mahogany case with accessories, the bronze triform base inscribed 'H.P. Aylward, 164 Oxford Rd., Manchester', c1900, 14in 35.5cm high.
£200–250
$300–350 ⋟ WW

A Schubert calculator, c1920, 11in (28cm) wide.
£200–230
$300–330 ⊞ ETO

▶ **A Lietl binocular microscope,** 1920–30, 14in (35.5cm) high, in a mahogany box with lenses.
£225–250
$320–360 ⊞ HEG

A brass inclinometer, c1910, 4in (10cm) high, in a leather case.
£65–75
$95–115 ⊞ FST
This instrument was used for measuring the intensity of the earth's magnetic force, as shown by the inclination of the magnetic needle.

A compass in a watch case, with chain, 1920.
£35–40
$50–60 ⊞ HO

A specific gravity thermometer, with full set of weights and ivory-mounted scale, 1920s, 7in (18cm) high, in a wooden box.
£55–65
$80–100 ⊞ FST

A wimshorst machine, c1920, 12in (30.5cm) high.
£340–380
$500–550 ⊞ ETO

A Fowler's long scale chrome slide rule, 1950s, 5in (12.5cm) diam, in leather case.
£40–50
$60–75 ⊞ TOM

A Bakelite and brass desk fan, 1940s, 9in (23cm) high.
£55–65
$80–100 ⊞ SPT

A Philips terrestrial globe, c1950, 19in (48.5cm) high.
£240–270
$350–400 ⊞ ETO

▶ **A British Aluminium Co cased advertising barometer,** 1950s, 6in (15cm) diam.
£30–35
$40–50 ⊞ RTW

A Sinclair ZX Spectrum, 128K, with printer and two microdrives, c1980, 12in (30.5cm) wide.
£80–100
$115–145 ⊞ CGX

Medical Instruments

A set of ivory-handled scalpels, and twin-bladed tortoiseshell bistoury, c1830, 7in (18cm) long, in a mahogany case.
£225–245
$330–360 ⊞ WAC

An amputation set, by Coxeter, London, including saws, scalpels and hammer, 19thC, 11in (28cm) wide, in a brass-bound mahogany box.
£370–450
$550–650 ⋟ RBB

A hand-blown yellow glass stethoscope, c1840, 10in (25.5cm) high.
£165–185
$250–280 ⊞ HO

A pair of cobalt-blue glass chemist's rounds, with red, black and gold-painted labels, 1850–60, 8½in (21.5cm) high.
£170–200
$250–300 ⋟ BBR

▶ **A brass enema set,** by Arnold & Sons, London, c1880, 52in (132cm) long, in a fitted case.
£250–275
$350–400
⊞ FST

◀ **A silver-plated brass ear trumpet,** with all-over leaf engraving, inscribed 'F.C. Rein & Son, Patentees, sole inventors and only makers, 108 Strand, London', 19thC.
£550–600
$800–880 ⋟ RBB

A Zeiss haemacytometer set, early 20thC, in a fitted box, 10in (25.5cm) wide.
£400–450
$580–650 ⊞ ETO
This apparatus was used for counting red and white blood cells.

A nurse's pulse-taking half-minute sand timer, 1910, 4in (10cm) long.
£20–25
$30–40 ⊞ HO

A Cressoline Vapo-Cresolena vaporizer inhaler, early 20thC, 7in (18cm) high.
£40–50
$60–75 ⊞ FST

Further reading

Miller's Collecting Science & Technology, Miller's Publications, 2001

◀ **A manometer,** c1925, 12in (30.5cm) high, in a wooden case.
£125–145
$180–200 ⊞ FST
This apparatus was used to test lung pressure.

Scripophily

A Tesoreria Nacional de Puerto Rico 25 pesos bond, authorized by the Provincial Junta, with a vignette of a coat-of-arms, 1813.
£100–120
$145–175 ⚒ P

A Geat Republic Gold & Silver Mining Co £50 bond, printed with vignettes of Lincoln, Queen Victoria, mining stamps, eagle and the White House, 1867.
£130–150
$200–220 ⚒ P

▶ **A Dock Sud de la Capital 100 pesos certificate,** printed in black with a vignette of a mythical female overlooking ships and a harbour, within a red border, Buenos Aires, 1889.
£55–65
$80–95 ⊞ GKR

An Indiana Coal and Railway Company $500 bond, printed in black and white, green seal, denomination underprint, coupons attached, 1881.
£30–35
$40–50 ⊞ SCR

A New York Central and Hudson River Railroad Company $1,000 bond, printed in orange and black with a vignette of a speeding loco passing ships in harbour, 1898.
£15–18
$20–25 ⊞ SCR

A Chemins de fer Ethiopiens bearer share, depicting the king on horseback with camels and followers waiting for a train to pass, printed in brown on a cream ground, Paris, 1899.
£200–225
$300–330 ⊞ SCR

◀ **A Sir James Laing & Sons £10 preference share,** depicting a wooden-hulled ship, printed in pink on a cream ground, 1899.
£60–70
$90–100 ⊞ GKR

A Canadian Mortgage Association bearer share, with vignettes of farming and city scenes, printed in brown, blue and beige, 1910.
£40–45
$60–70 ⊞ SCR

A Banco de Cartagena bond, depicting part of a Velazquez painting, printed in brown on a white ground, red revenue stamp, c1900.
£30–35
$40–50 ⊞ SCR

An Automobiles Charron Girardot & Voigt 100 franc share certificate, with vignettes of cars and a flying machine, printed in green and yellow, 1902.
£85–95
$125–145 ⊞ SCR

◄ **A Paris-France 500 franc bond,** with a vignette of five ladies by 'Mucha 98', four small hole cancellations, printed in brown on a buff ground, 1927.
£250–300
$350–450 ⚒ P

A Brazil Railway Company $100 share, with a vignette of a train on an iron bridge in a jungle, uncancelled, printed in black and pink on a cream ground, 1911.
£850–950
$1,250–1,350 ⚒ P

An A La Reine d'Angleterre share certificate, with a vignette of Queen Victoria during a visit to France in the 1840s, printed in pink and turquoise on a cream ground, 1924.
£30–40
$45–60 ⊞ GKR

► **A Republic of China Secured Sinking Fund $1,000 bond,** issued by J. P. Morgan, New York, countersigned by the Bank of China, 1937.
£600–650
$870–950 ⚒ P

► **An Electricas Reunidas de Zaragoza SA bearer share,** depicting a government building and a map of the area serviced by the company, printed in brown and black, 1968.
£16–18
$22–28 ⊞ SCR

◄ **A Casino des Fleurs de Beaulieu 500 franc share,** with a vignette of a casino overlooking the sea at Nice, with coupons, printed in pink and blue, dated 1929.
£30–35
$45–50 ⊞ GKR

Sewing

A pair of polished steel scissors, by C. A. Arnold, London, 19thC, 5½in (14cm) long.
£16–18
$22–28 ⊞ WAC

A cherrywood, maple and oak tri-leg yarn winder, with square wheel, 1780–1800, 42¾in (108.5cm) high.
£135–155
$200–225 ⊞ EON

A Victorian lady's papier mâché workbox, by Jennens & Bettridge, the black ground decorated with polychrome and gilt with floral arabesques inlaid with mother-of-pearl, the silk-lined interior fitted with small boxes, instruments and mother-of-pearl reels, impressed 'Jennens & Bettridge makers to the Queen', 12in (30.5cm) wide.
£450–500
$650–720 ⚒ HYD

Four mother-of-pearl thread winders, c1850, largest 1¾in (4.5cm) diam.
£20–40
$30–60 each ⊞ VB

◀ **A Continental lace-maker's glass lamp,** 6in (15cm) high.
£145–165
$200–250 ⊞ DHA

A green-painted pine sewing box, the revolving thread holder above a box with a drawer, decorated with a black wavy line, American, 19thC, 6½in (16.5cm) high.
£430–480
$630–700 ⚒ SK(B)

A Tunbridge ware pin cushion, c1870, 1in (2.5cm) high.
£80–90
$115–125 ⊞ AMH

A Mauchline ware needle holder, 1870, 8in (20.5cm) long.
£50–60
$75–90 ⊞ MB

A miniature pair of scissors, from an étui, 19thC, 2in (5cm) long.
£70–80
$100–125 ⊞ HO

A carved ivory sewing clamp, c1880, 5in (12.5cm) long.
£65–85
$100–125 ⊞ VB

A mother-of-pearl and abalone silver thimble case, c1880, 1½in (4cm) long.
£60–70
$90–100 ⊞ VB

A Bradbury & Co treadle sewing machine, for leather boots and shoes, with cast-iron frame and wooden table, c1884, 39in (99cm) high.
£600–640
$870–950 ⊞ WSM

A tape measure, in the shape of an iron, c1890. 2in (5cm) long.
£75–85
$110–125 ⊞ VB

A Celluloid tape measure, in the form of a Lifeboat man, c1900, 2¼in (5.5cm) high.
£90–100
$130–150 ⊞ VB

A tape measure, in the shape of a Highland terrier, c1900, 2in (5cm) high.
£80–100
$115–145 ⊞ VB

A silver thimble, Birmingham 1905, 1in (2.5cm) high.
£25–35
$30–50 ⊞ CoHA

Cross Reference
See Colour Review (page 313)

◄ A Singer 99K sewing machine, with a laminated wood carrying case, 1937, 19in (48.5cm) high.
£75–85
$110–125 ⊞ WSM

A tape measure, in the form of Edward, Prince of Wales, 1920s, 2¼in (5.5cm) high.
£85–95
$125–145 ⊞ VB

Shipping

A set of four handle plates, commemorating the Battle of Trafalgar, each depicting a tomb with a plaque inscribed 'Sacred to Nelson', beneath an anchor and 'Trafalgar', among war trophies, within a Greek key pattern border, handles missing, 1805, 3¼in (8.5cm) wide.
£445–485
$650–700 ⊞ TML

A Sherwood's ship's binnacle lamp, c1870, 11in (28cm) high.
£90–110
$130–160 ⊞ FST

Two cabinet cards, depicting *The Gypsy* shipwreck on the Avon estuary with *Sea King* rescue tug, c1880, 6½ x 4½in (16.5 x 11.5cm).
£20–25
$30–40 each ⊞ J&S

A diorama of a three-masted ship, in a glazed and ebonized case, c1900, 33in (84cm) wide.
£600–700
$870–1,000 ⚒ GH

◄ **A Royal Navy mess bucket,** with brass label, c1900, 16in (40.5cm) high.
£40–45
$60–65 ⊞ B&R

A brass ship's bell,
inscribed *Fragrant, 1908,*
10in (25.5cm) high.
£300–350
$450–500 ⊞ COB

Sheet music for 'The Ship that will Never Return', by F. V. St Clair, dedicated to the *Titanic* Relief Fund, c1912–13, framed and glazed.
£50–60
$70–90 ⋌ CDC

▶ **A water-colour of the *Empress of Ireland,*** blue, black, red and cream, in a seashell frame, 1914, 6½in (16.5cm) diam.
£50–60
$70–90 ⊞ RUSS

◀ **An RRS *Discovery II* wooden ship's register,** displaying a list of 17 ship's officers and crew with 'aboard' and 'ashore' slots, 1929, 17¼in (43.5cm) high.
£850–950
$1,250–1,350 ⊞ TML
The Royal Research Ship *Discovery II* was launched for the Antarctic from St Katharine's Dock in December 1929.

A US Navy theodolite,
by W. & L. E. Gurley, Troy, American, 1918, 15in (38cm) high.
£450–500
$650–720 ⊞ BoC

A Royal Navy ship's brass clock, 1929, 8in (20.5cm) diam.
£800–900
$1,200–1,300 ⊞ BoC

▶ **A White Star Line silver-plated napkin ring,** by Elkington, c1920, 2in (5cm) diam.
£25–30
$30–40 ⊞ CRN

A French Line silver and brass plaque, 1926, 8in (20.5cm) high.
£200–230
$300–330 ⊞ COB

A bronze ship's propellor, by Buntons, Sudbury, 1920s, 14in (35.5cm) diam.
£125–150
$180–220 ⊞ OLA

A set of eight Art Deco greetings cards, depicting life on board the great liners, printed in colour, c1920, 8½ x 6in (20.5 x 15cm).
£8–10
$12–15 ⊞ MAP

▶ **A model of a sailing dinghy,** carved from a single piece of cedar wood, 1930, 8in (20.5cm) long.
£180–200
$250–300 ⊞ BoC

◄ **A German African Lines timetable,** 1935, 8 x 6in (20.5 x 15cm).
£9–12
$14–18 ⊞ J&S

> **Cross Reference**
> See Colour Review (page 315)

A hand-built model boat, *Deglet Nour*, with diagonal planking and water-cooled diesel engine, painted cream and blue, 1940s, 36in (91.5cm) long.
£1,200–1,400
$1,800–2,000 ⊞ BoC

A Royal Navy Reserve poster, printed in red, white and blue, 1948, 38 x 20in (96.5 x 51cm).
£50–60
$70–90 ⊞ COB

An HM Yacht *Britannia* **embroidered blazer badge,** gold, red, green and blue on a black ground, 1990s, 4in (10cm) wide.
£10–15
$15–20 ⊞ COB

Four full colour *QEII* **first day postal covers,** 1969–82, 4 x 7in (10 x 18cm).
£10–15
$15–20 each ⊞ COB

Silver & Metalware
Silver

A Victorian silver and ivory travelling apple corer, Birmingham 1857, 5in (12.5cm) long.
£330–360
$450–500 ⊞ CoHA

▶ **A pair of Victorian silver and steel boot pulls,** by A. L. & S. and M. C., with foxes on the handles, 8in (20.5cm) long.
£600–650
$870–950 ⊞ BEX
These silver pulls were used for riding boots.

A Victorian engraved silver tankard, Exeter 1860, 4in (10cm) high.
£120–150
$175–225 ⚒ SWO

A Victorian silver vinaigrette, by Samson Mordan & Co, in the shape of a hunting horn, London 1889, 4in (10cm) long.
£370–420
$550–630 ⚒ P(L)

An engraved silver jam spoon, Sheffield 1895, 5in (12.5cm) long.
£20–25
$30–35 ⊞ HO

A silver pepper pot, 1882, 4in (10cm) high.
£50–55
$70–80 ⊞ HO

A silver three-piece tea service, on four compressed ball feet, teapot Birmingham 1897, cream jug and sugar basin Birmingham 1898, 40oz.
£320–360
$480–550 ⚒ CDC

Items in the Silver & Metalware section have been arranged in date order within each sub-section.

◀ **A silver box,** embossed with leaf scrolls, the domed lid with gadrooned edge, by W. N., Sheffield 1897, 4in (10cm) long.
£110–130
$150–200 ⚒ GAK

A pair of silver nut dishes, in the shape of leaves, with foliate-pierced and applied edges and cast pierced feet, by G. H., London 1899, 8in (20.5cm) wide, 15oz.
£200–250
$300–350 ⚒ GAK

A pair of pierced silver salts, with blue glass liners, Birmingham 1904, 2in (5cm) high.
£200–230
$300–330 ⊞ CoHA

A silver miniature pincushion, in the shape of a polar bear, 1909, 1½in (4cm) long.
£700–800
$1,000–1,200 ⊞ HCA

A silver miniature pepper pot, set with red and black Scottish stones, Birmingham 1904, 2in (5cm) high.
£120–150
$175–225 ⊞ HCA

A card marker, with silver base, used for bridge, 1909, 2½in (6.5cm) high.
£140–160
$200–230 ⊞ HCA

A set of four silver menu holders, by Mappin & Webb, depicting game birds, a gentleman with a shotgun and a gundog, Birmingham 1912–13, 1½in (4cm) high.
£700–775
$1,000–1,200 ⊞ HCA

Further reading

Miller's Silver & Plate Buyer's Guide,
Miller's Publications, 2001

◀ **A silver condiment set,** with blue glass liners, Chester 1930, pepper pot 3½in (9cm) high.
£280–330
$400–475
⊞ HCA

A five-bar silver toast rack,
Birmingham 1943, 4in (10cm) high.
£70–80
$100–120 ⊞ ASAA

A hand-beaten silver sugar bowl, cream jug and spoon, Birmingham 1968, spoon 4in (10cm) long.
£400–450
$580–650 ⊞ CoHA

A prototype textured silver pepper mill, by Stuart Devlin, with a central polished band between two chased textured bands, base stamped 'London 1975', 8in (20.5cm) high.
£500–600
$700–850 ⚒ P(Ba)

Silver Plate

A William IV Old Sheffield plate silver teapot, with a bone handle, c1830, 11in (28cm) long.
£180–220
$250–330 ⊞ ASAA

Miller's is a price GUIDE
not a price LIST

A Victorian silver-plated three-bar toast rack, by Elkington & Co, 4in (10cm) high.
£100–120
$145–175 ⊞ CoHA

A silver-plated bread fork, with a mother-of-pearl handle, c1910, 6in (15cm) long.
£18–20
$25–30 ⊞ HO

A set of engraved silver-plated teaspoons, with sugar tongs, c1920, in original box, 14in (35.5cm) wide.
£35–40
$50–60 ⊞ HO

Metalware

A brass and iron skimmer, c1770, 24in (61cm) long.
£200–225
$290–330 ⊞ SEA

A pewter salt, c1800, 4in (10cm) diam.
£50–55
$70–80 ⊞ HO

A painted metal tray, decorated with a mythical hunting scene in green, red, brown and cream, within a floral panelled border, 19thC, 30in (76cm) long.
£450–550
$650–800 ⋊ RBB

A branding iron, 'EH', 19thC, 15in (38cm) long.
£15–18
$20–25 ⊞ HCJ

▶ **A Victorian cast-iron free-standing heater,** by F. R. Embassy, 40in (101.5cm) high.
£200–250
$300–350 ⊞ CRN

A copper coffee pot, with swan-neck spout and turned ebony handle, the hinged domed cover with a bell metal acorn finial, mid-19thC, 12¾in (32.5cm) high.
£85–100
$125–145 ⋊ WW

A Victorian tin crumb pan, with turned wood handle, painted green with yellow pansies, 14in (35.5cm) long.
£10–12
$15–18 ⊞ VB

A Victorian clasp knife, by Joseph Rodgers & Sons, comprising 4¼in (11cm) blade, saw blade, 2½in (6.5cm) blade, hoof hook, corkscrew, awl and probe, the two-piece staghorn grip with vacant escutcheon containing tweezers and needle, marked, 5in (12.5cm) long closed.
£240–280
$350–420 ↗ WAL
The firm of Joseph Rodgers & Sons, Sheffield, was one of the leading producers of multi-bladed knives in the 19th century. In 1822, in order to celebrate their Royal appointment by George IV, Rodgers made a knife with 1822 blades, one for each year in the Christian calendar. For the Great Exhibition in 1851 they manufactured a giant knife with 75 blades and tools. The company's mark was a star and cross.

Two bronze drink measures, c1920, largest 3in (7.5cm) high.
£55–75
$80–110 ⊞ WAB

▶ **A chrome tray,** with orange Bakelite ends, 1930s, 15in (38cm) wide.
£55–65
$80–95 ⊞ LBe

A folding novelty pocket knife, the cover decorated with a chessboard motif, French, late 19thC, 1in (2.5cm) diam.
£45–50
$65–75 ⊞ MRW

A brass wine keg spigot, c1900, 8in (20.5cm) long.
£7–10
$10–15 ⊞ FST

Two lead models of cats, one black with a green bow, one ginger with an orange bow, beneath a green umbrella, German, 1920, 3in (7.5cm) high.
£110–140
$160–200 ⊞ HAL

A brass birdcage, c1880, 61in (155cm) high on stand.
£350–375
$500–550 ⊞ JACK

Two lead models of polar bears, on a block of soapstone, c1920, 2in (5cm) square.
£25–30
$35–45 ⊞ HAL

A lead model of a cat, possibly by Heyde, German, 1920s, 2in (5cm) high.
£40–50
$60–80 ⊞ HAL

Sixties & Seventies

A painted plywood Mark II book donkey, by Ernest Race for Isokon, on hardwood uprights, 1960s, 21in (53.5cm) long.
£150–170
$220–250 ⊞ ORI

In 1931 engineer Jack Pritchard and architect Wells Coates founded Isokon (Isometric Unit Construction), a progressive company that produced plywood furniture for the modernist 'minimum interior'. One of the company's best-known designs was the Penguin Donkey, so-called because it was specifically designed to hold the new paperback books pioneered in Britain by Sir Allen Lane's Penguin publishing imprint (established 1935). After WWII, the Penguin Donkey was remodelled for Isokon by the British designer Ernest Race (1913–64).

A Fornasetti ceramic calendar, 1963, 3¼in (8.5cm) high.
£25–30
$35–45 ⊞ DSG

A Sparklets chrome and black plastic soda syphon, 1960s, 12in (30.5cm) high.
£45–55
$65–80 ⊞ ZOOM

◄ **A Ridgway bowl,** decorated with Barbecue pattern, 1960s, 6¾in (17cm) diam.
£165–185
$240–270 ⊞ HSt

◄ **A Troika vase,** decorated with an abstract pattern in brown, oatmeal and blue, 1970, 8in (20.5cm) high.
£60–80
$90–115 ⋌ P(B)

A Portmeirion coffee pot, decorated with Majic City pattern, 1960s, 12½in (32cm) high.
£45–55
$65–80 ⊞ LEGE

A St Ives Pottery Troika wheel vase, decorated in oatmeal, brown and blue, c1965, 12in (30.5cm) diam.
£300–350
$450–500 ⊞ HUN

A pair of Grundig speakers, 1960s, 36in (91.5cm) high.
£450–500
$650–720 ⊞ HSt

LOCATE THE SOURCE
The source of each illustration in Miller's can be found by checking the code letters below each caption with the Key to Illustrations, pages 444–452.

▶ **Six Ironstone Pottery Beefeater mugs,** 1960s–70s, 3in (7.5cm) high.
£30–40
$45–60 ⋌ FLD

A Harvey Guzzini plastic picnic set, in the shape of a bowling ball, 1970s, 13in (33cm) diam.
£50–55
$75–80 ⊞ HSt

A Hornsea cream and black ashtray, 1970s, 6in (15cm) long.
£2–4
$4–6 ⊞ UNI

A chrome ceiling light, 1970s, 20in (51cm) high.
£200–250
$300–360 ⊞ ZOOM

A pair of red and black plastic chairs, on metal bases, Belgian, 1970s.
£400–450
$580–650 ⊞ HSt

A moulded plastic rock lamp, naturalistically coloured, internally lit, Italian, 1970s, 17in (43cm) diam.
£200–250
$300–360 ⋌ TREA

> **Cross Reference**
> See Lighting (page 272)

A Westclox chrome and plastic Big Ben clock, with a blue face, 1970s, 7½in (19cm) high.
£45–55
$65–80 ⊞ ZOOM

A Circle Sections B fabric panel, by Alexander Girard, light purple with purple silkscreen design, signed, slightly faded, 1972, 73in (185.5cm) long.
£220–270
$330–400 ⋌ TREA

A chrome and orange and white plastic lamp, Italian design, 1970s, 27in (68.5cm) diam.
£175–225
$250–320 ⊞ ZOOM

◀ **A San Marino ceramic plaque,** decorated with brown and black cats, c1970, 15in (38cm) long.
£40–50
$60–75 ⊞ DSG

A freestanding brown plastic ashtray, 1970s, 20½in (52cm) high.
£35–40
$50–60 ⊞ ZOOM

Smoking & Snuff Taking

An ivory snuff mull, the oval disc engraved 'WJ 1753', the lip with crescent-shaped mount engraved 'Isabella Moffatt, So.Shields', 2in (5cm) high.
£250–300
$360–440 ⚒ P(Ed)

An olive green glass snuff jar, with wide neck and rolled flared lip, pontil scar to base, 6¼in (16cm) high.
£100–120
$145–175 ⚒ BBR

A horn and brass snuff mull, c1780, 4in (10cm) long.
£250–300
$360–440 ⊞ HO

A birchwood tobacco-chopping board, 19thC, 6in (15cm) wide.
£60–75
$100–110 ⊞ NEW

▶ **A cedar cigar cabinet,** 19thC, 21in (53.5cm) high.
£200–250
$300–350 ⊞ OTT

A burr-mulberry and ebony-inlaid snuff box, 1790, 3½in (9cm) long.
£130–160
$200–230 ⊞ MB

A papier mâché and pewter-inlaid snuff box, 1840, 4in (10cm) long.
£50–60
$75–90 ⊞ MB

A Charles Stewart Parnell silver and gilt cigarette case, by W. W. and F. D., the lid inscribed with the arms of the Askwith family with motto 'Honesta Quam Splendida', the inside also inscribed, 1889, 3¼in (8cm) long, in original Carrington & Co presentation case.
£450–500
$650–720 ⊞ TML
George Ranken Askwith, Baron Askwith (1861–1942) was a barrister, arbitrator and member of many government committees and commissions.

A Great Exhibition clay pipe, by T. Blake, the bowl decorated with a view of the Crystal Palace exhibition buildings, 1851, 7in (18cm) long.
£100–120
$145–175 ⊞ TML

An ebony, ivory and silver pipe tamper, modelled as a truncheon, enclosing metal picker, 19thC, 3in (7.5cm) long.
£150–180
$220–280 ⊞ AEF

A Champagne E. Mercier & Co advertising cigar cutter, 1900, 2in (5cm) long.
£145–165
$200–240 ⊞ EMC

► A Gibson's Burslem hand-painted ashtray, decorated with black cats wearing red ribbons, 1910, 4in (10cm) wide.
£85–95
$125–140 ⊞ LBe

A Bollinger advertising cigar cutter, modelled as a champagne bottle, 1900, 2¼in (5.5cm) high.
£85–95
$125–140 ⊞ EMC

A brass lighter, depicting an airship, 1905, 2in (5cm) diam.
£85–95
$125–140 ⊞ SSM

◄ A jade and ebony cigarette holder, 1920s, 6in (15cm) long.
£30–35
$45–50 ⊞ AnS

► An IJOB metal cigarette-making machine, c1925, 10in (25.5cm) long.
£20–25
$30–35 ⊞ HUX

An Oriental-style brass smoking set, comprising cigarette holder, case and matchbox, 1930s, in a fitted case, 9 x 6in (23 x 15cm).
£40–50
$60–75 ⊞ AnS

◄ A lighter, with crocodile skin cover, 1940s, 4¼in (11cm) high.
£85–95
$125–140 ⊞ LBe

A brass and aluminium table cigarette lighter, 1940s, 4in (10cm) high.
£16–18
$20–25 ⊞ CRN

► A Bakelite seaside souvenir ashtray, 1940s–50s, 5in (12.5cm) diam.
£10–15
$15–20 ⊞ RTT

A chrome lift lighter, c1950, 3in (7.5cm) square.
£40–45
$60–65 ⊞ HarC

A brass and copper cigarette lighter, modelled as a lighthouse, 1940s, 8in (20.5cm) high.
£20–25
$30–35 ⊞ HarC

Sport

A leather dog fighting collar, with steel spikes, 18thC, 9in (23cm) long.
£55–65
$80–95 ⊞ SA

A silver-plated trophy, for Charing Cross Hospital athletics, 1897, 14in (35.5cm) high.
£75–85
$110–125 ⊞ SA

A Victorian mahogany revolving billiard cue stand, 44in (112cm) high.
£1,600–2,000
$2,300–3,000 ⚒ RBB

***Manual of Croquet,** its appointments and laws; by An Experienced Player,* published by Milner & Sowerby, original printed and decorated wrappers, rubbed and chipped, 1867, 12°.
£130–150
$200–220 ⚒ DW

A set of four bowling woods, 1900–10, 5in (12.5cm) diam.
£40–50
$60–75 ⊞ WaR

◄ **A set of four badminton rackets,** c1910, 27in (68.5cm) high.
£225–275
$330–400 ⊞ SMW

A silver-plated trophy, for Cambridge University Sports Club 100 yards race, 1891, 8in (20.5cm) high.
£50–55
$70–80 ⊞ SA

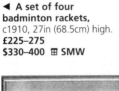

A 66th University Boat Race rudder, part-painted in Cambridge blue, the Cambridge University crew and 'Lost by 3 Lengths' inscribed in gilt, 1909, 18in (45.5cm) long.
£700–800
$1,000–1,150 ⚒ S

A set of badminton poles and net, 1920s–30s, poles 31in (78.5cm) long.
£60–75
$90–110 ⊞ SPA

◄ **A Stevengraph,** entitled 'The Meet', No. 165, c1910, 5 x 8in (12.5 x 20.5cm).
£100–120
$145–175 ⊞ VINE

A pair of brown and black leather cycling shoes, c1920.
£30–35
$45–50 ⊞ SA

A pair of wooden exercise clubs, 1920s, 18in (45.5cm) high.
£30–35
$45–50 ⊞ SPA

A black and white photograph of Clare College Athletes, 1925, framed and glazed, frame 14 x 16in (35.5 x 40.5cm).
£35–45
$50–65 ⊞ WAB

A pair of brown leather chaps, with rawhide fringes, c1930, 40in (101.5cm) long.
£100–125
$145–180 ⊞ SA

A pair of lady's brown leather cycling boots, 1920.
£90–110
$130–160 ⊞ PSA

▶ **A wood and leather lacrosse stick,** 1920s, 43in (109cm) long.
£30–40
$45–60 ⊞ SPT

A pair of men's brown leather running spikes, c1930.
£30–35
$45–50 ⊞ SA

▶ **A wooden rounders bat,** 1940s, 17in (43cm) long.
£35–45
$50–65 ⊞ SMW

A Whiff-Waff table tennis game, comprising vellum battledores, net with attachments and a tube of balls, c1922, in original box 20in (51cm) long.
£50–60
$75–90 ⚲ P(NW)

◀ **A pair of brown leather mountaineering boots,** with steel cleats, c1930.
£55–65
$80–95 ⊞ SA

A XIVth Olympiad official linen flag, printed in red, black, green, yellow and blue on a white ground, 1948, 47in (119.5cm) long.
£375–425
$560–620 ⚲ S

▶ **A pair of Jacques & Co mahogany croquet mallets,** with brass-ended square sections, c1950, 37in (94cm) long.
£150–175
$220–250 ⊞ SA

An Olympic Games table lamp, modelled as the Olympic torch, 1948, 25in (63.5cm) high.
£150–180
$220–260 ↗ P(NW)

A leather, plastic and steel bayonet fencing mask, 1950s, 15in (38cm) long.
£75–85
$110–125 ⊞ SA

A straw boater, with patent securing device, c1950, 15in (38cm) diam.
£30–35
$45–50 ⊞ SA

A traditional northern darts board, without 25 and triples, c1950, 18in (45.5cm) diam.
£25–30
$35–45 ⊞ SA

A leather medicine ball, 1950s, 14in (35.5cm) diam.
£55–65
$80–95 ⊞ PSA

A J. Salter & Son leather rugby ball, 1950s.
£55–65
$80–95 ⊞ PSA

▶ **A Sussex stoolball bat,** c1950, 18in (45.5cm) long.
£10–15
$15–20 ⊞ AL

An oak, steel and brass discus, c1950, 7¼in (18.5cm) diam.
£15–20
$20–30 ⊞ WAB

Ted's Idol — Babe Ruth

◀ **A 'Life of Ted Williams' baseball gum card,** depicting Babe Ruth, 1959.
£65–75
$95–110 ⊞ HALL

▶ **A wooden hurling stick,** c1960, 36in (91.5cm) long.
£10–15
$15–20 ⊞ WAB

Cricket

◄ A pair of white leather and leather-covered bamboo skeleton cricket pads, c1880–90, 23in (58.5cm) long.
£140–160
$200–230 ⊞ PEZ

A W. G. Grace Bakelite pipe bowl, embossed 'Centuplico', c1895, 4in (10cm) long.
£100–120
$145–175 ⚒ P(Ba)

W. G. Grace, 'W G', *Cricketing Reminiscences & Personal Recollections*, signed by L. C. H. Palairet, published by Bowden, 1899, 8°.
£140–180
$200–260 ⚒ VS

W. G. Grace, one page handwritten letter regarding a match between Worcester Park Beagles and London County, dated 22 May 1900.
£350–400
$500–580 ⚒ P(Ba)

The Eleventh Australian Tour 1902, with adverts and portraits, issued by *Cricket*.
£260–300
$380–440 ⚒ VS

◄ A pair of Staffordshire figures of cricketers, decorated in white with orange caps and bats and blue jackets, on oval bases, 20thC, 9¾in (25cm) high.
£200–250
$300–360 ⚒ RTo

A Geo. G. Bussey Sports Demon Driver cricket bat, with patent leather grip, c1910, 34in (86.5cm) long.
£90–100
$130–145 ⊞ PEZ

► A black and white photograph of the Australian Cricket Team, the mount signed by the team, framed and glazed, 1934, 15 x 20in (38 x 51cm).
£240–280
$350–400 ⚒ G(B)

Fishing

A steel eel gleave, c1830, 12in (30.5cm) long.
£50–55
$70–80 ⊞ SA

Three Victorian brass winches, largest 2in (5cm) diam.
£120–135
$170–200 ⊞ SA

◀ **A wooden hoop landing net,** with belt clip and brass end cap, 1880–1900, 37in (94cm) long.
£110–125
$160–180 ⊞ PEZ

A fishing silk, with a black and white print entitled 'The Angler's Companion', 1850, 17in (43cm) square.
£150–175
$220–250 ⊞ SA

▶ **A Britannia metal exhibitor's pass,** for the Great International Fisheries Exhibition, London, 1883, 2in (5cm) diam.
£50–80
$70–110 ⊞ OTB

A Nottingham 4in wood and brass spine-back reel c1880.
£50–55
$70–80 ⊞ SPA

An Eaton & Deller 2¾in brass Hercules-style trout fly reel, with nickel-silver pillars and centre screw, maker's logo, c1890.
£120–160
$175–225 ⊞ OTB

▶ **A Bernard & Son 4½in all brass salmon fly wheel,** with twin-pillared foot and black ebonite handle, c1910.
£60–90
$100–130 ⊞ OTB

A 3½in brass plate wind trout/salmon reel, c1900.
£50–60
$70–90 ⊞ PSA

▶ **A fly line greaser,** with tortoiseshell cover, felt-lined, 1910–30, 2¾in (7cm) long.
£20–30
$30–45 ⊞ OTB

A bottle of Hardy's Odourless Paraffin for Dry Flies, with wood-capped cork stopper, 1920–30, 2½in (6.5cm) high.
£100–120
$145–175 ⊞ OTB

A pair of brown leather and canvas wading and fishing boots, 1920s.
£40–45
$60–65 ⊞ SA

A black and white photograph of members of a fishermen's club, framed and glazed, c1910, 8 x 10in (20.5 x 25.5cm).
£40–45
$60–65 ⊞ SA

▶ **A hand-held wood and wire line drier,** 1920s, 4in (10cm) wide.
£20–30
$30–45 ⊞ OTB

A Nottingham 3½in aluminium-backed walnut reel, later catch, c1920.
£40–45
$60–65 ⊞ SA

A Scarborough 5in mahogany and brass fishing reel, with Slater catch mechanism, stamped 'Eton Son', 1920s.
£45–65
$60–95 ⊞ WAB

▶ **A 7in aluminium and brass big game reel,** c1930.
£65–75
$95–115 ⊞ SA

A Farlow Cairnton Killer nickel-silver priest, the head engraved with maker's name, c1930, 5¼in (13.5cm) long.
£80–100
$115–145 ⊞ OTB

A steel and brass fishing gaff, with mahogany handle and belt hook, 1930s, 21in (53.5cm) long.
£110–130
$160–190 ⊞ PEZ

A syringe-style plated brass sliding disgorger, patented 1928, 1930s, 9in (23cm) long.
£50–60
$75–90 ⊞ OTB

A leather-bound full reed angler's creel, with offset hole for catch, original strap, 1930s, 13in (33cm) long.
£100–120
$145–175 ⊞ PEZ

A Hardy fly box, in tortoiseshell effect, name stamped on lid, the interior with fitted chenille pipe-cleaner bars, 1930s, 6¼in (16cm) wide.
£50–60
$75–100 ⊞ OTB

Allcock's Anglers Guide and Abridged List of Fishing Tackle, 1937–38, 7 x 6in (18 x 15cm).
£40–50
$60–75 ⊞ AnS

Cross Reference
See Colour Review
(page 319)

A Modern Arms 4in Company mahogany and brass star-back sea reel, with brass-backed perforated drum, c1950.
£20–30
$30–45 ⊞ OTB

A Army & Navy 4½in perfect-style salmon fly reel, with rim-mounted drag adjustment and brass foot, 1930–40.
£100–120
$145–175 ⊞ PEZ

▶ **A Hardy Perfect 4in salmon fly reel,** with circular nickel-silver line guide, with grey enamel finish and scroll bordered straight line name, c1950.
£100–130
$145–190 ⊞ OTB

A fisherman's chrome folding penknife, c1950, 4in (10cm) long.
£40–45
$60–65 ⊞ SA

Football

A Newcastle United £100 share certificate, dated 12 November 1908, 7 x 10in (18 x 25.5cm).
£210–240
$300–350 ⚒ P(NW)

A County Football Match programme, Yorkshire v. Durham, 1876.
£230–260
$330–360 ⚒ DW

An FA Cup Final steward's badge, Bury v. Derby, gold lettering on a blue ground, 1903, 2in (5cm) diam.
£240–280
$350–400 ⚒ P(NW)

▶ **A wooden football supporter's rattle,** 1910, 13in (33cm) long.
£15–18
$20–25 ⊞ DQ

A brown leather football, c1920.
£150–200
$220–300 ⊞ SMW

A pair of brown leather football boots, 1940s.
£65–75
$90–110 ⊞ SPT

An International Match programme, England v. Wales, 13 April 1940, 7 x 6in (18 x 15cm).
£180–220
$275–325 ⚒ P(NW)

A pair of brown leather and cane shin pads, 1945. 9in (23cm) long.
£65–75
$90–110 ⊞ Mo

A home match programme, Arsenal v. Chelsea, 1 March 1947, fuel emergency edition, 4°.
£160–190
$230–280 ⚒ DW

▶ **A match programme,** Manchester United v. Grimsby, 31 August 1946, printed in black, white and red, repaired, 9 x 6in (23 x 15cm).
£150–180
$220–260 ⚒ P(NW)

A *Manchester Evening News* colour souvenir picture of Manchester United, signed by the team members, March 1957.
£550–650
$800–950 ↗ CDC

Three World Cup tickets, for Old Trafford, dated 13, 16 and 20 July 1966, 4in (10cm) square.
£320–360
$450–500 ↗ P(NW)

▶ **A photograph of Sir Stanley Matthews,** with later autograph, mounted, 1974, 16 x 10in (40.5 x 25.5cm).
£130–150
$200–220 ⊞ SSL

Golf

◀ **A Standard Golf Co Miles aluminium putter,** with hickory shaft, c1910, 36in (91.5cm) long.
£130–150
$200–220 ⊞ PEZ

▶ **A Smith patent anti-shank mashie golf club,** with hickory shaft, c1910, 39in (99cm) long.
£65–75
$90–110 ⊞ PEZ

A rubber core golf ball, decorated with concentric rings to six poles, the centres joined by straight lines, minor damage, early 20thC.
£500–600
$800–950 ↗ S

▶ **A pewter cigarette box,** with a square mesh golf ball and club on lid, c1930, 6in (15cm) wide.
£140–160
$200–230 ⊞ PEZ

A silver-plated cruet set, with golf clubs surmounted by a golf ball, blue glass liner in salt, c1910, 5in (12.5cm) high.
£90–110
$130–160 ⊞ SA

The Jimmy for Alex Patrick brassie golf club, with hickory shaft and leather grip, c1915, 36in (91.5cm) long.
£80–90
$115–135 ⊞ PEZ

◀ **A pair of Church's lady's golfing shoes,** in brown leather, c1950.
£50–55
$75–80 ⊞ SA

Tennis

Lawn tennis descended from 'Real Tennis', an indoor sport first played in medieval France and known as *Jeu de Paume* (palm game). The ball, which was made from sheepskin, and later from cloth, was first struck with the bare hand, then from the 15th century with a racket. Since the indoor court was bigger than a modern outdoor court, Real Tennis was the preserve of Royalty and the very wealthy. Henry VIII created a court at Hampton Court which is still in use today and in 1789, when Louis XVI locked the Third Estate out of their usual meeting place, the National Assembly of France retired to the King's tennis court at Versailles, where they swore the famous 'Tennis Court Oath', vowing never to disperse until France had a constitution.

It was another revolution, this time a technical one, that facilitated the emergence of lawn tennis the following century. Thanks to the developments in rubber, there was a new type of tennis ball and the invention of the lawn mower ensured you could have a smooth lawn. The man generally credited with inventing lawn tennis is Major Walter Wingfield who, in 1873 published a book of rules for 'Sphairistike or Lawn Tennis' and marketed kits for his new outdoor game. It was an instant success with both sexes, although women's long skirts and large hats meant that they were restricted to serving underarm. In 1875, the All-England Croquet Club at Wimbledon decided to set one of its lawns aside for tennis, and 1877 saw the first Wimbledon Tennis Championship.

An E. Nusser & Co fantail tennis racket, with convex wedge and scored handle, retailed by Harrods, early 20thC, 27in (68.5cm) long.
£55–65
$80–100 ⚘ P(NW)

A silver tennis trophy, probably for a British Army competition, inscribed with winners' names, cast with a band of palm leaves supported on three tennis rackets within a laurel wreath, on an ebonized plinth, Indian, c1895, 6½in (16.5cm) high.
£300–400
$440–580 ⚘ S

A mahogany tennis racket press, c1900, 12in (30.5cm) long.
£115–125
$170–180 ⊞ SA

◀ **A Talmo fish-tail tennis racket,** c1930, 27in (68.5cm) long.
£55–65
$80–100 ⊞ SA
The fish-tail tennis racket was designed to prevent the hand perspiring excessively.

A Spalding Pancho Gonzales autograph tennis racket, 1970s, 27in (68.6cm) long.
£25–30
$35–45 ⊞ SA

▶ **A box of Dunlop tennis balls,** 1965, 8in (20.5cm) long.
£15–20
$20–30 ⊞ HUX

Stanhopes

Stanhopes are named after Charles, 3rd Earl of Stanhope (1753–1816), British nobleman, statesman and inventor of a range of scientific devices including the Stanhope microscope lens. It was not until the second half of the 19th century, however, and with the development of micro-photography, that the custom emerged of placing a tiny Stanhope lens over a miniature photograph, and containing it in a piece of jewellery or a small souvenir. The man credited with first producing these decorative 'Stanhopes' in 1864, was the Victorian scientist Sir David Brewster, well-known for his optical work.

Queen Victoria herself was an early fan of Stanhope jewellery, and these novelty items soon became a popular craze. Stanhopes appear in many materials, from ivory to wood to minerals, and in every form from needlework tools to writing implements to brooches and charms. The majority contain photographs of favourite tourist attractions, and other subjects include portraits, famous events (such as major exhibitions) and, occasionally, naughty pictures, generally found on smoking implements or other objects likely to appeal to a male rather than female user.

Although Stanhopes were produced well into the 20th century, the golden age was the late Victorian and Edwardian periods. Values depend on material and design.

A Victorian wooden needlecase Stanhope, probably rosewood, 3½in (9cm) long.
£65–75
$90–110 ⊞ VB

A Victorian hoof letter opener Stanhope, 7½in (19cm) long.
£25–35
$30–50 ⊞ VB

A pen Stanhope, with bone handle, 1890–1900, 6in (15cm) long.
£85–95
$125–145 ⊞ MLa

A Victorian bog oak pig Stanhope, showing a view of Horsham, ½in (1.5cm) long.
£40–50
$60–75 ⊞ VB

A Victorian pen Stanhope, with bone handle, 7in (18cm) long.
£30–35
$45–50 ⊞ VB

A papier mâché spectacle case Stanhope, 1890–1900, 7in (18cm) long.
£180–200
$250–300 ⊞ MLa

A silver-plated propelling pencil Stanhope, 1890–1900, 3½in (9cm) long.
£100–120
$145–175 ⊞ MLa

► **A bookmark Stanhope,** showing views of Farnham, 1890–1900, 4in (10cm) long.
£100–120
$145–175 ⊞ MLa

Sunglasses & Lorgnettes

Sunglasses were developed in the second half of the 19th century to protect explorers on polar expeditions from snow blindness. In 1930, the Bausch and Lomb optical company (manufacturer of Ray-Bans) produced green-tinted lenses for US airforce pilots and in the ensuing decade, sunglasses took off as a fashion item, reflecting the new craze for sporting holidays and suntans. In 1937, Edwin

Land (inventor of the Polaroid Camera) set up the Polaroid Institution in Cambridge, Massachusetts, which produced polarized filters for spectacles and other items ranging from binoculars to military gunsights. In the 1950s, a huge range of extravagant designs were introduced and the post-war period saw 'shades' becoming an essential cool accessory sported by film stars, pop singers and celebrities.

A gold-rimmed lorgnette, with a lacquered case inlaid with mother-of-pearl, c1880, 3in (7.5cm) long.
£50–60
$75–90 ⊞ VB

A pair of men's side-panelled sunglasses, c1920, 6in (15cm) wide, with original case.
£70–80
$100–115 ⊞ MRW

A pair of Mardi Gras sunglasses, the plastic frames applied with fabric flowers, 1950s, 6in (15cm) wide.
£60–80
$90–115 ⊞ SpM

A pair of cat's-eyes sunglasses, the black plastic frames with diamanté trim, 1950s, 6in (15cm) wide.
£38–42
$55–60 ⊞ SpM

A pair of Swank sunglasses, the brown plastic frames with diamanté trim, French, 1950s, 5in (12.5cm) wide.
£35–40
$50–60 ⊞ SpM

A pair of cat's-eyes sunglasses, the blue plastic frames with red trim, 1950s, 6in (15cm) wide.
£30–35
$45–50 ⊞ SpM

▶ **A pair of Henri Guillet plastic sunglasses,** French, 1950s, 6in (15cm) wide.
£40–50
$60–75 ⊞ ZOOM

▶ **A black plastic lorgnette,** with mother-of-pearl and paste stone decoration, 1950–60, 10in (25.5cm) wide.
£60–70
$90–100 ⊞ SBL

A pair of Polaroid sunglasses, with blue plastic frames, c1960, 6in (15cm) wide.
£30–35
$45–50 ⊞ SBL

Teddy Bears & Soft Toys

A straw-filled teddy bear, with original eyes, wearing a black velvet jacket, c1915, 13¾in (35cm) high.
£175–200
$250–290 ⊞ BaN

A white mohair and straw-filled dog-on-wheels, with original eyes, c1920, 11¾in (29cm) high.
£250–300
$360–450 ⊞ BaN

A Chiltern blonde mohair teddy bear, with glass eyes, swivel head and jointed arms and legs, some restitching to pads, c1930, 15in (38cm) high.
£100–150
$145–220 ⚲ Bon(C)

A mohair and straw-filled Felix the Cat, with original boot button eyes, c1930, 19in (48cm) high.
£250–300
$360–440 ⊞ BaN

A Chiltern blonde mohair musical teddy bear, with orange glass eyes and tartan jacket, c1930, 16in (41cm) high.
£250–300
$360–440 ⚲ Bon(C)

▶ **A black cloth cat,** with mohair face, original red felt jacket and beige velvet trousers, buckled shoes and a cane, c1930, 15in (38cm) high.
£350–450
$500–650 ⊞ BaN

A Chiltern golden mohair teddy bear, with glass eyes, swivel head, jointed arms and legs, slight wear, c1930, 19in (48cm) high, with a framed photograph of it with its original owner.
£280–350
$400–500 ⚲ Bon(C)

> **Cross Reference**
> See Colour Review (page 385)

◀ **A Merrythought blonde mohair teddy bear,** with glass eyes, shaved muzzle, swivel head, jointed arms and legs, c1930, 21in (53cm) tall, with a photograph of the bear with its original owner.
£570–650
$800–950 ⚲ Bon(C)

A Farnell golden mohair teddy bear, with glass eyes, fully jointed body and tan Rexine pads, 1930s, 20in (51cm) high.
£450–550
$650–800 ✗ Bon(C)

A Dean's polar bear and cub, with original labels, 1949, 17in (43cm) high.
£400–450
$580–650 ⊞ DAn

A golden mohair teddy bear, possibly Chad Valley, with orange glass eyes, swivel head and jointed arms and legs, c1950, 29in (73.5cm) high.
£100–150
$145–220 ✗ Bon(C)

A Berg black cat, with red bow, Austrian, 1930s, 5½in (14cm) high.
£85–95
$125–140 ⊞ LBe

A soft toy bear, wearing a black hat and green sweater, 1930s–40s, 34in (86.5cm) high.
£60–80
$90–115 ✗ SWO

A Steiff spaniel, 'Cockie', with original chest and ear tags, original collar, German, c1960, 4¾in (12cm) high.
£50–60
$75–90 ⊞ TED

▶ **A Steiff tabby cat,** with original button and yellow tag in ear, original ribbon and bell, German, 1968–76, 4in (20cm) high.
£50–60
$75–90 ⊞ TED

A brown mohair teddy bear, possibly Chiltern, with glass eyes, shaved snout, slight wear and pads recovered, c1930, 21in (53.5cm) high, with a child's tapestry-seated wooden chair.
£250–300
$360–440 ✗ Bon

l. A Steiff golden artificial silk teddy bear, with brown-backed glass eyes, jointed arms and legs, squeeze voice-box, some repairs, German, c1947, 13½in (34cm) high.
£850–1,000
$1,250–1,500
r. A Steiff brown artificial silk teddy bear, with glass eyes, growler inoperative, German, c1949, 10¼in (26cm) high.
£800–950
$1,200–1,400 ✗ S(S)

Telephones

A Telefon Fabrik Automatic DO8 telephone, steel and brass with wooden handgrip, Danish, c1908.
£450–500
$650–720 ⊞ OTC

An Ericsson magneto corporation telephone, steel and brass with wooden handgrip, not converted for BT use, Swedish, 1920s.
£300–330
$440–480 ⊞ OTC

A cream Bakelite telephone, 1930s, 6in (15cm) high.
£300–350
$450–500 ⊞ HEG

A Bell Telephones black Bakelite telephone, with Bakelite and brass bell set No. 64d, converted for BT use, Belgian, 1930s–40s.
£200–240
$280–350 ⊞ OTC

◄ **A black Bakelite telephone,** converted for BT use, German, 1945–60, 6½in (16.5cm) high.
£80–100
$115–145 ⊞ HEG

Miller's is a price GUIDE not a price LIST

► **A Bakelite wall-mounted telephone,** c1950, 10in (25.5cm) high.
£100–125
$145–180 ⊞ AOY

◄ **A black Bakelite telephone,** with bell box, c1950, 7in (18cm) high.
£175–200
$250–280 ⊞ AOY

► **A black Bakelite telephone,** with Bell On/Bell Off switches, c1950, 6in (15cm) high.
£125–145
$180–200 ⊞ AOY

A Bell Telephones green
telephone, Belgian, 1956–66.
£125–150
$180–220 ⊞ OTC

A black telephone, converted for
BT use, French, 1950–60,
5½in (14cm) high.
£40–50
$60–75 ⊞ HEG

A white telephone, converted
for BT use, German, c1950s,
6½in (16.5cm) high.
£100–120
$145–175 ⊞ HEG

A copper and brass-finished
telephone, with black handset,
Belgian, 1956–1966, 5½in (14cm) high.
£85–95
$125–140 ⊞ HEG

A black thermoplastic telephone,
American, 1978–80, in original
sealed carton.
£80–90
$115–130 ⊞ OTC

A GPO Queen's Silver Jubilee
telephone, with type 64d bell
set, 1977.
£125–140
$180–200 ⊞ OTC

Textiles & Costume

A needlework panel of the Finding of Moses, worked in coloured wools and chenille on silk, with watercolour detailing, unfinished, early 19thC, 16½in (42cm) wide, in a wooden frame.
£160–200
$230–280 ✗ RTo

A sampler, by Elizabeth Cole, worked on silk, 1839, 13 x 10in (33 x 25.4cm), in a wooden frame.
£780–850
$1,100–1,250 ⊞ HIS

A sampler, worked by Ellan Christian Prosser, Aged 10 Years, 1840, in coloured thread, 13 x 12½in (33 x 32cm).
£120–150
$175–220 ✗ RTo

A sampler, by Mary Henry Macduff, decorated with a verse, flowers, birds, figures and religious artefacts, 1866, 19 x 15¾in (48.5 x 40cm), in a simulated rosewood frame.
£280–340
$400–500 ✗ AG

A collection of patchwork quilt squares, from the Bidwell Family & Friends Album, pieced and/or appliquéd cotton squares in various patterns and colours, most signed in ink by the maker, minor staining, American, c1860, largest 11½in (29cm) square.
£700–800
$1,000–1,150 ✗ SK(B)

A Victorian cotton patchwork quilt, Welsh, 66 x 65in (167.5 x 165cm).
£55–65
$80–95 ⊞ JJ

A narrow loom wool blanket, in orange and black on cream, Welsh, late 19thC, 70in (178cm) wide.
£65–75
$95–110 ⊞ JJ

A linen and hand-crocheted lace tablecloth, c1900, 54in (137cm) square.
£80–90
$115–130 ⊞ JuC

◄ **A linen and drawn thread-work tablecloth,** c1910, 51in (129.5cm) square.
£50–60
$75–90 ⊞ JuC

A Battenburg drawn threadwork and linen tablecloth, c1910.
£45–50
$65–75 ⊞ JuC

A linen and hand-crotcheted lace tablecloth, Mary Card design No. 68, 'The Garden Cloth', c1920, 52in (132cm) square.
£90–100
$130–150 ⊞ JuC

An Art Nouveau floral design pink quilt, with lemon-yellow reverse, c1900, 83 x 75in (211 x 190.5cm).
£400–500
$580–720 ⊞ JJ

A silk tea cosy, designed as a pierrot, with hand-painted face, 1920s, 14in (35.5cm) high.
£120–150
$175–220 ⊞ LBe

► A fake fur fabric tea cosy, designed as a poodle, with a green bow, 1930s, 13in (33cm) high.
£100–125
$145–180 ⊞ LBe

A black satin underwear case, with a lucky black cat panel, 1930s, 7in (18cm) square.
£20–25
$30–35 ⊞ LBe

A pair of Jolly Golly design curtains, multi-coloured on an orange ground, 1960s–70s, 72 x 48in (183 x 122cm).
£15–18
$20–30 ⚒ FLD

► A length of Deco Revival-style fabric, with male dancers in blue and green on a white ground, 1970s, 108 x 48in (274.5 x 122cm).
£35–40
$50–60 ⊞ HSt

A yellow and brown fringed wool blanket, Welsh, 1960, 94 x 72in (239 x 183cm).
£35–50
$50–75 ⊞ DE

Costume

Over the past few years, interest in vintage clothing has expanded considerably and become far more mainstream. Selfridges department store in London now includes a vintage section alongside its contemporary designer concessions. Top Shop, at their flagship store in Oxford Street, stocks vintage clothing next to the latest high street fashions. When Julia Roberts wore vintage Valentino to the Oscars ceremony, second-hand clothing became the ultimate in Hollywood glamour and today's fashion magazines continually mix old with new.

The great joy of collecting vintage clothes is the pleasure of wearing them. Some enthusiasts go the whole way, perhaps dressing top-to-toe in 1920s style, complete with make-up and hairstyle to match. Others simply accessorize contemporary outfits with a vintage scarf or handbag, using the past to enhance the present.

Buying clothes from an antique dealer or flea market is an adventure and you never know what you will find. Often people go for a period that suits their figure. Slim and leggy girls might chose 1960s or '20s, while the more curvaceous might try 1950s or even Edwardian. Some pieces (particularly pre-1900) can be too fragile to wear easily, and when buying vintage clothing it is always important to check condition. Clothes should also be tried on. Over the decades, our figures have changed and each generation grows bigger than the last. If you want to collect and wear 1920s shoes, for example, your feet will need to be far smaller than today's average size.

As the following selection shows, there is a huge range of antique clothing to choose from. Compared to their modern day, mass-produced equivalents, pieces are often far better made (if they weren't they wouldn't have lasted so long) and competitively priced (though as with modern fashion, expect to pay more for a good designer label). Finally, if you collect vintage clothing, not only do you have the enjoyment of wearing your collectables but you can virtually guarantee that no-one is going to turn up dressed exactly like you.

◄ A silk **Masonic apron,** embroidered in silk, chenille, metallic threads and sequins with Masonic symbols and initials 'J.B.' on a white ground, with yellow ribbon on a blue silk border, early 19thC, 18½in (47cm) high, mounted on blue velvet fabric in a giltwood frame.
£450–550
$650–800 ⚒ SK(B)

A child's Brussels lace *point de gaze* collar, c1890, 10in (25.5cm) wide.
£45–50
$65–75 ⊞ JuC

A child's cotton piqué coat, with mother-of-pearl buttons, c1900.
£60–65
$90–95 ⊞ JuC

A figured brown wool two-piece walking dress, with high neck, emphasized shoulder decoration and bustle back, c1890s.
£130–150
$190–220 ⊞ CCO

◄ An **electroplated nickel silver belt,** c1900, 26in (66cm) long.
£100–110
$145–160 ⊞ LBe

A taupe wool two-piece suit, the jacket with buttons down the back, 1930.
£40–50
$60–75 ⊞ DE

An eau-de-nil silk crêpe evening dress, with hand-painted flower detail, late 1930s.
£160–180
$230–260 ⊞ LaF

◄ **A red satin dress,** with a fur collar and self-fabric belt, 1950s.
£30–35
$45–50 ⊞ HSt

A Christian Dior black suit, 1950s.
£170–190
$250–275 ⊞ SBT

◄ **A pink silk dress and coat,** labelled 'Carnegie London', with self-fabric button loops and covered buttons, 1960.
£35–45
$50–65 ⊞ DE

◄ **A Western-style brown satin Occupied Japan souvenir shirt,** with a white panel embroidered with a golden dragon, 1940s–50s.
£150–175
$220–250 ⊞ SpM

A Crown Prince green gabardine bowling shirt, American, 1950s.
£65–75
$95–75 ⊞ SpM

◄ **A Jeannie Brand brown jersey cocktail dress,** 1950.
£25–35
$35–50 ⊞ DE

A Dianna Warren cream, blue and gold beaded and sequinned dress, dress shortened, 1960s.
£60–70
$90–100 ⊞ DE

A Cathy McGowan's Boutique purple tricel dress, 1970s.
£45–55
$65–80 ⊞ DE
In 1963, nineteen-year-old Cathy McGowan went from being a secretary earning £10 ($15) a week to star presenter on *Ready Steady Go* – the successful British TV pop programme. Dubbed 'Queen of the Mods', Cathy became a fashion icon for young girls, who imitated her long fringed hairstyle, theatrical makeup and clothes. Various products ranging from dresses to cosmetics were brought out under her name.

A green, black, purple and yellow psychedelic pattern skirt, labelled 'Dori, London', 1970s.
£10–15
$15–20 ⊞ DE

A Diane von Furstenberg red and white cotton jersey shirt dress, 1970s.
£125–145
$180–200 ⊞ SBT

A Biba green and black sequinned jacket, 1970s.
£175–195
$250–280 ⊞ SBT

A Jean Muir dark green wool crêpe two-piece suit, 1970s.
£300–350
$450–500 ⊞ SBT

A safari-style grey jersey suit, with flared trousers, 1970s.
£30–40
$45–60 ⊞ HarC

> **Cross Reference**
> See Colour Review (page 387)

A Today's Man short-sleeved cotton shirt, with a blue and green palm tree pattern, American, 1970s.
£20–25
$30–35 ⊞ HSt

A Vivienne Westwood punk jacket, c1976.
£450–500
$650–720 ⊞ IQ
This jacket is from her first shop, Let It Rock.

A Vivienne Westwood green cotton asymmetric shirt, with one sleeve, from the Witches Collection, c1983.
£200–250
$300–360 ⊞ ID

Coat Hangers & Hat Stands

A child's felt-covered golly coat-hanger, 1930s, 12in (30.5cm) wide.
£85–95
$125–140 ⊞ LBe

Miller's is a price GUIDE not a price LIST

A pair of wood and steel coat and hat hooks, French, c1910, 11in (28cm) high.
£70–90
$100–130 each ⊞ RUL

▶ A brass and wood robe-hanger, 1930s, 18in (45.5cm) high.
£25–30
$35–45 ⊞ SPT

A wooden hatstand, with a hand-painted figure of an Egyptian-style dancing girl, 1920s, 12in (30.5cm) high.
£150–175
$220–250 ⊞ LBe

◀ A wicker mannequin, 1950–60, 70in (178cm) high.
£65–75
$95–110 ⊞ NET

Hats

A Breton brown bonnet, with lace trim and taffeta bow, French, 18thC.
£180–200
$260–300 ⊞ JuC

A Victorian velvet and lace bonnet, trimmed with ostrich feathers.
£55–65
$80–95 ⊞ Ech

A Honiton bobbin-lace fall cap, c1860, 24in (61cm) wide.
£40–45
$60–65 ⊞ JuC

An Edwardian black velvet hat.
£85–95
$125–195 ⊞ LBe

A child's straw hat, trimmed with floral-printed ribbon, 1920s.
£80–100
$115–145 ⊞ Ech

◀ **A grey felt Homburg hat,** 1930s.
£20–30
$30–45 ⊞ DE

A black straw hat, decorated with felt flowers, c1930.
£35–40
$50–60 ⊞ DE

A black felt hat and veil, 1940s.
£30–35
$45–50 ⊞ CCO

A cast-iron flower press, with a wooden handle, c1920, 8¼in (21cm) long.
£100–120
$145–175 ⊞ MSB
These presses were used to mould silk flowers for hats.

A black straw hat, with silk netting and red grosgrain ribbon trim, 1940s.
£85–95
$125–140 ⊞ LBe

▶ **A black and white leather hat,** with leather flower decoration, 1960s.
£10–12
$15–18 ⊞ CCO

Shawls & Scarves

▶ **A Lancashire clogger's wool shawl,** late 19thC, 30 x 125in (76 x 317.5cm).
£55–65
$80–95 ⊞ DE

A red, black and blue paisley shawl, some damage, early 20thC, 66in (167.5cm) square.
£100–150
$145–220 ⊞ JPr

A brown and white printed wool shawl, with magenta border, c1860–70, 60 x 120in (152.5 x 305cm).
£85–95
$125–140 ⊞ DE

◀ **A multicoloured embroidered piano shawl,** Chinese, c1900, 66in (167.5cm) square.
£250–300
$350–450 ⊞ JuC

A red, gold and black scarf, inscribed 'Gay Times at Churchill's Club, 1940s, 35in (89cm) square.
£130–150
$190–220 ⊞ LBe

A Courtier rayon scarf, Nuits de Paris, multicoloured with blue border, 1939–45, 25in (63.5cm) square.
£50–60
$75–90 ⊞ REN

A Festival of Britain synthetic fabric scarf, with multicoloured London Views, 1951, 29in (74cm) square.
£50-60
$75–90 ⊞ REN

A yellow handkerchief, with black poodles, 1950s, 18in (45.5cm) square.
£8–10
$12–15 ⊞ LBe

An Oliver Messel silk scarf, with the Coronation coach, 1953, 35in (89cm) square.
£120–140
$175–200 ⊞ REN

A red, black and yellow Paloma Picasso scarf, 1980s, 34in (86.5cm) square.
£85–95
$125–140 ⊞ LBe

Shoes

▶ **A pair of pattens,** leather and wood mounted on an oval iron ring, c1780–1830.
£150–165
$220–250 ⊞ HO
Pattens were overshoes, worn to protect ordinary shoes from the mud and wet.

◀ **A pair of gentleman's silver shoe buckles,** by R. E., London 1813, 2½in (6.5cm) wide.
£100–120
$145–175 ⚒ PFK

A silver button hook, London 1887, 15in (38cm) long.
£500–550
$720–800 ⊞ SHa

An iron shoe stretcher, c1880, 15in (38cm) long.
£20–25
$30–35 ⊞ FST

A pair of wood clog bases, French, c1900.
£12–15
$17–20 ⊞ Cot

A pair of lady's black wool and leather ankle boots, by Delta, with button fastening, 1900.
£80–90
$115–130 ⊞ CCO

A pair of brown leather field boots, with trees, 1910.
£125–145
$180–200 ⊞ SPT

A pair of black leather shoes, 1920s.
£30–40
$45–60 ⊞ CCO

A pair of tan leather boots, with trees, 1910.
£85–95
$125–140 ⊞ SPT

A pair of black satin court shoes, with diamanté decoration to heels, 1920s.
£35–40
$50–60 ⊞ CCO

A pair of silver leather evening shoes, labelled 'Dolcis, Made in Budapest', c1930.
£30–35
$45–50 ⊞ CCO

◄ **A pair of child's Utility white buckskin boots,** 1940s.
£25–30
$35–45 ⊞ TT

A pair of white suede peep-toe shoes, by Physical Culture, 1940s.
£35–40
$50–60 ⊞ CCO

A pair of Utility snakeskin shoes,
1940–50.
£85–95
$125–140 ⊞ SpM

A pair of Perspex and plastic shoes,
with a 4in (10cm) heel,
late 1950s–60s.
£55–65
$80–95 ⊞ SpM

A pair of white leather shoes,
by Natale Ferrario, Italian, 1957.
£350–400
$500–580 ⊞ LBe
Rather than being supported
by a heel, these 'heel-less high-
heel shoes' have a metal sole
extension. Perhaps unsurprisingly,
this design was only produced
for a short period of time and
'invisible stiletto' shoes are now
very collectable.

**A pair of brown leather platform
boots,** with snakeskin decoration,
1970s.
£70–80
$100–115 ⊞ CCO

A pair of platform shoes, with
black patent plastic uppers and clear
Perspex bases, 1970.
£50–60
$75–90 ⊞ BEV

▶ **A pair of black suede shoes,**
by Salvatore Ferragamo, 1980s.
£65–75
$95–110 ⊞ SBT

Underwear

▶ **A pair of lady's embroidered
split-leg bloomers,** with lace
trim, c1920.
£35–40
$50–60 ⊞ JuC

A black lace corset, by Lady
Marlene, 1950s, in original box.
£55–65
$80–95 ⊞ LBe

**A pair of Mary Quant white
Tiffany Lace tights,** 1960s, original
package 9 x 7in (23 x 18cm).
£12–15
$15–20 ⊞ CCO

◀ **A pair of nylon Y-Front
underpants,** 1970s.
£4–5
$5–7 ⚲ FLD

Tiles

A set of majolica tiles, decorated in brown, orange and green, Dutch, 17thC, 5in (12.5cm) square.
£270–300
$390–440 ⊞ OLA

A Delft tile, with manganese border, the blue and white hexagonal centre with a horseman in a country landscape, Dutch, 18thC, 5in (12.5cm) square.
£90–100
$130–150 ⊞ JHo

A manganese tile, depicting a man resting on a bench in a country landscape, Dutch, 18thC, 5in (12.5cm) square.
£25–30
$35–45 ⊞ JHo

A Liverpool blue and white tile, depicting Moses and the Tablets, 1760, 5in (12.5cm) square.
£145–165
$200–240 ⊞ JHo

A London blue and white tile, depicting St Paul escaping, 1760, 5in (12.5cm) square.
£100–125
$145–180 ⊞ JHo

An encaustic floor tile, decorated in brown and white, 19thC, 6in (15cm) square.
£8–10
$10–15 ⊞ OLA

A set of 12 William de Morgan tiles, decorated with Persian-style stylized leaves and flowers in turquoise and green, impressed Merton Abbey marks, minor chips, 1880s, 6in (15cm) square.
£2,000–2,500
$2,900–3,600 ⚲ S(S)

Three Minton tiles, Spring, Autumn and Winter, late 19thC, 8in (20.5cm) square.
£90–100
$130–150 each ⊞ OLA

A Quimper tile/pot-stand, decorated with a Breton lady within a brown border, c1943, 8½in (21.5cm) square.
£60–70
$90–100 ⊞ SER

Tools

A wooden moulding plane, by J. Rogers, 1734–65, 9¾in (25cm) long.
£20–30
$30–45 ⊞ **WO**

A combination ebony-handled tool, comprising capped screwdriver, with pull-out turn screw revealing tweezers and nipple key, with a pricker at the end of the grip, 1840–50, 5½in (14cm) wide.
£80–100
$115–145 ⊞ **SPA**

A German silver and rosewood smoothing plane, with burr walnut infill, Scottish, c1870, 7in (18cm) long.
£325–375
$470–570 ⊞ **TOM**

A wheelwright's traveller, for measuring cartwheel circumference, c1880, 17in (43cm) high.
£55–65
$80–95 ⊞ **HCJ**

A Continental jeweller's or goldsmith's brass steelyard balance, early 19thC, 4in (10cm) long.
£85–95
$125–140 ⊞ **WO**

A barrister's ivory and steel hammer, c1870, 7in (18cm) long.
£55–65
$80–95 ⊞ **HO**

A Marples brass and ebony Ultimatum brace, 19thC, 13in (33cm) long.
£220–280
$320–420 ⊞ **WO**

LOCATE THE SOURCE

The source of each illustration in Miller's can be found by checking the code letters below each caption with the Key to Illustrations, pages 444–452.

A blacksmith-made cart jack, mid-19thC.
£35–40
$50–60 ⊞ **WO**

◄ **A beech plough plane,** by Sims, London, with brass fittings, 19thC, 9in (23cm) long.
£15–30
$20–45 ⊞ **WO**

A wood and iron adze, c1880, 30in (76cm) high.
£35–45
$50–65 ⊞ **HCJ**

◀ **A mitre shoot,** with wooden threads and multi-adjustment, German, 19thC, 32in (81.5cm) long.
£45–55
$65–80 ⊞ **WO**

▶ **A reciprocating drill,** by Goodell-Pratt, patent No. 1895, American, early 20thC.
£28–35
$40–50 ⊞ **WO**

A brass Lancashire-pattern shoulder plane, with a shaped mahogany handle, c1900, 9in (23cm) long.
£80–100
$115–145 ⊞ **TOM**

A cabinet-maker's tool chest, the painted exterior enclosing a mahogany interior with oval veneered panel to underside of lid, fitted with a variety of drawers and lidded compartments, early 20thC, 36½in (93cm) wide.
£300–350
$440–500 ⚒ **N**

Three gunmetal violin-maker's planes, by Ed. Preston, c1910, largest 2¼in (5.5cm) long.
£120–150
$175–220 each ⊞ **MRT**

A Stanley 45 plane, with rack of blades, early 20thC, 12in (30.5cm) long.
£65–85
$95–125 ⊞ **WO**

A billhook, by W. Bingham of Shadoxhurst, Kent, 20thC, 16½in (42cm) long.
£18–25
$27–35 ⊞ **WO**

Planes

Planes, used by carpenters for smoothing and moulding wooden surfaces, are among the most collectable woodworking tools. Examples have been found dating back to Roman times and over the centuries innumerable designs have been produced, both in terms of function (shaping different surfaces and objects) and decoration.

Five wood, brass and steel glass-cutters, c1930, largest 7in (18cm) long.
£8–15
$12–20 each ⊞ **WAB**

A general jobber's steel drill gauge, American, c1930, 6in (15cm) wide.
£15–18
$20–27 ⊞ **FST**

A boxwood and brass rope gauge, c1935, 5in (12.5cm) long.
£23–27
$35–40 ⊞ **FST**

A wood and brass travelling knife-grinder, with original paint-work, 1930, 79in (200.5cm) high.
£700–800
$1,000–1,200 ⊞ **MLL**

Toys

An acrobat toy, the two figures joined by mercury-filled bars, on folding stairs, the base with storage drawer, French, c1875, 7in (18cm) wide.
£950–1,100
$1,400–1,600 ⚘ SK(B)

A wooden stable, the exterior with brick-effect paper, with two skin-covered horses in full tack, and a tinplate and wood cart, painted blue and red, with wire rails and steering mechanism, 1880s, stable 10¾in (27.5cm) wide.
£150–200
$220–300 ⚘ Bon

▶ **A red Tri-ang scooter,** c1900, 32in (81.5cm) high.
£250–300
$360–440 ⊞ STE

◀ **A Dover Toys Mr Jolly articulated wooden toy,** with green hat and painted face, red and black striped socks, 1910, 12in (30.5cm) high, with original box.
£55–65
$80–95 ⊞ J&J

A filigree metal pram, German, 1898, 5in (12.5cm) wide.
£150–200
$220–300 ⊞ PSA

▶ **A tinplate clockwork exercising boy,** wearing a striped blue cap, grey sailor suit, red socks and black shoes, early 20thC, 7½in (19cm) high, in original box.
£425–475
$620–700 ⚘ Bea(E)

> **Cross Reference**
> See Colour Review
> (page 391)

A DRP Junior tin typewriter, with tin cover, German, 1920s, 8in (20.5cm) wide.
£55–65
$80–95 ⊞ JUN

A set of alphabet picture blocks, decorated with chromolithographed letters and pictures of animals and toys, German, c1920, box 15in (38cm) wide.
£450–550
$650–800 ✗ Bon

Two boxes of Wm Collins coloured magic lantern slides, 'The Pied Piper' and 'Night Before Christmas', from Disney's *Silly Symphony*, c1930, 6in (15cm) wide.
£10–15
$15–20 each ⊞ J&J

A papier mâché model of Bonzo, white on a green base, c1930, 6½in (16.5cm) high.
£45–50
$65–75 ⊞ MRW

▶ **A DRGM clockwork railway porter,** printed tin, pushing an opening trunk on a barrow, c1930, 6in (15cm) wide.
£50–60
$75–90 ✗ AH

A Tri-ang push-along dog-on-wheels, grey and white, 1930s, 18in (45.5cm) high.
£20–30
$30–45 ⊞ JUN

A tin bucket, decorated with anthropomorphic dogs playing on a beach, c1940, 5½in (14cm) high.
£30–35
$45–50 ⊞ HUX

A brown plastic nodding dog, 1950s–60s, 5in (12.5cm) long.
£15–20
$20–30 ⊞ RUSS

◀ **A wooden lesson board,** the paper roll operated by wind-round mechanism, c1950, 12in (30.5cm) wide.
£30–35
$45–50 ⊞ HO

A 'Riders of the Range' bagatelle game, based on the characters in *Eagle* comic, blue, yellow, red and brown on green, 1950s, 12in (30.5cm) high.
£20–25
$30–35 ⊞ J&J

A bronze-coloured plastic Citroen 2CV car, French, c1960, 6in (15cm) long.
£15–20
$20–30 ⊞ RTT

A Lumar 99 Evening Citizen white plastic competition yo-yo, early 1960s, 2¼in (5.5cm) diam.
£12–15
$17–20 ⊞ YO

A Thomas Damm Troll cow,
with brown mane, Danish, 1960s,
7in (18cm) high.
£25–35
$35–50 ⊞ PLB

A Thomas Damm Troll donkey,
with blonde mane, Danish, 1960s,
3in (7.5cm) high.
£25–35
$35–50 ⊞ PLB

A Peyo Smurf chimney-sweep,
blue with black clothes, 1960s–70s,
2¼in (5.5cm) high.
£10–12
$15–18 ⊞ CMF

**A Spectra Star yellow plastic yo-
yo,** with a Batman motif, American,
early 1970s, 2½in (5.5cm) diam.
£6–8
$9–12 ⊞ YO

**A Lionel 100th Anniversary train
clock,** the train revolving round the
clock once an hour, with authentic
railroad sounds, and light sensor to
switch off sound at night, American,
1980s, 14in (35.5cm) diam.
£30–35
$45–50 ⚒ LSK

**A Firebird Flying Shark computer
game,** for the Spectrum 48k/128k
computer, 1987, 5½ x 4in
(14 x 10cm) high.
£1–3
$2–5 ⊞ CGX

◄ **A McDonald's Smurf,** blue with
white hat, 1996, 2¼in (5.5cm) high.
£1–3
$2–5 ⊞ CMF

A Flintstones Wilma in car, multi-
coloured, 1993, 3in (7.5cm) high.
£1–2
$2–3 ⊞ CMF
This was a plastic free gift from
Burger King.

▶ **A Tom Kuhn Flying Camel
laser-carved rock maple yo-yo,**
American, 1996, 2¼in (5.5cm) diam.
£45–50
$65–75 ⊞ YO

**A Spectra Star glow-in-the-dark
plastic yo-yo,** with *Nightmare
Before Christmas* figure, 1996,
2¼in (5.5cm) diam.
£8–10
$12–15 ⊞ YO

Aeroplanes

A tinplate clockwork passenger monoplane, lithographed with red and black details and RAF roundels, and passengers at windows, German, 1920s, 9in (23cm) long.
£80–120
$115–175 ⚒ Bon(C)

A Lehmann tinplate model of a Heinkel HE 111 plane, painted in green, with swastikas to tail, original instruction booklet and box, c1938, 5in (12.5cm) wide.
£475–525
$690–750 ⊞ TOB

▶ **A Meccano single-engined biplane,** with seated pilot, silver finish with RAF roundels and tail markings, 1930s, wingspan 16in (40.5cm).
£70–90
$100–130
⚒ WAL

An Arnold tinplate clockwork Douglas DC6B aeroplane, in Scandinavian Airlines livery, 1950s, wingspan 11½in (29cm).
£160–190
$230–275 ⚒ VEC

Boats

A Hornby clockwork No. 2 Speedboat, 'Swift', with red hull and cream deck, original key and internal packing, 1930s.
£140–180
$200–260 ⚒ VEC

An A-class model yacht, 'Vanity', designed by Marine Models, clinker-built by F. Kemp, with wooden mast and boom, linen sails, brass and metal fixtures and painted wooden stand, with registration certificate, results for 1935, photographs and accessories, 1930–35, mast 9¾in (25cm) high.
£1,500–1,800
$2,150–2,600 ⚒ TRM
This yacht was raced under Model Yachting Association rules at Windermere Club.

A Gamages wooden pond yacht, the hull painted blue, c1930, 38in (96.5cm) high.
£300–350
$440–500 ⊞ PEZ

A Hornby Minic Ships diecast model of RMS *Queen Elizabeth*, scale 1:1200, 1972, 12in (30.5cm) long.
£50–55
$75–80 ⊞ FA

Diecast Vehicles

A diecast car, brown with red cross on door, American, c1910, 4in (10cm) long.
£45–50
$65–75 ⊞ MRW

A Dinky Toys Foden Diesel 8-wheel wagon, No 901, with second-type cab in red and fawn with red hubs, 1954–57, with original box.
£180–220
$260–320 ⚒ P(L)

▶ A Dinky Toys Foden Flat Truck, No. 903, second-type cab in blue, with orange flat-bed and light blue hubs, 1954–56, with original box.
£130–160
$190–230
⚒ P(L)

A Dinky Toys red Foden Flat Truck, No. 905, with chains, 1950s, 7in (18cm) long, with original box.
£245–275
$350–400 ⊞ UCO

▶ A Dinky Toys Trojan Esso van, No. 450, red, 1954–57, 3in (7.5cm) long, with original box.
£70–90
$100–130 ⊞ HAL

A Dinky Toys Motorway Police Car, No. 269, 1950s, 4in (10cm) long, with original box.
£100–120
$145–175 ⊞ UCO

▶ A Dinky Toys blue police box, late 1950s, 3in (7.5cm) high.
£30–35
$45–50 ⊞ UCO

A Corgi Toys Chipperfields Circus crane truck, 1960–68, 8in (20.5cm) long, with original box.
£70–80
$100–115 ⊞ WI

A Primo Renault Tour de France Waterman vehicle, cream with six cast-in blue ink-bottles to each side, red lettering, French, early 1960s, 5in (12.5cm) long, with original box.
£230–260
$330–380 ↗ WAL

▶ A Corgi Toys Chipperfields Circus animal cage, No. 1123, 1960–68, 4in (10cm) long, with original box.
£30–40
$45–60 ⊞ WI

A Dinky Toys AA Patrol Service Minivan, No. 274, early 1960s, 3in (7.5cm) long, with original box.
£130–150
$190–220 ⊞ UCO

▶ A Corgi Toys Superior Ambulance, No. 437, c1965, 5in (12.5cm) long, with original box.
£70–80
$100–115 ⊞ WI

A Dinky Supertoys Autobus Parisien ou Urbain, No. 889, made for the French market, early 1960s, 9in (23cm) long, with original box.
£180–200
$260–300 ⊞ UCO

l. A Corgi Toys Ferrari Berlinetta 250 Le Mans, 1960s, 4in (10cm) long, with original box.
£25–30
$35–50
r. A Corgi Toys Ferrari Berlinetta 250 Le Mans, worn, 1960s, 4in (10cm) long.
£4–6
$6–9 ⊞ HAL

A Dinky Toys Fourgon Peugeot J7 Dépannage Autoroutes, No. 570A, with figures and signs, made for the French market, mid-1960s, original box 10in (25.5cm) long.
£140–170
$200–250 ↗ P(WM)

A Matchbox Series Superfast
Mercedes 300SE Coupé, No. 46,
in trial colour of orange-yellow with
green tinted glass and off-white
interior, late 1960s–70s.
£280–320
$400–460 ⚡ VEC

A Matchbox Model of Yesteryear
1914 Prince Henry Vauxhall, red
with white upholstery, gold wire
wheels, 1960–70, 4in (10cm) long,
with original box.
£7–9
$10–15 ⊞ HAL

A Corgi Toy Green Hornet,
No. 268, early 1970s, 5in (12.5cm)
long, with original box.
£325–375
$450–550 ⊞ UCO

A Corgi Toys James Bond Toyota
2000GT, No. 336, red and black with
white interior, 1976, 4in (10cm) long,
with original box.
£85–95
$125–140 ⊞ UCO

A Corgi Toys The Monkees
Monkeemobile, No. 277, red and
white, with figures, 1969–70,
6in (15cm) long, with original box.
£325–375
$500–560 ⊞ UCO

An Airfix Micronauts Neon Orbiter,
with figure, 1976, 7¼in (18.5cm) long,
with original box.
£15–20
$20–30 ⊞ OW

A Corgi Batman gift set, No. 40, comprising Batmobile,
Batboat on trailer and Batcopter, 1977–80, with
original box.
£500–550
$700–800 ⚡ WAL

▶ A Corgi
James Bond 007
Secret Service
Game, No. 22,
comprising Space
Shuttle, Lotus
Esprit, Aston
Martin, rockets
and bandits,
1980–82.
£800–900
$1,200–1,300
⚡ Bon(C)

Model Soldiers & Figures

A Britains South Australian Lancers Set No. 49, with four Lancers and an Officer with sword on one-eared galloping horses, 1901–19, 3in (7.5cm) high.
£320–360
$450–500 ✗ P(L)

A Britains Pontoon Section of the Royal Engineers Set No. 203a, with four-horse team, light harness with two drivers in khaki service dress, flat wagon, pontoon and roadway section, 1928.
£400–450
$600–650 ✗ VEC

A Britains Zoological Series giraffe, No. 912, minor damage, 1929–41, with original box.
£200–220
$300–330 ✗ S(S)

A Britains motorcycle with sidecar, No. 641, with figures, minor damage, 1932–41.
£450–500
$650–720 ✗ Bon(C)

▶ **A set of white metal figures of Adolf Hitler and two SS guards,** Hitler wearing a tan coat and hat, the guards wearing black SS uniforms, c1938, 2in (5cm) high.
£15–20
$20–30 ⊞ IE

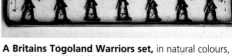

A Britains Togoland Warriors set, in natural colours, 1954–59, 2in (5cm) high, with original box.
£160–180
$230–260 ⊞ UCO

▶ **A Timpo Arctic set,** brown, cream and green, 1946, on original card.
£200–220
$300–330 ✗ WAL

◀ **A set of 10 white metal Royal Marines and mounted officer,** c1960, 2in (5cm) high.
£60–70
$90–100 ⊞ IE

Pedal Cars

A Eureka-style sepia tandem pedal car, probably Spanish, many parts missing, 1920s.
£1,500–2,000
$2,200–3,000 ⊞ CARS

A Tri-ang pedal car, red with white wheels, 1950s–60s.
£90–100
$125–145 ⊞ JUN

A pedal car, red with white trim, 1920s.
£550–650
$800–950 ⊞ JUN

▶ **A Tri-ang Austin A40 pedal car,** in blue pressed steel with opening bonnet showing dummy engine and spark plugs with leads, battery to power working lights and horn, opening boot and adjustable seat, 1960s, 48in (122cm) long.
£350–420
$500–620 ⊞ CARS

A Tri-ang Overlander pedal car, cream with red wheels, rusty, c1960.
£80–100
$115–145 ⊞ JUN

Robots

▶ **A Super Moon Explorer battery-operated plastic robot,** with black body and red feet, c1960, 12in (30.5cm) high, with original box.
£75–85
$115–125 ⊞ UCO

A battery-operated tin robot, with plastic fittings, Japanese, 1960s, 11in (28cm) high.
£60–70
$80–100 ⚒ AG

A battery-operated robot, Japanese, 1960s, 12in (30.5cm) high.
£125–150
$180–220 ⊞ HUX

Rocking Horses

A child's wooden horse, with original paint decoration, French, 18thC, 26in (66cm) high.
£750–850
$1,100–1,250 ⊞ FCL

A Victorian dapple grey rocking horse, on a green-painted stand, 46½in (118cm) high.
£800–1,000
$1,150–1,500 ↗ JNic

▶ **A Lines Brothers rocking horse,** restored to original dapple grey colouring, on a trestle and cruciform stand, 1900–10, 55in (140cm) long.
£700–800
$1,000–1,1500 ↗ HOLL

◀ **A dapple grey rocking horse,** with saddle, reins and stirrups, on a red and black trestle stand, c1890, 38in (96.5cm) high.
£100–125
$145–180 ⊞ GBr

A Lines Brothers rocking horse, on a bow rocker, c1880, 30in (76cm) high.
£800–900
$1,150–1,300 ⊞ STE

A Collinson rocking horse, with original hair and dapple grey paintwork, on a trestle stand, c1930.
£300–350
$450–500 ⊞ STE

A dapple grey rocking horse, on a trestle stand, early 20thC, 46in (117cm) high.
£550–650
$800–950 ⊞ KA

A painted pine rocking horse, with brass-tacked leather seat, on a trestle stand, early 20thC, 39½in (100.5cm) high.
£500–600
$720–870 ⚒ CGC

◀ A Collinsons rocking horse, with original hair and leather tack, on a trestle stand, c1940.
£400–500
$580–720 ⊞ STE

▶ A Tri-ang Mobo bucking bronco, on a red metal stand, restored, 1950, 35½in (90cm) high.
£675–750
$980–1,100 ⊞ AQ

Sci-Fi & TV

A Masuda tinplate battery-operated Sonicon Rocket, with attachable radar, and whistle which activates both vehicle and radar, Japanese, 1950s, 11in (28cm) long, in original box.
£330–360
$480–520 ⚒ Bon(C)

A battery-operated Star Roto Robot, 1970s, 14in (35.5cm) high, in original box.
£25–30
$35–45 ⊞ PLB

A Thunderbirds Parker porcelain figure, by English Porcelain Classics, 1999, 21in (53.5cm) high, in original box.
£250–300
$350–450 ⊞ UCO

A Daiya Astronaut Rocket Gun, blue and red, Japanese, 1960s, 9in (23cm) wide.
£70–80
$100–115 ⊞ HUX

◀ A Thunderbirds Parker figure, wearing brown jacket and striped trousers, 1966, 12in (30.5cm) high.
£80–90
$115–130 ⊞ UCO
If Parker still had his original chauffeur's hat the price would be doubled.

A Star Wars Millennium Falcon diecast model, c1980, 6½in (16.5cm) long.
£35–40
$50–60 ⊞ CMF

A Dr Who Mechanoid, by Herts Plastic Moulders, green plastic, 1965, 8in (20.5cm) high, in original packaging.
£350–400
$500–650 ⊞ WHO
In 1965, this Mechanoid sold for 4s 11d (just under 25p). Today it is extremely rare to find an unopened example. Smaller versions were produced by Cherilea Toys and these now attract a price range of £75–100 ($110–150).

> ### Cross Reference
> See Doctor Who (page 176)

A Space 1999 Eagle Transporter spaceship, original wood, Perspex, metal and plastic studio model, with accessories including Freighter Module, Space Mine and a nuclear waste container, 1975, 22in (56cm) long.
£8,500–9,500
$12,300–13,800 ⚒ FO

Five Star Wars plastic figures, c1980, largest 4in (10cm) high.
£4–8
$5–10 each ⊞ HAL

◀ A Star Wars Imperial Cruiser diecast model, with inner ship, c1980, 7½in (19cm) long.
£20–25
$30–35 ⊞ CMF

Tinplate

A tinplate clockwork Citroen coupé, maroon with tan roof, restored, c1925, 15¾in (40cm) long.
£270–300
$400–450 ⚒ S(S)

A blue Minic tinplate clockwork Chrysler Air-flow saloon car, some wear, 1930, 5in (12.5cm) long.
£50–60
$75–90 ⊞ HAL

A Tippco tinplate clockwork fire engine, with four firemen, 1930s, 9½in (24cm) long.
£230–275
$330–400 ⚒ P(WM)

A Tri-ang Minic clockwork Luton transport van, second series, No. 24M, red and blue, late 1940s, 6in (15cm) long, in original box.
£130–150
$190–220 ⚒ WAL

A Tri-ang Minic clockwork transport van, red and green, 85M, minor rusting, 1950s, 5in (12.5cm) long, in original box.
£75–95
$110–150 ⚒ WAL

A Tri-ang Minic clockwork articulated mechanical horse and trailer, No. 40M, red cab and dark green trailer with drop-down tailgate, 1950s, 7in (18cm) long, in original box.
£120–140
$175–200 ⚒ WAL

A Mettoy tinplate Indianapolis car, red and yellow, 1950s, 13in (33cm) long.
£285–325
$420–470 ⊞ JUN

Minics

The Minic range was launched by Tri-ang in 1935 and continued until 1963. Similar in size to diecast vehicles, Minics were made from tinplate with a clockwork mechanism (later models were fitted with a 'Push and Go' flywheel drive). Parts were high in quality and well detailed and the finished models were dipped in paint to achieve a high gloss finish. They were also scaled to fit with 0 gauge railway sets, hence their appeal to train collectors today. Minics were made in smaller quantities than their diecast rivals and the paint tended to chip easily, making examples in good condition hard to find. Tri-ang products are marked with a gold-coloured triangle or embossed mark, representing the partnership of the three Lines brothers who founded this offshoot of the family toy business in 1919.

◀ **A Tri-ang Minic clockwork mechanical horse and trailer,** No. 73M, red cab and green trailer with two cables, 1950s, 7in (18cm) long, with coloured leaflet and key.
£120–140
$175–200 ⚒ VEC

A Marusan tinplate battery-operated Smoky Joe red car and smoking driver, Japanese, 1950s, 10in (25.5cm) long, in original box.
£90–110
$130–160 ⚒ Bon(C)
The rubber-headed pipe-smoking driver has an opening by his mouth to allow the smoke to exit.

Wallpaper

Wallpaper is a subject new to this guide. Modern interest in interior design has stimulated demand both for architectural salvage and vintage décor. There is an established market for fine examples of historic wall coverings: *papiers peints* from the 18th century, original Arts and Crafts designs from the 19th. A strip of William Morris wallpaper from 1892, the floral pattern inscribed with pencilled notes, recently fetched £36,000 ($52,000) at a Glasgow auction. Such items appeal to the academic collector (for example design and architecture historians) and wallpaper fragments often end up being framed like paintings.

This section, however, is devoted to the more humble world of washable vinyl and is dominated by post WWII wallpaper. Such material is bought by those who wish to do up a room in a period style, or by enthusiasts with a specific collectable passion (ie Mabel Lucie Attwell or Thunderbirds).

A set of nine Mabel Lucie Attwell wallpaper cut-outs, by Sanderson, in reds, greens, yellows and blues, c1930, 10in (25.5cm) square.
£150–180
$220–260 ⊞ MEM

A roll of wallpaper, by Crown, printed with landmarks and modes of transport in yellow, green, red and blue, 1960, 20½in (52cm) wide, 17in (43cm) repeat.
£55–65
$80–95 per repeat ⊞ TWI

A roll of embossed wallpaper, depicting a historical scene in green, blue, yellow and grey, 1950, 21in (53.5cm) wide.
£30–35
$40–50 ⊞ TWI

A roll of wallpaper, by Crown, printed in brown and orange on a beige ground, 1960, 20¾in (52.5cm) wide, 21in (53.5cm) repeat.
£55–65
$80–95 per repeat ⊞ TWI

▶ **A roll of *Thunderbirds* wallpaper,** by ITC ENT, blue, yellow and red, 1992, 20½in (52cm) wide, 21in (53.5cm) repeat.
£45–50
$65–75 per repeat ⊞ TWI

◀ **A roll of wallpaper,** black, grey, cream and white, 1970, 21in (53.5cm) wide, 21in (53.5cm) repeat.
£65–75
$100–120 per repeat ⊞ TWI

A roll of wallpaper, printed with a French scene in red, green, yellow and blue on a white ground, 1960, 20½in (52cm) wide, 18in (45.5cm) repeat.
£75–85
$115–125 per repeat ⊞ TWI

A roll of wallpaper, by Crown, orange, brown, beige and white, 1970, 21in (53.5cm) wide.
£20–25
$30–40 ⊞ TWI

Watches & Clocks

A silver-plated pocket watch, c1895, 40mm diam.
£40–50
$60–75 ⊞ AOH

A Swiss lever half-hunter pocket watch, signed 'H Goodman 17 London Road Twickenham', London import mark and maker's mark 'GB', 1904, 20mm diam.
£250–290
$350–400 ⊞ PT

▶ **A silver pocket watch stand,** Birmingham 1904, 3in (7.5cm) high.
£50–60
$75–90 ⊞ AOH

A Goliath travelling watch, in a silver-fronted leather travelling case, key wind, enamel dial slightly damaged, Birmingham 1908, 5in (12.5cm) high.
£55–65
$80–95 ⊁ GAK

A stainless steel extra flat Universal mechanical pocket watch, with 17 jewel movement, c1930, 40mm diam.
£160–190
$225–275 ⊞ HARP

A Rolex Oyster wristwatch, the steel case with gold bezel, original dial, c1950.
£550–650
$800–1,000 ⊞ HARP

An Omega Constellation stainless steel wristwatch, officially certified chronometer, automatic day date, black dial, c1973.
£350–400
$500–600 ⊞ HARP

A Heuer mechanical stopwatch, c1980.
£80–100
$115–145 ⊞ HARP

A Heuer Regatta automatic wristwatch, with five minute indication on the dial for yacht racing, c1980.
£500–600
$720–870 ⊞ HARP

A Swatch plastic advertising wall-hanging battery-operated wristwatch, red, black and green, 1980s.
£70–80
$100–120 ⊁ BBR

▶ **A Longines silver wristwatch,** 1980s, 9in (23cm) long.
£400–450
$600–650 ⊞ LBe

◀ **A Seiko Chronograph RAF quartz wristwatch,** minor scratching, 1984.
£125–145
$180–220 ⊞ HARP

A KLG Plugs grey glass advertising wall clock, 1930s, 12in (30.5cm) high.
£300–350
$440–500 ⊞ MURR

A Bulle electric mantel clock, 1920s, 10in (25.5cm) high.
£90–110
$130–160 ↗ SWO

An oak mantel clock, in the manner of Gustave Serrurier-Bovy, with brass dial, striking on a gong, c1900, 14in (35.5cm) high.
£600–700
$875–1,000 ↗ S(S)

> Miller's is a price GUIDE not a price LIST

▶ **A Westclox Scotland wall clock,** yellow and white, with tin rim, 1960, 7½in (19cm) diam.
£70–80
$100–115 ⊞ Mo

A walnut longcase clock, with anodised dial, on cushion base and shaped square feet, 1930s, 77in (195.5cm) high.
£525–625
$750–900 ↗ DA

A Dartington Glass pyramid clock, 1980s, 3¾in (9.5cm) high.
£8–10
$12–15 ⊞ Law

World War II

A National Service information booklet, issued by HMSO, in red and white, 1939, 9 x 6in (23 x 15cm).
£6–10
$10–15 ⊞ J&S

Sheet music for *Thumbs Up,* in red, black and white, 1940, 12 x 9½in (30.5 x 24cm).
£4–5
$5–7 ⚒ RUSS

First Aid in Air Raids, with a foreword by Admiral Sir Edward Evans, KCB, DSO, yellow with black lettering, 1941, 7 x 5in (18 x 12.5cm).
£2–3
$5–6 ⊞ HUX

An ARP Home First Aid Case, by Boots Pure Drug Co, black with yellow lettering, 1940s, 12¾in (32.5cm) long.
£25–30
$35–45 ⊞ HUX

A brown RAF autograph book, 1941, 4 x 5in (10 x 12.5cm).
£35–45
$50–65 ⊞ COB

A metal Spitfire badge, 1939–45, 1½in (4cm) long.
£35–40
$50–60 ⊞ REN

A National Registration Identity Card, 1943, 8¾ x 5½in (22 x 14cm).
£1–2
$2–3 ⊞ HUX

Bristol Evening Post, Victory Day, 1945, 17 x 12in (43 x 30.5cm).
£5–8
$7–10 ⊞ J&S

A commemorative horse brass, 1945, 4in (10cm) diam.
£35–40
$50–60 ⊞ PJo

Writing

An ivory-handled steel ink eraser, 18thC, 6in (15cm) long.
£35–40
$50–60 ⊞ PPL

A Samuel Pemberton hand-engraved silver porte-crayon, with ruler, c1800, 4½in (11.5cm) long.
£125–150
$180–220 ⊞ PPL

A needlework card for postage stamps, c1860, 2½ x 3½in (6.5 x 9cm).
£20–30
$30–45 ⊞ VB

A silver novelty pencil, in the shape of a rifle, c1880, 4in (10cm) long.
£190–220
$275–325 ⊞ PPL

A Victorian cast-iron and glass inkwell, with pen holder, 5in (12.5cm) wide.
£130–150
$200–220 ⊞ MRW

A golden amber-coloured glass tea kettle inkwell, 2in (5cm) high.
£110–130
$160–200 ⋟ BBR

A bellowing man inkwell, the brown and tan salt-glazed face with quill hole to forehead, garland of grapes and vines to the edge, 3in (7.5cm) high.
£80–90
$115–135 ⋟ BBR

◀ **A Perry & Co glass inkwell,** with blue glass lid, c1890, 2in (5cm) high.
£50–60
$75–90 ⊞ PPL

A brass travelling inkwell, c1890, 2in (5cm) high.
£40–45
$60–65 ⊞ HO

▶ **A Sampson Mordan silver Popular desk pen and pencil set,** marked, c1890, 6½in (16.5cm) long, in original box.
£225–250
$320–360 ⊞ PPL

▶ **A seal/tamper,** with bone handle, 19thC, 1½in (4cm) long.
£15–20
$20–30 ⊞ WAC

◀ **A Victorian cast-iron documents spike,** 6in (15cm) long.
£25–30
$35–45 ⊞ HO

A Sampson Mordan gold carpenter's pencil, in a holder, hallmarked, 1920, 3½in (9cm) long.
£140–160
$200–230 ⊞ PPL

◀ **A brass seal,** with acorn handle, inscribed 'E', 1890–1910, 3in (7.5cm) long.
£28–32
$37–42 ⊞ WAC

An Onoto hard rubber pump-filler fountain pen, black with 18ct gold bands, 1920s, 6in (15cm) long.
£90–100
$130–145 ⊞ PPL

▶ **A Conway Stewart Dinkie red and black mottled fountain pen,** 1926, 3½in (9cm) long.
£60–80
$95–115 ⊞ RUS

A Swan Minor SM2.57 blue, black and gold marble fountain pen, 1920s, 5in (12.5cm) long.
£65–75
$95–110 ⊞ PPL

A Parker Lucky Curve True Blue fountain pen, 1920s, 5in (12.5cm) long.
£90–110
$130–160 ⊞ PPL

A Parker Falcon gold-plated Lattice fountain pen, 1979, 5in (12.5cm) long.
£100–120
$145–175 ⊞ RUS

An Ever-Sharp Skyline pen and pencil, 1940, 5in (12.5cm) long.
£110–130
$160–200 ⊞ AOH

Record Breakers

This section is devoted to objects that have made significant or record breaking prices at auction.

The world's first Christmas card, signed by Henry Cole, 1843, 3 x 5in (7.5 x 12.5cm).
World Record Price
£22,350
$32,400 ↗ HAld

▶ **A FA Cup winner's gold medal,** presented to Stanley Matthews in 1953, 2in (5cm) high.
World Record Price
£23,500
$34,000 ↗ S(O)
Stanley Matthews was one of Britain's most famous and respected football players. When his 1953 FA Cup winner's gold medal came up for auction at Sotheby's it sold for £23,500 setting a new world record for an FA Cup winner's medal. The purchaser was Nick Hancock, TV presenter and Stoke City fan.

A *Thunderbirds* puppet, Parker, wearing a pin-striped morning suit, white shirt and black bow-tie, 1960s, 20in (51cm) high, in later custom-made storage case.
World Record Price
£38,000
$55,000 ↗ FO
Parker was Gerry Anderson's favourite *Thunderbirds* character and he appeared in all 32 episodes of the television series. When it came up for auction at Fleetwood Owen's sale of film and TV memorabilia, this original Parker puppet from the series sold for £38,000. F.A.B.!

A Pelham clown string puppet, wearing a red hat and a camouflage suit, 1948–50, 12in (30.5cm) high.
World Record price
£1,350
$2,000 ↗ DN
Pelham puppets were extremely popular in the 1950s and '60s and many people still have one lurking in the attic. This clown came up for auction at Dreweatt Neate and was sold to a telephone bidder for a record price of £1,350, exceeding the figure paid earlier this year for a prototype tortoise puppet.

A Dunhill-Namiki Giant *maki-e* lacquer fountain pen, decorated with two dragons, signed 'Shogo', 1928–30, 6in (15cm) long.
World Record Price
£183,000
$265,000 ↗ Bon

▶ **A coffin-shaped cobalt-blue glass poison bottle,** embossed 'Patent 5658 Poison' within a shield, entwined initials within a circle, c1871, 6½in (16.5cm) high.
World Record Price
£9,750
$14,000 ↗ BBR
This is perhaps the rarest of all poison bottles. In 1871, G. F. Langford was granted provisional patent protection for a bottle in the shape of a coffin. It appears not to have been a popular design and was soon dropped from production. Only three were known to exist until a bottle digger excavated this example from a Pontefract dump. Sold by bottle specialists BBR, it fetched an auction record of £9,750.

Baca

BRITISH ANTIQUES AND COLLECTABLES AWARDS

presented by

MILLER'S

In association with

Celebrating the Winners of BACA 2001

The Dorchester Hotel played host to the second of the British Antiques and Collectables Awards on Tuesday 19th June 2001. These Awards are designed to recognize excellence across the Antiques and Collectables industry. This year saw the inclusion of eight new Awards, and it is envisaged that over the following years BACA will rotate its Awards and/or Categories to include all areas of the trade.

How to Vote for 2002

The voting process for the 2002 Awards begins now and will end in March 2002. For a voting form, please write to BACA or log on to the website:

BACA/Miller's
2-4 Heron Quays
London E14 4JP
www.baca-awards.co.uk

To date, BACA have received an overwhelming response – be it nominations, ideas, support and sponsorship. We would be very interested to hear from you on the subject of new Categories and new Awards for 2002 - but most importantly of course, we want your vote!

PROUDLY SPONSORED BY

The **BACA** *Winners...*

CATEGORY 1
General Antiques Dealer

LONDON (INSIDE M25)
sponsored by

Windsor House Antiques
28-29 Dover Street, Mayfair, London W1X 3PA

UK (OUTSIDE M25) *sponsored by*
David J. Hansord & Son
6 & 7 Castle Hill, Lincoln,
Lincolnshire LN1 3AA

CATEGORY 2
Specialist Antiques Dealers

FURNITURE
Norman Adams
8-10 Hans Road, Knightsbridge, London SW3 1RX

CERAMICS
Roderick Jellicoe
3a Campden Street, off Kensington Church St,
London W8 7EP

CLOCKS, WATCHES & SCIENTIFIC INSTRUMENTS
Brian & Joy Loomes
Calf Haugh Farmhouse, Pateley Bridge, Harrogate,
N. Yorks HG3 5HW

SILVER & PLATE
Nicholas Shaw Antiques
Great Grooms Antiques Centre, Parbrook,
Billingshurst, West Sussex RH14 9EU

COLLECTABLES
Ropewalk Antiques
Rye, East Sussex TN31 7NA

TOYS & DOLLS
Yesterday's Child
Angel Arcade, 118 Islington High Street,
London N1 8EG

JEWELLERY
N. Bloom & Son
The New Bond St Antiques Centre,
124 New Bond Street, London W1S 1DX

ARMS & ARMOUR
Trident Arms
96-98 Derby Road, Nottingham NG1 5FB

COSTUMES & TEXTILES
Linda Wrigglesworth Ltd
34 Brook Street, London W1K 5DN

ARCHITECTURAL & GARDEN
LASSCO
The London Architectural Salvage
and Supply Co, St Michael's Church,
Mark Street, London EC2 4ER

CATEGORY 3
Auction Houses

LONDON (INSIDE M25)
Phillips
101 New Bond Street, London W1S 1SR

UK (OUTSIDE M25)
Tennants Auctioneers
The Auction Centre, Leyburn,
N. Yorkshire DL8 5SG

CATEGORY 4
Associated Awards

 For a significant
contribution to the
popular appreciation
of Antiques

The BBC Antiques Roadshow

FAIR OF THE YEAR
Olympia Fine Art & Antiques Fair
June 2000, Olympia, London

BEST IN-HOUSE EXHIBITION *sponsored by* Antiques Trade
Pelham Galleries GAZETTE
"East and West:
Masterpieces of Lacquer Furniture",
24-25 Mount Street, London W1Y 5RB

AUCTIONEER OF THE YEAR
Ben Lloyd
Mallams, Bocardo House, St Michael's Street,
Oxford OX1 2DR

BEST ANTIQUES WRITER *sponsored by* freeserve
Christopher Wood
Christopher Wood Gallery, 20 Georgian House,
10 Bury Street, London SW1Y 6AA

SERVICES AWARD: BEST FREIGHT CARRIER *sponsored by* CHRISTIE'S
Lockson
29 Broomfield Street, London E14 6BX

 BEST ANTIQUES TOWN/VILLAGE
Horncastle, Lincolnshire

Directory of Specialists

If you require a valuation for an item it is advisable to check whether the dealer or specialist will carry out this service, and whether there is a charge. Please mention Miller's when making an enquiry. Having found a specialist who will carry out your valuation, it is best to send a description and photograph of the item to them, together with a stamped addressed envelope for the reply. A valuation by telephone is not possible. Most dealers are only too happy to help you with your enquiry, however, they are very busy people and consideration of the above points would be welcomed.

Berkshire

Collect It!, Unit 11, Weller Drive, Hogwood Industrial Estate, Finchampstead RG40 4QZ
Tel: 0118 973 7888
sales@collectit.co.uk www.collectit.co.uk
Magazine for Collectors.

Mostly Boxes, 93 High Street, Eton, Windsor SL4 6AF
Tel: 01753 858470
Fax: 01753 857212
Antique wooden boxes.

Special Auction Services, The Coach House, Midgham Park, Reading RG7 5UG
Tel: 0118 971 2949
Fax: 0118 971 2420
www.invaluable.com/sas/
Commemoratives, pot lids & Prattware, Fairings, Goss & Crested, Baxter & Le Blond prints.

Cambridgeshire

Antique Amusement Co, Mill Lane, Swaffham Bulbeck CB5 0NF
Tel/Fax: 01223 813041
www.aamag.co.uk
Vintage amusement machines also auctions of amusement machines, fairground art and other related collectables.

Cloisters Antiques, 1A Lynn Road, Ely CB7 4EG Tel: 01353 668558
info@cloistersantiques.co.uk
www.cloistersantiques.co.uk
Sewing, writing, heavy horse and antiquarian books.

Canada

Waddington's, 111 Bathurst Street, Toronto, ON M5V 2R1
Tel: 416 504 9100 Fax: 416 504 0033
www.waddingtonsauctions.com
Auctioneers.

When The Hammer Goes Down, 440 Douglas Avenue, Toronto, ONT M5M 1H4 Tel: 416 787 1700
BIDCALR@home.com
www.bidcalr.com
Auctioneers.

Cheshire

The Antique Garden, Grosvenor Garden Centre, Wrexham Road, Belgrave, Chester CH4 9EB
Tel: 01244 629191
Mobile: 07976 539 990
Fax: 01829 733802
info@antique-garden.co.uk

www.antique-garden.co.uk
Original antique garden tools and accessories.

Collector's Corner, PO Box 8, Congleton CW12 4GD
Tel: 01260 270429
Tel/Fax: 01260 298996
dave.popcorner@ukonline.co.uk
Beatles and pop memorabilia.

Dollectable, 53 Lower Bridge Street, Chester CH1 1RS
Tel: 01244 344888/679195
Fax: 01244 679469
Antique dolls.

On The Air, The Vintage Technology Centre, The Highway, Hawarden, (Nr Chester), Deeside CH5 3DN
Tel/Fax: 01244 530300
www.vintageradio.co.uk
Vintage radios.

Sweetbriar Gallery, Robin Hood Lane, Helsby WA6 9NH Tel: 01928 723851
Mobile 07860 907532
Tel: 01928 724153
sweetbr@globalnet.co.uk
www.sweetbriar.co.uk
Paperweights.

Charles Tomlinson, Chester
Tel/Fax: 01244 318395
charles.tomlinson@lineone.net
charles.tomlinson@btinternet.com
www.lineone.net/-charles.tomlinson
Scientific instruments.

Cleveland

Vectis Auctions Ltd/Barry Potter Auctions, Fleck Way, Thornaby, Stockton-on-Tees TS17 9JZ
Tel: 01642 750616 Fax: 01642 769478
admin@vectis.co.uk
admin@barrypotterauctions.com
www.vectis.co.uk
www.barrypotterauctions.co.uk
Toy auctions.

Cornwall

Gentry Antiques, Little Green, Polperro PL13 2RF Tel: 01503 272 361
info@cornishwarecollector.co.uk
www.cornishwarecollector.co.uk
Cornish ware. Also at Gray's Antique Market Mews, London W1
Tel: 020 7792 1402

Derbyshire

Bear Hugs Restoration - On Tired Old Bears, Bev McNab, Long Cottage, Eggington Road, Etwall DE65 6NB

Tel/Fax: 01283 734147
bevmcnab@talk21.com
www.bear-hugs.co.uk
Superior restoration on Yesterdays Bears! Have your Teddy Bear restored back to life!

Devon

The Pen and Pencil Lady
Tel: 01647 231619
penpencilady@aol.com
www.penpencilady.com

Dorset

Ancient & Gothic Tel: 01202 431721
Antiquities.

Books Afloat, 66 Park Street, Weymouth DT4 7DE Tel: 01305 779774
Books on all subjects, liner and naval memorabilia, shipping company china, ships bells, old postcards, models, paintings.

The Crow's Nest, 3 Hope Square, opp. Brewers Quay, Weymouth DT4 8TR
Tel: 01305 786930
peter.ledger3@btopenworld.com
Nautical collectables.

Dalkeith Auctions Ltd, Dalkeith Hall, Dalkeith Steps, Rear of 81 Old Christchurch Road, Bournemouth BH1 1YL Tel: 01202 292905
how@dalkeith-auctions.co.uk
www.dalkeith-auctions.co.uk
Auctions of postcards, cigarette cards, ephemera and collectors items.

Hardy's Collectables, 862 Christchurch Road, Boscombe, Bournemouth BH7 6DQ Tel: 07970 613077
www.poolepotteryjohn.com
Poole pottery.

Murrays' Antiques & Collectables
Tel: 01202 309094
Shipping, motoring, railway, cycling items always require. Also advertising related items, eg showcards, enamel signs, tins & packaging and general quality collectables. Anything old and interesting.

Old Button Shop Antiques, Lytchett Minster, Poole BH16 6JF
Tel: 01202 622169
Buttons & collectables.

Poole Pottery, Sopers Lane, Poole BH17 7PP Tel: 01202 666200
Fax: 01202 682894
www.poolepottery.com
Poole Pottery.

www.collectorsworld.net, PO Box 4922,
Bournemouth BH1 3WD
Mobile 07860 791588
info@collectorsworld.biz
www.collectorsworld.net
www.collectorslondon.com
www.collectorsworld.biz
19th and 20th century watches,
clocks, cameras. Toys, Dinky, Corgi
and diecast. TV/film related, tinplate
cars, boats, planes, robots, dolls and
teddy bears. Disneyana, memorabilia.
Open 24 hours and on the web.

Essex

Brandler Galleries, 1 Coptfold Road,
Brentwood CM14 4BN
Tel: 01277 222269 Fax: 01277 222786
john@brandler-galleries.com
www.brandler-galleries.com

Nick Garner Tel: 07970 206682
or 01245 261863
nickgarner@btinternet.com
www.ngarners.co.uk
Sally Tuffin, Dennis china, Dartington,
Highland stoneware, Roger Cockram,
Moorcroft, and more. Antiques and
collectables. Outlets in Chipping Ongar
and Ipswich. Ring for details.

GKR Bonds Ltd, PO Box 1, Kelvedon
CO5 9EH Tel: 01376 571711
Fax: 01376 570125
Old bonds and share certificates.

Haddon Rocking Horses Ltd, 5 Telford
Road, Clacton on Sea CO15 4LP
Tel: 01255 424745 Fax: 01255 475505
millers@haddonrockinghorses.co.uk
www.haddonrockinghorses.co.uk
Rocking horses.

Megarry's and Forever Summer, Jericho
Cottage, The Duckpond Green,
Blackmore CM4 0RR
Tel: 01277 821031 or 01277 822170
Antiques, Arts & Crafts. 11am–5pm
Wed–Sun closed Mon and Tues. Member
Essex Antiques Dealers Association.

The Old Telephone Company, The Old
Granary, Battlesbridge Antiques
Centre, Nr Wickford SS11 7RF
Tel: 01245 400601
Fax: 01245 401054
gp@theoldtelephone.co.uk
www.theoldtelephone.co.uk
Period telephones.

Gloucestershire

Bread & Roses, Durham House Antique
Centre, Sheep Street, Stow on the
Wold GL54 1AA Tel: 01451 870404
or 01926 817342
Kitchen antiques 1800–1950s.

Grimes House Antiques, High Street,
Moreton-in-Marsh GL56 0AT
Tel/Fax: 01608 651029
grimes_house@cix.co.uk
grimeshouse.co.uk cranberryglass.co.uk

Olliff's Architectural Antiques, 19–21
Lower Redland Road, Redland, Bristol
BS6 6TB Tel: 0117 923 9232

Fax: 0117 923 9880
marcus@olliffs.com
www.olliffs.com

Park House Antiques & Toy Museum,
Park Street, Stow-on-the-Wold
GL54 1AQ Tel: 01451 830159
info@thetoymuseum.co.uk
www.thetoymuseum.co.uk
Come and see one of the best private
collections of old toys in the country.
Admission £2, OAPs £1.50. Summer
10am–1pm, 2–5pm. Winter 11am–1pm,
2–4pm. Closed Tues and all May. Please
ring to confirm if travelling long distance.
We buy old toys and teddy bears.

Specialised Postcard Auctions, 25
Gloucester Street, Cirencester GL7 2DJ
Tel: 01285 659057 Fax: 01285 652047
Sales of early postcards and ephemera.

Telephone Lines Ltd, 304 High Street,
Cheltenham GL50 3JF
Tel: 01242 583699 Fax: 01242 690033
Telephonelines.freeserve.co.uk
www.telephonelines.net
Antique telephones.

Hampshire

Classic Amusements Tel: 01425 472164
pennyslot@aol.com
www.classicamusements.net

Cobwebs, 78–80 Old Northam Road,
Southampton SO14 0PB
Tel/Fax: 023 8022 7458
www.cobwebs.uk.com
Ocean liner memorabilia. Also naval
and aviation items.

Goss & Crested China Centre &
Museum, incorporating Milestone
Publications, 62 Murray Road,
Horndean PO8 9JL Tel: (023) 9259 7440
Fax: (023) 9259 1975
info@gosschinaclub.demon.co.uk
www.gosscrestedchina.co.uk
Goss & Crested china.

The Old Toy Shop, PO Box 4389,
Ringwood BH24 1YN
Tel: 01425 470180
djwells@btinternet.com
www.TheOldToyShop.com
Clockwork, steam & electric vintage
toys & memorabilia and figures.

Romsey Medal Centre, PO Box 169,
Romsey SO51 6XU
Tel: 01794 324488 Fax: 01794 324411
post@romseymedals.co.uk
www.romseymedals.co.uk
Orders, decorations & medals.

Solent Railwayana Auctions
Tel: 01489 584633
Railway relics and model railway items.
Also Railwayana auctions.

Hertfordshire

Brown & Merry, Tring Market
Auctions, Brook Street, Tring HP23 5EF
Tel: 01442 826446 Fax: 01442 890927
sales@tringmarketauctions.co.uk
www.tringmarketauctions.co.uk

Forget-Me-Knot Antiques, Over the
Moon, 27 High Street, St Albans
AL3 4EH Tel: 01727 848907
Tel/Fax: 01923 261172
Jewellery.

Isle of Wight

Nostalgia Toy Museum, High Street,
Godshill, Ventnor PO38 3HZ
Tel: 01983 730055 Fax: 01983 821296
Diecast toys specialist and museum.

Kent

20th Century Marks, 12 Market Square,
Westerham TN16 1AW
Tel: 01959 562221
Mobile 07831 778992
Fax: 01959 569385
lambarda@btconnect.com
www.20thcenturymarks.co.uk
Original 20th century design.

Chris Baker Gramophones, All Our
Yesterdays, 3 Cattle Market, Sandwich
CT13 9AE Tel: 01304 614756
cbgramophones@aol.com
Specialist dealer in gramophones and
phonographs.

Beatcity, P O Box 229, Chatham
ME5 8WA Tel/Fax: 01634 200444
Mobile: 07770 650890
Darrenhanks@beatcity.co.uk
www.beatcity.co.uk
Beatles and rock & roll memorabilia.

Candlestick & Bakelite, PO Box 308,
Orpington BR5 1TB
Tel: 020 8467 3743/3799
candlestick.bakelite@tesco.net
www.candlestickandbakelite.co.uk
Telephones.

Dragonlee Collectables
Tel: 01622 729502
Noritake.

Paul Haskell Tel: 01634 891796
Mobile: 07774 781160
www.antiqueslotmachines.inuk.com
Old mechanical slot machines.

Stuart Heggie, 14 The Borough,
Northgate, Canterbury CT1 2DR
Tel/Fax: 01227 470422
Vintage cameras, optical toys and
photographic images.

J & M Collectables Tel: 01580 891657
jandmcollectables@tinyonline.co.uk
Postcards, Crested china, Osborne
(Ivorex) plaques and small collectables
including Doulton, Wade, etc.

Lambert & Foster, 102 High Street,
Tenterden TN30 6HT
Tel: 01580 762083 Fax: 01580 764317
lf@tenterden14.freeserve.co.uk
www.lambertandfoster.co.uk
Antique auction rooms.

Barbara Ann Newman, London House
Antiques, 4 Market Square, Westerham
TN16 1AW Tel: 01959 564479
Antique dolls, Teddy bears and
collectables.

The Old Tackle Box, PO Box 55, High
Street, Cranbrook TN17 3ZU
Tel & Fax 01580 713979
tackle.box@virgin.net
Old fishing tackle.

Pretty Bizarre, 170 High Street, Deal
CT14 6BQ Tel: 07973 794537
1920s–1970s ceramics and collectables.

The Neville Pundole Gallery, 8A & 9
The Friars, Canterbury CT1 2AS
Tel: 01227 453471
www.pundole.co.uk
*Moorcroft and contemporary pottery
and glass.*

Stevenson Brothers, Bethersden, Ashford,
Kent TN26 3AP Tel: 01233 820363 /
07000 Dobbin Fax: 01233 820580
sales@stevensonbros.com
www.stevensonbros.com
Makers and restorers of rocking horses.

Wenderton Antiques
Tel: 01227 720295 (by appt only)
Kitchenware.

Woodville Antiques, The Street,
Hamstreet, Ashford TN26 2HG
Tel: 01233 732981
woodvilleantiques@netscapeonline.co.uk
Tools.

Lancashire

Decades, 20 Lord St West, Blackburn
BB2 1JX Tel: 01254 693320
*Original Victorian to 1970s clothing,
accessories, jewellery, decorative
textiles, and more.*

Jazz Art Deco.com Tel: 07721 032277
jazzartdeco@btinternet.com
www.jazzartdeco.com
Art Deco.

Tracks, PO Box 117, Chorley PR6 0UU
Tel: 01257 269726 Fax: 01257 231340
sales@tracks.co.uk
Beatles and pop memorabilia.

Leicestershire

Pooks Transport Bookshop, Fowke
Street, Rothley LE7 7PJ
Tel: 0116 237 6222 Fax: 0116 237 6491
pooks.motorbooks@virgin.net
Motoring books and automobilia.

Lincolnshire

Cleethorpes Collectables, 34 Alexander
Road, Cleethorpes DN35 8LF
Tel: 01472 291952
www.cleethorpescollectables.co.uk
Dealers in modern fine arts to antiques.

Junktion, The Old Railway Station,
New Bolingbroke, Boston PE22 7LB
Tel: 01205 480068/480087
*Advertising and packaging, automobilia,
slot machines, pedal cars, etc.*

Skip & Janie Smithson
Tel/Fax: 01754 810265
Mobile: 07831 399180
Kitchenware.

London

Angling Auctions, P O Box 2095,
W12 8RU Tel: 020 8749 4175
Mobile: 07785 281349
Fax: 020 8743 4855
neil@anglingauctions.demon.co.uk
Angling auctions.

The Antique Dealer, 115 Shaftesbury
Avenue, WC2H 8AD
Tel: 020 7420 6684
Fax: 020 7420 6685
info@theantiquedealer.co.uk

Banana Dance Ltd, 16 The Mall,
Camden Passage, 359 Upper St,
Islington N1 0PD Tel: 020 8699 7728
Mobile: 07976 296987
jonathan@bananadance.com
www.bananadance.com
*Decorative Arts of the 1920s and the
1930s. Also at Northcote Road
Antiques Market, Unit 20, 155A
Northcote Road, Battersea, SW11*

Beverley, 30 Church Street/Alfie's
Antique Market, Marylebone NW8 8EP
Tel/Fax: 020 7262 1576
Mobile: 07776 136003
*Art Deco furniture, glass, figures,
metalware and pottery.*

Biblion, Grays Antique Market,
1–7 Davies Mews, Mayfair W1Y 2LP
Tel: 020 7629 1374
info@biblion.co.uk
www.biblion.com
Antiquarian books, maps & prints.

Bloomsbury Book Auctions, 3 & 4
Hardwick Street, Off Rosebery Avenue,
EC1R 4RY Tel: 020 7833 2636/7
or 020 7636 1945
Fax: 020 7833 3954
info@bloomsbury-book-auct-.com
www.bloomsbury-book-auct.com
Book auctions.

Bonhams, 101 New Bond Street,
W1S 1SR Tel: 020 7629 6602/7468 8233
www.bonhams.com
Auctioneer.

Christie's South Kensington Ltd,
85 Old Brompton Road, SW7 3LD
Tel: 020 7581 7611 info@christies.com
www.christies.com
Auctioneers.

The Collector, Tom Power, 4 Queens
Parade Close, Friern Barnet N11 3FY
Tel: 020 8361 7787/020 8361 4143
collector@globalnet.co.uk
*Contemporary collectables including
Royal Doulton, Beswick, Pendelfin,
Worcester, Lladro, Border Fine Art,
Wade, Wedgwood, Coalport, Bossons,
Lilliput Lane, David Winter, etc.*

Comic Book Postal Auctions Ltd,
40–42 Osnaburgh Street, NW1 3ND
Tel: 020 7424 0007
Fax: 020 7424 0008
comicbook@compuserve.com
www.compalcomics.com
Comic book auctions.

Dix-Noonan-Webb, 1 Old Bond Street,
W1S 4PB Tel: 020 7499 5022
Fax: 020 7499 5023
auctions@dnw.co.uk
www.dnw.co.uk
*Auctioneers and valuers of Orders,
decorations and medals, coins, tokens
and banknotes.*

eBay International AG, Unit 6, Dukes
Gate, Acton Lane, Chiswick W4
Tel: 020 7384 6717
Fax: 020 7384 9728
ebay.co.uk

Michael German Antiques Ltd,
38B Kensington Church Street, W8 4BX
Tel: 020 7937 2771
www.antiquecanes.com
Walking canes, arms and armour.

Gooday Gallery, 14 Richmond Hill,
Richmond TW10 6QX
Tel: 020 8940 8652
Mobile: 077101 24540
goodaygallery@aol.com
*Arts & Crafts, Art Deco, Art Nouveau,
Tribal, 1950s and 60s.*

Harlequin House Puppets & Masks,
3 Kensington Mall, W8 4EB
Tel: 020 7221 8629
*Best collection of Pelham puppets, also
antique rod puppets from Polka Theatre
Wimbledon, old ventriloquist dummies,
Czech puppets, Punch & Judy.
Open Tues, Fri and Sat 11am–5.30pm.*

Adrian Harrington, 64a Kensington
Church Street, W8 4DB
Tel: 020 7937 1465
Fax: 020 7368 0912
rare@harringtonbooks.co.uk
www.harringtonbooks.co.uk
Antiquarian books, prints and maps.

David Huxtable Tel: 07710 132200
david@huxtablesoldadv.demon.co.uk
*Old advertising collectables. Also now
at Portobello Road on Sats, Basement
Stall 11/12, 288 Westbourne Grove W11*

Charles Jeffreys Posters & Graphics,
12 Octavia Street, SW11 3DN
Tel: 020 7978 7976
Mobile: 07836 546150
Fax: 020 7978 6315
charlie@cjposters.com
www.cjposters.com
*Specialising in selling original, rare and
collectable posters from the birth of
modernism through bauhaus to the
60s and 70s pop art and psychedelic
culture including contemporary posters.*

Francis Joseph Publications, 5 Southbrook
Mews, SE12 8LG
Tel: 020 8318 9580
office@francisjoseph.com
Books on 20thC ceramics and glass.

Timothy Millett Ltd, Historic Medals
and Works of Art, PO Box 20851,
SE22 0YN Tel: 020 8693 1111
Mobile: 07778 637 898
tim@timothymillett.demon.co.uk

Murray Cards (International) Ltd,
51 Watford Way, Hendon Central,
NW4 3JH Tel: 020 8202 5688
Fax: 020 8203 7878
murraycards@ukbusiness.com
www.murraycards.com/
Cigarette & trade cards.

Colin Narbeth & Son Ltd, 20 Cecil
Court, Leicester Square, WC2N 4HE
Tel: 020 7379 6975

Onslow's, The Depot, 2 Michael Road,
SW6 2AD Tel: 020 7371 0505
*19th and 20th century posters,
railwayana, motoring, aviation, Titanic
and ocean liner collectors items. Sales
held twice a year, usually April
and October.*

Stevie Pearce, Stand G144, Alfies
Antique Market, 13–25 Church Street,
Marylebone NW8 8DT
Tel: 020 7723 2526/5754
Fax: 020 7724 5404
Stevie@steviepearce.co.uk
www.SteviePearce.co.uk
*Antique costume jewellery and fashion
items 1900–1970.*

Rumours, 10 The Mall, Upper Street,
Camden Passage, Islington N1 0PD
Tel/Fax: 01582 873561
Mobiles 07836 277274/07831 103748
Rumdec@aol.com
Moorcroft pottery.

Totem Records, 168 Stoke Newington,
Church Street, N16 0JL
Tel: 020 7275 0234
Fax: 020 7275 0111
sales@totemrecords.com
www.totemrecords.com
*Secondhand records, tapes, CDs
bought, sold and exchanged.*

Twinkled, Units 28/29, Village Market,
Stockwell Street, Greenwich SE10
Tel: 0208 4880930/07940 471574
Fax: 020 7207 8596
info@twinkled.net
www.twinkled.net
*Sat & Sun only. Also at High St
Antiques Centre, 39 High St, Hastings
Old Town, East Sussex TN34
01424 460068 (closed Weds).*

Unique Collections, 52 Greenwich
Church Street, SE10 9BL
Tel: 020 8305 0867 Fax: 020 8853 1066
glen@uniquecollections.co.uk
www.uniquecollections.co.uk
Old toys bought and sold.

Nigel Williams Rare Books, 22 & 25 Cecil
Court, WC2N 4HE Tel: 020 7836 7757
*Books. First editions, illustrated,
childrens and detective.*

Wimbledon Sewing Machine Co Ltd
and The London Sewing Machine
Museum, 292–312 Balham High Road,
Upper Tooting, SW17 7AA
Tel: 020 8767 4724 Fax: 020 8767 4726
wimbledonsewingmachinecoltd@btinte
rnet.com
www.sewantique.com

*Antique sewing machines bought
and sold. Collection of antique
sewing machines.*

Yesterday Child, Angel Arcade,
118 Islington High Street, N1 8EG
Tel: 020 7354 1601
Tel/Fax: 01908 583403
Antique dolls and dolls house miniatures.

Middlesex

Hobday Toys Tel: 01895 636737
Fax: 01895 621042
wendyhobday@freenet.co.uk
Tinplate toys, trains and dolls houses.

John Ives, 5 Normanhurst Drive,
Twickenham TW1 1NA
Tel: 020 8892 6265 Fax: 020 8744 3944
jives@btconnect.com
*Reference books on antiques
and collecting.*

Norfolk

Roger Bradbury Antiques, Church Street,
Coltishall NR12 7DJ Tel: 01603 737444
Fax: 01603 737018
*Chinese blue and white porcelain
circa 1690–1820.*

Cat Pottery, 1 Grammar School Road,
North Walsham NR28 9JH
Tel: 01692 402962
Winstanley cats.

Northamptonshire

The Old Brigade, 10A Harborough Road,
Kingsthorpe, Northampton NN2 7AZ
Tel: 01604 719389 Fax: 01604 712489
theoldbrigade@easynet.co.uk
www.theoldbrigade.co.uk
Military antiques.

Nottinghamshire

T. Vennett-Smith, 11 Nottingham Road,
Gotham NG11 0HE Tel: 0115 983 0541
Fax: 0115 983 0114
info@vennett-smith.com
www.vennett-smith.com
*Ephemera and sporting
memorabilia auctions.*

Oxfordshire

Dauphin Museum Services, PO Box 602,
Oxford OX44 9LU Tel: 01865 343542
sales@Dauphin.co.uk
www.Dauphin.co.uk
Mount-making and conservation.

Michael Jackson Antiques, The Quiet
Woman Antiques Centre, Southcombe,
Chipping Norton OX7 5QH
Tel: 01608 646262
Mobile: 07831 402238
mjcig@cards.fsnet.co.uk
www.our-web-site.com/cigarette-cards
Cigarette cards.

Otter Antiques, 20 High Street,
Wallingford OX10 0BP
Tel: 01491 825544
www.antique-boxes.com
*Sale and restoration of antique wooden
boxes, always over 100 in stock.*

Alvin Ross Tel: 01865 772409
vintage.games@virgin.net
Pelham puppets.

Stone Gallery, 93 The High Street,
Burford OX18 4QA
Tel: 01993 823302
mail@stonegallery.co.uk
www.stonegallery.co.uk
*Specialist dealers in antique and
modern paperweights, gold and silver
designer jewellery and enamel boxes.*

Teddy Bears of Witney, 99 High Street,
Witney OX8 6LY
Tel: 01993 702616
Teddy bears.

Pembrokeshire

Arch House Collectables, St George
Street, Tenby SA70 7JB
Tel: 01834 843246
archhouse@onetel.net.uk
Pen Delfins.

Republic of Ireland

Michelina & George Stacpoole, Main
Street, Adare, Co Limerick
Tel: 00 353 6139 6409
stacpool@iol.ie
Pottery, ceramics, silver and prints.

Scotland

Bow Well Antiques, 103 West Bow,
Edinburgh EH1 2JP
Tel: 0131 225 3335
Specialists in all things Scottish.

Courtyard Antiques,
108A Causewayside, Edinburgh EH9 1PU
Tel: 0131 662 9008

Edinburgh Coin Shop, 11 West
Crosscauseway, Edinburgh EH8 9JW
Tel: 0131 668 2928/667 9095
Fax: 0131 668 2926
Coins, medals, militaria and stamps.

Shropshire

Decorative Antiques, 47 Church Street,
Bishop's Castle SY9 5AD
Tel/Fax: 01588 638851
enquiries@decorative-antiques.co.uk
www.decorative-antiques.co.uk
*Decorative objects of the 19th
and 20thC.*

Mullock & Madeley, The Old Shippon,
Wall-under-Heywood, Nr Church
Stretton SY6 7DS
Tel: 01694 771771
Fax: 01694 771772
auctions@mullockmadeley.co.uk
www.mullockmadeley.co.uk
Sporting auctions.

Somerset

Bath Antiques Online, Bartlett Street
Antiques Centre, Bartlett Street,
Bath BA1 2QZ
Tel: 01225 311061
Tel/Fax: 0117 939 1333
info@bathantiquesonline.com
www.BathAntiquesOnline.com

Bookbasket.co.uk, 30A Monmouth
Street, Bath BA1 2AN
Tel: 01225 484877 Fax: 01225 334619
www.bookbasket.co.uk
*Specialising in books on antiques and
collectable subjects at discount prices.*

Lynda Brine, Assembly Antiques,
5–8 Saville Row, Bath BA1 2QP
Tel: 01225 448488
lyndabrine@yahoo.co.uk
www.scentbottlesandsmalls.co.uk
Perfume bottles.

Cottage Collectibles, Pennard House,
East Pennard, Shepton Mallet BA4 6TP
Tel: 01749 860731
Sheila@cottagecollectibles.co.uk
www.cottagecollectibles.co.uk
*Open Mon–Sat 9.30–5.30pm and by
appointment. English and Continental
country antiques and kitchenalia.*

Julia Craig, Bartlett Street Antiques
Centre, 5–10 Bartlett Street, Bath
BA1 2QZ Tel: 01225 448202/310457
Mobile: 07771 786846
Textiles.

Richard Dennis Publications, The Old
Chapel, Shepton Beauchamp, Ilminster
TA19 OLE Tel: 01460 240044
Fax: 01460 242009
richarddennispublications.com
www.richarddennispublications.com
Publisher.

Philip Knighton, 11 North Street,
Wellington TA21 8LX
Tel: 01823 661618
gramman@msn.com
*Wireless, gramophones and all valve
equipment.*

The London Cigarette Card Co Ltd,
Sutton Road, Somerton TA11 6QP
Tel: 01458 273452 Fax: 01458 273515
cards@londoncigcard.co.uk
www.londoncigcard.co.uk
Cigarette and trade cards.

Joanna Proops Antique Textiles &
Lighting, 34 Belvedere, Lansdown Hill,
Bath BA1 5HR Tel: 01225 310795
*Antique textiles and vast selection of
chandeliers and wall lights.*

Richard Twort Tel/Fax: 01934 641900
Mobile: 077 11 939789
*Barographs and all types of
meteorological instruments.*

Staffordshire

Peggy Davies Ceramics, Freepost Mid
16669, Stoke-on-Trent ST4 1BJ
Tel: 01782 848002 Fax: 01782 747651
rhys@kevinfrancis.co.uk
www.kevinfrancis.co.uk
*Ceramics-Limited edition Toby jugs
and figures.*

Keystones, PO Box 387, Stafford
ST16 3FG Tel/Fax: 01785 256648
gkey@keystones.demon.co.uk
www.keystones.co.uk
Denby pottery.

Gordon Litherland, 25 Stapenhill Road,
Burton on Trent DE15 9AE
Tel: 01283 567213
Fax: 01283 517142
pubjugs@aol.com
*Bottles, breweriana and pub jugs,
advertising ephemera and
commemoratives.*

The Potteries Antique Centre,
271 Waterloo Road, Cobridge,
Stoke on Trent ST6 3NR
Tel: 01782 201455
Fax: 01782 201518
www.potteriesantiquecentre.com
Collectable ceramics.

Trevor Russell Vintage fountain pens,
PO Box 1258, Uttoxeter ST14 8XL
gtantiques@onetel.net.uk
*Buying, selling and repairing
fountain pens.*

Suffolk

Jamie Cross, PO Box 73, Newmarket
CB8 8RY jamiecross@aol.com
www.thirdreichmedals.com
*We buy and sell, value for probate and
insurance British, German and foreign
war medals, badges and decorations.*

W. L. Hoad, 9 St. Peter's Road, Kirkley,
Lowestoft NR33 0LH
Tel/Fax: 01502 587758
William@whoad.fsnet.co.uk
www.cigarettecardsplus.com
Cigarette cards.

Surrey

David Aldous-Cook, PO Box 413,
Sutton SM3 8SZ Tel/Fax: 020 8642 4842
*Reference books on antiques
and collectables.*

British Notes, PO Box 257, Sutton
SM3 9WW Tel/Fax: 020 8641 3224
pamwestbritnotes@compuserve.com
www.west-banknotes.co.uk
Banking collectables.

Childhood Memories Tel: 01252 793704
Fax: 01252 793704
maureen@childhood-memories.co.uk
www.childhood-memories.co.uk
Antique Teddies, dolls and miniatures.

Julian Eade Tel: 01491 575059
Mobile: 07973 542971
*Doulton Lambeth stoneware and
signed Burslem wares.*

Howard Hope, 19 Weston Park, Thames
Ditton KT7 0HW Tel: 020 8398 7130
Fax: 020 8398 7630
phonoking@virgin.net
www.gramophones.uk.com
*Specialising for 30 years in gramophones,
phonographs, anything related to the
history of recorded sound and other
mechanical/musical items. Dealing by
correspondence only, please no visits -
call first. Colour pictures of any item in
stock can be sent on request by email.
Exporting worldwide. Shipping
quotations given for any machine.*

East Sussex

Tony Horsley Tel: 01273 550770
Fax: 01273 550855
*Candle extinguishers, Royal Worcester
and other porcelain.*

Ann Lingard, Ropewalk Antiques,
Rye TN31 7NA Tel: 01797 223486
Fax: 01797 224700
ann-lingard@ropewalkantiques.freeserve.
co.uk
Antique pine furniture and kitchenware.

Mad about Mabel, P O Box 900,
Lewes BN7 1TF Tel: 01273 477246
*All Mabel Lucie Attwell creations from
bathroom plaques to original artwork.
Bi-annual mail order available.*

Twinkled, High St Antiques Centre,
39 High Street, Hastings TN34
Tel: 01424 460068
info@twinkled.net www.twinkled.net
*Closed Weds. Also at Greenwich Sat &
Sun, see entry under London.*

Wallis & Wallis, West Street Auction
Galleries, Lewes BN7 2NJ
Tel: 01273 480208
Fax: 01273 476562
auctions@wallisandwallis.co.uk
www.wallisandwallis.co.uk
*Specialist auctioneers of militaria, arms,
armour, coins and medals. Also die-cast
and tinplate toys, Teddy bears, dolls,
model railways, toy soldiers and models.*

West Sussex

Limited Editions, 2 Tarrant Street,
Arundel BN18 9DG
Tel: 01903 883950
Fax: 01903 883518
limited@editions-shop.freeserve.co.uk
www.limitededitionsshop.co.uk
*Ceramics including Kevin Francis, David
Winter, Lilliput Lane, J. P. Editions,
Moorcroft, Royal Doulton, Pendelfin,
Belleek, Lladro, etc.*

USA

Antique European Linens, Emil &
Pandora Balthazar, PO Box 789, Gulf
Breeze, FL 32562-0789, 14 North
Palafox St, Pensacola, FL 32501
Tel: 850 432 4777
Textiles, inc pillows and duvets.

Dragonflies Antiques and Decorating
Center, Frank & Cathy Sykes,
24 Center Street, Wolfeboro, New
Hampshire 03894 Tel: 603 569 0000

M. Finkel & Daughter, 936 Pine Street,
Philadelphia, Pennsylvania 19107-6128
Tel: 215 627 7797
mailbox@finkelantiques.com
www.finkelantiques.com
Antique samplers and needlework.

Randy Inman Auctions, PO Box 726,
Waterville, Maine 04903
Tel: 207 872 6900 Fax: 207 872 6966
inman@inmanauctions.com
www.inmanauctions.com
*Auctioneer specialising in advertising,
coin-op, gambling devices, automata,*

Directory of Markets & Centres

Cheshire

Davenham Antique Centre, 461 London Road, Davenham, Northwich CW9 8NA Shop Tel: 01606 44350
Fax: 01606 782317 maxwells@connectfree.co.uk
www.antiques-atlas.com/davenham

Derbyshire

Alfreton Antique Centre, 11 King Street, Alfreton DE55 7AF
Tel: 01773 520781 www.alfretonantiques.supanet.com
30 dealers on 2 floors. Antiques, collectables, furniture, books, militaria, postcards, silverware. Open 7 days Mon–Sat 10am–4.30pm, Sun 11am–4.30pm.

Chappells Antiques Centre, King Street, Bakewell DE45 1DZ
Tel: 01629 812496 ask@chappellsantiquescentre.com
www.chappellsantiquescentre.com
Over 30 dealers inc BADA & LAPADA members. Quality period furniture, ceramics, silver, plate, metals, treen, clocks, barometers, books, pictures, maps, prints, textiles, kitchenalia, lighting, furnishing accessories, scientific, pharmaceutical and sporting antiques from the 17th–20thC. Open Mon–Sat 10am–5pm, Sun 11am–5pm. Closed Christmas Day, Boxing Day, New Year's Day.

Heanor Antiques Centre, Ilkeston Road, Heanor DE75 7AE
Tel: 01773 531181 sales@heanor.co.uk
Open 7 days. 10.30am–4.30pm. 70+ dealers.

Matlock Antiques, Collectables & Riverside Café, 7 Dale Road, Matlock DE4 3LT Tel: 01629 760808 Proprietor W. Shirley.
www.matlock-antiques-collectable.cwc.net
Over 70 dealers.

Devon

Quay Centre, Topsham, Nr Exeter EX3 0JA
Tel: 01392 874006 www.antiquesontopshamquay.co.uk
80 dealers on 3 floors. Antiques, collectables and traditional furnishings. Ample parking. Open 7 days, 10am–5pm.

Gloucestershire

Durham House Antiques Centre, Sheep Street, Stow-on-the-Wold GL54 1AA Tel: 01451 870404
30+ dealers. Town and country furniture, metalware, books, ceramics, kitchenalia, silver, jewellery, sewing ephemera and samplers. Mon–Sat 10am–5pm, Sun 11am–5pm. Stow-on-the-Wold, Cotswold home to over 40 antique shops, galleries and bookshops.

Gloucester Antiques Centre, The Historic Docks, 1 Severn Road, Gloucester GL1 2LE Tel: 01452 529716
www.antiques.center.com
Open Mon–Sat 10am–5pm, Sun 1pm–5pm

Hampshire

Lymington Antiques Centre, 76 High Street, Lymington SO41 9AL Tel: 01590 670934 *30 dealers. Open Mon–Fri 10am–5pm, Sat 9am–5pm. Clocks, watches, silver, glass, jewellery, toys & dolls, books, furniture, textiles.*

Herefordshire

The Hay Antique Market, 6 Market Street, Hay-on-Wye HR3 5AF Tel: 01497 820175
Open 6 days 10am–5pm, Sun 11am–5pm. 17 separate units on 2 floors selling pine, country and period furniture. Rural and rustic items. China, glass, jewellery, linen and period clothes. Pictures, lighting, brass and collectables.

Mulberry's Antiques & Vintage Costume, Hereford HR1 2NH
Tel: 01432 350101 mulberrysantiques@hotmail.com
A wide range of antiques and collectables on 2 floors - furniture, fine china, porcelain, silver, jewellery, textiles, pre-1930s clothing and accessories, objets d'art, prints, oils and watercolours. Trade Welcome.

Humberside

Hull Antique Centre, Anderson Wharf, Wincolmlee, Hull HU2 8AH Tel: 01482 609958 www.@thehullantiquecentre.com
Open Mon–Fri 9am–5pm, Sat & Sun 10am–4pm

Kent

Castle Antiques, 1 London Road (opposite Library), Westerham TN16 1BB Tel: 01959 562492
Open Mon–Sat 10am–5pm . Phone for Sunday times. 4 rooms of antiques, small furniture, collectables, rural bygones, costume, tools, glass, books, linens, jewellery, kitsch, retro-clothing. Services: advice, valuations, theatre props, house clearance, talks on antiques.

Malthouse Arcade, High Street, Hythe CT21 5BW
Tel: 01303 260103

Lancashire

GB Antiques Centre, Lancaster Leisure Park, (the former Hornsea Pottery), Wyresdale Road, Lancaster LA1 3LA
Tel: 01524 844734 *140 dealers in 40,000 sq ft of space. Porcelain, pottery, Art Deco, glass, books, linen, mahogany, oak and pine furniture. Open 7 days 10am–5pm.*

The Antique & Decorative Design Centre, 56 Garstang Road, Preston PR1 1NA Tel: 01772 882078 Fax: 01772 252842
Paul@antiquecentre.co.uk
antique_centre@antiqueweb.co.uk
www.antiqueweb.co.uk/centre/ Paulallisonantiques.co.uk
Open 7 days a week 10am–5pm. 25,000 sq.ft. of quality antiques, objets d'art, clocks, pine, silverware, porcelain, upholstery, French furniture for the home & garden.

Kingsmill Antique Centre, Queen Street, Harle Syke, Burnley BB10 2HX Tel: 01282 431953 Fax: 01282 839470

Leicestershire

Oxford Street Antiques Centre, 16-26 Oxford Street, Leicester LE1 5XU Tel: 0116 255 3006
30,000 sq.ft. on 4 floors. Extensive range of Victorian, Edwardian and later furniture etc. Open Mon–Fri 10am–5.30pm, Sat 10am–5pm, Sun 2–5pm.

Lincolnshire

Cleethorpes Collectables, 34 Alexander Road, Cleethorpes DN35 8LF Tel: 01472 291952

St Martins Antiques Centre, 23a High Street, St Martins, Stamford PE9 2LF Tel: 01780 481158 peter@st-martins-antiques.co.uk www.st-martins-antiques.co.uk

London

Alfie's Antique Market, 13–25 Church Street NW8 8DT Tel: 020 7723 6066 post@eAlfies.com www.eAlfies.com

Covent Garden Antique Market, Jubilee Market Hall, Covent Garden WC2 Tel: 020 7240 7405 *Every Monday*

Grays Antique Market, 1–7 Davies Mews W1K 5AB Tel: 020 7629 7034 grays@clara.net www.graysantiques.com

Northcote Road Antique Market, 155a Northcote Road, Battersea SW11 6QB Tel: 020 7228 6850 *Open 7 days. 30 dealers offering a wide variety of antiques & collectables.*

Palmers Green Antiques Centre, 472 Green Lanes, Palmers Green N13 5PA Tel: 020 8350 0878 Mobile: 0785 506 7544 *Over 40 dealers. Specialising in furniture, jewellery, clocks, pictures, porcelain, china, glass, silver & plate, metalware, kitchenalia and lighting, etc. Open 6 days a week, closed Tues. Weekdays & Sats 10am–5.30pm, Sun 11am–5pm, open Bank Holidays. Removals & house clearances, probate valuations undertaken, quality antiques and collectables sold on commission basis.*

Norfolk

Tombland Antique Centre, Augustine Steward House, 14 Tombland, Norwich NR3 1HF Tel: 01603 619129 or 761906 *Open Mon–Sat 10am–5pm.*

Northamptonshire

The Brackley Antique Cellar, Drayman's Walk, Brackley NN13 6BE Tel: 01280 841841

Situated under the Co-op supermarket. Open 7 days 10am–5pm. Very large range of antiques and collectables. 30,000 sq.ft. of showroom with up to 100 dealers.

Nottinghamshire

Newark Antiques Centre, Regent House, Lombard Street, Newark NG24 1XP Tel: 01636 605504

Oxfordshire

Antiques on High, 85 High Street, Oxford OX1 4BG Tel: 01865 251075 *Open 7 days a week 10am–5pm. Sundays & Bank Holidays 11am–5pm. 35 dealers with a wide range of quality stock.*

Jackdaw Antiques Centres Ltd, 5 Reading Road, Henley-on-Thames RG9 0AS Tel: 01491 572289 sales@jackdaw-antiques.co.uk www.jackdaw-antiques.co.uk *Approx 1,000 sq ft of collectables (modern & discontinued), furniture, books, specialist areas, Carlton Ware, Doulton, Beswick.*

Lamb Arcade Antiques Centre, High Street, Wallingford OX10 0BS Tel: 01491 835166 *Open 10am–5pm daily, Sat till 5.30pm, Bank Holidays 11am–5pm. Furniture, silver, porcelain, glass, books, boxes, crafts, rugs, jewellery, lace and linens, pictures, tin toys, motoring and aviation memorabilia, antique stringed instruments, sports and fishing items, decorative and ornamental items.*

Shropshire

Stretton Antiques Market, Sandford Avenue, Church Stretton SY6 6BH Tel: 01694 723718 *60 dealers under one roof.*

Somerset

Bartlett Street Antique Centre, 5–10 Bartlett Street, Bath BA1 2QZ Tel: 01225 466689 info@antiques-centre.co.uk www.antiques-centre.co.uk

Staffordshire

Rugeley Antique Centre, 161 Main Road, Brereton, Nr Rugeley WS15 1DX Tel: 01889 577166 info@rugeleyantiquecentre.co.uk www.rugeleyantiquecentre.co.uk *Open Mon–Sat 9am–5pm, Sun & Bank Holidays 12 noon–4.30pm.*

Tutbury Mill Antiques Centre, Tutbury Mill Mews, Tutbury DE13 9LU Tel: 01283 520074 www.antiquesplus.co.uk *Open Mon–Sat 10am–5pm, Sun 12 noon–5pm*

Surrey

Maltings Monthly Market, Bridge Square, Farnham GU9 7QR General tel: 01252 726234 Mkt Organiser Tel: 01252 717434 FarnMalt@aol.com www.farnhammaltings.com *9.30am–4pm first Sat of the month.*

East Sussex

High Street Antiques, 39 High Street, Hastings TN34 3ER Tel: 01424 460068

West Sussex

Roundabout Antiques Centre, 7 Commercial Square, Haywards Heath RH16 7DW Shop Tel: 01444 417654 *Several specialist dealers with good quality extensive stock. Open Tues–Sat 10am–5pm. Specialising in musical instruments - ring Angie 01273 835926.*

Tyne & Wear

The Antique Centre, 2nd floor, 142 Northumberland St, Newcastle-upon-Tyne NE1 7DQ Tel: 0191 232 9832 timeout-antiques@btinternet.co.uk www.timeout-antiques.co.uk *Mon–Sat 10am–5pm.*

Wales

Offa's Dyke Antique Centre, 4 High Street, Knighton, Powys LD7 1AT Tel: 01547 520145

The Works Antiques Centre, Station Road, Llandeilo, Carmarthenshire SA19 6NH Tel: 01558 823964 *Closed Mon. 5,000sq ft. 49 dealers. Ample parking. Free tea & coffee.*

Warwickshire

Barn Antiques Centre, Station Road, Long Marston, Nr Stratford-upon-Avon CV37 8RB Tel: 01789 721399 *One of the largest traditional Antique Centres in the Midlands. Now over 13,000 sq ft. Open 7 days 10am–5pm. Antique furniture, antique pine, linen and lace, old fireplaces and surrounds, collectables, pictures and prints, silver, china, ceramics and objet d'art.*

Dunchurch Antiques Centre, 16a Daventry Road, Dunchurch (Nr Rugby) Tel: 01788 522450 *Open 7 days 10am–5pm. 11 dealers specialising in furniture, china, glass, books, postcards, stamps, clocks, toys, trains.*

Stratford Antiques Centre, 59-60 Ely Street, Stratford-upon-Avon CV37 6LN Tel: 01789 204180

West Midlands

Birmingham Antique Centre, 1407 Pershore Road, Stirchley, Birmingham B30 2JR Tel: 0121 459 4587 Fax: 0121 689 6566 *Open 7 days.*

Worcestershire

Worcester Antiques Centre, Unit 15, Reindeer Court, Mealcheapen Street, Worcester WR1 4DS Tel: 01905 610680 *Open Mon–Sun 10am–5pm, Mon–Sat 10am–5pm (Dec). Porcelain, silver, jewellery, Art Nouveau, Arts & Crafts, leather.*

Yorkshire

Cavendish Antique & Collectors Centre, 44 Stonegate, York YO1 8AS Tel: 01904 621666 sales@yorkantiquescentre.co.uk www.yorkantiquescentre.co.uk *Open 7 days 9am–6pm. Over 50 dealers on 3 floors.*

Stonegate Antiques Centre, 41 Stonegate, York YO1 8AW Tel: 01904 613888 sales@yorkantiquescentre.co.uk www.yorkantiquescentre.co.uk *Open 7 days 9am–6pm. Over 110 dealers on 2 floors.*

York Antiques Centre, 1a Lendal, York YO1 8AA Tel: 01904 641445 *15 dealers. General antiques. Open Mon–Sat 10am–5pm*

USA

Antique Village, North of Richmond, Virginia, on Historic US 301, 4 miles North of I-295 Tel: 804 746 8914 *Mon, Tues, Thurs, Fri 10am–5pm, Sat 10am–6pm, Sun 12 noon–6pm, Closed Wed. 50 dealers specialising in Art Pottery, country & primitives, Civil War artifacts, paper memorabilia, African art, toys, advertising, occupied Japan, tobacco tins, glassware, china, holiday collectibles, jewellery, postcards.*

Antiques at Colony Mill Marketplace, 222 West Street, Keene, New Hampshire 03431 Tel: (603) 358 6343 www.antiques.colonymill.com *Open Mon–Sat 10am–9pm, Sun 11am–6pm. Over 200 booths. Period to country furniture, paintings & prints, Art Pottery, glass, china, silver, jewellery, toys, dolls, quilts, etc.*

The Coffman's Antiques Markets, at Jennifer House Commons, Stockbridge Road, Route 7, PO Box 592, Great Barrington, MA 01230 Tel: (413) 528 9282/(413) 528 9602 www.coffmansantiques.com

Michiana Antique Mall, 2423 S. 11th Street, Niles, Michigan 49120 michianaantiquemall@compuserve.com www.michianaantiquemall.com *Open 7 days a week 10am–6pm.*

Quechee Gorge Antiques & Collectibles Center, Located in Quechee Gorge Village Tel: 1 800 438 5565 *450 dealers. Open all year, 7 days a week. Depression glass, ephemera, tools, toys, collectibles, Deco, primitives, prints, silver and fine china.*

Showcase Antique Center, PO Box 1122, Sturbridge, MA 01566 Tel: 508 347 7190 www.showcaseantiques.com *Open Mon, Wed, Thurs 10am–5pm, Fri, Sat 10am–5pm, Sun 12 noon–5pm, closed Tues. 170 dealers.*

Key to Illustrations

Each illustration and descriptive caption is accompanied by a letter code. By referring to the following list of Auctioneers (denoted by *) and Dealers (•), the source of any item may be immediately determined. Inclusion in this edition in no way constitutes or implies a contract or binding offer on the part of any of our contributors to supply or sell the goods illustrated, or similar articles, at the prices stated. Advertisers in this year's directory are denoted by (†).

If you require a valuation for an item, it is advisable to check whether the dealer or specialist will carry out this service and if there is a charge. Please mention Miller's when making an enquiry. Having found a specialist who will carry out your valuation it is best to send a photograph and description of the item to the specialist together with a stamped addressed envelope for the reply. A valuation by telephone is not possible. Most dealers are only too happy to help you with your enquiry; however, they are very busy people and consideration of the above points would be welcomed.

A&H • Architectural & Historical Salvage, Spa Street, Ossett, Wakefield, Yorkshire WF5 0HJ Tel: 01924 262831

A&J • A & J Collectables, Bartlett Street Antique Centre, 10 Bartlett Street, Bath, Somerset BA1 2QZ Tel: 01225 466689

AEF • A & E Foster Tel: 01494 562024

AEL • Argyll Etkin Ltd, 1–9 Hills Place, Oxford Circus, London W1R 1AG Tel: 020 7437 7800 argyll.etkin@btconnect.com

AG * Anderson & Garland (Auctioneers), Marlborough House, Marlborough Crescent, Newcastle-upon-Tyne, Tyne & Wear NE1 4EE Tel: 0191 232 6278

AH * Andrew Hartley, Victoria Hall Salerooms, Little Lane, Ilkley, Yorkshire LS29 8EA Tel: 01943 816363

AHa •† Adrian Harrington, 64a Kensington Church Street, London W8 4DB Tel: 020 7937 1465 rare@harringtonbooks.co.uk www.harringtonbooks.co.uk

AHJ •† Arch House Collectables, St George Street, Tenby, Pembrokeshire SA70 7JB Tel: 01834 843246 archhouse@onetel.net.uk

AL •† Ann Lingard, Ropewalk Antiques, Rye, East Sussex TN31 7NA Tel: 01797 223486 ann-lingard@ropewalkantiques.freeserve.co.uk

ALA • Alexander Antiques, Post House, Small Dole, Henfield, West Sussex BN5 9XE Tel: 01273 493121

ALiN • Lineham, Andrew Fine Glass, The Mall, Camden Passage, London N1 8ED Tel: 020 7704 0195 andrew@andrewlineham.co.uk www.andrewlineham.co.uk

AM • Alison Massey, MBO 32/33 Grays Antiques, 1–7 Davies Mews, London W1K 5AB Tel: 020 7629 7034

AMC • Amelie Caswell Tel: 0117 9077960

AMH • Amherst Antiques, Monomark House, 27 Old Gloucester Street, London WC1N 3XX Tel/Fax: 01892 725552 Mobile: 07850 350212 amherstantiques@monomark.co.uk

AMR • Amron Antiques Tel: 01782 566895

ANA * Anthemion Auctions, 2 Llandough Trading Park, Penarth Road, Cardiff Wales CF11 8RR Tel: 029 2071 2608

AND * Anderson's Auction Rooms Ltd, Unit 7, Prince Regent Business Park, Prince Regent Road, Castereagh, Belfast, Northern Ireland BT5 6QR Tel: 028 9040 1888

ANG •† Ancient & Gothic Tel: 01202 431721

Ann • Annie's Dolls & Teddies Tel: 01424 882437 anniestoys@btinternet.com www.anniestoys.com

AnS • The Antique Shop, 30 Henley Street, Stratford upon Avon, Warwickshire CV37 6QW Tel: 01789 292485

AOH • Antiques on High, 85 High Street, Oxford OX1 4BG Tel: 01865 251075

AOT • Annie's Old Things, PO Box 6, Camphill, Queensland 4152, Australia Tel: 0061412353099 annie@fan.net.au

AOY • All Our Yesterdays, 3 Cattle Market, Sandwich, Kent CT13 9AE Tel: 01304 614756 chrisbaker@uk.packardbell.org

APC • Antique Photographic Company Ltd Tel: 01949 842192 alpaco@lineone.net www.thesaurus.co.uk/cook

AQ • Antiquated, 10 New Street, Petworth, West Sussex GU28 0AS Tel: 01798 344011

ARB • Arbour Antiques Ltd, Poet's Arbour, Sheep Street, Stratford-on-Avon, Warwickshire CV37 6EF Tel: 01789 293453

ARo •† Alvin Ross Tel: 01865 772409 vintage.games@virgin.net

ASA • A. S. Antiques, 26 Broad Street,Pendleton, Salford, Greater Manchester M6 5BY Tel: 0161 737 5938

ASAA • ASA Antiques, 5–10 Bartlett Street, Bath, Somerset BA1 2QZ Tel: 01225 421037/312781

ASB * Andrew Spencer Bottomley, The Coach House, Thongs Bridge, Holmfirth, Yorkshire HD7 2TT Tel: 01484 685234 andrewbottomley@compuserve.com

ASH • Ashburton Marbles, Great Hall, North Street, Ashburton, Devon TQ13 7QD Tel: 01364 653189

ATH • Apple Tree House Tel: 01694 722953

AU • Auto Suggestion Tel: 01428 722933

AVT • Alexander von Tutschek Tel: 01225 465532

B&R •† Bread & Roses, Durham House Antique Centre, Sheep Street, Stow on the Wold, Gloucestershire GL54 1AA Tel: 01451 870404 or 01926 817342

BAJ • Beaulieu Autojumble, Beaulieu, Hampshire

BaN •† Barbara Ann Newman, London House Antiques, 4 Market Square, Westerham, Kent TN16 1AW Tel: 01959 564479

BAO •† Bath Antiques Online, Bartlett Street Antiques Centre, Bartlett Street, Bath, Somerset BA1 2QZ Tel: 01225 311061 info@bathantiquesonline.com www.BathAntiquesOnline.com

BAY • George Bayntun, Manvers Street, Bath, Somerset BA1 1JW Tel: 01225 466000 EBayntun@aol.com

BBA *† Bloomsbury Book Auctions, 3 & 4 Hardwick Street, Off Rosebery Avenue, London EC1R 4RY Tel: 020 7833 2636/7 or 020 7636 1945

info@bloomsbury-book-auct-.com
www.bloomsbury-book-auct.com

BBR *† BBR, Elsecar Heritage Centre, Wath Road,
Elsecar, Barnsley, Yorkshire S74 8HJ
Tel: 01226 745156
sales@bbrauctions.co.uk
www.onlinebbr.com

BD • Banana Dance Ltd, 16 The Mall, Camden Passage,
359 Upper St, Islington, London N1 0PD
Tel: 020 8699 7728 Mobile: 07976 296987
jonathan@bananadance.com
www.bananadance.com

BDA • Briar's C20th Decorative Arts, Skipton
Antiques & Collectors Centre, The Old
Foundry, Cavendish Street, Skipton, Yorkshire
BD23 2AB Tel: 01756 798641

Bea(E) * Bearnes, St Edmund's Court, Okehampton
Street, Exeter, Devon EX4 1DU
Tel: 01392 422800

BEV •† Beverley, 30 Church Street/Alfie's Antique
Market, Marylebone, London NW8 8EP
Tel: 020 7262 1576 Mobile: 07776136003

BEX • Daniel Bexfield Antiques, 26 Burlington
Arcade, London W1V 9AD Tel: 020 7491 1720

BIB •† Biblion, Grays Antique Market, 1–7 Davies
Mews, Mayfair, London W1Y 2LP
Tel: 020 7629 1374 info@biblion.co.uk
www.biblion.com

BiR • Bill Robson Tel: 01434 270206

BKS * Bonhams, Montpelier Street, Knightsbridge,
London SW7 1HH Tel: 020 7393 3900
www.bonhams.com

BLH * Ambrose, Ambrose House, Old Station Road,
Loughton, Essex IG10 4PE Tel: 020 8502 3951

BLM • Bill Little Motorcycles, Oak Farm, Braydon,
Swindon, Wiltshire SN5 0AG
Tel: 01666 860577

BND • Brian Barnfield, Bourbon Hanby Antiques
Centre, 151 Sydney Street, Chelsea, London
SW3 6NT Tel: 020 7565 0002

BoC • Bounty Antiques Centre, 76 Fore Street,
Topsham, Devon EX3 0HQ Tel: 01392 875007
Mobile: 07939 526504

Bon * Bonhams, Montpelier Street, Knightsbridge,
London SW7 1HH Tel: 020 7393 3900
www.bonhams.com

Bon(C) * Bonhams, 65–69 Lots Road, Chelsea, London
SW10 0RN Tel: 020 7393 3900
www.bonhams.com

BONA • Bonapartes, 13 George Street, Bath, Somerset
BA1 2EN Tel: 01225 423873

BRG •† Brandler Galleries, 1 Coptfold Road, Brentwood,
Essex CM14 4BM Tel: 01277 222269

BRT • Britannia, Grays Antique Market, Stand 101,
58 Davies Street, London W1Y 1AR
Tel: 020 7629 6772

BRU • Brunel Antiques, Bartlett Street Antiques
Centre, Bath, Somerset BA1 2QZ
Tel: 0117 968 1734

BSA • Bartlett Street Antique Centre, 5/10 Bartlett
Street, Bath, Somerset BA1 2QZ
Tel: 01225 466689
info@antiques-centre.co.uk
www.antiques-centre.co.uk

BSa • Ben Satterthwaite Tel: 07811 128689

BTC •† Beatcity, P O Box 229, Chatham, Kent
ME5 8WA Tel/Fax: 01634 200444
Mobile: 07770 650890
Darrenhanks@beatcity.co.uk
www.beatcity.co.uk

BUR • House of Burleigh Tel: 01664 454570
HousBurl@aol.com

BWA • Bow Well Antiques, 103 West Bow,
Edinburgh, Scotland EH1 2JP
Tel: 0131 225 3335

C&R • Catchpole & Rye, Saracen's Dairy, Pluckley,
Ashford, Kent TN27 0SA Tel: 01233 840457

CAL • Cedar Antiques Ltd, High Street, Hartley
Wintney, Hampshire RG27 8NY
Tel: 01252 843252

CAm • Classic Amusements Tel: 01425 472164
pennyslot@aol.com
www.classicamusements.net

CARS • C.A.R.S. (Classic Automobilia & Regalia
Specialists), 4–4a Chapel Terrace Mews, Kemp
Town, Brighton, East Sussex BN2 1HU
Tel: 01273 60 1960

CAu * Cotswold Auction Company, Chapel Walk
Saleroom, Chapel Walk, Cheltenham,
Gloucestershire GL50 3DS Tel: 01242 256363

CB • Christine Bridge Antiques, 78 Castelnau,
London SW13 9EX Tel: 07000 445277

CBGR •† Chris Baker Gramophones, All Our Yesterdays,
3 Cattle Market, Sandwich, Kent CT13 9AE
Tel: 01304 614756 or 614756
cbgramophones@aol.com

CBP *† Comic Book Postal Auctions Ltd, 40–42
Osnaburgh Street, London NW1 3ND
Tel: 020 7424 0007
comicbook@compuserve.com
www.compalcomics.com

CCB • C. Bowdell, PO Box 65, Grantham,
Lincolnshire NG31 6QR Tel: 01476 563206

CCC •† The Crested China Co, The Station House,
Driffield, Yorkshire YO25 7PY
Tel: 01377 257042
dt@thecrestedchinacompany.com
www.thecrestedchinacompany.com

CCO • Collectable Costume Tel: 07980 623926

CDC * Capes Dunn & Co, The Auction Galleries,
38 Charles Street, Off Princess Street, Greater
Manchester M1 7DB Tel: 0161 273 6060/1911

CGC * Cheffins, 2 Clifton Road, Cambridge CB2 4BW
Tel: 01223 213343 www.chefins.co.uk

CGX • Computer & Games Exchange, 65 Notting Hill
Gate Road, London W11 3JS
Tel: 020 7221 1123

CHA • Chislehurst Antiques, 7 Royal Parade,
Chislehurst, Kent BR7 6NR Tel: 020 8467 1530

CJP • Charles Jeffreys Posters & Graphics, 12 Octavia
Street, London SW11 3DN Tel: 020 7978 7976
Mobile: 07836 546150
charlie@cjposters.com
www.cjposters.com

CMF • Childhood Memories Tel: 01252 793704
maureen@childhood-memories.co.uk
www.childhood-memories.co.uk

CMS * Calcutt Maclean Standen, The Estate Office,
Stone Street, Cranbrook, Kent TN17 3HD
Tel: 01580 713828

CoA • Country Antiques (Wales), Castle Mill,
Kidwelly, Carms, Wales SA17 4UU
Tel: 01554 890534

COB •† Cobwebs, 78–80 Old Northam Road,
Southampton, Hampshire SO14 0PB
Tel/Fax: 023 8022 7458
www.cobwebs.co.uk

CoCo • Country Collector, 11–12 Birdgate, Pickering,
Yorkshire YO18 7AL Tel: 01751 477481

CoHA • Corner House Antiques and Ffoxe Antiques By
appointment Tel: 01367 252007
jdhis007@btopenworld.com

CORD • Corder Collectible Radios
paul@pcorder.freeserve.co.uk

Cot • Cottage Collectibles, Pennard House, East Pennard, Shepton Mallet, Somerset BA4 6TP Tel: 01749 860731 sheila@cottagecollectibles.co.uk www.cottagecollectibles.co.uk

CrF • Crowdfree Antiques, Fairview, The Street, Stanton, Suffolk IP31 2DQ Tel: 0870 444 0791 info@crowdfree.com

CRIS • Cristobal, 26 Church Street, London NW8 8EP Tel: 020 7724 7230 Mobile: 07956 388194

CRN •† The Crow's Nest, 3 Hope Square, opp. Brewers Quay, Weymouth, Dorset DT4 8TR Tel: 01305 786930

CS • Christopher Sykes, The Old Parsonage, Woburn, Milton Keynes, Bedfordshire MK17 9QM Tel: 01525 290259 www.sykes-corkscrews.co.uk

CTO •† Collector's Corner, PO Box 8, Congleton, Cheshire CW12 4GD Tel: 01260 270429 dave.popcorner@ukonline.co.uk

CWO • www.collectorsworld.net, PO Box 4922, Bournemouth, Dorset BH1 3WD Mobile: 078 60 791588 info@collectorsworld.biz www.collectorsworld.net www.collectorslondon.com www.collectorsworld.biz

CYA • Courtyard Antiques, 108A Causewayside, Edinburgh, Scotland EH9 1PU Tel: 0131 662 9008

DA * Dee, Atkinson & Harrison, The Exchange Saleroom, Driffield, Yorkshire YO25 7LD Tel: 01377 253151 www.dee-atkinson-harrison.co.uk

DAD • Decorative Arts @ Doune, Stand 26, Scottish Antique and Arts Centre, By Doune, Stirling, Scotland FK16 6HD Tel: 01786 461 439 Mobile: 07778 475 974 gordonfoster@excite.co.uk fionamacsporran@btinternet.com

DAn • Doll Antiques Tel: 0121 449 0637

DBo • Dorothy Bowler, Ely Street Antique Centre, Stratford-on-Avon, Warwickshire CV37 6LN Tel: 01789 204180

DCA • Devon County Antique Fairs, The Glebe House, Nymet Tracey, Crediton, Devon EX17 6DB Tel: 01363 82571

DD * David Duggleby, The Vine St Salerooms, Scarborough, Yorkshire YO11 1XN Tel: 01723 507111 www.davidduggleby.com

DE •† Decades, 20 Lord St West, Blackburn, Lancashire BB2 1JX Tel: 01254 693320

DEC •† Decorative Antiques, 47 Church Street, Bishop's Castle, Shropshire SY9 5AD Tel: 01588 638851 enquiries@decorative-antiques.co.uk www.decorative-antiques.co.uk

DFA • Delvin Farm Antiques, Gormonston, Co Meath, Republic of Ireland Tel: 00 353 1 841 2285 info@delvinfarmpine.com john@delvinfarmpine.com www.delvinfarmpine.com

DgC • Dragonlee Collectables Tel: 01622 729502

DHA • Durham House Antiques Centre, Sheep Street, Stow-on-the-Wold, Gloucestershire GL54 1AA Tel: 01451 870404

DHAR • Dave Hardman Antiques, West Street, Witheridge, Devon EX16 8AA Tel: 01884860273 Mobile: 0797 973 7126 hardmanantiques@talk21.com

DID • Didier Antiques, 58–60 Kensington Church Street, London W8 4DB Tel: 020 7938 2537/07836 232634

DLP • The Dunlop Collection, P.O. Box 6269, Statesville NC 28687, U.S.A. Tel: (704) 871 2626 or Toll Free Telephone (800) 227 1996

DMC * Diamond Mills & Co, 117 Hamilton Road, Felixstowe, Suffolk IP11 7BL Tel: 01394 282281

DMG • DMG Fairs, PO Box 100, Newark, Nottinghamshire NG24 1DJ

DN * Dreweatt Neate, Donnington Priory, Donnington, Newbury, Berkshire RG14 2JE Tel: 01635 553553

DNo/ • Desmond & Amanda North, The Orchard, 186
DNO Hale Street, East Peckham, Kent TN12 5JB Tel: 01622 871353

DNW *† Dix-Noonan-Webb, 1 Old Bond Street, London W1S 4PB Tel: 020 7499 5022 auctions@dnw.co.uk www.dnw.co.uk

DOL •† Dollectable, 53 Lower Bridge Street, Chester CH1 1RS Tel: 01244 344888/679195

DOR • Dorset Reclamation, Cow Drove, Bere Regis, Wareham, Dorset BH20 7JZ Tel: 01929 472200 info@dorsetrec.u-net.com www.dorset-reclamation.co.uk

DP • No 7 Antiques, 7 High Street, Dulverton, Somerset TA22 9HB Tel: 01398 324457

DPO • Doug Poultney, 219 Lynmouth Ave, Morden, Surrey SM4 4RX Tel: 020 8330 3472

DQ • Dolphin Quay Antique Centre, Queen Street, Emsworth, Hampshire PO10 7BU Tel: 01243 379994 www.antiquesbulletin.com/dolphinquay

Dri • Drivepast Automobilia Tel: 01452 790672

DRJ • The Motorhouse, DS & RG Johnson, Thorton Hall, Thorton, Buckinghamshire MK17 0HB Tel: 01280 812280

DSG • Delf Stream Gallery, 14 New Street, Sandwich, Kent CT13 9AB Tel: 01304 617684 www.delfstreamgallery.com

DW *† Dominic Winter Book Auctions, The Old School, Maxwell Street, Swindon, Wiltshire SN1 5DR Tel: 01793 611340 info@dominicwinter.co.uk www.dominicwinter.co.uk

E * Ewbank, Burnt Common Auction Room, London Road, Send, Woking, Surrey GU23 7LN Tel: 01483 223101 www.ewbankauctions.co.uk

Ech •† Echoes, 650a Halifax Road, Eastwood, Todmorden, Yorkshire OL14 6DW Tel: 01706 817505

EH * Edgar Horn Fine Art Auctioneers, 46–50 South Street, Eastbourne, East Sussex BN21 4XB Tel: 01323 410419 www.edgarhorns.com

EMC • Sue Emerson & Bill Chapman, Bourbon Hanby Antiques Centre, Shop No 18, 151 Sydney Street, Chelsea, London SW3 6NT Tel: 020 7351 1807

EMP • The Emporium Antique Centre Too, 24 High Street, Lewes, East Sussex BN7 2 LU Tel: 01273 477979

EON • Eugene O'Neill Antique Gallery, Echo Bridge Mall, 381 Elliot Street, Newtown Upper Falls MA 02164, U.S.A. Tel: (617) 965 5965

ERC • Zenith Antiques (Elizabeth Coupe), Hemswell Antiques Centre, Caenby Corner Estate, Hemswell Cliff, Gainsborough, Lincolnshire DN21 5TJ Tel: 01427 668389

ES • Ernest R Sampson, 33 West End, Redruth, Cornwall TR15 2SA Tel: 01209 212536

ET • Early Technology, 84 West Bow, Edinburgh, Scotland EH1 2HH Tel: 0131 226 1132

ETO • Eric Tombs, 62a West Street, Dorking, Surrey RH4 1BS Tel: 01306 743661

EV • Marlene Evans, Headrow Antiques Centre, Headrow Centre, Leeds, Yorkshire Tel: 0113 245 5344. Also at Red House Antiques Centre, Duncombe Place, York Tel: 01904 637000

EXC • Excalibur Antiques, Taunton Antique Centre, 27–29 Silver Street, Taunton, Somerset TA1 3DH Tel: 01823 289327

F&C * Finan & Co, The Square, Mere, Wiltshire BA12 6DJ Tel: 01747 861411

FA • Fagin's, Old Whiteways Cider Factory, Hele, Exeter, Devon EX5 4PW Tel: 01392 882062

Fai • Fair Finds Antiques, Rait Village Antiques Centre, Rait, Perthshire, Scotland PH2 7RT Tel: 01821 670379

FCL • French Country Living, Rue de Remparts & 21 rue de L'Eglise, 06250 Mougins, France Tel: 00 33 4 93 75 53 03 F.C.L.com@wanadoo.fr

FL • Falling Leaves Antiques, Mailing address only: 79 Valley Road, Westport CT 06880, U.S.A. fl@TIAS.com www.tias.com

FLD • Flying Duck, 320/322 Creek Road, Greenwich, London SE10 9SW Tel: 020 8858 1964 Mobile: 07831 273303

FMa • Francesca Martire, Stand F131–137, Alfie's Antique Market, 13–25 Church Street, London NW8 0RH Tel: 020 7724 4802

FO * Fleetwood Owen, 25 Ivor Place, London NW1 6HR Tel: 0207 563 5400

FST • Curiosities and Collectables, Gloucester Antiques Centre, he Historic Docks, 1 Severn Road, Gloucester GL1 2LE Tel: 01452 529716

G(B) * Gorringes Auction Galleries, Terminus Road, Bexhill-on-Sea, East Sussex TN39 3LR Tel: 01424 212994 bexhill@gorringes.co.uk www.gorringes.co.uk

G(L) * Gorringes inc Julian Dawson, 15 North Street, Lewes, East Sussex BN7 2PD Tel: 01273 472503 auctions@gorringes.co.uk www.gorringes.co.uk

G&CC •† Goss & Crested China Centre & Museum incorporating Milestone Publications, 62 Murray Road, Horndean, Hampshire PO8 9JL Tel: (023) 9259 7440 info@gosschinaclub.demon.co.uk www.gosscrestedchina.co.uk

GAA • Gabrian Antiques Tel: 01923 859675 gabrian.antiques@virgin.net

GaB • Garden Brocante Tel: 0118 9461905

GAC •† Gloucester Antiques Centre, The Historic Docks, 1 Severn Road, Gloucester GL1 2LE Tel: 01452 529716 www.antiques.center.com

GAD • Decodence Tel: 07831 326326 gad@decodence.demon.co.uk

GAK * Aylsham Salerooms, 8 Market Place, Aylsham, Norfolk NR11 6EH Tel: 01263 733195

GAZE * Thomas Wm Gaze & Son, Diss Auction Rooms, Roydon Road, Diss, Norfolk IP22 3LN Tel: 01379 650306 www.twgaze.com

GBr • Geoffrey Breeze Antiques, 6 George Street, Bath, Somerset BA1 2EH Tel: 01225 466499

GeN •† Gentry Antiques, Little Green, Polperro, Cornwall PL13 2RF Tel: 01503 272 361/020 7792 1402 info@cornishwarecollector.co.uk www.cornishwarecollector.co.uk

GH * Gardiner Houlgate, The Bath Auction Rooms, 9 Leafield Way, Corsham, Nr Bath, Somerset SN13 9SW Tel: 01225 812912 gardiner-houlgate.co.uk www.invaluable.com/gardiner-houlgate

GKR •† G.K.R. Bonds Ltd, PO Box 1, Kelvedon, Essex CO5 9EH Tel: 01376 571711

GLa • Glassdrumman Antiques, 7 Union Square, The Pantiles, Tunbridge Wells, Kent TN4 8HE Tel: 01892 538615

Gle * Glendinings & Co, 101 New Bond Street, London W1Y 9LG Tel: 020 7493 2445

GM •† Philip Knighton, 11 North Street, Wellington, Somerset TA21 8LX Tel: 01823 661618 gramman@msn.com

GRa •† Grays Antique Market, 1–7 Davies Mews, London W1K 5AB Tel: 020 7629 7034 grays@clara.net www.graysantiques.com

GRI •† Grimes House Antiques, High Street, Moreton-in-Marsh, Gloucestershire GL56 0AT Tel/Fax: 01608 651029 grimes_house@cix.co.uk www.grimeshouse.co.uk www.cranberryglass.co.uk

GRo • Geoffrey Robinson, GO77–78 (Ground floor), Alfies Antique Market, 13–25 Church Street, Marylebone, London NW8 8DT Tel: 020 7723 0449

GV • Garth Vincent, The Old Manor House, Allington, Nr Grantham, Lincolnshire NG32 2DH Tel: 01400 281358

GWR • Gwen Riley, Stand 12, Bourbon Hanby Antique Centre, 151 Sydney Street, Chelsea, London SW3 6NT Tel: 020 7352 2106

HaG • Harington Glass, 2 Queen Street, Bath, Somerset BA1 1HE Tel: 01225 482179

HAK •† Paul Haskell Tel: 01634 891796 Mobile: 07774 781160 www.antiqueslotmachines.inuk.com

HAL •† John & Simon Haley, 89 Northgate, Halifax, Yorkshire HX1 1XF Tel: 01422 822148/360434 toysandbanks@aol.com

HALB • Halbzwolf, Eschstrabe 21b, 32257 bunde, Germany Tel: 00 49 05223 52 58

HAld * Henry Aldridge & Son, Unit 1, Bath Road Business Centre, Devizes, Wiltshire SN10 1XA Tel: 01380 729199

HALL • Hall's Nostalgia, 389 Chatham Street, Lynn MA 01902, U.S.A. Tel: 001 781 595 7757 playball@hallsnostalgia.com www.hallsnostalgia.com

HAM * Hamptons International, 93 High Street, Godalming, Surrey GU7 1AL Tel: 01483 423567 fineart@hamptons-int.com www.hamptons.co.uk

HaR • Mr A. Harris Tel: 020 8906 8151 Mobile: 079 56 146083

HarC •† Hardy's Collectables, 862 Christchurch Road, Boscombe, Bournemouth, Dorset BH7 6DQ Tel: 07970 613077 www.poolepotteryjohn.com

HARP •† Harpers Jewellers Ltd, 2/6 Minster Gates, York YO1 7HL Tel: 01904 632634 harpersjewellers@btinternet.com www.vintage-watches.co.uk

HBr • www.horsebrass.co.uk, Diane Wilkinson, Cuddington Lane, Northwich, Cheshire CW8 2SY Tel/Fax: 44 (0) 1606 882555 brasses@horsebrass.co.uk www.horsebrass.co.uk/

HCA • Hilltop Cottage Antiques, 101 Portobello Road, London W11 Tel: 01451 844362 Mobile: 0777 365 8082 noswadp@AOL.com

HCJ • High Class Junk

HEG •† Stuart Heggie, 14 The Borough, Northgate, Canterbury, Kent CT1 2DR Tel: 01227 470422

HEL • Helios Gallery, 292 Westbourne Grove, London W11 2PS Tel: 077 11 955 997 heliosgallery@btinternet.com www.heliosgallery.cpm

HIS • Erna Hiscock & John Shepherd, Chelsea Galleries, 69 Portobello Road, London W11 Tel: 01233 661407 Mobile: 0771 562 7273

HO • Houghton Antiques, Houghton, Cambridgeshire Tel: 01480 461887 Mobile: 07803 716842

HOB •† Hobday Toys Tel: 01895 636737 wendyhobday@freenet.co.uk

HOLL * Holloways (RICS), 49 Parsons Street, Banbury, Oxfordshire OX16 5PF Tel: 01295 817777 enquiries@hollowaysauctioneers.co.uk www.hollowaysauctioneers.co.uk

HON • Honan's Antiques, Crowe Street, Gort, County Galway, Republic of Ireland Tel: 00 353 91 31407

HOP •† The Antique Garden, Grosvenor Garden Centre, Wrexham Road, Belgrave, Chester CH4 9EB Tel: 01244 629191 Mobile: 07976 539 990 info@antique-garden.co.uk www.antique-garden.co.uk

HSt • High Street Antiques, 39 High Street, Hastings, East Sussex TN34 3ER Tel: 01424 460068

HT • Heather's Treasures Tel: 01202 624018

HUM • Humbleyard Fine Art, Unit 32 Admiral Vernon Arcade, Portobello Road, London W11 2DY Tel: 01362 637793

HUN • Huntercombe Manor Barn, Henley-on-Thames, Oxfordshire RG9 5RY Tel: 01491 641349 wclegg@thecountryseat.com www.thecountryseat.com

HUX •† David Huxtable, Sats at Portobello Road, Basement Stall 11/12, 288 Westbourne Grove, London W11 Tel: 07710 132200 david@huxtablesoldadv.demon.co.uk

HYD * Hy Duke & Son, Dorchester Fine Art Salerooms, Dorchester, Dorset DT1 1QS Tel: 01305 265080

I&M • I & M Collectables Tel: 01942 205688 Mobile: 07768551801 kben@tinyworld.co.uk

ID • Identity, 100 Basement Flat, Finsborough Road, London SW10 9ED Tel: 020 7244 9509

IE • Imperial Echoes, The Antique Centre, 59–60 Ely Street, Stratford-upon-Avon, Warwickshire CV37 6LN Tel: 01789 204180

IQ • Cloud Cuckooland, 12 Fore Street, Mevagissey, Cornwall PL26 6UQ Tel: 01726 842364 inkquest@dial.pipex.com www.inkquest.dial.pipex.com/

IS • Ian Sharp Antiques, 23 Front Street, Tynemouth, Tyne & Wear NE30 4DX Tel: 0191 296 0656

IW • Islwyn Watkins, Offa's Dyke Antique Centre, 4 High Street, Knighton, Powys, Wales LD7 1AT Tel: 01547 520145

J&J • J & J 's, Paragon Antiquities Antiques & Collectors Market, 3 Bladud Buildings, The Paragon, Bath, Somerset BA1 5LS Tel: 01225 463715

J&S • J.R & S.J Symes of Bristol Tel: 0117 9501074

JACK •† Michael Jackson Antiques, The Quiet Woman Antiques Centre, Southcombe, Chipping Norton, Oxfordshire OX7 5QH Tel: 01608 646262 Mobile: 07831 402238 mjcig@cards.fsnet.co.uk www.our-web-site.com/cigarette-cards

JAK • Clive & Lynne Jackson Tel: 01242 254375 Mobile: 0410 239351

JBB • Jessie's Button Box, Great Western Antique Centre, Bartlett Street, Bath, Somerset BA1 5DY Tel: 0117 929 9065

JBL • Judi Bland Tel: 01276 857576

JE •† Julian Eade Tel: 01491 575059 Mobile: 07973 542971

JEB • Jenni Barke, Scottish Antique and Arts Centre, Carse of Cambus, Doune, Perthshire, Scotland FK16 6HD Tel: 01786 841203

JEZ • Jezebel, 14 Prince Albert Street, Brighton, East Sussex BN1 1HE Tel: 01273 206091

JHa • Jeanette Hayhurst Fine Glass, 32a Kensington Church Street, London W8 4HA Tel: 020 7938 1539

JHo • Jonathan Horne, 66 Kensington Church Street, London W8 4BY Tel: 020 7221 5658

JJ • Jen Jones, Pontbrendu, Llanybydder, Ceredigion, Wales SA40 9UJ Tel: 01570 480610

JM * Maxwells of Wilmslow, 133A Woodford Road, Woodford, Cheshire SK7 1QD Tel/Fax: 0161 439 5182

JMC • J & M Collectables Tel: 01580 891657 jandmcollectables@tinyonline.co.uk

JMW • JMW Gallery, 144 Lincoln Street, Boston MA02111, U.S.A. Tel: 001 617 338 9097 www.jmwgallery.com

JNic * John Nicholson, The Auction Rooms, Longfield, Midhurst Road, Fernhurst, Surrey GU27 3HA Tel: 01428 653727

JOL • Kaizen International Ltd, 88 The High Street, Rochester, Kent ME1 1JT Tel: 01634 814132

JP • Janice Paull, Beehive House, 125 Warwick Road, Kenilworth, Warwickshire CV8 1HY Tel: 01926 855253

JPr •† Joanna Proops Antique Textiles & Lighting, 34 Belvedere, Lansdown Hill, Bath, Somerset BA1 5HR Tel: 01225 310795

JU • Jukebox Showroom, 9 Park Parade, Gunnersbury Avenue, London W3 9BD Tel: 020 8992 8482/3

JuC • Julia Craig, Bartlett Street Antiques Centre, 5–10 Bartlett Street, Bath, Somerset BA1 2QZ Tel: 01225 448202/310457 Mobile: 07771 786846

JUN •† Junktion, The Old Railway Station, New Bolingbroke, Boston, Lincolnshire PE22 7LB Tel: 01205 480068/480087 Mobile: 07836 345491

JW • Julian Wood, Exeter Antique Lighting, Cellar 15, The Quay, Exeter, Devon EX2 4AY Tel: 01392 490848

KA • Kingston Antiques Centre, 29–31 London Road, Kingston-upon-Thames, Surrey KT2 6ND Tel: 020 8549 2004/3839 enquiries@kingstonantiquescentre.co.uk www.kingstonantiquescentre.co.uk

KES •† Keystones, PO Box 387, Stafford ST16 3FG Tel: 01785 256648 gkey@keystones.demon.co.uk www.keystones.co.uk

KNI * Knight's, Cuckoo Cottage, Town Green, Alby, Norwich, Norfolk NR11 7HE Tel: 01263 768488

L&E * Locke & England, 18 Guy Street, Leamington Spa, Warwickshire CV32 4RT Tel: 01926 889100 www.auctions-online.com/locke

LaF • La Femme Tel: 0117 950 4983 jewels@joancorder.freeserve.co.uk

Law • Malcolm Law Collectables, Greenways Garden Centre, Bethersden, Kent Mobile: 07977 3211603

LBe • Linda Bee Art Deco, Stand L18–21, Grays Antique Market, 1–7 Davies Mews, London W1Y 1AR Tel: 020 7629 5921

LCC •† The London Cigarette Card Co Ltd, Sutton Road, Somerton, Somerset TA11 6QP Tel: 01458 273452 cards@londoncigcard.co.uk www.londoncigcard.co.uk

LDC • L & D Collins Tel: 020 7584 0712

LeB • Le Boudoir Collectables, Bartlett Street Antique Centre, Bath, Somerset BA1 2QZ Tel: 01225 311061 www.bathantiquesonline.com

LEGE • Legend Tel: 0117 926 4637

LF *† Lambert & Foster, 77 Commercial Road, Paddock Wood, Kent TN12 6DR Tel: 01892 832325

LIB • Libra Antiques Tel: 01580 860569

LSK * Lacy Scott and Knight, Fine Art Department, The Auction Centre, 10 Risbygate Street, Bury St Edmunds, Suffolk IP33 3AA Tel: 01284 763531

Ma • Marie Antiques, Stand G136–138, Alfie's Antique Market, 13–25 Church Street, London NW8 8DT Tel: 020 7706 3727 marie136@globalnet.co.uk www.marieantiques.co.uk

MAP • Marine Art Posters, 71 Harbour Way, Merchants Landing, Victoria Dock, Port of Hull, Yorkshire HU9 1PL 01482 321173

MAr • Mint Arcade, 71 The Mint, Rye, East Sussex TN31 7EW Tel: 01797 225952

MARK •† 20th Century Marks, 12 Market Square, Westerham, Kent TN16 1AW Tel: 01959 562221 Mobile: 07831 778992 lambarda@btconnect.com www.20thcenturymarks.co.uk

MB •† Mostly Boxes, 93 High Street, Eton, Windsor, Berkshire SL4 6AF Tel: 01753 858470

MCC • M.C. Chapman Antiques, Bell Hill, Finedon, Northamptonshire NN9 5NB Tel: 01933 681260

MD • Much Ado About Deco, The Antiques Centre, 59–60 Ely Street, Stratford-upon- Avon, Warwickshire CV37 6LN Tel: 01789 204180

MED * Medway Auctions, Fagins, 23 High Street, Rochester, Kent ME1 1LN Tel: 01634 847444

MEM •† Memories UK, Mabel Lucie Attwell Club, Abbey Antiques, 63 Great Whyte, Ramsey, Nr Huntingdon, Cambridgeshire PE26 1HL Tel: 01487 814753

MFB • Manor Farm Barn Antiques Tel: 01296 658941 Mobile: 07720 286607 mfbn@btinternet.com www.btwebworld.com/mfbantiques

MGC • Midlands Goss & Commemoratives, The Old Cornmarket Antiques Centre, 70 Market Place, Warwick CV34 4SO Tel: 01926 419119

MGe • Michael German Antiques Ltd, 38B Kensington Church Street, London W8 4BX Tel: 020 7937 2771 www.antiquecanes.com

MI • Mitofsky's, 101 Terenure Road East, Dublin 6, Republic of Ireland Tel: 00 353 1 492 0033 info@mitofskyartdeco.com www.mitofskyartdeco.com

Mit * Mitchells, Fairfield House, Station Road, Cockermouth, Cumbria CA13 9PY Tel: 01900 827800

ML • Memory Lane, Bartlett Street Antiques Centre, 5/10 Bartlett Street, Bath, Somerset BA1 2QZ Tel: 01225 466689

MLa • Marion Langham Tel: 020 7730 1002 mlangham@globalnet.co.uk ladymarion@btinternet.co.uk

MLL • Millers Antiques Ltd, Netherbrook House, 86 Christchurch Road, Ringwood, Hampshire BH24 1DR Tel: 01425 472062 mail@millers-antiques.co.uk www.millers-antiques.co.uk

MLu • Michael Lucas Antiques, Admiral Vernon Antiques Arcade, Portobello Road, London W11 Tel: 020 8650 1107 Mobile: 07850 388288

Mo • Mr Moore

MRT • Mark Rees Tools Tel: 01225 837031

MRW • Malcolm Welch Antiques, Wild Jebbett, Pudding Bag Lane, Thurlaston, Nr. Rugby, Warwickshire CV23 9JZ Tel: 01788 810 616

MSB • Marilynn and Sheila Brass, PO Box 380503, Cambridge MA 02238-0503, U.S.A. Tel: 617 491 6064

MUR •† Murray Cards (International) Ltd, 51 Watford Way, Hendon Central, London NW4 3JH Tel: 020 8202 5688 murraycards@ukbusiness.com www.murraycards.com/

MURR • Murrays' Antiques & Collectables Tel: 01202 309094

MVX • Music & Video Exchange, 1st Floor, 38 Notting Hill Gate, London W11 3HX Tel: 020 7243 8574

MW • Malcolm Wells Tel: Miller's 01580 766411

N * Neales, 192–194 Mansfield Road, Nottingham NG1 3HU Tel: 0115 962 4141

NET • Nettlebed Antique Merchants, 1 High Street, Nettlebed, Henley on Thames, Oxfordshire RG9 5DA Tel: 01491 642062

NEW • Newsum Antiques, 2 High Street, Winchcombe, Gloucestershire GL54 5HT Tel: 01242 603446/07968 196668

NP • The Neville Pundole Gallery, 8A & 9 The Friars, Canterbury, Kent CT1 2AS Tel: 01227 453471 www.pundole.co.uk

OCAC • Old Cornmarket Antiques Centre, 70 Market Place, Warwick CV34 4SO Tel: 01926 419119

OCB • The Old Children's Bookshelf, 175 Canongate, Edinburgh, Scotland EH8 8BN Tel: 0131 558 3411

OD • Islwyn Watkins, Offa's Dyke Antique Centre, 4 High Street, Knighton, Powys, Wales LD7 1AT Tel: 01547 520145

OLA • Olliff's Architectural Antiques, 19–21 Lower Redland Road, Redland, Bristol, Gloucestershire BS6 6TB Tel: 0117 923 9232 marcus@olliffs.comwww.olliffs.com

OND • Ondines, 14 The Mall, Camden Passage, London N1 Tel: 01865 882465

ONS * Onslow's, The Depot, 2 Michael Road, London SW6 2AD Tel: 020 7371 0505 Mobile: 078 31 473 400

OO • Pieter Oosthuizen, Unit 4 Bourbon Hanby Antiques Centre, 151 Sydney Street, London SW3 6NT Tel: 020 7460 3078

OPB • Olde Port Bookshop, 18 State Street, Newburyport, Massachusetts 01950, USA Tel: 001 978 462 0100 Oldeport@ttlc.net

ORI • Origin 101, Gateway Arcade, Islington High Street, London N1 Tel: 07769 686146/07747 758852 David@origin101.co.uk www.naturalmodern.com www.origin101.co.uk

OTA •† On The Air, The Vintage Technology Centre, The Highway, Hawarden, (Nr Chester), Deeside, Cheshire CH5 3DN Tel/Fax: 01244 530300 www.vintageradio.co.uk

OTB •† The Old Tackle Box, PO Box 55, High Street, Cranbrook, Kent TN17 3ZU Tel/Fax 01580 713979 tackle.box@virgin.net

OTC •† The Old Telephone Company, The Old Granary, Battlesbridge Antiques Centre, Nr Wickford, Essex SS11 7RF Tel: 01245 400601 gp@theoldtelephone.co.uk www.theoldtelephone.co.uk

OTT • Otter Antiques, 20 High Street, Wallingford, Oxfordshire OX10 0BP Tel: 01491 825544 www.antique-boxes.com

OVE • Chuck Overs

OW • Off World, Unit 20, Romford Shopping Halls, Market Place, Romford, Essex RM1 3AT Tel: 01708 765633

P *† Bonhams, 101 New Bond Street, London W1S 1SR Tel: 020 7629 6602/7468 8233 www.bonhams.com

P(B) * Bonhams, 1 Old King Street, Bath, Somerset BA1 2JT Tel: 01225 310609

SCM • Scarabond & The Moon, Scottish Antique and Arts Centre, Carse of Cambus, Doune, Perthshire, Scotland FK16 6HD Tel: 01786 841203

SCR • Herzog, Hollender Phillips & Company, The Scripophily Shop, PO Box 14376, London NW6 1ZD Tel/Fax: 020 7433 3577 hollender@dial.pipex.com Currency.dealers-on-line.com/ScripophilyShop

SDP • Stage Door Prints, 9 Cecil Court, London WC2N 4EZ Tel: 020 7240 1683

SEA • Mark Seabrook Antiques, 9 West End, West Haddon, Northamptonshire NN6 7AY Tel: 01788 510772

SEE • Liz Seeber Old Cookery, Food & Wine Books, The Old Vicarage, 3 College Road, Brighton, East Sussex BN2 1JA Tel: 01273 684949 seeber.books@virgin.net www.lizseeberbooks.co.uk

SER • Serendipity, 125 High Street, Deal, Kent CT14 6BQ Tel: 01304 369165/01304 366536 dipityantiques@aol.com

SEY • Mike Seymour, The Directors Cut, The Antiques Centre, Ely Street, Stratford-upon-Avon, Warwickshire CV37 6LN Tel: 07931 345784 mike@seymour.gsbusiness.co.uk

SHA • Shambles, 22 North Street, Ashburton, Devon TQ13 7QD Tel: 01364 653848

SK * Skinner Inc, The Heritage On The Garden, 63 Park Plaza, Boston MA 02116, U.S.A. Tel: 001 617 350 5400

SK(B) * Skinner Inc, 357 Main Street, Bolton MA 01740, U.S.A. Tel: 001 978 779 6241

SLL • Sylvanna Llewelyn Antiques, Unit 5, Bourbon-Hanby Antiques Centre, 151 Sydney Street, Chelsea, London SW3 6NT Tel: 020 7598 1278

SMI •† Skip & Janie Smithson Tel/Fax: 01754 810265 Mobile: 07831 399180

SMW • Sporting Memorabilia of Warwick, 13 Market Place, Warwick CV34 4FS Tel: 01926 410600 sales@sportantiques.com www.sportsantiques.com

SOL *† Solent Railwayana Auctions Tel: 01489 584633

Som • Somervale Antiques, 6 Radstock Road, Midsomer Norton, Bath, Somerset BA3 2AJ Tel/Fax: 01761 412686 Mobile: 07885 088022 ronthomas@somervaleantiquesglass.co.uk www.somervaleantiquesglass.co.uk

SPA • Sporting Antiques, 10 Union Square, The Pantiles, Tunbridge Wells, Kent TN4 8HE Tel: 01892 522661

SpM • Sparkle Moore, The Girl Can't Help It!/Cad Van Swankster, G100 & G116 Ground Floor, Alfies Antique Market, 13–25 Church Street, Marylebone, London NW8 8DT Tel: 020 7724 8984 Office: 0208 809 3923 sparkle.moore@virgin.net www.grays.clara.net

SPT • Sporting Times Gone By, Warehouse (Clubhouse) Tel: 01903 885656 Mobile: 07976 942059 www.sportingtimes.co.uk

SPU • Spurrier-Smith Antiques, 28, 30, 39 Church Street, Ashbourne, Derbyshire DE6 1AJ Tel: 01335 343669/342198

SRA *† Sheffield Railwayana Auctions, 43 Little Norton Lane, Sheffield, Yorkshire S8 8GA Tel: 0114 274 5085 ian@sheffrail.freeserve.co.uk www.sheffieldrailwayana.co.uk

SSL • Star Signings Ltd, Unit E16/E17 Grays in the Mews, 1–7 Davies Mews, London W1K 5AB Tel: 020 7491 1010 Mobile: 07973 840625

SSM • Sue Scott Motoring Memorabilia Tel: 01525 372757

StC • St Clere Carlton Ware, P O Box 161, Sevenoaks, Kent TN15 6GA Tel: 01474 853630 stclere@aol.com www.stclere.co.uk

STE •† Stevenson Brothers, The Workshop, Ashford Road, Bethersden, Ashford, Kent TN26 3AP Tel: 01233 820363 sales@stevensonbros.com www.stevensonbros.com

STP •† Stevie Pearce, Stand G144, Alfies Antique Market, 13–25 Church Street, Marylebone, London NW8 8DT Tel: 020 7723 2526/5754 Stevie@steviepearce.co.uk www.SteviePearce.co.uk

SWB •† Sweetbriar Gallery, Robin Hood Lane, Helsby, Cheshire WA6 9NH Tel: 01928 723851 Mobile: 07860 907532 sweetbr@globalnet.co.uk www.sweetbriar.co.uk

SWO * G E Sworder & Sons, 14 Cambridge Road, Stansted Mountfitchet, Essex CM24 8BZ Tel: 01279 817778 www.sworder.co.uk

T&D • & Dolls, 367 Fore Street, Edmonton, London N9 0NR Tel: 020 8807 3301

TAC • Tenterden Antiques Centre, 66–66A High Street, Tenterden, Kent TN30 6AU Tel: 01580 765655/765885

TB • Millicent Safro, Tender Buttons, 143 E.62nd Street, New York NY10021, U.S.A. Tel: (212) 758 7004 Fax: (212) 319 8474 Author of BUTTONS

TBoy • Toy Boy, G64–65 Alfies Antique Market, 13–25 Church Street, Marylebone, London NW8 8DT Tel: 020 7723 5613

TCG • 20th Century Glass, Kensington Church Street Antique Centre, 58–60 Kensington Church Street, London W8 4DB Tel: 020 7938 1137 Tel/Fax: 020 7729 9875 Mobile: 07971 859848

TED •† Teddy Bears of Witney, 99 High Street, Witney, Oxfordshire OX8 6LY Tel: 01993 702616

TEN * Tennants, The Auction Centre, Harmby Road, Leyburn, Yorkshire DL8 5SG Tel: 01969 623780

TF * Tayler & Fletcher, London House, High Street, Bourton-on-the-Water, Cheltenham, Gloucestershire GL54 2AP Tel: 01451 821666 www.tayler-and-fletcher.co.uk

TMA *† Brown & Merry, Tring Market Auctions, Brook Street, Tring, Hertfordshire HP23 5EF Tel: 01442 826446 sales@tringmarketauctions.co.uk www.tringmarketauctions.co.uk

TMa • Tin Man, St Ives, Cambridgeshire Tel: 01480 463891 john.lambden@virgin.net

TMi • T. J. Millard Antiques, Bartlett Street Antiques Centre, Bath, Somerset Tel: 01225 469785

TML • Timothy Millett Ltd, Historic Medals and Works of Art, PO Box 20851, London SE22 0YN Tel: 020 8693 1111 Mobile: 07778 637 898 tim@timothymillett.demon.co.uk

TOB •† The Old Brigade, 10A Harborough Road, Kingsthorpe, Northampton NN2 7AZ Tel: 01604 719389 theoldbrigade@easynet.co.uk www.theoldbrigade.co.uk

TOM •† Charles Tomlinson Tel/Fax: 01244 318395 charles.tomlinson@lineone.net charles.tomlinson@btinternet.com www.lineone.net/~charles.tomlinson

TOT •† Totem, 168 Stoke Newington, Church Street, London N16 0JL Tel: 020 7275 0234 sales@totemrecords.com www.totemrecords.com

TPC • Pine Cellars, 39 Jewry Street, Winchester, Hampshire SO23 8RY Tel: 01962 777546/867014

TRA • Tramps, Tuxford Hall, Lincoln Road, Tuxford, Newark, Nottinghamshire NG22 0HR Tel: 01777 872 543 info@trampsuk.com

TREA * Treadway Gallery, Inc., 2029 Madison Road, Cincinnati, Ohio 45208, U.S.A. Tel: 001 513 321 6742 www.treadwaygallery.com

TRM * Thomson, Roddick & Medcalf, 60 Whitesands, Dumfries, Scotland DG1 2RS Tel: 01387 255366

TRO •† The Troika Man Tel: 01535 667294 thetroikaman@aol.com www.troikapottery.org

TT • Treasures in Textiles Tel: 01244 328968

TUN • Tunbridge Wells Antiques, 12 Union Square, The Pantiles, Tunbridge Wells, Kent TN4 8HE Tel: 01892 533708

TWAC • Talbot Walk Antiques Centre, The Talbot Hotel, High Street, Ripley, Surrey GU23 6BB Tel: 01483 211724

TWI •† Twinkled, Units 28/29, Village Market, Stockwell Street, Greenwich, London SE10 Tel: 0208 4880930/07940471574 info@twinkled.net www.twinkled.net Also at: High St Antiques Centre, 39 High Street, Hastings, East Sussex TN34 Tel: 01424 460068 info@twinkled.net www.twinkled.net

TWr • Tim Wright Antiques, Richmond Chambers, 147 Bath Street, Glasgow G2 4SQ Tel: 0141 221 0364

TYL * John Taylors, 14–18 Cornmarket Chambers, Louth, Lincolnshire LN11 9PY Tel: 01507 603648

UCO •† Unique Collections, 52 Greenwich Church Street, London SE10 9BL Tel: 020 8305 0867 glen@uniquecollections.co.uk www.uniquecollections.co.uk

UNI • No longer trading

UTP • Utility Plus, 66 High Street, West Ham, Pevensey, East Sussex BN24 5LP Tel: 01323 762316 07850 130723

V&S • No longer trading

VB • Variety Box Tel: 01892 531868

VBo • Vernon BowdenTel: 01202 763806

VCL • Vintage Cameras Ltd, 256 Kirkdale, Sydenham, London SE26 4NL Tel: 020 8778 5416 info@vintagecameras.co.uk www.vintagecameras.co.uk

VEC *† Vectis Auctions Ltd/Barry Potter Auctions, Fleck Way, Thornaby, Stockton-on-Tees, Cleveland TS17 9JZ Tel: 01642 750616 admin@vectis.co.uk admin@barrypotterauctions.com www.vectis.co.uk www.barrypotterauctions.co.uk

VINE • Vine Antiques Tel: 01235 812708

VP • VintagePostcards.com, 60–C Skiff Street, Suite 116, Hamden CT 06517, U.S.A. Tel: 001 203 248 6621 quality@VintagePostcards.com www.VintagePostcards.com

VS *† T. Vennett-Smith, 11 Nottingham Road, Gotham, Nottinghamshire NG11 0HE Tel: 0115 983 0541 info@vennett-smith.com www.vennett-smith.com

VSP * Van Sabben Poster Auctions, PO Box 2065, 1620 EB Hoorn, Netherlands Tel: 31 229 268203 uboersma@sabbenposterauctions.nl www.vsabbenposterauctions.nl

WAB • John Lambden Tel: 01480 463891 john.lambden@virgin.net

WAC • Worcester Antiques Centre, Unit 15, Reindeer Court, Mealcheapen Street, Worcester WR1 4DF Tel: 01905 610680

WAL *† Wallis & Wallis, West Street Auction Galleries, Lewes, East Sussex BN7 2NJ Tel: 01273 480208 auctions@wallisandwallis.co.uk www.wallisandwallis.co.uk

WaR • Wot a Racket, 250 Shepherds Lane, Dartford, Kent DA1 2PN Tel/Fax: 01322 220619 wot-a-racket@talk21.com

WBH * Walker, Barnett & Hill, Cosford Auction Rooms, Long Lane, Cosford, Shropshire TF11 8PJ Tel: 01902 375555

WCa • Wendy Carmichael, S126–129 Alfies Antique Market, 13–25 Church Street, London NW8 8DT Tel: 020 7723 6066

WD * Weller & Dufty Ltd, 141 Bromsgrove Street, Birmingham, West Midlands B5 6RQ Tel: 0121 692 1414 wellerdufty@freewire.co.uk www.welleranddufty.co.uk

WED • Wedgewood, Barlaston, Stoke on Trent, Staffordshire ST12 9ES Tel: 0800 317 412

WHO • The Who Shop International Ltd, 4 Station Parade, High Street North, East Ham, London E6 1JD Tel: 020 8471 2356 Mobile: 07977 430948 whoshop@hilly.com www.the whoshop.com

WI • David Winstone, Bartlett Street Antique Centre, 5–10 Bartlett Street, Bath, Somerset BA1 2QZ Tel: 01225 466689 Mobile: 07979 506415 winstampok@netscapeonline.co.uk

WilP * W&H Peacock, 26 Newnham Street, Bedford, MK40 3JR Tel: 01234 266366

WO • Woodville Antiques, The Street, Hamstreet, Ashford, Kent TN26 2HG Tel: 01233 732981 woodvilleantiques@netscapeonline.co.uk

WP •† British Notes, PO Box 257, Sutton, Surrey SM3 9WW Tel: 020 8641 3224 pamwestbritnotes@compuserve.com www.west-banknotes.co.uk

WRe • Walcot Reclamations, 108 Walcot Street, Bath, Somerset BA1 5BG Tel: 01225 444404

WSA • West Street Antiques, 63 West Street, Dorking, Surrey RH4 1BS Tel: 01306 883487

WSM •† Wimbledon Sewing Machine Co Ltd and The London Sewing Machine Museum, 292–312 Balham High Road, Upper Tooting, London SW17 7AA Tel: 020 8767 4724 wimbledonsewingmachinecoltd@btinternet.com www.sewantique.com

WW * Woolley & Wallis, 51–61 Castle Street Salisbury, Wiltshire SP1 3SU Tel: 01722 424500/01722 411854

YEST • Yesterday's, V.O.F. Yesterday's, Maaseikerweg 202, 6006 AD Weert, The Netherlands Tel: 0475 531207

YO • Martin Burton, 201 Hull Road, York YO10 3JY Tel: 01904 415347 yoyomonster@jugglers.net

YR • Yorkshire Relics of Haworth, 11 Main Street, Haworth, Yorkshire BD22 8DA Tel: 01535 642218 Mobile: 07971 701278

ZOOM • Zoom, Arch 65 Cambridge Grove, Hammersmith, London W6 Tel: 07000 9666 2001 Mobile: 07958 372975 eddiesandham@hotmail.com www.retrozoom.com

Index to Advertisers

Index

Italic page numbers denote colour pages; **bold** numbers refer to information and pointer boxes